NARRATORIAL COMMENTARY IN
THE NOVELS OF GEORGE ELIOT

LUND STUDIES IN ENGLISH 114

Editor

Marianne Thormählen

LUND STUDIES IN ENGLISH was founded by Eilert Ekwall in 1933. Published by the Centre for Languages and Literature at Lund University, the series consists of books on the English language and on literature in English.

Narratorial Commentary in the Novels of George Eliot

Sara Håkansson

LUND
UNIVERSITY

LUND STUDIES IN ENGLISH

NARRATORIAL COMMENTARY IN THE NOVELS OF GEORGE ELIOT
Sara Håkansson

LUND STUDIES IN ENGLISH 114
ISBN 978-91-976935-1-6
ISSN 0076-1451

Publisher:
Centre for Languages and Literature, Lund University
English Studies
P.O. Box 201
SE-221 00 LUND
Sweden

Typesetting *Ilgot Liljedahl*
Printed by Media-Tryck
Lund University, Sweden
2009

Table of Contents

Acknowledgements

Throughout the process of writing this book I have been lucky enough to have had people around me whose support and encouragement have made it a wholly rewarding experience. First and foremost, it is with sincere gratitude that I thank my supervisor, Professor Marianne Thormählen, who has followed this project from its initial stumbling steps to its last, with perceptive insight, invaluable criticism and inexhaustible encouragement. Her tactful guidance, her dedication beyond the call of duty and her unfailing enthusiasm have been truly inspiring, providing the work with focus and precision and the worker with the strength to press on.

I am indebted to the members of the English literary seminar at the Centre for Languages and Literature in Lund, who offered searching questions as well as fruitful suggestions and advice as my work moved through its various stages; they also provided a dynamic and constructive working environment, not to mention delicious wine and cheese on a weekly basis. I especially wish to thank Anna Lindhé, Dr Claes Lindskog, Dr Eivor Lindstedt, Marie Wallin, Stefan Ekman, Staffan Johansson, Kiki Lindell, Cecilia Kraitiss, Lisa Larsson and Dr Birgitta Berglund for their invaluable assistance and encouragement. A special thank you to Stefan Ekman for proofreading the manuscript on its final lap.

In my first year as a doctoral student, I gratefully received financial support from Knut och Alice Wallenbergs Stiftelse which allowed me to pursue my research on a fulltime basis. I would like to thank The New Society of Letters (Vetenskapssocieteten) at Lund and STINT (Stiftelsen för internationalisering av högre utbildning och forskning) for munificent grants which allowed me to spend a full year of research at the University of Oxford, as well as Hjalmar Gullberg och Greta Thotts stipendiefond, which awarded me a generous grant during my last year of research.

Without my friends and family, this project would never have left the ground. My heartfelt thanks go out to them all for their unswerving support and encouragement, for picking me up when I was down, for making me laugh through the sometimes despairing moments of thesis work and for providing tea, cakes, and long chats about exceedingly non-academic things, never letting me forget that there really is a life outside the moulting-cage.

Finally, my greatest debt I owe to my parents, Veronica and Bengt. Their love and support have known no bounds; they have carried me through it all – I thank them for everything, but most of all I thank them for walking the difficult paths so that I can walk the easy ones. This book is dedicated to them.

Introduction

> [T]he only effect I ardently long to produce by my writings, is that those who read them should be better able to *imagine* and to *feel* the pains and the joys of those who differ from themselves in everything but the broad fact of being struggling erring human creatures.[1]

In 1859, when George Eliot wrote this characteristic statement, she had already published two works of fiction but was still only at the outset of her writing career. The statement nevertheless epitomises her literary enterprise: endeavouring to affect her readers towards sympathy and feeling was an undertaking to which she remained devoted throughout her life as a writer. The narratological and rhetorical techniques Eliot used to accomplish this project are manifold, including elements as diverse as free indirect discourse and epigraphy. This investigation studies the means by which Eliot used one such technique – the narratorial comment – to shape her reader's responses to the text.

George Eliot had been a writer for many years before embarking on a novelistic career. As translator of David Friedrich Strauss's *The Life of Jesus* and Ludwig Feuerbach's *The Essence of Christianity*, and as the author of numerous essays spanning a wide field of topics, Marian Evans established her reputation as an intelligent and erudite London journalist, editor and critic well before the publication of her first fictional work, *Scenes of Clerical Life*, in 1857.[2] However, it was not until she became a novelist that the pseudonym George Eliot came into being, and it was only then that

---

1   George Eliot to Charles Bray, 5 July 1859, *The George Eliot Letters*, ed. by Gordon S. Haight, 9 vols (New Haven: Yale University Press, 1954-1978), iii, 111. Hereafter cited as *Letters*.

2   Among the works that George Eliot translated was Baruch Spinoza's *Ethics*, completed in 1856 but, to her disappointment, never published. Of course, before 4 February 1857, it was not George Eliot whose name appeared in translations and essays, but Marian Evans. For more on George Eliot's names, see Rosemarie Bodenheimer, 'A Woman of Many Names', in *The Cambridge Companion to George Eliot*, ed. by George Levine (Cambridge: Cambridge University Press, 2001), pp. 20-37.

the powerful intellect which was to be associated with that name found its full expression. Almost all Eliot's novels were immediate successes, and the author was commended for managing to interweave warm human sympathy with a sharp critical intellect. This correlation between artistic genius and human emotion is particularly clearly seen in Eliot's narratorial commentary. By intruding on descriptive narrative, remarking on courses of events and characters, the narrators in all Eliot's novels present running commentary which serves to shape and shift the reader's interpretation.

Although the practice of what was called 'author's intrusions' was no novelty by the time Eliot wrote her novels, and although several of her contemporaries shared the habit, Eliot's intrusions have come in for much criticism on account of their alleged obtrusiveness. Some readers have regarded Eliot's intrusions as manifestations of moralism and as explicit demonstrations of authorial control. George Steiner, for example, has argued that '[b]y interfering constantly in the narration George Eliot attempts to persuade us of what should be artistically evident'.[3] W. J. Harvey also expressed reservations, contending that Eliot's 'omniscient technique only becomes objectionable when the author intrudes directly into her fiction'.[4] A later observation derives from F. B. Pinion, who finds Eliot's commentary 'irritating' and indicative of the 'author's lack of restraint'.[5] Then again, other critics have noticed the powerful artistic effects of commentary. K. M. Newton, for example, views intrusions as part of an anti-dramatic function which detaches and distances in order to make readers 'more capable of active participation'.[6] Newton regards Eliot's commentary as part of a total structure, and it is clear that Eliot herself was intensely concerned with formal aspects and with presenting her works as artistic wholes. Worrying that Alexander Main's compilation of *Wise, Witty, and Tender Sayings* might have made people think that her comments could be separated from her novels and regarded as independent moralising excerpts, Eliot argued: 'Unless my readers are more moved towards the ends I seek by my works as wholes than by an assemblage of extracts, my writings are a mistake'.[7] The present study proceeds from the contention that while many narratorial comments offer reflections on the world outside

3 F. George Steiner, 'A Preface to *Middlemarch*', *Nineteenth-Century Fiction*, 9 (1955), 262-279 (p. 271).
4 W. J. Harvey, *The Art of George Eliot* (London: Chatto & Windus, 1961), p. 69.
5 F. B. Pinion, *A George Eliot Companion: Literary Achievement and Modern Significance* (London: Macmillan, 1981), p. 200.
6 K. M. Newton, 'The Role of the Narrator in George Eliot's Novels', *The Journal of Narrative Technique*, 3 (1973), 97-107 (p. 104)
7 *Letters*, v, 458-459. See Alexander Main, *Wise, Witty, and Tender Sayings in Prose and Verse, Selected from the Works of George Eliot* (London: Blackwood & Sons, 1872).

the novels, their principal purpose – to shape the reader's response to the text by changing perspectives and adding depth – is in fact achieved within the context of Eliot's narratives.

The notion that narratorial commentary in Eliot's novels influences reader response is nothing new in Eliot criticism, nor is the general study of commentary. Ever since the publication of *Adam Bede*, reviewers and critics have explored Eliot's commentary, accumulating a solid body of scholarship from which later scholars have benefited.[8] However, this scholarship has not provided any precise definition of narratorial commentary.

Furthermore, although most Eliot criticism agrees that narratorial commentary serves to shape the reader's responses to the narrative, little has been said in the way of *how* this process is implemented.

Consequently, the first aim of this study was to formulate a definition of narratorial commentary. The first chapter presents a set of concepts by which narratorial commentary is demarcated from other modes of narrative, focusing on the ways in which these comments steer the dynamic relationship between narrator and reader. Distance, both spatial and temporal, is a central factor in this interaction. A new pair of concepts, 'story-time now' and 'narration now', elucidates the interplay between narrator and reader, clarifying the means by which the narrator conditions the reader's interpretation. That is the second and main aim of this study. By defining narratorial commentary and investigating the modes in which it operates, the present investigation provides Eliot criticism with a comprehensive view of how narratorial commentary actually functions in the reading process.

It is important to note that the research presented here does not claim to describe the potential effects of Eliot's narratorial commentary; rather, it analyses the *means* by which comments operate to affect reader response. Whether or not the reader *is* affected, or indeed what effect (if any) Eliot's comments have on him or her, is up to each reader to consider.

After the introductory conceptual review, each chapter in this dissertation discusses an Eliot novel in chronological order. Every chapter adheres to the same bipartite structure. The first line of inquiry is technically orientated, analysing commentary in Eliot's novels from a narratological perspective. This is where the constituents of commentary are identified and analysed, where the narratological-technical groundwork is performed, as it were. The second part of each chapter is thematically orientated.

Although Eliot had authorised the first edition of Main's compilation, she was doubtful about a second edition.

8   *Scenes of Clerical Life* has, of course, also been studied, but *Adam Bede* is the first of Eliot's works of fiction to gain any serious critical response on a large scale.

Identifying and investigating the most prominent thematic concerns addressed in narratorial commentary, this section situates narratological analyses in the thematic context of each novel. By identifying pressing thematic concerns as discussed in commentary, these sections not only emphasise narratorial attitudes towards specific issues, but also illustrate how commentary works in relation to those issues.

All Eliot's novels include a large number of comments, rendering the task of isolating a few for analysis a difficult one. However, the comments included for analysis here meet either of two criteria: the first is that they form good general examples of a specific mechanism, that is, they are illustrative of how commentary as a device is implemented in the text; the second is that they deviate from the general form of the narrative, demonstrating some exceptionality which renders them particularly interesting for analysis. In other words, both representativeness and particularity have been brought into the process of selection, with a view to conveying as inclusive a survey as possible of the different types of commentary in Eliot's novels and of the variations which appear within those types.

***

When George Eliot died on 22 December 1880, she was celebrated as one of the greatest English novelists of her times. As was the case with many other Victorian writers, however, her fame subsided with the emergence of literary modernism. The 1940s saw a reappraisal of Eliot's novels in the works of F. R. Leavis and Joan Bennett, though, Leavis's *The Great Tradition* (1948) marking something of a turning-point in Eliot's critical reputation. Leavis challenged earlier contentions that Eliot, although recognised as sharp and intellectual, was drab, didactic and unimaginative. Joan Bennett's *George Eliot: Her Mind and Art*, published the same year, also reassessed Eliot's work, examining her novels from the perspectives of formal coherence and moral vision. Two other studies were published around the same time, Gerald Bullet's *George Eliot: Her Life and Books* (1947) and Basil Willey's *Nineteenth-Century Studies* (1949), indicating that George Eliot's critical reputation was changing.[9] Several seminal works followed in the wake of this critical resurgence, two of which – Barbara Hardy's *The Novels of George Eliot: A Study in Form* (1959) and W. J. Harvey's *The Art of George Eliot* (1961) – provided modern Eliot criticism with indispensable critical groundwork.

---

9 For more on George Eliot's critical reputation during her lifetime, just after her death and up till the 1940s, see *George Eliot: The Critical Heritage*, ed. by David Carroll (London: Routledge, 1971).

The revival of interest in George Eliot's novels entailed new attention to formal and thematic coherence as well as to the functions of Eliot's narrators. Most early critical works acknowledged narratorial commentary as a mode of presentation associated with the nineteenth-century novel. However, opinions on its *raison d'être* varied a good deal. Joan Bennett, for instance, argued that Eliot's comments were shortcomings, indicating the author's distrust in her own creative power.[10] In defence of 'the omniscient author convention', W. J. Harvey examined Eliot's 'intrusiveness', distinguishing statements that serve as stage directions and moral 'preaching' from comments that express 'those basic facts of life that underlie all human situations, real or imaginary'.[11] The latter, Harvey argued, are not obtrusive; rather, they serve as bridges between the reader's world and the world of the novel. Barbara Hardy regarded Eliot's commentary as attempts at imparting greater intensity to unexciting material; the comments are, she argued, devices for explaining and analysing characters who are too dull to analyse themselves. In this sense, the comment – unsatisfactorily, in Hardy's view – fills 'the gap between character and creator'.[12] Although Hardy did not develop these arguments on commentary further, she did elaborate a distinction between three major types of authorial voice, one of which is germane to the study of Eliot's commentary. The 'intimate voice', Hardy claimed, 'addresses a living reader', provides a context of intimacy between characters and readers and situates the reader inside the experience of characters. The study at hand will show that Hardy's delineation of the 'intimate voice' coincides with some of the functions inherent in narratorial commentary.

In the 1970s a number of critics investigated the relationship between the reader and the *Middlemarch* narrator. Isobel Armstrong examined George Eliot's 'sayings', which she defined as detachable 'sage-like, discursive generalizations about the nature of human relationships'.[13] Studying Eliot's 'sayings' in terms of function, Armstrong observed how they 'turn outwards towards the reader [...] to invoke a general body of [...] experience' (120). Concurring in W. J. Harvey's bridge image, Armstrong recognised Eliot's generalising statements, considering them as links between the unknown world of the novel and the reader's known world. Although

---

10 See Joan Bennett, *George Eliot: Her Mind and Her Art* (Cambridge: Cambridge University Press, 1948).
11 W. J. Harvey, *The Art of George Eliot* (London: Chatto & Windus, 1961), p. 83.
12 Barbara Hardy, *George Eliot's Novels: A Study in Form* (London: Athlone, 1959), p. 19.
13 Isobel Armstrong, ' "Middlemarch": A Note on George Eliot's "Wisdom" ', in *Critical Essays on George Eliot*, ed. by Barbara Hardy (London: Routledge & Kegan Paul, 1970), pp. 116-132 (p. 116).

Armstrong's article provides no classification of functions, only discussing a handful of randomly selected 'sayings', her essay constitutes one of the first attempts to analyse narratorial commentary as a literary technique serving to shape the reader's interpretation of the text.

In 1977, Jane S. Smith published an article on *Middlemarch* which concentrated on the reader's participation in the text. Smith studied the discursive plot in the novel – that is, the plot which 'lies in the implicit conversation between the narrator and the reader'.[14] Smith's essay is indicative of a critical development moving towards reader-response-orientated analyses, focusing on how the text conditions the reader's distance to and participation in the narrative. Smith is thus primarily interested in what she describes as the 'fictive reader', but naturally includes the phenomenon of commentary within her discussion. One year after the publication of Smith's article, Carol Howe Spady published an essay which also analyses *Middlemarch* from a reader-response-orientated perspective. Howe Spady devotes special attention to the reader's responses to narratorial commentary, attempting to show that commentary forms part of 'Eliot's purpose to humanize the reader'.[15] Howe Spady's analyses of some commentary components have been useful to the present study, but her predetermined purpose – to show that Eliot's comments aim to 'humanize' the reader – makes her essay somewhat reductive.

In the above-mentioned article 'The Role of the Narrator in George Eliot's Novels' (1973), K. M. Newton takes issue with earlier investigations that equate Eliot's narrators with the author herself. Regarding the narrator as an essential part of narrative structure, Newton proposes that Eliot's narrators should be studied according to what role they play in the text rather than according to whether, and how, they might be identified with the author. This distinction may seem self-evident to twenty-first-century scholars, but it was by no means self-evident at the time of Newton's article.

The studies cited above are all concerned with narratorial commentary to some degree, but Suzanne Graver's *George Eliot and Community* (1984) is the first work of scholarship to devise a methodically organised survey of functions within narratorial commentary. Although Graver's investigation is limited to the study of direct reader addresses, excluding other types of comments, her discussions of patterns within Eliot's reader addresses have been valuable for the present study. Tracing the development of the reader

14 Jane S. Smith, 'The Reader as Part of the Fiction: *Middlemarch*', *Texas Studies in Literature and Language*, 19 (1977), 188-203 (p. 194).
15 Carol Howe Spady, 'The Dynamics of Reader-Response in *Middlemarch*', *Rackham Literary Studies*, 9 (1978), 64-75 (p. 64).

address from *Adam Bede* to *Daniel Deronda*, Graver investigates how the narrator's direct appeal to the reader is modelled in each novel. Like several scholars before her, Graver understands the function of reader addresses as serving to evoke the reader's sympathy, bringing him or her into a community of feeling through sympathetic agreement.[16]

Another systematic investigation appeared in 1986 with the publication of Carl D. Malmgren's 'Reading Authorial Narration'. Malmgren elaborates a scheme for the classification of what he calls 'authorial narration', a narrative device manifested in the use of 'commentaries'.[17] Malmgren's categorisation of commentary into four types of statement – the deictic, personal, ideological and metalingual – elaborates on those 'bridges' between known and unknown worlds which W. J. Harvey and Isobel Armstrong outlined some twenty years before. Although Malmgren's definition and classification of 'commentaries' do not correspond directly with the survey of commentary provided here, his study is nevertheless relevant to the investigation of narratorial commentary in Eliot's novels.

Robyn Warhol's term 'engaging narrator' has also inspired some discussions of commentary in this book. Arguing that engaging narrators function as 'their author's surrogates in earnestly trying to foster sympathy for real world sufferers', Warhol identifies five methods by which engaging narrators evoke sympathy from readers.[18] Constituting a review of the engaging narrator's characteristic properties, Warhol's discussion complements earlier research by its inquiry into and application of narratological concepts and ideas.

While Graver, Malmgren and Warhol have elaborated some principles of organisation for commentary, by far the most ambitious attempt to systematise narratorial mediation in George Eliot's novels is Ansgar Nünning's magisterial study *Grundzüge eines kommunikationstheoretischen Modells der erzählerischen Vermittlung: Die Funktionen der Erzählinstanz in den Romanen George Eliots*, published by Wissenschaftlicher Verlag Trier in 1989. Nünning's book presents a highly complex conceptual structure geared to covering the entire range of narratorial phenomena in Eliot's fiction. His scope is thus very much wider than that of the present study, and it proved impossible to extrapolate narratorial commentary from his theoretical model to serve as a basis for the investigation at hand. However,

---

16 Suzanne Graver, *George Eliot and Community: A Study in Social Theory and Fictional Form* (Berkeley: University of California Press, 1984).

17 See Carl D. Malmgren, 'Reading Authorial Narration', *Poetics Today*, 7 (1986), 471-494 (p. 476).

18 Robyn R. Warhol, 'Toward a Theory of the Engaging Narrator: Earnest Interventions in Gaskell, Stowe, and Eliot', *PMLA*, 101 (1986), 811-818 (p. 813).

Nünning's chapters on the individual novels often provide enlightening discussions of passages that are also analysed here, as a number of references testify.

A few unpublished dissertations deserve some attention. Jerome David Cartwright's doctoral thesis from 1969, 'Authorial Commentary in the Novels of George Eliot as Primarily Exemplified in *Adam Bede*, *The Mill on the Floss*, and *Middlemarch*', examines commentary in terms of Eliot's aesthetic and philosophical teaching. Cartwright is thus principally interested in commentary in relation to ideas and theories rather than as a narratological device. Steven Berrien juxtaposes commentary in two works, Eliot's *Middlemarch* and Honoré de Balzac's *Illusions Perdues*, emphasising shared and distinctive qualities in the commentary of both novels. Although Berrien examines commentary in terms of function, his primary purpose is to justify narrative comments as integral elements in the novels as wholes.[19] Finally, Arundhati Maitra Sanyal's doctoral dissertation from 2000 investigates the narrator's addresses to a reader/narratee from a Bakhtinian perspective. Studying the narrator-narratee relationship, Sanyal focuses on dialogue and opposition in Eliot's novels within the context of reader-response theories.[20]

All the works mentioned above have inspired research on Eliot's narratorial commentary in some way. The contribution that this book hopes to make is the elaboration of an inclusive survey of the narratological devices constituting commentary and a comprehensive analysis of *how* these operate to shape reader response.

***

Chapters 2 to 7 of this study analyse Eliot's novels from *Adam Bede* to *Daniel Deronda*. *Scenes of Clerical Life* is not included in the investigation, partly because of its status as a compilation of short stories and partly because it constitutes something of a dress-rehearsal for Eliot's more ambitious literary achievements. Moreover, although intriguing in their own right, narratorial comments in the three stories that form *Scenes of Clerical Life* are such extreme versions of the commentary embedded in Eliot's later novels that they contribute little to the understanding of narratorial commentary in Eliot's oeuvre as a whole. For similar reasons, *Romola*, often regarded as something of a fictional experiment on Eliot's part, is excluded from the investigation proper although brief references to this

19 See Steven Berrien, 'Narrative Commentary in *Illusions Perdues* and *Middlemarch*' (unpublished doctoral dissertation, Harvard University, 1989).

20 See Arundhati Maitra Sanyal, 'Written in Opposition: Narrator-Narratee Relationship in the Major Novels of George Eliot' (unpublished doctoral dissertation, City University of New York, 2000).

novel occur throughout the book. Set in late-fifteenth-century Florence, *Romola* diverges from the temporal and spatial settings of Eliot's other novels, all of which are set in provincial middle England a generation or two before the time of writing. The narrator's relation to the world of *Romola* is consequently not only distinct from the corresponding relation in other novels, but also a complex feature in the novel itself. An analysis of *Romola* within the scope of this investigation would therefore not contribute to the understanding of commentary in terms of how this narrative technique progresses from Eliot's first novel to her last.

As was pointed out above, the first chapter of this study presents a review of theories and concepts relevant to analyses of narratorial commentary, serving as a conceptual introduction to the book and equipping it with a definition of narratorial commentary. Chapter 2 focuses on Eliot's first full-length novel, *Adam Bede*, a key work with regard to the narratorial function in Eliot's fiction. The narrator in *Adam Bede* is specifically male, unlike narrators in subsequent novels, and is consequently referred to as 'he' in the discussion here. This pronoun is retained for the narrators in the gender-neutral later novels: the reader is 'he or she' throughout; 'she' is the natural choice for the author, George Eliot/Marian Evans; and it seemed convenient to use the same pronoun for the narrator throughout the book to avoid confusion. Subsequent chapters discuss *The Mill on the Floss*, *Silas Marner*, *Felix Holt*, *Middlemarch* and *Daniel Deronda*. The novels are studied chronologically in order to convey a general view of the evolution of narratorial commentary in Eliot's novels from her first to her last. This study hopes to show that although the aim of George Eliot's literary enterprise remained constant during her entire career – to inspire her readers towards sympathy – the methods by which she sought to achieve that aim kept developing throughout the two decades that saw her establish herself as a major novelist.

1. Narrators, Readers and Meanings: A Conceptual Review

Story-Time Now and Narration Now

This study examines functions of narratorial commentary in George Eliot's novels by means of a set of implements, derived from the field of narratology, which provides theoretical approaches and terminology particularly suited to the investigation of narrative strategies and techniques. The purpose of this chapter, which proceeds from discussions in literary theory on the idea of authorial presence and reader response, is to present a theoretical apparatus facilitating analysis and to introduce those narratological concepts which will be employed in the book.

The definition of narratorial commentary is vital to this investigation. In general, narratorial commentary is identified by the narrator's calling attention to his or her own voice. This can be accomplished by a departure from the narrative mode in the form of shifts in tense, person or syntax, by generalisations and rhetorical questions or by the use of a first-person pronoun – all devices which draw the reader's attention to a narratorial presence. But it is possible to define narratorial commentary even more exactly by looking at temporal states in the text.

As early as 1817, Charles Lamb raised the issue of present tenses, indicating in a letter to a friend that 'My Now' at the time of writing is different from 'Your Now' at the time of reading. Lamb argued that '[t]his confusion of tenses, this grand solecism of two presents, is in a degree common to all postage'.[1] The idea of 'two presents' – a narrative present

---

1 *Distant Correspondants*, quoted in A. A. Mendilow, *Time and the Novel* (London: Peter Neville, 1952), p. 99.

and the reader's present – has occupied many literary theorists and produced various systems for distinguishing and labelling narrative time and
reading time. Seymour Chatman distinguishes between what he calls 'dis-
course-time' and 'story-time', the former indicating the time it takes an
actual reader to read a text and the latter signifying the period of time it
takes for events to unfold in the story.[2] Chatman's concepts were inspired
by Günther Müller's elaboration of Erzählzeit and Erzählte Zeit, which
discriminates between the time it takes to represent events in the narrative
and the time that is narrated.[3] Paul Ricoeur extends Müller's scheme by
adding a third dimension which is not essentially textual but produced by
the structure, assortment and distribution of pivotal episodes in the text
– what he calls 'the time of life'.[4] These considerations of time, however,
are concerned with the temporal structure of the narrative act versus that
of the time narrated.[5] A. A. Mendilow notices a further dimension to the
perception of time in the narrative. Observing that narratives establish
a sense of 'now' in the story, irrespective of whether it is narrated in the
past or present tense, Mendilow perceives two 'nows' in the narrative: the
'now' of the story and the 'now' of the discourse, the latter referring to the
time occupied by the narrator who steps out from the 'imaginary frame of
the novel to address the reader in person'.[6] These addresses to the reader,
Mendilow continues, 'recall [the reader] from the "Relative Now" of the
characters to his own "Absolute Now"'.

Mendilow's suggestion of 'two presents' is helpful in the development of a precise definition of narratorial commentary. Proceeding from
Mendilow's two 'nows', this study introduces the concepts *story-time now*

---

2   Seymour Chatman, *Story and Discourse: Narrative Structure in Fiction and Film* (Ithaca:
    Cornell University Press, 1978), p. 62. Monika Fludernik questions the story vs.
    discourse dichotomy as the focal point of narratology as, she argues, the definition of
    the concept 'story' becomes 'nearly impossible in reference to the twentieth-century
    novel'; see *Towards a 'Natural' Narratology* (London: Routledge, 1996), p. 335.
3   Günther Müller, *Morphologische Poetik* (Tübingen: Max Niemeyer, 1968).
4   Ricoeur calls for a 'three-tiered scheme: utterance-statement-world of the text, to which
    correspond a time of narrating, a narrated time, and a fictive experience of time projected
    by the conjunction/disjunction between the time it takes to narrate and narrated time';
    see *Time and Narrative*, 2 vols., trans. by Kathleen McLaughlin and David Pellauer
    (Chicago: University of Chicago Press, 1984), p. 77.
5   Applying these ideas of temporality to film, Christian Metz explains the differences in
    narrative time as the 'time of the thing told' compared to 'the time of the narrative';
    Film Language: A Semiotics of the Cinema, trans. by Michael Taylor (New York: Oxford
    University Press, 1974), p. 18. Gérard Genette breaks the idea of narrative time down
    further into classifications of order, duration and frequency, but each of these categories
    remains intrinsically textual. See *Narrative Discourse: An Essay in Method*, trans. by Jane
    E. Lewin (Ithaca: Cornell University Press, 1980).
6   Mendilow, p. 99.

and *narration now*. Story-time now comprises the events and developments of the actual story, the present in the narrative in which the reader
is engrossed. Encouraging the latter to enter a fictional world at a time and
place removed from his or her own present, story-time now invites the
reader into an imagined world in which principles, value systems, community structures and languages may be different from what he or she is
familiar with. This type of now, which corresponds to Mendilow's 'relative
now', allows the reader to open up to new worlds and explore fresh pos-
sibilities within the boundaries set by the narrative. The second now in
Eliot's novels appears as the reader is unexpectedly pulled away from the
succession of events and directly addressed by the narrator.

These direct addresses force the reader into an awareness of self, offering
the illusion of a possible dialogue with the narrator and of the existence
of another now which is present in the narrative but separated from the
development of the story. This now, the narration now, is a present shared
by the narrator and the reader; it constitutes an ontological level which is
detached from the story but also detached from the reader's actual temporal constrictions, as it allows reader and narrator to 'meet' in an exclusive
sphere. Narration now thus differs from Mendilow's 'absolute now' in that
it does not jolt the reader into his or her own 'here and now' in the sense
that the reader becomes concretely aware of his or her own existing place
and time, that is, his or her 'absolute now'. Rather, it offers an exclusive
and timeless now which is shared by reader and narrator only. Hence, the
reader is still engrossed in the reading and part of the reading world, but
propelled onto a different ontological level with the narrator. Accordingly,
narratorial commentary in Eliot's novels occurs when the narrator halts
story-time now, taking the reader into a narration-now sphere where he or
she is invited into communication with the narrator.

With regard to the operations of commentary, Ansgar Nünning's differ-
entiation between four groups of narratorial functions forms an important
recent development. Nünning delineates a technical function, an analytical
function, a synthetic function and functions orientated towards the act of
narration. These functions serve as descriptions, explanations, corrections,
analyses and evaluations of, and generalisations on the texts in which they
are embedded, being inspired by Roman Jakobson's elaboration of six functions which describe the communication processes within narrative texts.[7]

7 Ansgar Nünning, 'Steps towards a Discourse-Oriented Narratology of the Fairy Tale:
   On the Functions of the Narrator in Hans Christian Andersen's Fairy Tales', in *When
   We Get to the End…: Towards a Narratology of the Fairy Tales of Hans Christian Andersen*,
   ed. by Per Krogh Hansen and Marianne Wolff Lundholt (Odense: University Press of
   Southern Denmark, 2005), pp. 27-51.

Although Nünning's model of narratorial functions is elaborate and illuminating, it will not be emphasised in the ensuing analyses of Eliot's novels as these functions do not exclusively relate to commentary, but include such narratorial functions as the presentation of fictional worlds through descriptions of settings and characters. Additionally, Nünning's investigation is primarily concerned with pinpointing categories from a narratological point of view rather than with distinguishing the *ways* in which narratorial comments operate to shape reader response. Furthermore, Nünning's categorisation does not engage the temporal dimension which sets narratorial commentary apart from other modes of narratorial expression. Consequently, this study acknowledges and makes use of Nünning's categorisation, but adduces the temporal dimension which is essential to the definition of narratorial commentary.

The Narrator

The practice of what has been termed 'the author's intrusion' has existed in literature since ancient times. In 'modern' English literature, Anthony Trollope's and William Makepeace Thackeray's novels offer some of the most striking examples of authorial intrusions. Henry Fielding also indulged in the habit but would occasionally ask for the reader's 'pardon for this short appearance, by way of chorus on the stage'.[8] Authorial intrusions were not an unproblematic feature of the early novel, however, as novelists in the late nineteenth century became aware.[9] Objections to narrative intervention increased as literary critics started to question the idea of the 'author's' presence in a fictional text. Henry James, for example, was severe

8   Henry Fielding, *The History of Tom Jones*, vol. 1 (London: Everyman's Library, 1962), p. 93. Ian Watt criticises Fielding's authorial intrusions, alleging that they strip the narrative of authenticity. He claims that they 'break with almost every narrative precedent, beginning with that set by Homer, whom Aristotle praised for saying "very little in *propria persona*" '. *The Rise of the Novel: Studies in Defoe, Richardson and Fielding* (London: Chatto & Windus, 1957; repr. London: Pimlico, 2000), p. 286.

9   Indeed, George Eliot herself was conscious of critical attitudes towards the convention of narratorial intrusions, commenting in her 'Leaves' on Sterne: 'The objections to Sterne's wild way of telling "Tristram Shandy" lie more solidly in the quality of the interrupting matter than in the fact of interruption. The dear public would do well to reflect that they are often bored from the want of flexibility in their own minds. They are like the topers of "one liquor" '; see 'Leaves from a Note-Book', in *Essays of George Eliot*, ed. by Thomas Pinney (London: Routledge & Kegan Paul, 1963), pp. 437-451 (p. 446). Hereafter cited as *Essays*.

in his criticism, commenting that '[c]ertain accomplished novelists have a habit of giving themselves away which must often bring tears to the eyes of people who take their fiction seriously'.[10] James argued that narratives should unfold visibly without the author stepping in to remind the reader of the text's fictionality. He was followed by Joseph Warren Beach, who coined the phrase 'exit author' to describe a new self-sufficiency on the part of the text.[11] In 1921 Percy Lubbock outlined a new approach to literature which drew on the opposition between 'showing' and 'telling', anticipating formalist and neocritical approaches which value structural complexity and language over fidelity to life and mimetic considerations.[12] These more recent attitudes towards the author's relation to the narrative have been incorporated into modern literary theory to such an extent that the author's absence from the narrative text is often tacitly assumed.[13] Even so, the question of who speaks in the text remains. If the author is not the speaking agent, then instances in the text which call attention to a narrative presence raise questions about who the speaker is, what relation he/she bears to the author and what position he/she occupies in the world of the story.

---

10 Henry James, 'The Art of Fiction', in *Partial Portraits* (London: Macmillan, 1899), pp. 375-408 (p. 379). It is important to note that James does not object to commentary *per se*; for example, he praises Balzac's historical tone, which is primarily achieved through commentary. James's issue is with the type of commentary or intrusion which reminds the reader that he or she is involved in a fabrication of events and characters, that is, that the narrative he or she is reading is fictitious.

11 See Joseph Warren Beach, *The Twentieth-Century Novel: Studies in Technique* (New York: Appleton-Century-Crofts, 1932), pp. 14-24.

12 See Percy Lubbock, *The Craft of Fiction* (London: Jonathan Cape, 1921), *passim*.

13 The discussion of the author's relation to the text continued throughout the twentieth century and particularly with the emergence of post-structuralist theories on literature. The apex of the debate was Roland Barthes' essay 'The Death of the Author', which attacks the critical practice of regarding the author as the supreme source of explanation of a text. Barthes argues that the author's 'death' means that the author's own identity is put on hold in the act of writing. It is language which speaks, not the author, as he or she is only the instance writing, not the instance speaking or meaning. See Roland Barthes, 'The Death of the Author', in *The Rustle of Language*, trans. by Richard Howard (New York: Hill & Wang, 1986), pp. 49-55. Andrew Bennett argues that Roland Barthes and Michel Foucault 'laid the foundations for later literary-critical and theoretical thinking about authors', maintaining that their essays challenge readers and critics to analyse the 'relationship between text or work or oeuvre and the historical agent'; *The Author* (London: Routledge, 2005), p. 28. However, it could be argued that these foundations were laid already with Wimsatt's and Beardsley's intentional and affective fallacies or even with T. S. Eliot's contention in 'Tradition and the Individual Talent' that 'the poet has, not a "personality" to express, but a particular medium, which is only a medium and not a personality'. See T. S. Eliot, *Selected Essays*, 3rd enlarged edition (London: Faber and Faber, 1951), pp. 19-20 (first publ. in *The Egoist*, 1919).

The early twentieth century saw a complete division between the author and the narrator. In *Aesthetics*, Monroe Beardsley contends that 'the speaker of a literary work cannot be identified with the author – and therefore the character and condition of the speaker can be known by internal evidence alone'.[14] Gérard Genette upholds a distinction between narrators and authors by declaring that 'the role of narrator is itself fictive, even if assumed directly by the author', explaining by means of an example that 'the narrator of *Père Goriot* "is" not Balzac, even if here and there he expresses Balzac's opinions, for this author-narrator is someone who "knows" the Vauquer boarding-house, its landlady and its lodgers, whereas all Balzac himself does is imagine them'.[15] As early as 1872, Edward Dowden commented on the separateness between Eliot as a person and the narrative voice in her novels, referring to that ' "second self" who writes her books, and lives and speaks through them'.[16] The idea of the author's second self was adopted by Wayne Booth, who regards it as the novelist's constructed image of himself in the narrative. This 'second self' Booth translated into the implied author, who exists in the narrative as the author's 'implied version of "himself" '.[17] According to Booth, the implied author is distinct from the narrator as he/she does not narrate events and situations but rather exists behind the scenes, assuming responsibility for the structure of the narrative and for the 'values and cultural norms it adheres to'.[18] Seymour Chatman explains the implied author as 'the principle that invented the narrator, along with everything else in the narrative', an entity which 'instructs us silently, through the design of the whole'.[19] Chatman argues that the distinction between narrator and implied author is most evident when the narrator is unreliable. In fact, the narrator's unreliability, Chatman maintains, is most clearly discerned when his or her values obviously diverge from those of the implied author.[20] According to Chatman, the implied author has no voice, 'no direct means of communication' (148), which means that he/she cannot be accountable for the interac-

---

14 Monroe Beardsley, *Aesthetics: Problems in the Philosophy of Criticism* (New York: Harcourt, Brace & World, 1958), p. 240.

15 Genette, pp. 213-214.

16 Edward Dowden, 'George Eliot', in *A Century of George Eliot Criticism*, ed. by Gordon S. Haight (London: Methuen & Co Ltd, 1965), pp. 64-73 (p. 64). Dowden's essay was first publ. in *The Contemporary Review*, 20 (1872), 403-422.

17 Wayne Booth, *The Rhetoric of Fiction* (Chicago: The University of Chicago Press, 1961), p. 70.

18 Gerald Prince, *A Dictionary of Narratology* (Lincoln: University of Nebraska Press, 2003), p. 42.

19 Chatman, p. 148.

20 Chatman, p. 149. The idea of the reliable and unreliable narrator was first expressed in Wayne Booth's *Rhetoric of Fiction*.

tion between text and reader brought about by narratorial commentary.[21] Hence, although the implied author is responsible for the 'design' of the narrative and although – in Shlomith Rimmon-Kenan's words – it is a 'construct inferred and assembled by the reader from all the components of the text', the implied author possesses no voice and cannot communicate with the reader. Consequently, the implied-author concept will not be employed in the following analyses.[22]

The narrative voice in a literary text derives from one or several narrators, if not from fictional characters. This voice has been explored in detail by Genette who elaborated a typology of narrative levels, each signifying 'the level at which an existent, event, or act of recounting is situated with regard to a given diegesis'.[23] Recounting the events of the diegesis at a narrative level above the diegetic, the narrators in George Eliot's novels usually appear on the extradiegetic level; they are consequently extradiegetic narrators.[24] The notion of the extradiegetic narrator is defined by the narrative level at which he/she is positioned in relation to the diegesis. The extradiegetic narrator is hence external to the story he/she narrates and positioned at a level above it. In contrast, the intradiegetic narrator is part of the narrated story and situated on the same level as the diegesis. Genette also defines narrators according to the relationship they have to the story. A narrator who does not tell his/her own story is defined as heterodiegetic; that is, he/she is absent from the events and situations recounted in the narrative. The opposite phenomenon is termed, logically, homodiegetic,

---

21 Booth, however, speaks about the various versions of the author's self in a text which 'are most evident when the second self is given an overt, speaking role in the story' (71). Booth goes on to explain that when 'Fielding comments, he gives us explicit evidence of a modifying process from work to work' but then defines the narrator as a dramatised spokesperson for the implied author (71-72). As Booth speaks of Fielding's, that is, the actual author's, commentary and is somewhat unclear on the differences between the enunciator of commentary, the author's second self and the narrator, I have chosen to understand the 'implied author' concept as it is explained by Seymour Chatman and Shlomith Rimmon-Kenan.

22 Shlomith Rimmon-Kenan, *Narrative Fiction: Contemporary Poetics* (London: Routledge, 1983), p. 87.

23 Prince, *A Dictionary of Narratology*, p. 20. It is possible, as Richard Walsh does, to pursue the question of who speaks further by questioning who the narrator really is. Walsh suggests that the narrator can only be the author or a character, a proposition interesting to compare with Jonathan Culler's idea of authors and narratives. Following Barthes' notion of the death of the author, Culler objects to what he considers a 'naturalisation' of the narrator, arguing that narratives indicate the impersonality of language itself. Rather than representing a personal voice, Culler maintains, narrative is simply language or 'writing'. See Jonathan Culler, *Structuralist Poetics* (Ithaca: Cornell University Press, 1975), p. 201, and Richard Walsh, 'Who Is the Narrator?', *Poetics Today*, 18 (1997), 495-513.

24 Some exceptions occur, but these will be discussed in the respective chapters below.

signifying a narrator who is also a character in the narrative he/she relates. Eliot's narrators thus exist in an extradiegetic-heterodiegetic sphere; that is, they appear on a separate ontological level from the characters in the diegesis and have no part in the diegesis themselves. Genette's terminology consequently schematises the positions that Eliot's narrators occupy in relation to the texts, as well as their level of presence in or absence from those texts.[25]

The extradiegetic-heterodiegetic sphere in which Eliot's narrators appear should not be confused with the idea of the narrator's omniscience. This concept has prevailed for a long time in literary criticism, signifying a narrator who is ubiquitous and all-knowing, able to penetrate characters' thoughts as well as see into the future and past of the narrative. The idea of the omniscient narrator has come under debate, however, as critics have questioned the adequacy of the term. Martin Wallace argues that the notion of omniscient narration 'becomes a kind of dumping-ground filled with a wide range of distinct narrative techniques' and calls for new terminology by which to distinguish the relevant techniques.[26] Similarly, Jonathan Culler heightens the complexity of the concept by questioning just how far the narrator's all-pervading knowledge extends and why the narrator chooses to reveal only parts of this omniscient knowledge. Culler suggests that there may be additional levels in between 'ordinary human limitations' and omniscience, arguing, like Wallace, that an alternative vocabulary is needed.[27] Commenting on George Eliot's fiction in particular, Culler remarks that her novels belong to the kind that would make the best cases for the notion of omniscient narration, as their narrators convey the authority of sages who reflect 'on the foibles of humankind' (31). But contradicting this impression is the narrator's tendency to reflection and rumination which, according to Culler, renders his omniscience abortive compared to the idea of an omniscient God, who 'should not need to reflect at all: he simply knows' (31). Monika Fludernik, however, regards omniscience as a 'narratorial privilege [. . .] that one most wishes a narrator to have, since it affords the reader the comforting illusion of reliability, objectivity and absolute knowledge'.[28]

---

25 Jeffrey Williams criticises Genette's idea of narrative levels, arguing that it builds on the premise that the diegesis is 'a stable or definitive category', which Williams contends it is not. See *Theory and the Novel: Narrative Reflexivity in the British Tradition* (Cambridge: Cambridge University Press, 1998), p. 37.

26 Martin Wallace, *Recent Theories of Narrative* (Ithaca: Cornell University Press, 1986), p. 146.

27 Jonathan Culler, 'Omniscience', *Narrative*, 12 (2004), 22-34 (p. 28).

28 Fludernik, *Towards a Natural Narratology*, pp. 167-168.

Referring to the narrator as 'nobody', Elizabeth Deeds Ermarth suggests that the omniscient narrator is in actuality a collective consciousness which exists 'everywhere and nowhere, brooding over the realistic work like an energy source'.[29] J. Hillis Miller maintains that the narrators in Eliot's novels take on the 'role of a collective mind', insisting that the 'term "omniscient narrator" has tended to obscure clear understanding of the narrating voice in Victorian fiction' as it comes with theological connotations.[30] Miller argues that omniscience, as evinced by Victorian novelists, refers to a 'pervasive presence' rather than a 'transcendent vision' (64) and is defined by a 'human awareness which is everywhere at all times within the world of the novel' (64).

The idea of the omniscient narrator as used in the present study takes Miller's description as a point of departure. The narrator harbours no Godlike qualities, nor is he positioned at a higher level as a supreme onlooker who sees, knows and judges characters from a distance.[31] Rather, the narrator's omniscience in Eliot's novels is revealed through a consciousness of characters' minds and through the control which the narrator displays when meta-narratively commenting on the narrating act or when referring to forthcoming narrative actions and situations. In Rimmon-Kenan's words, omniscience denotes characteristics such as 'familiarity, in principle, with the character's innermost thoughts and feelings; knowledge of past, present and future [...] and knowledge of what happens in several places at the same time' (95).[32] The narrator's omniscience is connected to his control of the narrative; that is, he is not analogous to an all-knowing creator of the cosmos in the sense that his knowledge about the world he depicts is all-pervading, or that he knows everything there is to know about the story down to the colour of each character's eyes. Rather, he is

29 Elizabeth Deeds Ermarth, *Realism and Consensus in the English Novel* (Edinburgh: Edinburgh University Press, 1998), pp. 66-67.

30 J. Hillis Miller, *The Form of Victorian Fiction: Thackeray, Dickens, Trollope, George Eliot, Meredith and Hardy* (Notre Dame: University of Notre Dame Press, 1968), p. 63.

31 Traditionally 'omniscience' has been considered, in Scholes and Kellogg's words, as 'not a descriptive term so much as a definition based on the presumed analogy between the novelist as creator and the Creator of the cosmos, an omniscient God'. Qualifying that traditional definition by pointing to the narrator's boundaries in space and time, Scholes and Kellogg's notion of omniscient narration is continually being revised, developed and questioned by narrative theorists. See *The Nature of Narrative* (London: Oxford University Press, 1966), p. 272.

32 Audrey Jaffe points out that the characteristics which define omniscience are dependent on what is not omniscience in order for the reader to understand them; that is, 'when omniscient narration demonstrates the ability to transcend the boundaries that confine characters, it must construct the very boundaries it displays itself transcending'. *Vanishing Points: Dickens, Narrative and the Subject of Omniscience* (Berkeley: University of California Press, 1991), p. 6.

omniscient in the sense that the narrative is his to control – the structure, the offering and holding back of information, the delineation of plot, the attitudes towards characters and situations all contribute to the idea of the narrator's privileged position vis-à-vis the text; and it is this position, this licence of narrative control, that will be referred to as the narrator's omniscience in this study.

The idea of narratorial omniscience is connected to concepts such as 'point of view', 'perspective' and 'focalisation'. In 1943 Cleanth Brooks and Robert Penn Warren distinguished between 'focus of narration' (who writes?) and 'focus of character' (who perceives?).[33] This distinction was developed by Genette, who posed the questions 'who speaks?' and 'who sees?'. The distinctions were necessary, as discussions of point of view in twentieth-century literary analyses were becoming increasingly unclear, giving rise to a plurality of signification which included perceptual as well as conceptual considerations.[34] Genette offered alternative terminology to 'point of view' by distinguishing between the speaker's voice and the perspective through which fictional phenomena were filtered, that is, the focalisation – a notion which has been developed and extended to form the concepts focaliser and focalised, referring to the active medium through which fictive episodes are perceived and the object of that perception.[35]

In order to avoid unnecessary complications when considering perspective, this investigation will distinguish between focalisation and perspective: the former signifies perceptual aspects only, that is, the consideration of a visual position; and the latter involves both perceptual and conceptual aspects, that is, the consideration of attitudes or conceptual mechanisms without regard to physical positioning. Therefore, when Eliot's narrators bring in alternative perspectives, they present the reader with matters of

---

33 Cleanth Brooks and Robert Penn Warren, *Understanding Fiction* (New York: Appleton-Century-Crofts, 1943), pp. 586-594.

34 Seymour Chatman identifies three senses in which 'point of view' can be understood: the literal sense which indicates perception, the figurative sense which indicates conception and the point of interest which indicates the egoistic vantage-point of a particular subject, pp. 151-152.

35 Genette himself made no distinction between focaliser and focalised. To him focalisation is the prism through which a story is mediated, a prism which has a degree of abstractness and cannot be attributed to a single agent in the text. Mieke Bal has developed Genette's theory of focalisation to include the notion of a focalising and focalised agent; see *Narratology: Introduction to the Theory of Narrative*, trans. by Christine Van Boheemen (Toronto: Toronto University Press, 1985). See also *Narrative Discourse Revisited*, trans. by Jane E. Lewin (Ithaca: Cornell University Press, 1988), for Genette's response to Bal's discussion on focalisation. Monika Fludernik argues that 'focalisation' is an unsatisfactory term as the narrator is not a 'seer' in the story, but rather the 'producer' of it; see *Towards a Natural Narratology*, p. 345.

cognition, ideology or sentiment which add new dimensions to the reader's interpretation of fictive episodes. Significantly, however, alternative perspectives may be presented through focalisation, allowing the reader to view situations and events through the 'eyes' of characters or narrators and thereby shaping his or her interpretation of the text. Perspective and focalisation are thus interconnected terms, impossible to separate absolutely. But the distinction between the concepts is useful in the study of narratorial commentary in Eliot's novels which often serves to shift viewpoints, presenting the reader with alternative perspectives as well as with new mediums of focalisation.

According to Genette's classification of mood, distance is another factor – along with perspective – which controls narrative information. In Genette's understanding, distance refers to the imagined span between the particularities of the narrative and their narration. The more concealed the narrating medium and the more plentiful the details of the narrative, the less distance is believed to exist between the narrative and its narration; if the narratorial presence is explicit and the details of narrative situations limited, the distance between narration and narrative is thought to be enhanced. But the idea of distance can also be used to denote the metaphorical space between narrator and reader, between the narrator and characters or fictive events as well as between reader and events and characters. Booth shows that this type of distance can be moral, intellectual or emotional and can vary in degree within the body of the novel.[36] Discussions of distance in this study are indebted to Booth's understanding of the term. Considering the narrator's and the reader's relation to diegetic properties, distance will be discussed as the narrator's or reader's imagined moral, intellectual or emotional closeness to the narrative, but also in terms of the imagined closeness between narrator and reader. Through narratorial commentary, the narrator in Eliot's novels adjusts the reader's distance to the properties of the text in order to shape his or her understanding of particular phenomena. This distance, then, is a measure of the reader's emotional, intellectual or moral involvement in the text which is continually modified along with the narrator's variable commentary.

Genette has also coined the term metalepsis which denotes the intrusion of a persona from one diegesis into another level of diegesis, i.e. the combining of two distinct diegetic levels. For instance, when the extradiegetic narrator unexpectedly appears as a character in the diegesis or indi-

---

36 See Booth, pp. 155-159.

cates the reader's capacity to 'see' characters or events, metalepsis occurs.[37] In Eliot's fiction this phenomenon belongs primarily to the early novels, where it is related both to the narrator's participation as a character in the narrative body and to the reader's imagined tangible access to narrative properties. Disregarding ontological limitations, the narrator may refer to the reader's ability to look through a fictive window or see the shape of a hand. The narrator thus transgresses the boundaries between the reader's world and the imagined world of the narrative, giving the impression that ontological limitations can be overcome, i.e. suggesting that the reader has direct sensory access to the narrative.

As a preliminary to analysing the functions of narratorial commentary in Eliot's novels, it is interesting to look at Genette's classification of narratorial functions in any piece of fiction. Genette distinguishes five narratorial functions in a text. The first and most obvious relates to the act of narrating, which he calls the 'narrative function'. The second is connected to the structural organisation of the text and identified as a 'directing function', and the third, the function of communication, concerns the narrator's interaction with the reader (or narratee). Genette's fourth function relates to the narrator's own association with the narrative, a 'testimonial function' which indicates the narrator's affective, moral and intellectual relation to the story. Finally, the fifth function, which Genette calls 'ideological', constitutes the 'narrator's interventions, direct or indirect', which may 'take the more didactic form of an authorized commentary on the action'.[38] The present analysis, however, will show that these interventions in Eliot's novels possess much more than an ideological function and that narratorial comments, or what Genette calls interventions, serve all five types of functions. Indeed, narratorial commentary forms part of the narrator's most overt presence in the text, so it seems only reasonable that these instances of narratorial presence should involve direction, communication and testimony as well as ideology.

---

37 Genette is suspicious of this phenomenon, claiming that 'any intrusion by the extradiegetic narrator or narratee into the diegetic universe [...] produces an effect of strangeness that is either comical [...] or fantastic' (235). The statement is a value-judgment difficult to argue with, as it is based on personal opinion. But it should be noted that examples of metalepsis are not unusual in Eliot's early novels, none of which have, in general critical opinion, been accused of including elements of the fantastic.

38 Genette, p. 256. See also Carl D. Malmgren, who identifies three types of commentary in Eliot's novels: the personal statement, the ideological statement and the metalingual statement. While these three types of commentary certainly appear in Eliot's novels, Malmgren's classification is somewhat reductive, leaving out types of commentary which further affect the reader's understanding of the text.

The Reader

Throughout literary history authors have been aware that every narrative involves a rhetorical situation, its means of subsistence depending on its being read or heard by an audience. This awareness was developed in the second half of the twentieth century within the framework of what is now referred to as reader-oriented theories.[39] Emphasising the reader's, viewer's or hearer's active involvement in the act of interpretation and complementing the scrutiny of the narrator's division into implied, omniscient, reliable and unreliable, literary criticism in the 1960s saw an increasing interest in questions pertaining to the identity and role of the reader. Founded on the premise that narrative meaning is never self-formulated, reader-oriented theories maintain that readers must engage with the textual material in order to create meaning – in other words, meaning is not inscribed in the text for the reader to receive passively, but produced through his or her active participation in the reading process.[40]

However, reader-oriented criticism is not a single field of study but an interlacing of often contradictory trails that cover a substantial section of the critical landscape. Several different approaches in literary criticism can be discerned under the umbrella of reader-response theory; to name a few, it includes rhetorical, structural, phenomenological and hermeneutic approaches. These methods of analysis are not absolute systems in themselves; each of them in turn comprises a number of variations and their advocates. The following section reviews those aspects of reader-oriented criticism which are relevant to the examination of narratorial commentary in Eliot's novels. Its aim is therefore not to provide an exhaustive account

---

39 The 1960s saw an explosion of literary theories which were concerned with the reader's role in the narrative situation, but these concerns were by no means original. For example, in 'The Novels of George Eliot', published as early as 1866, Henry James states: 'In every novel the work is divided between the writer and the reader; but the writer makes the reader very much as he makes his characters. When he makes them ill, that is, makes him indifferent, he does no work; the writer does all. When he makes him well, that is, makes him interested, then the reader does quite half the labor'. In *A Century of George Eliot Criticism*, ed. by Gordon Haight (London: Methuen, 1965), pp. 43-54 (p. 48): first publ. in the *Atlantic Monthly*, 18 (1866), 479-492.

40 A central problem for reader-oriented theories concerns the question of whether the narrative itself activates the reader's act of interpretation or whether the reader's own interpretative approach, that is, the preconceived attitudes he or she incorporates, is imposed on the text. Umberto Eco has proposed a solution, suggesting that texts can be either 'open' or 'closed'. An open text, Eco argues, encourages the reader's involvement in the construction of meaning, whereas a closed text predetermines the reader's interpretation. See *The Role of the Reader: Explorations in the Semiotics of Texts* (Bloomington: Indiana University Press, 1979).

of reader-response or reception theories, but to broach ideas pertaining to the reader which are especially relevant to an analysis of narratorial commentary. The types of reader-oriented analyses which are particularly interesting to the study at hand are those approaches which construct theories based on questions concerning who the reader is, what role he or she plays in the act of interpretation and how narrative meaning is produced.

Concerned with the identity of the recipient of a narratorial address, Gerald Prince recognises how texts produce their own readers. The narratee, he states, is a fictional construct, produced by the text as an imaginary character whom the narrator addresses. Distinguished from the 'actual' flesh-and-blood reader and functioning as an interlocutor to the narrator, the narratee may be specified in terms of gender, class, age or other particulars and may also be identified through more or less overt signals, such as the narrator's questions and solicitations to or attacks on an imagined reader.[41] Attempting to answer questions about how the narratee can be identified and what narrative tasks he or she performs, Prince considers the narrator's direction of attention, proposing that narration may be directed to a receiver represented as a character or a receiver who exists in the narrative as a silent listener or reader. Alternatively, narration may be directed first at one receiver, then at another and so on, or it may be intended for one receiver but unintentionally fall into the hands of another. Significantly, Prince suggests, narration may be directed at a receiver who is not represented as a character but who exists as a 'real-life receiver'.[42] The narratee, however, being always the receiver of the narratorial address and the one narrated to, should not be confused with the 'real-life receiver', that is, the actual reader. As the narratee is a textual construct, it is a constant element in the narrative which has a fixed set of narratees but can have an illimitable amount of actual readers.[43] Prince furthermore distinguishes between

---

41 See Gerald Prince, *Narratology: The Form and Functioning of Narrative* (Berlin: Mouton Publishers, 1982), p. 57. Robyn R. Warhol proceeds from Prince's idea of the narratee when coining the phrase 'engaging narrator'. According to Warhol, the engaging narrator promotes the notion of an engaging narratee. In Warhol's scheme the engaging narrator attempts to reduce the distance or gap between the narratee, the addressee and the receiver in order to stimulate actual readers to identify with the narratee in the text. Warhol argues that, encouraging the reader to identify fully with the engaging narratee, Eliot's narrators (as well Harriet Beecher Stowe's and Elizabeth Gaskell's) – by serving as 'their author's surrogates in earnestly trying to foster sympathy for real-world sufferers – work to engage "you" through the substance and, failing that, the stance of their narrative interventions and addresses to "you" ' (813).

42 Gerald Prince, 'On Readers and Listeners in Narrative', *Neophilologus*, 55 (1971), 117-122 (p. 119).

43 Michael Kearns accepts Prince's notion of the narratee but qualifies it, arguing that the term should be restricted to those instances when an audience is explicitly referred to or

the narratee and the 'virtual reader', who is the reader on whom the narrator 'bestows […] certain qualities, faculties, and inclinations according to his opinion of men in general' – that is, the type of reader that the author imagines for his or her narrative.[44] Moreover, the narratee is different from the 'ideal reader', the reader who understands and sympathises with the author's every move.

Developments in reader-response criticism have triggered debates about the recipients of narratorial addresses, elaborating on as well as qualifying Prince's seminal investigation of the narratee. Some of these discussions regarding the reader are important to consider in connection with George Eliot's narratorial commentary, as instances of reader address naturally imply information about the reader, or, in Prince's view, about the narratee. According to Prince, as was pointed out above, narration is addressed to a narratee who should not be confused with the reader. The narratee is also distinct from what Wolfgang Iser calls the 'implied reader'. The implied reader constitutes the implied author's audience and is inferable from the text. Inscribed into the text like the narratee, the implied reader is distinguished from the narratee because he/she does not serve as an addressee for the narrator. Moreover, the notion of the implied reader should be distinguished from the actual reader, as the former is textually constructed and the latter is not. Constituting an arrangement of response-inviting schemes which incline readers to make specific interpretations of the text, the implied reader is the reader whom the text fashions for itself. In Iser's view, the notion of the implied reader is closely related to meaning-production in the reading process. Iser argues that the presentation of the novel as a genre in the eighteenth century aspired to the effect of involving readers in the world of the novel through which they could arrive at a better understanding of their own world. The novel genre contends with historical norms and social values, but does so by situating them in new contexts which change their functions, eventually leading to a questioning rather than a substantiation of their legitimacy. This confusion and negation of norms forces the reader to participate actively in the construction of meaning in the novel. This is where the term 'implied reader' comes in, defined by Iser as 'both the prestructuring of the potential meaning by the text, and the reader's actualization of this potential through the reading

---

addressed. See *Rhetorical Narratology* (Lincoln: University of Nebraska Press, 1999), pp. 114-117.

44 Gerald Prince, 'Introduction to the Study of the Narratee', in *Reader-Response Criticism: From Formalism to Post-Structuralism*, ed. by Jane P. Tompkins (Baltimore: Johns Hopkins University Press, 1980), pp. 7-25 (p. 9).

process'.[45] The 'implied reader' thus, Iser argues, 'refers to the active nature of this process – which will vary historically from one age to another – and not to a typology of possible readers' (xii).

The idea of the implied reader has replaced what Walker Gibson referred to as the 'mock reader'. According to Gibson, the mock reader is a fictional construct 'whose mask and costume the individual takes on in order to experience the language' of the text.[46] Put simply, the text invites the reader to identify with the mock reader in order for him or her to experience the full impact of the narrative. Gibson maintains that the language of the text recreates the living, breathing reader into a mock reader, a role which incorporates a 'set of attitudes and qualities' which the reader must assume in his or her capacity as mock reader. Should the reader choose not to assume this role, the narrative becomes unreadable.[47]

The development of reader-response theories has given rise to an abundance of terms dedicated to identifying the receiving party of a narrative text. The most important concepts regarding the reader in the present context, the narratee and the implied reader, have been discussed above in some detail; but it is also useful to mention a few further concepts with a bearing on the identity of the reader which, although not directly material to the study at hand, form natural parts of a review of theoretical discussions pertaining to the reader in the context of the narrative.

A number of concepts concern the type of reader the author wishes for. Mention has already been made of Prince's 'ideal reader', sometimes referred to as the 'optimal reader' who, as the term suggests, is a hypothetical reader highly equipped, in terms of understanding, experience and insight, for discerning the utmost potential in the text. Associated with the ideal reader is Michael Riffaterre's 'super-reader' who is familiar not only with the text itself, but with all the possible interpretations, analyses and debates it has generated. In a sense the super-reader incorporates the sum of reactions to a particular text, with which he/she re-approaches it to pursue meaning beyond the surface.[48] The 'model reader' is a concept coined by

45 Wolfgang Iser, *The Implied Reader: Patterns of Communication in Prose Fiction from Bunyan to Beckett* (Baltimore: The Johns Hopkins University Press, 1974), p. xii.

46 Walker Gibson, 'Authors, Speakers, Readers, and Mock Readers', in *Reader-Response Criticism: From Formalism to Post-Structuralism*, ed. by Jane P. Tompkins (Baltimore: Johns Hopkins University Press, 1980), pp. 1-6 (p. 2), first publ. in *College English*, 11 (1950), 265-269.

47 Gibson, p. 1.

48 See Michael Riffaterre, *Semiotics of Poetry* (London: Methuen, 1978). Riffaterre is concerned with meaning-production principally and argues for a type of narrative analysis that goes beyond and below the surface level to decipher ways in which grammatical and phonemic patterns in narratives (Riffaterre's studies mainly apply to poetry) deviate from standard representation. By being 'literary competent', Riffaterre

Umberto Eco, who imagines that the author construes a model reader in order to establish communication between text and reader. This potential reader reads in accordance with the interpretative strategies constructed by the text. While it is up to the actual reader to interpret the narrative in any way he or she chooses, the model reader's interpretation, Eco argues, suggests itself as an exemplary reading.[49] Stanley Fish defines the best possible reader as the 'informed reader' who possesses a number of qualities, ranging from an intrinsic knowledge of the language of which the text is constructed to a literary competence which he explains as the reader's internalised understanding of literary conventions. The informed reader, Fish argues, is 'neither an abstraction nor an actual living reader, but a hybrid – a real reader (me) who does everything within his power to make himself informed'.[50]

As a rejoinder to these theories of idealised readers, some critics have proposed that interpretation should involve the reader's defiance of potential authoritarian structures of power inscribed in the text. An 'oppositional reading' is required to contest possible interpretative strategies encoded in the text. For example, Judith Fetterley suggests that women should read classic literature critically and judiciously in order to resist reading as men.[51] Rather than speaking of readers, Peter J. Rabinowitz refers to audiences and distinguishes between three kinds: the 'actual audience' corresponds to the actual reader, the living breathing person reading a text; the 'authorial audience' is an imaginary group of interpreters to whom the author addresses himself; and, finally, the 'narrative audience', Rabinowitz suggests, constitutes the role which the text imposes on the reader.[52]

Theories on who the reader is and what role he or she plays in the interpretative process thus abound, making it almost impossible to distinguish between the many definitions of readers that have emerged from the vast field of reader-response theory. In respect of narratorial commentary in George Eliot's novels, the notions of narratee and implied reader are, as was mentioned above, the most important ones, as these concepts not only embrace several of the types of readers described above but also function

---

maintains, the reader will be impelled to decode grammatical deviations which will eventually lead to an uncovering of another level of significance in the text.

49 See Eco, pp. 204-217.

50 Stanley Fish, 'Literature in the Reader: Affective Stylistics', in *Is There a Text in This Class? The Authority of Interpretive Communities* (Cambridge, MA: Harvard University Press, 1980), p. 49.

51 See Judith Fetterley, *The Resisting Reader: A Feminist Approach to American Fiction* (Bloomington: Indiana University Press, 1978), pp. xi-xxvi.

52 See Peter J. Rabinowitz, *Before Reading: Narrative Conventions and the Politics of Interpretation* (Ithaca: Cornell University Press, 1987).

as accepted models for the notion of a responding reader in the realm of narratology.

With regard to narratorial commentary, the notion of the implied reader as receiver of and respondent to addresses is problematic given that the implied reader is explained as a fictional construct that responds to the implied author and not to the narrator. The text creates the implied reader for itself as an arrangement of response-inviting structures, influencing readers to make particular interpretations. It does not, however, create the implied reader as addressee for the narrator's comments. Instead, the narrator addresses himself to a narratee – a fictional construct that can be more or less specified in terms of gender, class or age.

However, the notion of a responding narratee appears slippery, as commentary generally serves to shape the reactions of an imagined respondent in some way. In Eliot's novels, moreover, the narratee is usually unspecified, and any signs which might embody information about him or her are concealed. Prince acknowledges that narratees can be either overt or covert but does not elaborate further on this distinction. Genette claims that the extradiegetic narrator 'can aim only at an extradiegetic narratee, who merges with the implied reader and with whom each real reader can identify'.[53] Considering these ambiguities regarding the narratee – that is, with regard to the indistinct relation between overt and covert narratees, and to the idea of a merging extradiegetic narratee and implied reader – this study will refer to the responding party of narratorial commentary as, simply, the reader. This reader is defined, in accordance with Genette's understanding, as the amalgam of extradiegetic narratee and implied reader with which the actual reader identifies.[54] This reader, furthermore, serves as a general everyman reader; hence the concept does not claim to encompass the potential responses of all possible readers, but serves as a representative idea of a reader. The notion of the narratee, in this study, accords with Michael Kearns's proposal that the concept applies to those instances where the recipient is clearly and distinctly specified in terms of actual characteristics such as age, dress or class – all other narratorial addresses will be considered

---

53 Genette, p. 260.

54 The idea of the implied reader is also discussed by Wayne Booth, who regards the concept as a counterpart to his idea of the implied author. Booth argues that for a successful reading the actual reader must agree with the implied reader's values and norms, regardless of his or her own 'beliefs and practices' (138). Susan R. Suleiman rightly points out that such agreements or identifications with the implied reader might be difficult or even impossible in certain literary works. See 'Introduction: Varieties of Audience-Oriented Criticism', in *The Reader in the Text: Essays on Audience and Interpretation*, ed. by Susan R. Suleiman and Inge Crosman (Princeton: Princeton University Press, 1980).

as directed to the reader.[55] It is important to understand, however, that this study is concerned with analysing the methods by which narratorial commentary shapes the reader's responses rather than with analysing the actual effects that narratorial commentary has on readers. In other words, the investigation focuses on narrative method rather than on narrative effect.

Several reader-oriented theories explore the question of how meaning is produced. Although this study is not directly concerned with the reader's perception of meaning it is useful, as a backdrop to discussions on narratorial commentary, to review some of the principal notions concerning the production of meaning in narrative texts. Employing a phenomenological approach to the reader's relation to the text, Iser regards 'meaning' as constituted in the reading process by the reader's continuous amendments and considerations of preconceived expectations. Iser conceives of a dialectical relationship between the reader and the text, a relationship which is constituted by the text's stipulation as to how it should be read and the experiences that the reader brings into the reading process. Attempting to resolve the contradictions between his or her own experience, the interpretations set up by the text and the various perspectives which appear in it, the reader fills in what Iser calls 'gaps', explained as elements of indeterminacy, with his or her own creative imagination and by so doing incorporates the text into his or her experience, thereby producing meaning.[56]

Iser's phenomenological approach, although decontextualised and de-historicised, is inspired by, among others, Hans-Georg Gadamer, who argues that meaning in any literary text depends on and varies with the historical and situational context of the reader. Maintaining that meaning issues from a dialogue between past and present, Gadamer regards the interpretation of texts as conditioned by the cultural environment in which they happen to exist at any given time. The understanding of any literary text, he argues, is relative and involves regarding it from past as well as present perspectives.[57] Like Gadamer, Hans Robert Jauss – an exponent

---

55 See Kearns, pp. 114-117.

56 See Wolfgang Iser, *The Act of Reading: A Theory of Aesthetic Response* (London: Routledge & Kegan Paul, 1978), pp. 165-169. It remains unclear, however, whether Iser regards meaning as being ultimately produced by the text itself or by the reader, that is, whether he asserts the reader's pre-eminence in the role as creator, thus allowing for an innumerable quantity of individual interpretations, or whether he regards the reader's interpretation as being immanent in the text.

57 See Hans-Georg Gadamer, *Truth and Method*, trans. by Garret Barden and John Cumming (New York: Seabury Press, 1975), *passim*. Gadamer's study of texts proceeds from Heidegger's theories on the individual's subjection to and incorporation of situational and historical contexts. Hermeneutics has traditionally been identified as an approach which objects to subjective interpretation, instead endeavouring to arrive at universally valid readings of texts. Gadamer, however, subscribes to an alternative and

of 'reception theory', particularly associated with the German school of reader-oriented criticism – is concerned with general, rather than individual, responses to literary texts. [58] Coining the term 'aesthetic distance' to denote the difference of interpretation a text effects when it is first published as compared to the present day, Jauss suggests that the value of a literary text depends on how much its interpretations change over time. He devises a second term, 'horizon of expectations', to designate a collective set of assumptions and expectations attributable to any given generation of readers. The 'horizon of expectations', which changes with passing time, serves as a set of criteria for readers by which to value literary texts. In Jauss's view, then, as in Gadamer's, meaning is relative and can never be universally fixed since the 'horizon of expectations' – that is, the principles by which meaning can be ascertained – is in a state of flux, changing from one generation to the next.[59]

Similarly to Jauss's 'horizon of expectations', Stanley Fish's idea of 'interpretive communities' conceives of interpretation as something determined on a communal level. An 'interpretive community', according to Fish, includes a group of readers who share a set of strategies and conventions by which they interpret literary works. Each interpretive community, he claims, produces its own approach to the text, by implication indicating that there can be no correct or absolute interpretation. The validity of any reading will depend on the conjectures and strategies which readers share with other members of a particular interpretive community.[60] Recognising that readers construct different interpretations of texts, Jonathan Culler argues that these various readings are exactly what needs to be explained by literary theory. He claims that although readings deviate in terms of what values individuals extract from particular texts, the conventions of

more recent form of hermeneutics which springs from the hypothesis that the idea of universally valid interpretations is inconceivable.

58 Robert C. Holub describes reception theory as a 'cohesive, conscious and collective undertaking' which originated as a group effort among German scholars and primarily among scholars at the University of Constance, whereas reader-response theory, he argues, is used as a post-dated umbrella term for a collection of scholars working independently throughout the world with no intended connection to each other. See *Reception Theory: A Critical Introduction* (London: Methuen, 1984), p. xiii.

59 See Hans Robert Jauss, *Toward an Aesthetic of Reception*, trans. by Timothy Bahti (Brighton: Harvester Press, 1982), p. 142 *et passim*.

60 See Stanley Fish, pp. 167-173. Susan Suleiman points out that the idea of 'interpretive communities' represents a departure from Fish's earlier attempts to describe universal processes of competent reading. She maintains that 'whereas his earlier work affirmed there was but one road to salvation where reading and criticism are concerned [...] here he argues that how one reads is entirely a matter of shared conventions or interpretive strategies, none of which is better than another'. See *The Reader in the Text*, p. 20, n29.

interpretation which readers employ to understand meaning are shared. Therefore readers, although sharing the same conventions of reading, apply those conventions to texts in dissimilar ways and also interpret particular practices of reading differently, thus allowing for different levels and models of interpretative conventions.[61] Structuralist poetics, however, as Culler affirms, is not principally interested in extracting new interpretations from texts or charging them with meaning, but rather concerned with deciphering the codes and conventions which make the text's 'readability' possible.

Objecting to structuralist attempts at uncovering systems of codes within texts, Roland Barthes differentiates between two types of text. The 'readerly' (lisible) text, he claims, refers to the type of narrative which presents an easily recognisable world. This type of text renders the reader's response passive as he or she can, without much effort, accept meaning the way it is inscribed in the text. The realistic novel, for example, Barthes argues, offers the reader little scope for imagination as it insists on a specific meaning. The 'writerly' (scriptible) text, on the other hand, places demands on the individual reader's capacity for decoding and interpreting the text, encouraging him or her to produce meaning. These texts turn the reader into producer and creator as well as receiver, thereby allowing for as many variations of meaning as there are readers and contexts.[62]

Deconstructionist critics question the possibility of a single, cohesive construction of reading and claim that attempts at establishing meaning evade several major difficulties, not least the contradictions within the text itself. Derrida's deconstructionist enterprise sets out to undermine belief in the text as one coherent whole, or as a formatted medium of communication serving to transmit meaning between addresser and addressee. Accusing structuralist critics of being caught up in 'logocentrism', that is, in the belief that all texts contain a centre of meaning of some sort, Derrida subverts the traditional notion of textual unity, maintaining that texts contain merely differences and traces of traces.[63] Inspired by Derrida, the American deconstructionist critic Paul de Man investigates the phenomenon which occurs when a text presents readers with two possible interpretations. De Man terms the conflict which arises between two possible and equally appropriate interpretations the 'impossibility of reading'.

---

61 See Jonathan Culler, *The Pursuit of Signs: Semiotics, Literature, Deconstruction* (London: Routledge & Kegan Paul, 1981).

62 See Roland Barthes, *S/Z*, trans. by R. Miller (New York: Hill & Wang, 1970). Cf. Eco's discussion of 'open' and 'closed' texts.

63 See Jacques Derrida, *Of Grammatology*, trans. by Gayatri Chakravorty Spivak (Baltimore: Johns Hopkins University Press, 1976).

These conflicts emanate from a set of assertions which 'compel [readers] to choose while destroying the foundations of any choice'.[64] According to de Man, it is within the spaces of such impossible contradictions that reading can be most forcefully scrutinised.

Consequently, the notion of textual meaning has undergone and continues to undergo investigation in literary theory. Ranging from criticisms which conceive of meaning as produced within the reader's individual, subjective psyche via theories which consider meaning to be contextually moored and communally conditioned to notions of the impossibility of meaning, these divergent lines of reasoning form part of a vibrant spectrum the whole of which falls under the label reader-oriented theories. With regard to analyses of narratorial commentary these discussions are, as was pointed out above, not directly pertinent; but an acknowledgment of how literary theorists have addressed the production of meaning is nevertheless relevant to the present study. After all, it aims to show that narratorial commentary serves to shape the reader's responses in specific ways, which by implication suggests that narratorial commentary, in effect, compels readers to construct meaning in accordance with a particular set of structures devised by the text.

The Realist Novel

Realism as a term for describing a mode of fictional writing subsists in literary criticism as an unsatisfactory appellation, its connotations seemingly endless and eternally equivocal. What assumptions about the real world this term involves remains an intensely debated area in the field of literary criticism, expanding into several other fields of discussion such as philosophy, ideology and politics. Still, it is necessary, and generally accepted, to consider realism – as Ian Watt does in his seminal work on the history of the English novel – as a particular mode of representation.[65] Often described as narratives which concern themselves with everyday events, with the plight of ordinary human beings, with the documentation of demonstrable facts and with the narration of recognisable political and

---

64 Paul de Man, *Allegories of Reading: Figural Language in Rousseau, Nietzsche, Rilke, and Proust* (New Haven: Yale University Press, 1979), p. 245.

65 See Ian Watt, *The Rise of the Novel*. For a comprehensive discussion of 'realism' in the Victorian novel and the debates it has sparked in literary criticism, see *The Victorian Novel*, ed. by Francis O'Gorman (Oxford: Blackwell Publishing, 2002), pp. 94-148.

social movements, George Eliot's novels have been cited as prime examples of the classic realist novel. These novels concentrate on creating illusions of reality which serve to persuade readers that they are reading about 'real' life. For Victorian writers such as Trollope, Thackeray and Eliot, these illusions – viewed as attempts to maintain a relationship of similarity between art and life – are the responsibility of the artist. In 'The Natural History of German Life', Eliot argues that 'our social novels profess to represent the people as they are, and the unreality of their representations is a grave evil'.[66] She praised John Ruskin's *Modern Painters* for the importance it placed on truth to nature, commenting in the *Westminster Review* that the 'truth of infinite value that he teaches is *realism*'.[67] She firmly believed that realism in art promoted human solidarity and sympathy between humans and argued that '[a]rt is the nearest thing to life; it is a mode of amplifying experience and extending our contact with our fellow-men beyond the bounds of our personal lot'.[68] The adequate depiction of feelings and perceptions was, to Eliot, as much part of realistic representation as veracious illustrations of the 'concrete' world. For Eliot, 'truth', art and realistic representation were intrinsically intertwined, and she readily subscribed to George Henry Lewes's contention that art 'always aims at the representation of Reality, i.e. of Truth'.[69] Her notion of realistic representation stretches from the external world to the internal world of individual consciousness, expanding the realist project to include questions pertaining to the philosophy of the human mind. Eliot's novels thus demonstrate her unwillingness to separate representational exactitude from psychological conditions and moral substance.

Eliot was, however, conscious of the elusive nature of the 'realistic' idea.[70] She saw the inevitability of mediation as an inescapable impediment to ab-

---

66 *Essays*, pp. 266-299 (p. 270), first publ. in *Westminster Review*, lxvi (1856), 51-79.

67 George Eliot, 'John Ruskin's *Modern Painters*, Vol. III', in *George Eliot's Selected Critical Writings*, ed. by Rosemary Ashton (Oxford: Oxford University Press, 1992), pp. 247-259 (p. 248), first publ. in *Westminster Review*, lxv (1856), 628-633.

68 *Essays*, p. 271.

69 See *The Literary Criticism of George Henry Lewes*, ed. by Alice R. Kaminsky (Lincoln: University of Nebraska Press, 1964), pp. 87-89.

70 By acknowledging the complexities attached to realistic representation, Eliot pre-empted much of the objections raised in later literary criticism. Several post-structuralist critics, for example, regard realism as an approach to narrative which neglects the inescapable alteration of the 'real' when it is transferred into art. Catherine Belsey, for example, criticises the classic realist novel, claiming that these texts simply attempt to imitate notions of reality without recognising the complexity of language or the unreliability of the narrating medium; see *Critical Practice* (London: Methuen, 1980), pp. 67-84. Colin MacCabe argues that the classic realist text disregards its own status as writing and that it establishes a hierarchy of language, situating the narrator's language at the top from which that language serves as a lens through which 'reality' is regarded; *James Joyce and*

solute representation, commenting on her own role as mediator: 'I only try to exhibit some things as they have been or are, seen through such a medium as my own nature gives me'.[71] Although her *Adam Bede* narrator professes faithfully to represent 'men and things as they have mirrored themselves in my mind' (xvii, 175), the enterprise is qualified by the humble admission that 'the mirror is doubtless defective' (xvii, 175). Eliot was also susceptible to the complexities which language as a medium encompasses. Remarking on how it can shape individual ideas, yet misrepresent reality, the narrator in *Middlemarch* states: 'we all of us, grave or light, get our thoughts entangled in metaphors, and act fatally on the strength of them' (x, 79). Eliot also understood the impossibility of single perspectives, realising that subjectivity relentlessly influences interpretation. Perception, perspective and interpretation form integral and important themes in each novel, and Eliot's treatment of these concerns demonstrates the intellectual sophistication with which she recognised their complexities.

Much of Eliot's writing, moreover, explores the limits of realistic representation, exposing it to scrutiny and challenging its premises. Evident narratorial presences in the form of commentary and metalepses, for example, disturb the boundaries of the classic realist form and often serve to remind the reader of the text's fictionality. The first chapter of *The Mill on the Floss* introduces the narrative as a reverie in the narrator's memory, and in *Adam Bede* a whole chapter is dedicated to a discussion of the principles on which the novel is constructed – neither example embodying typical traits of the realist text. Other features in Eliot's novels, such as epilogues and allusions, advertise the textuality of her narratives and point towards relations with other texts and genres which further indicate deviations from the classic realist mould.

Accordingly, although Eliot's novels remain essentially within the conventions of nineteenth-century realism, the author herself was acutely aware of the restrictions and ambiguities that this mode of writing entailed. But her commitment to realistic representation derived from an ardent desire to encourage, through the extension of sympathy, an understanding of the world that could bridge gaps between people of diverse classes and cultures. Her realistic enterprise should thus be regarded not as

---

the *Revolution of the Word*, 2nd edn (Houndmills: Palgrave Macmillan, 2003), pp. 13-27. Two well-known articles by J. Hillis Miller, 'Narrative and History', *EHL*, 41 (1974), 455-473 and 'Optic and Semiotic in *Middlemarch*', in *The Worlds of Victorian Fiction*, ed. by Jerome Buckley (Harvard: Harvard University Press, 1975), pp. 125-145, suggest that in *Middlemarch*, Eliot demonstrates a full awareness of the problematic nature of language and offers a deconstruction of classic realism.

71 *Letters*, ii, 362.

a naïve attempt to reproduce received values and norms in a particular so-cial environment, but as an instrument by which she subjected represented reality to scrutiny, analysis and criticism.

2. *Adam Bede*

Adam Bede was published in three volumes in 1859, just one year after the publication of *Scenes of Clerical Life*.[1] As George Eliot's first full-length novel, *Adam Bede* resumes many of the characteristic features of *Scenes of Clerical Life* such as the author's concentration on 'ordinary' life, the extent of her humanitarian concern, her sympathy and humour in commentary and dialogue and her carefully crafted evocation of a time past. Indeed, *Adam Bede* was originally intended as a fourth story in *Scenes of Clerical Life*; but Eliot soon realised that the principal subject of this fourth 'Scene' would not fit in under the heading 'Clerical Life' and so resolved to make it into a novel.[2] *Adam Bede* was an immediate success with the public and also with most critics, who commended Eliot's ability to stir the reader's emotions and applauded her original powers of observation.[3] However, some criticism was levelled against the novel's explicit 'realism' in terms of Hetty's pregnancy, trial and expulsion, and against what was felt to be a forbidding picture of rustic existence. The representation of commonplace life, with all its potential awfulness, was, however, Eliot's purpose. She recognised what she considered to be a deficiency in English fiction, a deficiency she addressed in her essay on the German sociologist

1   Contemporary critics agreed that *Scenes of Clerical Life* was written in a remarkable style that had not been seen before. George Eliot was praised for her manner of faithfully depicting 'ordinary' lives and scenes, and for investing them with a significance that affected the reader deeply. *Scenes of Clerical Life* was George Eliot's literary debut, albeit not Marian Evans's. It made an immediate impression on William Makepeace Thackeray and Charles Dickens. The latter not only praised the author but was quick to detect a feminine dimension despite the masculine pseudonym.

2   In a letter to her publisher John Blackwood, Eliot introduced the idea of writing a full-sized novel: 'I have a subject in my mind which will not come under the limitations of the title "Clerical Life," and I am inclined to take a large canvas for it, and write a novel'; see *Letters*, ii, 381.

3   At the time, of course, it was generally supposed (with the exception of a few suspicious minds such as Dickens's and Barbara Bodichon's) that George Eliot was a man, an assumption which survived until after the publication of *Adam Bede* when Marian Evans had to reveal her cover to ward off rumours that Joseph Liggins had written her books.

Wilhelm Heinrich von Riehl. Arguing that contemporary novels wanted 'a real knowledge of the People', and that the reader should be 'taught to feel, not for the heroic artisan or the sentimental peasant, but for the peasant in all his coarse apathy, and the artisan in all his suspicious selfishness', George Eliot set out to introduce a new mode of representation in *Adam Bede*.[4]

Living up to the expectation of being a 'country story – full of the breadth of cows and the scent of hay' (*Letters*, ii, 387), *Adam Bede* combines the representation of country life and pastoral landscapes with close investigations into modes of living in contrasting environments. The thematic concerns in the novel include considerations of past and present, of human suffering and of idealism versus 'realism'. The novel is 'realistic' in the sense that it aspires to give a 'faithful account of men and things' (*Adam Bede*, xvii, 175), taking 'ordinary' people in humble and agrarian settings as its subject matter. Hence, *Adam Bede* is 'realistic' in terms of both subject and procedure.[5] In other words, it is a novel which tells a story; but it also tells about telling a story.[6]

This investigation of narratorial commentary in *Adam Bede* proceeds, like all subsequent chapters, from an analysis of the movement between the particular and the general in the text. As the shift from particular depictions in story-time now to general reflections in narration now is characteristic of most comments, regardless of whatever other functions they may serve, the study of these transfers is important for an understanding of the general function of commentary in the novel. Narratorial commentary is also concerned with the reader's presence in the reading situation. The ensuing discussions hence consider ways in which the *Adam Bede* narrator refers to and addresses the reader, remarking on his or her expected response, manipulating his or her distance to the diegesis and playing with his own

---

4   'The Natural History of German Life', in *Essays*, pp. 271-272 (first publ. in *Westminster Review*, lxvi (1856), 51-79).

5   For a discussion of the distinction between 'realism of subject' and 'realism of procedure' as well as of types of procedural 'realisms' in *Adam Bede*, see Ian Adam, 'The Structure of Realisms in *Adam Bede*', *Nineteenth- Century Fiction*, 30 (1975), 127-149. Some critics argue that *Adam Bede* contradicts its own realistic enterprise by its idealistic delineation of Adam and by treating the 'real' as 'ideal', i.e. by sneaking the 'ideal' into the 'real'. U. C. Knoepflmacher, for example, considers the ideal depictions of Adam and Dinah in relation to Eliot's claim of representing 'ordinary' people. See *George Eliot's Early Novels: The Limits of Realism* (Berkeley: University of California Press, 1968), pp. 97-99. See also Sarah Gates, ' "The Sound of the Scythe Being Whetted": Gender, Genre, and Realism in *Adam Bede*', *Studies in the Novel*, 30 (1998), 20-45.

6   In his introduction to *Adam Bede* in the World's Classics edition, Valentine Cunningham begins: 'The distinction of *Adam Bede* is to tell a story, and also to tell about telling the story' (vii).

role as extradiegetic narrator. The technically orientated part of this chapter ends with a discussion of meta-narrative comments. The second part of the chapter adopts a thematic rather than a narratological-technical approach. It is introduced by an examination of chapter 17 which creates a hiatus in the book, interrupting the story to discuss the complexities of representation. Chapter 17 is important in the present context for two reasons. First, it constitutes one very long narratorial comment dealing with the reader's expected reaction to the author's mode of representation and subject matter. Second, chapter 17 forms what has come to be called Eliot's 'aesthetic manifesto' and therefore has a bearing on her fiction as a whole. This chapter on *Adam Bede* ends with an examination of the most pressing thematic concerns broached in narratorial commentary in the novel.

Particular-General-Particular

The movement from a depiction of particular phenomena in story-time now to general reflections in narration now is fundamental to narratorial commentary in George Eliot's novels. By regarding a particular situation or character from a general perspective, one which the reader is invited to recognise, the narratorial comment appeals to the reader's sympathy and/or understanding. The general reflection serves to stimulate the reader's sense of recognition, bringing him or her into an experience in order to inspire a further understanding of the characters and situations in the narrative. Having recognised the pertinence of the general reflection in his or her own world, the reader returns to the particular situation in the text and relates his or her experience to the narrated instance. The transfer from particular to general and back is thus a circular process, the general reflection serving to rouse the reader's recognition in order for him or her to understand and relate to fictional phenomena.[7] Recognising a situation

---

7 The narrative movement between particular and general has occasioned some observations among Eliot scholars. Barbara Hardy speaks of Eliot's 'personal voice [which] puts the author – and the reader – inside the experience and not above it or outside it'; *The Novels of George Eliot*, p. 161. Isobel Armstrong notices Eliot's 'capacity to move beyond the moral universe of the novel, turn outwards toward the reader and to invoke a general body of moral and psychological knowledge or, rather, *experience*, which can be the corporate possession of both writer and reader' (p. 120). Furthermore, Carl D. Malmgren distinguishes between three types of commentary: personal, ideological and metalingual. The ideological statements, Malmgren claims, 'locate the fictional world somewhere within the "real world"' (473). These comments,

or event does not, however, necessarily involve first-hand experience. As a phenomenon, recognition can be considered to have two dimensions: an experientially orientated dimension based on actual experiences, and an imaginatively orientated dimension based on a consciousness which is able to inhabit states of mind, feelings and beliefs. Both dimensions are part of the reader's sphere of experience; and even if they cannot be kept separate in the reader's mind, they are nonetheless possible to distinguish as strands making up a whole.

In *Adam Bede*, as in all Eliot's novels, the movement between particular and general serves to intensify and add new dimensions to the reading experience, as happens in chapter 15 which juxtaposes Hetty and Dinah in their respective bed-chambers.[8] Describing Hetty's complete pre-oc-cupation with her own appearance and her visions of a luxurious future away from farm life, the narrator contemplates her obliviousness of those who have fed and reared her: 'There are some plants that have hardly any roots: you may tear them from their native nook of rock or wall, and just lay them over your ornamental flower-pot, and they blossom none the worse' (xv, 154).[9] The image serves to amplify the reader's understand-ing of Hetty's character, providing an illustration of Hetty's (dis)regard for her environment. It is an ambiguous image, however. The plant blossoms regardless of being uprooted and cannot be blamed for prospering despite having been pulled up; Hetty, on the other hand, seems to be subject to the narrator's disapproval, as he remarks that '[i]t was wonderful how little she seemed to care about waiting on her uncle, who had been a good father to her' (xv, 154).[10] The comment reveals the narrator's dual attitude towards

---

Malmgren continues, 'are predicated on the assumption that the fictional world and real world are contiguous and congruent' (474). However, these critics emphasise the linear movement of the reading process, disregarding the fact that the reader returns to the text and story-time now with the experience of locating the contents of the narrative within his or her own sphere of recognition.

8 On the contrasts and similarities between the two young women, see Nünning, pp. 168-169.

9 Nina Auerbach points out that both Hetty and Dinah are disapproved of in the community of the novel because of their rootlessness. She interprets the 'botanical analogy' of the image above as the narrator's instruction to the reader to disapprove of Hetty. See 'The Rise of the Fallen Woman', *Nineteenth-Century Fiction*, 35 (1980), 29-52 (p. 46). While I appreciate the understanding that plant imagery is belittling to the character and agree with Auerbach that the community of Hayslope disapproves of Dinah's and Hetty's wandering natures (which does not necessarily entail the narrator's disapproval), I cannot see the uprooted yet surviving flower image in those terms and rather understand it as an indication of the narrator's ambiguous relation to Hetty.

10 A great deal of critical analysis has been devoted to the narrator's attitude towards Hetty. Dorothy Van Ghent argues that Eliot attempts to 'load the dice' against Hetty; see *The English Novel: Form and Function* (New York: Rinehart & Company, 1953), p.

Hetty, simultaneously disparaging and fascinated. Comparing Hetty to a blossoming uprooted plant, the general reflection suggests admiration, whereas its context implies criticism. The narration-now comment thus contributes a qualifying perspective to the narrator's attitude toward Hetty in the particular, suggesting the complexity of the narrator's stance as regards this character.

In chapter 36, once more considering Hetty in a general comment, the narrator again appeals to the reader's recognition, but this time with reference to Hetty's situation rather than to her character. Chapter 36 depicts Hetty's 'journey in hope', and by this time the narrator's attitude towards her, even in narrative description, has gradually progressed from censure to sympathy for her desperate situation. As Hetty is caught out in the rain, afraid, alone and despondent, the narrator comments: 'The beginning of hardship is like the first taste of bitter food – it seems for a moment unbearable; yet, if there is nothing else to satisfy our hunger, we take another bite and find it possible to go on' (xxxvi, 373). Alerting the reader to the transitoriness of Hetty's emotion, the general statement appeals to the reader's experience, stimulating him or her to relate to the phenomenon which allows Hetty to dry her tears and resolve to rally 'her fainting courage' (xxxvi, 373). Involving the reader, and human kind in general, in the experience by the use of the first-person pronoun, the narrator hints at a common condition by which the reader can relate to Hetty and so sympathise with her. In this manner, the general statement decreases the distance between Hetty and the reader, which is necessary in order for the

402. U. C. Knoepflmacher refers to the 'author's pretended pity for this seventeen-year old child'; *George Eliot's Early Novels*, p. 119, and W. J. Harvey comments that Hetty is an easy target for the narrator's vicious attacks, which adds to the reader's 'sense of unjustified hostility on the part of the author'; *The Art of George Eliot*, p. 87. Jennifer Uglow suggests that Hetty is punished by the narrator not for 'her sensuality, as several critics have suggested, but for her compulsive dreaming'; *George Eliot* (London: Virago, 1987), p. 109. Mary Ellen Doyle argues that Hetty must be portrayed somewhat unsympathetically in order for Adam's progress through suffering towards sympathetic feeling to materialise, but not too unsympathetically so that the reader cannot empathise with her tragic fate. However, Doyle continues, Eliot had not yet mastered the technique of narrative, for '[h]ad the narrator's aggressive tactics worked, we would all but despise this girl'; *The Sympathetic Response: George Eliot's Fictional Rhetoric* (London: Associated University Presses, 1981), p. 40. Gillian Beer, however, maintains that the character of Hetty 'permeates the language of narration, refusing to be inscribed and contained, teasing the author's project'. This irritation, Beer suggests, inclined Eliot to return to related characters such as Rosamond Vincy and Gwendolen Harleth, developing the character's egoism to become 'a principle of self-discovery and intelligence'; *George Eliot* (Brighton: The Harvester Press, 1986), p. 73. Reiterating Beer's contention, Nina Auerbach claims that Hetty is a 'more challengingly complex figure than the narrator wants her to be' (40) and claims that the rhetoric of the novel 'forbids the reader to like Hetty'; 'The Rise of the Fallen Woman', p. 45.

reader fully to appreciate the ensuing tragedy. The generalisation hence forms part of a narrative strategy which guides the reader towards gradual sympathy with Hetty in order to intensify the impact of the imminent calamity.[11]

The link between story-time now and narration now, i.e. between particular and general, is often signalled by typographical devices. For instance, general reflections are frequently attached to descriptive sentences by means of semi-colons. An example appears in chapter 26, which depicts the 'dance' at Arthur's birthday feast. Having waited to dance with Arthur for what seems an eternity to her, Hetty is finally in his arms, wishing the dance will never end, whereupon the narrator comments:

> Arthur wished it too; it was the last weakness he meant to indulge in; and a man never lies with more delicious languor under the influence of a passion, than when he has persuaded himself that he shall subdue it to-morrow (xxvi, 288).

Introducing Arthur's psychological make-up, presenting the reader with information about Arthur's resolve which the character himself is ignorant of, the comment signals the futility of his resolution. It operates as a presentiment by which the reader is informed of the continuation of Hetty's and Arthur's relationship and by which the particular details presented in story-time now are qualified. Besides, the comment indicates the narrator's privileged position in relation to the narrative, demonstrating not only his knowledge of the failure of Arthur's determination but also his access to the character's psychological processes. The narrator's familiarity with these processes, however, is presented as generalised; that is, Arthur's particular mindset is considered as a general phenomenon common to people in his situation. The proverb-like tone of the comment, moreover, serves to reinforce the narrator's authority as well as to substantiate the veracity of the argument. In this case, then, the movement from particular to general appeals to the reader's recognition not in order to elicit sympathy for a particular character or situation, but to suggest that Arthur's mental processes are common to human nature.

The conjunctions 'for' and 'but' are devices allowing the narrator to move between story-time now and narration now. 'For' works as a causal conjunction, introducing a clause of reason which explicates whatever has

---

11 Barbara Hardy compares Hetty to Amos Barton and Silas Marner, arguing that there is 'no evolution' in either character's tragedy. Hardy contends that the reader is 'made to pity the unheroic figure who is equipped neither to understand what is happening to him, nor to endure and grow'; *Novels of George Eliot*, p. 33. For more on Hetty's tragedy, see also Felicia Bonaparte, *Will and Destiny: Morality and Tragedy in George Eliot's Novels* (New York: New York University Press, 1975), pp. 180-189.

gone before. Introducing either primary clauses or secondary clauses, it serves as an indication of the transition between story-time now and narration now. Chapter 2 includes an example which shows how the general statement introduced by the causal conjunction can be wedged in between elements of narrative description. With regard to the travelling horseman's observation of Dinah's sermon on the green, the narrator remarks:

> The stranger, who had been interested in the course of her sermon, as if it had been the development of a drama – for there is this sort of fascination in all sincere unpremeditated eloquence, which opens to one the inward drama of the speaker's emotions – now turned his horse aside (ii, 32).

Signalling that the particular will be clarified, 'for' introduces a general statement which lends depth to narrative description. Placed within a descriptive sentence, the comment elucidates, as if in passing, the reasons for the traveller's interest in Dinah. It also reinforces the idea that Dinah's sermon is of superior quality. By dwelling on the reason for the horseman's fascination, the comment indirectly underlines the impact Dinah has on the people she is speaking to. Although purporting to concern itself with the horseman, then, the comment is implicitly concerned with shaping the reader's interpretation of Dinah.

The passage is also a good example of the harmonious transition between story-time now and narration now which is so characteristic of Eliot's narratorial commentary. Developing the particular subject matter and sentence into the general narration-now statement, the narrator accomplishes the transition from particular to general and back without disrupting the structure of the passage: within one sentence, the reader's focus is guided from the particular diegetic moment to a general consideration by which his or her understanding of a phenomenon is appealed to, and then back to the particular episode again.

'For' may also introduce primary clauses and has more varied functions in this position. In a passage preceding Adam's discovery of Arthur and Hetty about to kiss in the woods, 'for' is used as a conjunction to introduce two successive general statements. The chapter has been introduced by a picturesque description of how the August weather imbues the people of Hayslope and Broxton with feelings of joy and brightness, but the description ends with an ominous suggestion of the transitoriness of those emotions: 'And yet a day on which a blighting sorrow may fall upon a man' (xxvii, 292). Moving into narration now, the narrator continues:

> For if it be true that Nature at certain moments seems charged with a presenti-
> ment of one individual lot, must it not also be true that she seems unmindful,
> unconscious of another? For there is no hour that has not its births of gladness and
> despair, no morning brightness that does not bring new sickness to desolation as
> well as new forces to genius and love. There are so many of us, and our lots are so
> different (xxvii, 292).

The first 'for' leads into a rhetorical question by introducing a supposition from which the ensuing argument can issue. This 'for' establishes a
consensus between the reader and the narrator, presupposing the veracity
of the first statement as a point of departure for the second. The rhetorical question invites the reader's active participation, calling on him or her
to contemplate, together with the narrator, the unfathomable element of
erratic Nature. The second 'for' is more directly causal, introducing assertions about which the narrator is certain. Although the two 'for's differ
formally, they both function as causal conjunctions, introducing general statements which appeal to the reader's sense of recognition. Inviting
the reader's participation in the considerations of Nature, the passage as
a whole anticipates the crisis which Adam will experience on what is described as a beautiful summer day. By encouraging the reader to recognise
the unpredictable ways in which humans are exposed to joys and sorrows,
and by inducing him or her to contemplate the phenomenon, the passage
serves to prepare the reader for the particular details that ensue. It also elevates the details of the particular onto a philosophical level.[12] The reader
is encouraged to view what will happen as a part of the grand scheme of
things, an outcome of unpredictable but natural processes to which all
humans are subject. The transition between particular and general in this
example thus serves to shape the reader's understanding of ensuing events
even before they take place. It is important to note, however, that the
comment includes the narrator's promotion of fellow-feeling under these
circumstances. Humans must accept the undemocratic nature of personal
lots and help one another deal with the consequences. Empathy for fellow

---

12 Commenting on the passage, Bernard J. Paris contends that it relates to the theme of
egoism in the novel. According to Eliot, all humans are egoistic, Paris argues, and all are
eventually awakened in one way or another to the severity of life. The first lesson learnt
from that awakening, Paris continues, is that 'nature is indifferent to human beings, that
its appearance of being friendly or hostile is the product of a limited, subjective point
of view'. See *Experiments in Life: George Eliot's Quest for Values* (Detroit: Wayne State
University Press, 1965), p. 133. U. C. Knoepflmacher notices the 'opposing moods of
two-faceted Nature' which the passage presents and reads this as corresponding to the
characters of Hetty and Dinah. The two girls are 'incomplete halves', Knoepflmacher
argues, Dinah the caring element of Nature, capable of 'presentiment', and Hetty
heedless and 'unconscious of another' (*Adam Bede*, xxvii, 292); *George Eliot's Early
Novels*, p. 118.

human beings is the ultimate argument of the generalisation, which then moves into story-time now and starts from the beginning of what happened to Adam on that eventful August day.

As a conjunction, 'but' introduces sentences which signal a degree of opposition or re-direction of argument. It functions in the same manner as 'for' to mark a transition between story-time now and narration now and again, like 'for', it can be employed to introduce primary clauses as well as secondary ones. Contrary to 'for', however, 'but' does not facilitate a subtle transition between the particular and general. Rather, it commands the reader's attention, making him or her alert to a contradiction of some sort. Introducing general comments, the 'but'-conjunction ushers the reader in another direction which may be in opposition to the particularities of story-time now, or which may expand the reader's perspective of the particular. An example of a comment in which 'but' introduces a secondary clause appears in chapter 22. The chapter depicts Arthur's birthday feast and the narrator remarks on the 'high spirits' (xxii, 254) and good looks of the young Captain on his special day, but checks his own perception with a reservation: 'So open-looking and candid, too; but candid people have their secrets, and secrets leave no lines in young faces' (xxii, 254). The 'but'-clause reminds the reader of the dark deceit underlying Arthur's bright face, challenging the depiction in preceding passages by 'lifting the veil', as it were, on Arthur's seemingly carefree façade. The statement works as a note to the reader, not letting him or her forget the grim realities lurking behind fair exteriors.

By remarking in a general fashion on the deceptive nature of appearances, the comment not only elicits the reader's recognition; it also includes other characters, apart from Arthur, into the reflection. Most significantly, of course, Hetty matches the observation, her face being not only young but also beautiful – a trait which the narrator repeatedly equates with innocence.[13] Although Hetty is never depicted as candid-looking – the narrative portrays her as reticent – her appearance, like Arthur's, is presented as an effective camouflage of dark secrets. Consequently, the conjunction alerts the reader to a narratorial reservation, encouraging his or her recognition, a recognition which qualifies the particular details presented in

13 See, for example, the introduction of Hetty into the novel, part of which reads: '[T]here is one order of beauty which seems made to turn the heads not only of men, but of all intelligent mammals, even of women. It is a beauty like that of kittens, or very small downy ducks making gentle rippling noises with their soft bills, or babies just beginning to toddle and to engage in conscious mischief – a beauty with which you can never be angry, but that you feel ready to crush for inability to comprehend the state of mind into which it throws you. Hetty Sorrel's was that sort of beauty' (vii, 83-84).

story-time now and brings the principle of deceptive appearances into play involving not only Arthur but also Hetty.

Introducing primary clauses, 'but' works in the same manner as the secondary-clause conjunction to qualify or challenge a particular argument and to expand the reader's perspective on it. In chapter 54, referring to Adam's disinclination to be thankful for Arthur's and Hetty's misfortunes, the narrator reflects generally on the selfishness of which that kind of thankfulness would be indicative. Following this contention, however, the narrator suggests what Adam *can* be thankful for:

> But it is not ignoble to feel that the fuller life which a sad experience has brought us is worth our own personal share of pain: surely it is not possible to feel otherwise [...] The growth of higher feeling within us is like the growth of faculty, bringing with it a sense of added strength: we can no more wish to return to a narrower sympathy, than a painter or a musician can wish to return to his cruder manner, or a philosopher to his less complete formula (liv, 530).

The passage turns the preceding argument around to some extent, substantiating the claim that another's misfortune should not be the basis for gratitude, but suggesting that the pain other people's actions have caused can be. Through the suffering which Hetty and Arthur inflicted on Adam, his character developed from hardness towards fellow-feeling.[14] The suffering Adam has endured, then, is part of a process of growth which is a prerequisite for the 'higher feeling' that not only leads him to sympathy with his fellow human beings, but also causes him to fall in love with Dinah.[15]

---

14 The idea of arriving at fellow-feeling through suffering is thought to derive from Ludwig Feuerbach's *Das Wesen des Christenthums* (*The Essence of Christianity*) which Eliot had translated under her real name in 1854. Feuerbach argues that a 'being without suffering is a being without a heart'; see *The Essence of Christianity*, trans. by George Eliot (New York: Prometheus Books, 1989), p. 62. U. C. Knoepflmacher refers to the ' "mental and moral" education of her protagonist' as a progress toward the 'Feuerbachian "religion of suffering" '; *Religious Humanism and the Victorian Novel: George Eliot, Walter Pater, and Samuel Butler* (Princeton: Princeton University Press, 1965), pp. 56-57. Bernard Paris argues that Eliot regarded suffering as humanising and observes a three-stage pattern of moral development in her novels, in which egoistic characters move from selfishness through shock and dejection caused by hardship to empathy and sympathy. See *Experiments in Life*, p. 128 *et passim*.

15 Analysing the Wordsworthian elements in *Adam Bede*, and arguing that a principle of compensation which can be detected in Wordsworth's visionary poetry also applies to Eliot's novel, Jay Clayton comments on the phrase 'higher feeling' in the passage above, contending that Eliot's defence of this higher feeling in fact 'amounts to a defense of her "higher" art' which 'exalts a wider sympathy, a sophisticated principle of compensation, and a complex theory of vision'; see 'Visionary Power and Narrative Form: Wordsworth and *Adam Bede*', *ELH*, 46 (1979), 645-672 (pp. 669-670).

The first-person pronoun in the comment above refers to human nature in general while specifically appealing to the reader's personal experience. He or she is directly implicated in the 'we' and 'us', pronouns which serve to reduce the distance between narrator, reader and characters. The 'surely', moreover, reinforces the element of opposition suggested by the 'but'-conjunction while appealing to the reader's sense of logic. Eventually the passage acquires a tone of authority which establishes the narrator's confidence, serving as an informative reflection rather than an idea offered for the reader's approval or agreement. The tone of the passage thus alters gradually with the progression of the general argument.

This passage is important for the reader's 'right' understanding of Adam's happiness. Seemingly anxious in case the reader misinterprets Adam's gladness as deriving from satisfaction over the dispensation of justice, the narrator is careful to explain the motives behind it. At the same time it is important for the 'happy ending' of the novel, and for the success of Adam's moral development, that the reader believes that he is truly happy. The narration-now passage hence forms part of a narrative strategy which aims to persuade the reader that the suffering which Adam's love for Hetty causes constitutes a prerequisite for the 'higher' love he has for Dinah.[16]

Consequently, this passage, along with other instances of movement between story-time now and narration now in *Adam Bede*, shows how the movement between the particularities of diegetic elements and general reflection expands, lends depth to and invites a conceptualisation of phenomena in order to elicit the reader's recognition and understanding

---

16 Several critics have commented on the credibility of the happy ending in *Adam Bede*. Both Hetty's rescue and Adam's marriage to Dinah have been singled out as imperfections in the novel. Henry James expressed reservations early on, regretting George Eliot's consent to having the two characters marry, which was apparently George Henry Lewes' suggestion. See *Partial Portraits* (London: Macmillan,1899), p. 53. John Diekhoff presents a detailed analysis of the whole ending and is not happy with it. Nor is Dorothy Van Ghent, who argues that the marriage is a disappointing consolation for the 'tragedy of Hetty'; see 'The Happy Ending of *Adam Bede*', *ELH*, 3 (1936), 221-227 and *The English Novel: Form and Function* (New York: Rinehart & Company, 1953), pp. 180-181. Bruce K. Martin, on the other hand, considers Adam's and Dinah's marriage as contributing to the unity of the novel. See 'Rescue and Marriage in *Adam Bede*', *Studies in English Literature*, 12 (1972), 745-763. The problem for most critics who object to the marriage, however, concerns Dinah rather than Adam. Adam's motives for loving Dinah are clear, as the passage above shows; but Dinah's sudden 'conversion' is not as well accounted for in the novel. Reva Stump argues that the novel has not helped readers perceive the slow preparations of 'conversion' in Dinah's character; see *Movement and Vision in George Eliot's Novels* (Seattle: University of Washington Press, 1948), p. 65. W. J. Harvey finds her sudden change of principle arbitrary and discomforting; see *The Art of George Eliot*, p. 180.

of nuances in the narrative. Such a movement is often effected through typographical devices which allow smooth transitions between narratorial levels and which serve as indications of the reader's entering another diegetic level.

References and Addresses to the Reader

Narratorial comments, including the general reflections discussed above, are in a sense always concerned with the reader's response to the narrative. All commentary in Eliot's novels could therefore be regarded as 'referring to' the reader. However, the references and addresses discussed in this section focus on those narratorial comments which make direct references to the reader's presence in the narrative context – that is, those comments in which the narrator approaches the reader directly, acknowledging his or her part in the interpretative process. In *Adam Bede* the narrator, although most often operating on an extradiegetic level, is immediately present in the narrative: he repeatedly refers to his own presence as 'I' and frequently offers opinions on the unfolding of events or the make-up of characters. This animated presence is also manifested in the narrator's addresses to the reader whose presence is, in turn, inscribed in the text in a correspondingly perceptible manner. Emphasising the reader's active part in the process of interpretation, the direct reader address demonstrates the narrator's attention to the precise depiction of characters and events, signalling his concern with the reader's response as well as indicating his self-awareness.[17] Like other comments, these references and addresses serve to shape the reader's response to the narrative, but with the difference that the method of manipulation is overt and presented in the form of active communication between narrator and reader.

Describing Adam's appreciation of Hetty in chapter 15, the narrator devotes a long passage to the power of Hetty's beauty, contemplating the widely shared tendency to align physical beauty with the possession of

---

17 *Adam Bede* and *The Mill on the Floss* include a large number of direct addresses. In *Silas Marner* and *Felix Holt* the reader address is less frequent, whereas in *Middlemarch* it figures extensively. Suzanne Graver explains Eliot's irregular employment of the direct address as owing to the author's susceptibility to audience reactions. Graver contends that Eliot refrained from the direct address in the novels following the 'two books [*The Mill on the Floss* and *Middlemarch*] that had caused her contemporaries to question her sympathy, suspect her irony, and be wary of her sincerity' (279).

a fine spirit. The passage interrupts Hetty's night-time preening in her bed-chamber and assumes the tone of an awe-struck observer. Concluding the eulogy, the narrator remarks: 'It was very much in this way that our friend Adam Bede thought about Hetty' (xv, 153).[18] Then, as if uncertain whether the tangible irony might incline the reader to disparage Adam, the narrator attempts to forestall his or her interpretation:

> Before you despise Adam as deficient in penetration, pray ask yourself if you were ever predisposed to believe evil of any pretty woman – if you ever *could*, without hard head-breaking demonstration, believe evil of the *one* supremely pretty woman who has bewitched you. No: people who love downy peaches are apt not to think of the stone, and sometimes jar their teeth terribly against it (xv, 153).

Anticipating disapproval of Adam, the comment serves to moderate the reader's reaction by involving him or her in the example; a principle of 'he who casts the first stone' is employed to restrain the reader's sense of superiority over the character. Encouraging the reader to recognise Adam's response to Hetty's beauty, the address seems at first to imply a male audience. Pleading with his male reader to recognise the power of female beauty, the narrator reduces the distance between himself and his male audience yet retains an ironical tone. The second section after the colon, however, refers to human beings in general, presenting a recognisable image in the proverb-like rhetoric which reinforces the narrator's authoritarian tone and sage-like status.[19]

In another address, the narrator contrastingly discourages the reader's attempts to understand or rationalise. Again referring to Hetty's appearance but this time to her fascination with wearing ornaments, the narrator remarks:

---

18 The identity of the speaker, venerating Hetty's beauty and thinking of her as a 'prize' (xv, 152) for the man who wins her and thereby becomes the envy of all other men, is ambiguous and has caused much discussion among critics. Mary Ellen Doyle identifies the speaking voice as the personality of 'an unpleasant, waspish woman who dislikes men and takes satisfaction in their painful awakening from delusion'. The reader, Doyle continues, is 'clearly a man, one of the deceived lot who will deserve what they get' (39). Arundhati Maitra Sanyal, on the other hand, regards the passage as ironic, the narrator mimicking a general male reaction to feminine beauty in order to have the reader understand Adam's response to Hetty. See 'Written in Opposition: Narrator-Narratee Relationship in the Major Novels of George Eliot' (unpublished doctoral dissertation, The City University of New York, 2000), pp. 122-124. This seems a reasonable interpretation, corroborated by the conclusion to the passage and by the ensuing narratorial comment.

19 Barbara Hardy notices that the narrator's reflection here is reiterated by another character in the novel, namely Mrs Poyser, who says of Hetty: 'It's my belief her heart's as hard as a pibble' (xv, 156). See *Novels of George Eliot*, p. 159.

> Do not reason about it, my philosophical reader, and say that Hetty, being very
> pretty, must have known that it did not signify whether she had on any ornaments
> or not [...] you will never understand women's natures if you are so excessively ra-
> tional. Try rather to divest yourself of all your rational prejudices, as much as if you
> were studying the psychology of a canary bird, and only watch the movements of
> this pretty round creature as she turns her head (xxii, 248).20

Rather than admonishing the reader for an expected response, this comment discourages him or her from attempting to rationalise Hetty's behaviour. The comment presupposes a continuously interpreting reader who
actively endeavours to understand characters and situations but who is, in
this instance, encouraged to discard analysis and engage in mere observation – the same activity, in fact, that Adam has been accused of in previous
sections. This kind of narratorial instruction to the reader is actually rare
in Eliot's novels. The comment serves as a good example of narratorial ambivalence in *Adam Bede*: this is the voice of a narrator who is concerned to
establish his male identity, and whose comments run the risk of alienating
groups of readers. Both rhetoric and argument thus jeopardise the reader's
confidence in the narrator's authority and in his respect for characters and
readers.[21]

The comment dissuades the reader from analysing Hetty's reasons for
ornamentation, arguing that her nature, and women's in general, is in-
comprehensible to overly commonsensical men. The distance between the
diegetic character and the reader is a long one here, the narrator acting as
a controlling mediator on whose instructions the reader is dependent. The
comment gives the impression that the narrator understands things which
the reader does not, and need not. The narrator thus seems to be on a
higher diegetic level from which the reader is excluded.

A different scenario appears in chapter 19, which gives a detailed description of 'Adam on a working day' (xix, 207). Having described Adam's
appearance and physiognomy, the narrator turns to the reader, commenting: 'Perhaps, if you had not been already in the secret, you might not have

---

20 So far, the examples of narratorial commentary in *Adam Bede* have shown that Hetty has
  been compared to an uprooted plant, a peach and a canary bird. For further discussion
  on the imagery used for Hetty, see Nina Auerbach's article 'The Rise of the Fallen
  Woman' in which she argues that Hetty's 'association with small, spiritually non-existent
  forms of life seems to deprive her fall of a corresponding ascent we can admire' (45). See
  also Felicia Bonaparte, pp. 180-189.

21 Isobel Armstrong claims that George Eliot is a 'comfortable – or at least comforting
  – novelist' in the sense that she, as opposed to Thackeray, does 'not play ambiguously
  with our responses'. The quotation above, however, constitutes one example (albeit one
  of very few) where Eliot's narrator gives rise to more discomfort than comfort. See
  Armstrong, p. 122.

guessed what sad memories, what warm affection, what tender fluttering hopes, had their home in this athletic body' (xix, 211). Here, the narrator refers to information which he shares with the reader, inviting him or her onto a mutual level, inspiring a confidence between them which serves to reduce the reader's distance to the narrator and to both increase and decrease the reader's distance to Adam. The decrease is effected by the reader's recognition of Adam's 'sad memories' and 'fluttering hopes' and the increase by the acknowledgement of the reader's acquisition of information and secrets which the character is ignorant of. The closeness between reader and narrator established through this type of comment is repeatedly reinforced, appearing again in the following chapter when the narrator refers to Adam's misinterpretation of Hetty's feelings: 'And Hetty? You know quite well that Adam was mistaken about her' (xx, 220).

Consequently, direct references to reader response in *Adam Bede* modify the reader's distance both to the characters in the text and to the narrator. The comments which address part of the readership only – here, in *Adam Bede*, male readers intrigued by female beauty – carry the risk of alienating some readers, and Eliot refrained from these types of comments in her subsequent novels. However, the type of comment which invites the reader onto an exclusive level with the narrator on the basis of a shared body of information recurs in all Eliot's novels. By involving the reader in 'secrets' – putting his arm around him or her, as it were – the narrator seemingly flatters the reader and by doing so makes him or her amenable to manipulation. This decrease of distance between reader and narrator serves to facilitate the narrator's control of the reader's interpretation of characters and events.

An effect of these references and addresses to the reader is that they ensure the reader reaches the 'right' interpretation – that is, the interpretation inscribed in the text. The narrator in *Adam Bede* employs several methods by which he seeks to inspire the reader to attain the 'correct' reading. A further approach makes use of the reader's remembrance and imagination, acknowledging the fact that the reader belongs to a sphere beyond the diegesis. One example of this approach pertains to the depiction of Arthur Donnithorne's appearance, which occasions the narrator to summon the reader's remembrance:

> If you want to know more particularly how he looked, call to your remembrance some tawny-whiskered, brown-locked, clear-complexioned young Englishman whom you have met with in a foreign town, and been proud of as a fellow-countryman [...] I will not be so much of a tailor as to trouble your imagination with

the difference of costume, and insist on the striped waistcoat, long-tailed coat, and low-top boots (v, 61).[22]

By appealing to the reader's recognition of young Englishmen in his or her own world, the narrator acknowledges the divide between the reader's actual world and the world of the narrative. Situating diegetic elements within the reader's world, the comment not only emphasises the reader's customary position outside the diegesis but also underpins the 'realistic' nature of the narrative. Arthur, the statement implies, is as 'real' as any young man existing in the reader's memory. Like many other references to the reader's response, the quoted comment encourages the reader to incorporate personal experiences into the interpretation of the narrative. The difference here, however, is that the comment refers to the reader's 'tangible' and visual world, rather than to his or her potential recognition of philosophical or ideological phenomena. Hence, the reader's own visual experiences are brought into the description of Arthur's appearance. In this sense, the narrator is engaging *with* the reader as well as engaging his or her world *in* the interpretative process.

The comment moves from invoking the reader's remembrance to appealing to his or her imagination as the narrator reveals his concern with the 'right' interpretation by making sure that the reader's impression of Arthur is wearing the right attire. By claiming not to insist on the specifics of garb, the narrator is, of course, tongue in cheek, ensuring that these details of costume are indeed included in the reader's mental image of Arthur.[23] Hence, the passage shows that the narrator's concern with the reader's response in *Adam Bede* relates to matters of external description as well as to moral and philosophical issues, the comments endeavouring to shape the reader's mental images as well as his or her understanding.

References to the reader in George Eliot's novels regularly involve the use of the first-person pronoun. By including the reader and human nature in general in a 'we', 'our' or 'us', the narrator induces a sense of community and solidarity between reader, narrator and characters, on the basis of the notion that these agents can be linked through the recognition of experiences common to all humans. Characters, narrator and reader are thus participants in a shared body of experiences by which the reader is stimulated to recognise phenomena and sympathise with characters. In *Adam Bede* the first-person pronoun is used extensively, continually bringing the read-

---

22 See a similar comment in *Middlemarch*: 'If you want to know more particularly how Mary looked, ten to one you will see a face like hers in the crowded street to-morrow' (xl, 382).
23 Cf. Nünning, p. 163.

er's own recognition of experiences into the interpretative process. Late in the novel, after Hetty's trial and expulsion, the narrator remarks on Adam's psychological pain and sorrow which, the narrator states, he 'had not out-lived' (l, 487), and then comments:

> Do any of us? God forbid. It would be a poor result of all our anguish and our wrestling, if we won nothing but our old selves at the end of it [...] Let us rather be thankful that our sorrow lives in us as an indestructible force, only changing its form, as forces do, and passing from pain into sympathy – the one poor word which includes all our best insight and our best love (l, 487).

By addressing the reader directly through the rhetorical question, the narrator enforces the reader's active participation in the narrative. Albeit rhetorical, the question obliges the reader to position himself or herself in relation to it. The reader is then included in the argument by the use of the first-person plural by which characters, narrator and reader are linked, each being equally subject to the mechanisms of human nature.[24] The pronoun adds weight to the argument, implying that it applies as well outside as inside the domain of the novel – that it reveals 'truths' not only about the characters in the diegesis, but also about the reader. In the fashion of a generalised statement, it incorporates the particular details of Adam's situation into general phenomena applicable to all mankind.[25] The particular passage above, however, contains an additional element. Rather than merely including the reader in the first-person pronoun, the comment is advisory, proposing a principle by which to live. Like many other inclusive statements it reflects on human nature, but moves from observation of the mechanisms determining human suffering to an exhortation which implores the reader to regard suffering as a means towards sympathy.[26]

---

24 Suzanne Graver argues that narratorial commentary in *Adam Bede* follows a tripartite pattern which involves 'an appeal to "our" common experience, a plea for a sympathetic response to a fictional character, and a reminder that what "we" are witnessing is authentic' (279-280). According to Graver, the passage above serves as an example of a comment which includes all three elements. Although these elements are very common in *Adam Bede*, Graver's tripartite pattern is reductive in the sense that it disregards nuances in the different comments. For example, it does not acknowledge ironical comments which serve to reduce the distance between reader and narrator, nor does it allow for meta-narrative comments. Furthermore, the pattern excludes comments which bring up social, political or religious themes, encouraging the reader to sympathise with issues rather than characters.

25 Commenting on this particular passage, Barbara Hardy claims that it shows George Eliot discarding the narrator's 'fictitious mask'. The comment, Hardy argues, communicates George Eliot's voice 'at its calmest and most intense, without disguise, exaggeration, or arch humour'; *Novels of George Eliot*, p. 160.

26 Jay Clayton argues that Adam's sorrow which changes its form, 'passing from pain into sympathy' (l, 487), is a 'psychological form of sublimation' (649). Again, the comment is

Urging the reader to recognise the processes by which sorrow is transformed into sympathy, the comment not only elicits the reader's recognition but itself gives the impression of recognising the reader's experience
of sorrow. In this respect, if the reader can agree with the argument, the
comment conveys a sense of comfort – which in turn, of course, serves to
persuade the reader to identify with Adam.

The narrator in *Adam Bede* has a high level of presence in the sense that
he frequently comments on diegetic elements, offers opinions and evaluations of characters and addresses the reader directly, as mentioned above.
This presence is also manifested in the narrator's references to himself.
Calling himself 'I', the narrator acknowledges his role in the narrative, providing it with a persona which has a notable function in the diegesis while
still mainly operating on an extradiegetic-heterodiegetic level. In *Adam
Bede* the personalised 'I' often serves to reinforce the narrator's authority
by establishing opinions and evaluations which indicate his commanding
presence.[27] For example, with regard to Adam's work the narrator comments on Adam's tendency to get satisfaction out of knowing that he has
produced something: 'And I believe the only people who are free from
that weakness are those who have no work to call their own' (xxvii, 294).
Compared to Adam's contention: 'I hate to see a man's arms drop down as
if he was shot, before the clock's fairly struck, just as if he'd never a bit o'
pride and delight in 's work' (i, 11), the narrator's argument seems almost
to assume Adam's voice. The two statements show how close the narrator is
to Adam in terms of moral conviction.[28] But the comment gives the added
impression of forestalling the reader's potential censure of Adam, as if wor-
ried that the reader might find Adam's job-satisfaction selfish and haughty.

---

reminiscent of Feuerbach's 'religion of suffering': 'Love does not exist without sympathy,
sympathy does not exist without suffering in common'; *The Essence of Christianity*, p.
54. Bernard Paris has explored Eliot's principle of suffering and argues that her letters,
journals, essays and novels all promote this contention that 'suffering, if it does not
simply embitter, leads us to be sympathetic with the suffering of others, and our
sympathy leads us to behave so that others will not suffer as we have'; see *Experiments in
Life*, p. 69.

27 As subsequent discussions will show, the 'I' in Eliot's later novels often serves,
contrastingly, to indicate a degree of narratorial prudence which undermines the
impression of authoritative control.

28 Several critics argue that Mr Irwine is George Eliot's spokesperson in the novel. See, for
example, John Goode, '*Adam Bede*', in *Critical Essays on George Eliot*, ed. by Barbara
Hardy (London: Routledge & Kegan Paul, 1970), pp. 19-41 (p. 29). Whether or not
Mr Irwine is Eliot's spokesperson, it is certainly true that his utterances on several issues
coincide with the narrator's arguments. However, in the passage above it is noticeable
that the narrator also has much in common with Adam.

Again, the narrator rationalises Adam's emotions, but here without eliciting the reader's sympathy; instead, he or she is warned not to judge.

Another passage indicative of a personal involvement on the narrator's part again refers to Adam Bede. In chapter 33, with Arthur gone and Hetty becoming more reconciled to the prospect of marrying Adam, the narrator contemplates Adam's misinterpretation of Hetty. Addressing the reader first, the narrator remarks: 'Possibly you think that Adam was not at all sagacious in his interpretations' (xxxiii, 353) and eventually goes on to offer his own evaluation:

> For my own part, however, I respect him none the less: nay, I think the deep love he had for that sweet, rounded, blossom-like, dark-eyed Hetty, of whose inward self he was really very ignorant, came out of the very strength of his nature, and not out of any inconsistent weakness (xxxiii, 353).

Continually attempting to vindicate Adam Bede, even going so far as to interpret his inability to see through Hetty's exterior as a strength, the narrator is adamant in his high regard for Adam.[29] Anticipating the reader's disrespect for Adam's inability to see beyond Hetty's beauty, the narrator gradually builds up his argument. First, the reader's expected opinion is met by a reminder that to every rule or convention there is an exception. The passage then moves into the narrator's personal evaluation, as evinced by the quotation above. Having established his own attitude the narrator returns to focusing on the reader's experiences, putting questions to him or her regarding aesthetics and morality.[30] The passage then moves into general reflections on aspects of beauty, drawing the reader into the statement and connecting him or her with Adam by the use of 'we'. Finally the passage is concluded by the transfer into story-time now – a transfer

---

29 As a character, Adam has a good deal in common with Daniel Deronda, who is also the object of the narrator's high and unwavering regard. Mary Ellen Doyle objects to the narrator's treatment of both characters, maintaining that the insistence on Adam's eminence makes him 'look not less but more foolish'. With reference to the reader's response, Doyle continues: 'Once the narrator demanded that the mock-reader make too little of Hetty; now he insists on making too much of her in order to make much of Adam. In both cases he stands to lose the real reader' (51).

30 See Caroline Levine's 'Women or Boys? Gender, Realism and the Gaze in *Adam Bede*', *Women's Writing*, 3 (1996), 113-127 for a reading of this passage as a manifestation of Kantian love. Adam's love for Hetty and Dinah respectively, Levine claims, is possible to read as a movement from Kantian to Hegelian considerations of beauty. Doyle maintains that the passage in its entirety is inspired by 'Feuerbach's religion of humanity, in which God is the idea of human perfection'. Acting as a representative of the divine qualities which constitute human perfection, one person, Doyle claims, 'becomes the object of a worship imbued with the noblest religious emotion'. Doyle argues that this is the way in which Adam regards Hetty. See Doyle, pp. 50-51.

introduced by '[o]ur good Adam' (xxxiii, 354), which implies that narrator and reader share an affection and sympathy for Adam. The whole passage, consequently, moves from anticipating the reader's criticism of Adam to assuming his or her sympathy for him. The narrator's 'I' is, of course, part of this process. The arguments which he puts forward in this long passage are the principal means by which the reader's response is shaped; but the rhetorical developments, progressing from the reader's 'you' to the narrator's 'I' back to the reader's 'you' and then into 'we' and 'our', also form a significant part of extensive response manipulation. Moreover, the narrator's exposition of his own opinion – whether or not one regards it as undercut by irony ('most sensible men will choose sensible women') – further affects the reader's distance to the diegesis. By aligning with Adam and demonstrating his loyalty to him, the narrator not only reduces his own distance to the character but invites the reader to do so, too.

References and addresses to the reader occur to a greater extent in *Adam Bede* than in Eliot's later novels. By addressing the reader directly, including him or her in the first-person pronoun and establishing an authoritative narratorial 'I', the narrator not only shapes and controls the response of the reader, but also engages him or her into active participation in the narrative.

Metalepses

The narrator in *Adam Bede* is not fixedly extradiegetic. Occasionally he inscribes himself into the narrative, figuring as an unidentified yet participating character. This narratorial participation in the diegesis renders the narrator temporarily intradiegetic as he purports to take part in the narrative, but heterodiegetic as he remains with the original story – that is, he does not tell his own story, but the story of Adam Bede.[31] The most evident example of narratorial metalepsis appears in chapter 17, where the narrator professes to be on speaking terms with Adam. The scene depicts Adam in his old age, reminiscing on old times and in particular on Mr Irwine's preaching practices. Introducing his conversation with Adam, the narrator states: 'But I gathered from Adam Bede, to whom I talked of these

31 For a discussion of the relations between George Eliot, the narrator and *Adam Bede*, see Cynthia Huggins, '*Adam Bede*: Author, Narrator and Narrative', *The George Eliot Review: Journal of the George Eliot Fellowship*, 23 (1992), 35-39.

matters in his old age' (xvii, 179). The notion of the narrator's direct access to characters conveys the impression that the story told is 'true to life' – that is, that it is historically accurate and that the characters in the text are actually 'real' people.

The last passage of chapter 17 presents another 'spin' on the narrator's presence in the text. Here the narrator assumes an almost homodiegetic nature; that is, he starts recounting his own narrative, enlightening the reader as to his own experiences of discussions on the ideal and 'real' with 'accomplished and acute gentlemen' (xvii, 183) and of a conversation he has had with a 'Mr Gedge, the landlord of the Royal Oak' (xvii, 183). These scenes are not part of the story of *Adam Bede*; rather, they form part of an argument regarding the representation of ideal versus commonplace characters, settings and situations. In this respect, then, the last part of chapter 17 concerns the narrator's own story, rendering his nature homodiegetic and intradiegetic in this final passage.

Chapter 17, however, is unique, as it constitutes a disruption in the course of the story-telling in order for the narrator to pursue a discussion of the principles on which the novel is constructed. The narrator's defection from the extradiegetic-heterodiegetic level therefore seems appropriate to the unusual nature of the chapter as a whole. However, narratorial metalepsis occurs elsewhere in the novel as well. A well-known example appears in chapter 35, which depicts Hetty's journey to Treddleston during which she resolves to run away. This chapter also gives the first indications as to Hetty's pregnancy, suggested by her overwhelming fear of imminent shame. Describing Hetty's trip to Treddleston, the narrator interrupts the account by directing the reader's attention to a scene in which the narrator himself is indirectly present:

> What a glad world this looks like, as one drives or rides along the valleys and over the hills! I have often thought so when, in foreign countries, where the fields and woods have looked to me like our English Loamshire [...] I have come on something by the roadside which has reminded me that I am not in Loamshire: an image of a great agony – the agony of the Cross. [...] and surely, if there came a traveller to this world who knew nothing of the story of man's life upon it, this image of agony would seem to him strangely out of place in the midst of this joyous nature. He would not know that hidden behind the apple-blossoms, or among the golden corn, or under the shrouding boughs of the wood, there might be a human heart beating heavily with anguish: perhaps a young blooming girl (xxxv, 363-364).

The passage, included in the chapter entitled 'The hidden dread', forebodes the ensuing tragedy. It is the first indication of Hetty's condition and also one of the first comments to approach her intensely and sympathetically, without any ironic overtone.[32] Moving from the narrator's familiarity with the scene to his understanding of Hetty's consciousness, the comment constitutes an exceptional piece of narrative structure in Eliot's oeuvre. It begins in the present tense as a first signal to alert the reader to a change in narrative form. In the first sentence the narrator not only describes the Loamshire setting, but suggests that he can actually see it. The second sentence conducts the reader through the narrator's remembrance, still keeping the reader's focus with the narrator as protagonist. The narrator's memory, however, leads the reader to the image of the Cross, by which the focus of the passage is directed away from the narrator's presence onto a potential traveller. By introducing the traveller into the scene, the narrator resumes his extradiegetic status – the only position he can assume if he is to enter into Hetty's consciousness.[33] The purpose of the narrator's intradiegetic presence in this passage is to introduce the symbolism of the Cross into the setting of Protestant England. The image is, of course, anomalous in the Loamshire countryside and therefore has to be presented in a fashion which does not disrupt the authentic depiction of English life.[34]

Apart from bringing in the image of the Cross, by which Hetty's suffering is foreboded, the narrator's metalepsis serves to authenticate the 'realness' of the Loamshire district. By suggesting that the narrator is familiar with this district, the comment reinforces the veracity of the narrative. The metalepsis thus diminishes the sense of fictionality by situating the extradiegetic narrator himself in the diegetic setting.[35] His implicit claim to be speaking of 'real' characters is particularly significant in conjunction with the semi-revelation of Hetty's pregnancy. Sensing the 'realness'

---

32 Jay Clayton regards the passage as the most intense in the novel. The narrative, he claims, 'almost seems to internalize Hetty's anguish, take her pain into itself through the symbol of the cross, much as Adam internalizes Hetty's suffering. Like Adam, the story performs an act of sublimation' (655).

33 It is significant that the narrator's focus is passed on to the notion of a traveller, as this hypothetical traveller enters immediately prior to Hetty's decision to run away, as well as just before a series of journeys which make travellers out of several characters. Hetty journeys in hope and despair, Adam travels to find her, Dinah travels to where she thinks she is most needed and Arthur goes to Ireland and back. Every literal journey has a metaphorical counterpart, as each character's travelling involves emotional change.

34 David Carroll regards the image of the Cross in this passage as one of several instances of anamorphism, that is, 'objects, characters, attitudes, and values which will not fit in to the conventional perspective the novel seems to assume'. See *George Eliot and the Conflict of Interpretations* (Cambridge: Cambridge University Press, 1992), p. 74.

35 Robyn Warhol also regards these instances of metalepsis in *Adam Bede* as substantiating the reader's impression that the characters and scenes depicted in the novel are somehow 'real'. Therefore, she also opposes Genette's view that metalepsis yields an incongruous effect in the text. See 'Toward a Theory of the Engaging Narrator', p. 815 and *Narrative Discourse*, pp. 234-235.

of Hetty's despair, the reader is more apt to sympathise with her character. Additionally, through the symbolism of the Cross, by which the narrator reflects on the agony which is concealed under beauty, the reader is encouraged to modify his or her preconceived idea of Hetty's beauty and instead see it as a veil which shrouds real suffering.[36]

Metalepsis involves not only the narrator's transgression of diegetic levels, but also the reader's imagined participation inside the diegesis. Several instances in *Adam Bede* convey a sense of the reader's actual physical presence in the diegetic world, assuming his or her visual access to the characters and settings in the text.[37] Introducing Mr Irwine and his mother, the narrator invites the reader into the diegetic realm:

> Let me take you into that dining-room, and show you the Rev. Adolphus Irwine […] We will enter very softly, and stand still in the open doorway, without awaking the glossy-brown setter who is stretched across the hearth, with her two puppies beside her (v, 54).

Pulling the reader into the narrative, the narrator turns both himself and the reader into voyeurs, capable of disrupting the status quo of the fictive world. The reader is situated within the diegetic realm, in which he or she can *see* characters and also *be seen*, or there would be no point in insisting that the reader enter 'softly'. Implying the reader's potential for physical disturbance, this cautionary remark serves to affect the reader's state of mind, inspiring him or her to assume an attitude of prudence and discretion. As the reader becomes part of the diegesis, his or her distance to the characters is of course radically diminished. Moreover, by assuming that the reader can see and physically affect the diegetic scene, the narrator counteracts the impression of fictionality and instead promotes the notion that the characters are so 'real' that they cannot only be seen by the reader, but can actually return the gaze.[38]

---

36 Charles Palliser makes this point as well, arguing that in the same way as the traveller must rethink his understanding of the beauty of nature, so the reader must modify his or her expectations. Palliser goes on to argue that the comment accuses Adam, as well as the hypothetical traveller and the reader, 'of failing to perceive this concealed and harsh dimension of reality'. See '*Adam Bede* and "the Story of the Past" ', in *George Eliot: Centenary Essays and an Unpublished Fragment*, ed. by Anne Smith (London: Vision Press, 1980), pp. 55-76 (p. 72).

37 Although metalepsis occurs in Eliot's later novels it is never as frequently employed as in *Adam Bede*, nor does it position the reader as fully in the diegesis as in the examples above.

38 This type of metalepsis is exceptional to *Adam Bede*. Although Eliot's narrators in subsequent novels invite the reader into the diegesis, there are no indications of a hypothetical two-way communication between the reader and the characters.

Introducing the Rector of Broxton through the reader's imagined presence in the scene, the passage from the very start establishes a reduced
distance between Mr Irwine and the reader, whose potential disapproval
of the unconventional clergyman is counteracted. The Rector's (lack of)
theological enthusiasm and doctrinal discipline is a matter of great concern
in the novel, not least in chapter 17; so as this character is introduced, it is
important that the reader interpret him 'correctly'. By reducing the reader's
distance to him, rendering him almost 'real' and ostensibly 'tangible', and
by emphasising his noble, compassionate character – one that values ethics and reason over dogmatic principle – the passage serves to incline the
reader towards Mr Irwine, encouraging him or her to perceive the clergyman's lax attitude towards his calling as secondary to his considerate and
intelligent character.[39]

Instead of 'meeting' the reader in narration now, the example of metalepsis above shows how the 'contact' between narrator and reader takes
place in story-time now. The passage is therefore not a narratorial comment as defined by the narration-now framework, but part of story-time
now and of the particularities of the story. Nevertheless, the passage serves
to shape the reader's response in the same manner as narratorial commentary, and it establishes the same type of connection between narrator and
reader as is often generated through commentary.

The Hall Farm and its inhabitants are introduced in the following
chapter, and again the device of metalepsis is employed. The reader is assumed to have visual access to diegetic elements, as the narrator states: 'by
putting our eyes close to the rusty bars of the gate, we can see the house
well enough' (vi, 71). This invitation retains the idea that the reader can be
part of the diegetic world and that he or she can overcome the ontological divide which separates the world of the novel from the reader's world.
However, this notion is soon qualified by another instance of metalepsis:

> Yes, the house must be inhabited, and we will see by whom; for imagination is a
> licensed trespasser: it has no fear of dogs, but may climb over walls and peep in at

---

39 Jennifer Uglow argues that both Dinah and Mr Irwine are connected to the narrator
   in their 'ability to love the ordinary people' (101). Considering the narrator's concern
   with Mr Irwine's superior qualities, Suzanne Graver remarks that '[o]verstatement
   occurs because the point was so important to George Eliot and because Mr Irwine's
   ecclesiastical standing was of great concern to her Victorian readers' (281). George R.
   Creeger, on the other hand, sees the delineation of Mr Irwine not as an overstatement,
   but as Eliot's presentation of a character who possesses a fine balance between head and
   heart – a characteristic which, Creeger argues, Mr Irwine shares with Bartle Massey
   and Mrs Poyser; see 'An Interpretation of Adam Bede', in George Eliot: A Collection of
   Critical Essays, ed. by George R. Creeger (London: Prentice-Hall, 1970), pp. 86-106 (p.
   92).

windows with impunity. Put your face to one of the glass panes in the right-hand window: what do you see? (vi, 71-72).

Here the reader need not worry about entering softly or disturbing the dogs, as it is only his or her imagination that enters the scene. The idea that the reader's physical being can be incorporated into the diegetic setting has thus been abandoned, and the narrator acknowledges the barrier which separates the reader's world from the world of the narrative. Serving as a 'licensed trespasser', however, the reader's imagination is regarded as a medium through which the details of the narrative can be communicated, suggesting that the reader's 'mind's eye' can 'see' the scene depicted. Again the reader is imagined to be positioned at a vantage-point from which he or she can take part in the fictive world, but with the difference that it is through his or her imagination that this participation takes place. Visualising the scene rather than physically seeing it, the reader's imagination is acknowledged as crucial to the interpretation of narrative detail.

The occurrences of metalepsis in *Adam Bede* do not, however, adhere to any straightforward line of development. Examples of metalepsis which refer to the reader's physical presence in diegetic scenes alternate with instances which recognise the impossibility of that notion. The reader's imagined ability actually to see characters is, for example, revived again in chapter 19, where the narrator asks the reader to '[l]ook at Adam through the rest of the day [...] Look at this broad-shouldered man with the bare muscular arms, and the thick firm black hair' (xix, 211). This example of metalepsis, like others, establishes the tacit understanding that the narrator and reader are on the same narrative level, that is, they share the same visual access to the narrative. Indicating the authenticity of narrative components and implying that the reader is able to gaze on Adam, the appeal to 'look' at him reduces the distance between him and the reader and reinforces the impression of Adam's physical and aesthetic superiority. In the effort to promote Adam's spiritual soundness, then, the narrator extols his physical attributes.

Consequently, instances of metalepsis, which occur more frequently in *Adam Bede* than in any other Eliot novel, primarily serve to reduce the distance between the reader's world and the world of the narrative in order for the reader to feel connected to and sympathetic towards particular characters. Although most examples of metalepsis remain within story-time now and cannot be defined as commentary *per se*, the communication between reader and narrator which they induce makes them operate in much the same way as narratorial commentary.

Meta-Narrative Comments

Any comment which draws attention to the narrating act accentuates the status of the narrative as an artefact and displays a sense of narratorial self-consciousness with regard to the relationship between fiction and 'reality'. Reminding the reader of the fictionality of the text, the meta-narrative comment indicates the narrator's role as director and implies how the text should be understood.[40] The most well-known meta-narrative comment in *Adam Bede* is also the comment by which the novel is introduced:

> With a single drop of ink for a mirror, the Egyptian sorcerer undertakes to reveal to any chance comer far-reaching visions of the past. This is what I undertake to do for you, reader. With this drop of ink at the end of my pen I will show you the roomy workshop of Mr Jonathan Burge, carpenter and builder in the village of Hayslope, as it appeared on the eighteenth of June, in the year of our Lord 1799 (i, 5).

The comment introduces not only the novel, but also two conflicting perspectives by which the reader may approach it: one, as a fabrication narrated by an immediately present narrator; and two, as a mimetic account of actual historical characters and events. The comment thus presents a window on the narrative which can be understood in dissimilar ways. In addition, the comment introduces the idea of a sorcerer – an image which invests the understanding of the premises on which the narrative is constructed with even greater complexity, and which also complicates the reader's understanding of the narrator's position in relation to the text.[41] The narrator's authority as controller and director is established by the meta-narrative element of the comment, but the sorcerer analogy implies an aspect of deception which to some degree destabilises that impression of authority and credibility.[42]

---

40 According to Gerald Prince, meta-narrative comments serve several functions such as interpreting the text, slowing down the rhythm of the narrative and revealing the narrator's attitude towards his audience. Additionally, Prince argues, the meta-narrative comment can 'help define a narrator, his narratee and their relationship'. See 'Metanarrative Signs', in *Metafiction*, ed. by Mark Currie (London: Longman, 1995), pp. 55-68 (p. 65).

41 The sorcerer image is ambiguous in that sorcerers in stories and fairytales are conventionally associated with black magic, that is, with people who perform magic by using the power of evil spirits. Besides, the idea of a sorcerer brings a metaphysical element into the understanding of the novel, which is atypical of Eliot's 'realistic' fiction (*The Lifted Veil* excepted). Moreover, sorcerers are generally associated with visions of the future rather than of the past. The analogy thus gives rise to a sense of incongruity, as the parallel seems incompatible with the narrator's role.

42 Lucie Armitt notices the discrepancies in this opening paragraph and explains it as Eliot's deconstruction of her own text. Armitt argues: 'In reminding us of her trickery

The mirror image is interesting for other reasons, too. Presenting the novel as a mirror which reflects the diegetic world, the narrator endeavours to promote the authenticity of the narrative.[43] The mirror image provides the narrative with a visual accent, as does the idea of the sorcerer. But whereas the mirror promotes authenticity, the sorcerer analogy indicates the supernatural, thus investing the whole image with ambiguity.

Consequently, the introductory comment serves to introduce the narrator persona and to establish his authority in the text. In addition, it establishes a sense of narrative authenticity, encouraging the reader to understand the fiction as a historical account. Challenging these objectives, however, the comment also includes a meta-narrative element which qualifies the impression of authenticity and a sorcerer analogy which attaches an uneasy sense of trickery and supernaturalism to both narrator and narrative. Hence, in the very introduction to the novel, the reader is made aware of a narratorial complexity which signals the narrator's elusive and variable position in the narrative.

Further references to the act of narrating can be found in chapter 7, where Hetty is introduced. Here attention is drawn to the narrator's control by his evaluations of what elements of the story are 'of use' to describe. The narrator claims that 'it is of little use' for him to describe Hetty's beauty and magnetism unless the reader has had first-hand experience of 'a woman who affected you as Hetty affected her beholders' (vii, 84). Representation cannot measure up to 'reality'; description cannot do first-hand experience justice; and so the reader is reminded of the limits of imagination.[44] Ironically, however, the narrator's claim to refrain from description does not prevent him from delving into detailed descriptions of Hetty's physiognomy. Every 'it is of little use for me to tell you' (vii, 84) is followed by an exhaustive account of exactly what it is that is of little use

---

at the same time as she seduces us with the verisimilitude of her fictions, Eliot draws attention to the precarious role played by the narrative authority within realism'. See *George Eliot: A Reader's Guide to Essential Criticism*, ed. by Lucie Armitt (Cambridge: Icon Books, 2000), p. 24. According to Janice Carlisle, the sorcerer image makes the reader 'aware of his distance from the world of Hayslope'. See *The Sense of an Audience: Dickens, Thackeray and George Eliot at Mid-Century* (Brighton: Harvester Press, 1982), p. 196.

43 The reader will learn later, in chapter 17, that the 'mirror is doubtless defective' (xvii, 175); but in the comment above the mirror constitutes a mimetic representation which is only disturbed by the figure of the sorcerer.

44 These indications of the reader's limited imagination can be compared to the passage in the previous chapter, where imagination is referred to as a 'licensed trespasser' – an image which, contrarily, suggests the limitlessness of imagination.

to tell.[45] Hence, the narrator refers to the alleged futility of narration as a rhetorical means towards narration.

The narrator's emphasis on the act of narration in these examples underpins his function as controller, reminding the reader that what he or she 'sees' of the story is what the narrator has chosen for him or her to 'see'. Furthermore, these instances of meta-narration elevate Hetty's beauty to an inaccessible level beyond the reader's imagination and thus also beyond his or her critical judgement. The 'fact' of Hetty's beauty is thereby made incontestable and immune to the reader's personal evaluation. In this case, then, the meta-narrative references, although drawing attention to the act of narration, indicate the authenticity of the narrative which, they suggest, is so intense and 'real' that it cannot even be justly represented. Rather than highlighting fictionality, then, these meta-narrative indications emphasise the authenticity of diegetic details, thereby tending to persuade the reader of the credibility of the principal idea on which the major plot-line is founded.

In Which the Story Pauses a Little

Adam Bede's famous chapter 17 can be regarded as one very long meta-narrative comment. The chapter constitutes the narrator's vindication of 'realistic' representation and is more or less detached from story-time now and the unfolding of events. Instead it presents an argument for the principles on which the narrative is constructed and as such creates a hiatus in the novel.[46] Several aspects of narratorial commentary which have been

---

45 Maintaining that representation cannot do 'reality' justice, this passage contradicts Eliot's assertions in her essay 'The Natural History of German Life' in which she argues that '[a]rt is the nearest thing to life'. Art, Eliot reasoned, stimulates feeling in such a way that the emotions which may spring from experience can, through art, be understood without actually living the experience. See *Essays*, p. 271.

46 Critical opinion cannot seem to agree on the usefulness of this chapter, but it is often regarded as George Eliot's aesthetic manifesto. As early as 1948, Joan Bennett considered the chapter detrimental to the reader's 'total experience of the book' and thought the narrator's pronouncement of artistic aims completely unnecessary, as these 'reveal themselves in their achievement' (107). W. J. Harvey finds the chapter to be an extreme instance of intrusion and accuses the author of tactlessness; see *The Art of George Eliot*, p. 70. Lucie Armitt argues that the only function the chapter serves is to 'entertain us with Eliot's own sleight of hand' and maintains that Eliot's aim to draw attention to the mechanisms of realism falls short, as it 'also draws attention to the *limits and limitations* of realism – and does so by overstepping them' (43). However,

mentioned above pervade chapter 17; the meta-narrative aspect is the most prominent one, as the purpose of the chapter is to justify not only the narrated contents but also the ways in which those contents are communicated. Studying the chapter from a meta-narrative perspective, it is possible to discern two distinct sections in it. The first section concerns representation from a general perspective. Here, the argument derives from an extradiegetic narrator who seems to be in dialogue with a specific narratee. Addressing this narratee on a narration-now level, this section could be regarded as a full narratorial comment. The second section returns to the diegetic world of the narrative but to a time when Adam has entered old age, and it places the narrator as a character within the diegesis. This second section is therefore not strictly meta-narrative, although it remains with the argument of representation started in the first section.[47]

Although the meta-narrative element in the first section draws attention to the narrating act, the chapter as a whole serves to justify the representation of commonplace and imperfect characters – characters who are, the narrator insists, 'real', historical people. Employing the mirror image again, the narrator regards the novel as a reflection of something 'real', suggesting that his own narrating task consists of communicating the reflections 'as they have mirrored themselves in my mind' (xvii, 175). By using the mirror image to illustrate his own narrating task, the narrator emphasises the authenticity of the narrative while drawing the reader's attention to the narrating act. The analogy is somewhat modified, however, as the narrator adds: 'The mirror is doubtless defective; the outlines will sometimes be disturbed; the reflection faint or confused' (xvii, 175). Again, the act

---

in his essay 'George Eliot Provoked', Roland F. Anderson emphasises the 'discrepancy between principle and practice', arguing that Eliot's reasons for writing the chapter should be seen in context before critics offer opinions on its *raison d'être*. Having inspected the correspondence between George Eliot and her publisher John Blackwood, between roughly 1857 and 1859, Anderson appreciates the conflicting views Eliot and Blackwood held with regard to artistic representation. In his letters, Blackwood would frequently object to Eliot's realistic mode of representation and press for a more idealised, softened touch to characters and events. Equally frequently, Eliot would either ignore Blackwood's criticism or respond with a concise and well-aimed rebuff. However, according to Anderson, criticism as to Eliot's style of 'realism' continued to mount, and not only from Blackwood, so that Eliot eventually felt that there was no choice for her but to 'assert her own artistic aims' once and for all. See 'George Eliot Provoked: John Blackwood and Chapter 17 of *Adam Bede*', *Modern Philology*, 71 (1973), 39-47 (p. 46).

47 Janice Carlisle observes that the narrator's attitude changes in the two sections. In the first part he 'poses as the creator, the preacher, the measure of moral values', whereas in the second part 'he becomes, like the mock-reader, a fallible man in need of moral guidance' (201). It is a little peculiar, however, that Carlisle should identify the mock-reader as a 'man', when the narratee in the first section of the chapter is a woman.

of mediation is underlined as the narrator acknowledges the impossibility of objectivity and admits to having a subjective perspective. But even this qualification reinforces the authenticity of the narrative, as the narrator speaks of a connection between events as they are mirrored in his mind and the events as they 'really' happened. The meta-narrative element of chapter 17 thus serves to substantiate the impression of veracity in the text and to establish the narrator's role as a historical chronicler.[48]

The meta-narrative element is the predominant over-all function of the first section in chapter 17; but as mentioned above, this exceptional chapter embraces most features of commentary, such as movements between particular and general, addresses and references to the reader and instances of metalepsis. The principal transition between particular and general in the chapter relates to Mr Irwine, who, the narrator assumes, will be subject to the reader's censure. By anticipating the reader's dissatisfaction with the unconventional clergyman, the chapter develops from discussing his particular character to discussing representation in general and then resumes his particular case in the second section of the chapter, which begins: 'And so I come back to Mr Irwine, with whom I desire you to be in perfect charity' (xvii, 179). In effect, the chapter in its entirety constitutes one full circular development from particular to general and back to particular. But here, unlike other instances of commentary which proceed in this manner, the narrator's intentions are patent as he frankly discloses how he wishes the reader to respond.

The reader address is equally patent. In fact, the chapter is introduced by the narrator's mimicry of a hypothetical reader response: ' "This Rector of Broxton is little better than a pagan!" I hear one of my lady readers exclaim' (xvii, 175). The specified narratee in the first part of the chapter is, as the quotation shows, a woman, and her gender is indicated again when the narrator refers to 'your excellent husband himself, who has other irritating habits besides that of not wiping his shoes' (xvii, 176). Mimicry of the narratee's possible interjections is a means by which the narrator approaches the discussion of representation. Realistic representation versus idealistic depiction was a crucial issue for Eliot, who had received much criticism for her descriptions of imperfect clergymen and commonplace

---

48 Caroline Levine draws an interesting parallel between the narrator's mirror as described in chapter 17 and Hetty's mirror. Observing that the narrator's mirror reflects his own mind, Levine also notices that Hetty's mirror 'reflected the particularity of her own mind, rather than a perfect flawless reflection'. Commenting on this parallel, Levine argues that both 'Hetty's unethical self-consciousness and the ethical realism of the narrative [...] attest to the limited particularity of the spectator, refusing to claim universal, neutral, or *impersonal* status' (Levine's italics; 'Women or Boys?', 124).

characters in *Scenes of Clerical Life* and who, during the time of writing *Adam Bede*, was engaged in a continuous debate with John Blackwood concerning the prevalence of less than ideal characters in her new novel.[49] Aware of the fact that some of her readers were predisposed to disapprove of flawed characters (and of Mr Irwine in particular), Eliot has her narrator undermine the authority of these potential readers. The mimicry serves a satirical function, making fun of the narratee even before her argument is dealt with. In this case, the reader is not supposed to identify with the narratee who is, it is implied, a prim and ignorant woman.[50]

The idea of a woman narratee is abandoned as the narrator advances into a general discussion on the matter of representation. Here the reader is referred to as 'you', as if in dialogue with the narrator, and as the discussion progresses the narrator keeps endeavouring to reduce the distance between himself and the reader.

The second section of chapter 17 deals with the same arguments regarding representation, but with the difference that they are included in story-time now and emanate from the intradiegetic narrator's conversation with Adam.[51] In effect, Adam becomes the narrator's mouthpiece, as his vindication of Mr Irwine's character is made to support the representation of the 'realistic'. This second section also identifies the narrator as an experienced man of the world who can move as easily among gentry as among plebeians. The specification of the narrator's identity and gender as masculine was abandoned with the later novels, once Eliot's cover had been revealed.[52] In *Adam Bede*, however, the narrator's maleness and Eliot's pseudonym tell of a Victorian standard which saw a contradiction between female status and narrative authority.[53] By establishing the narrator as male

---

49 See Anderson's article 'George Eliot Provoked'.

50 Cf. Roy Pascal's discussion of Free Indirect Discourse (FID) which, he claims, often involves mimicry of characters' speech in order to convey satire and irony. See *The Dual Voice: Free Indirect Speech and Its Function in the Nineteenth-Century European Novel* (Manchester: Manchester University Press, 1977), pp. 79-80.

51 Janice Carlisle notes about the transition in chapter 17 that 'George Eliot moves from a dialogue between the narrator and a mock-reader [...] to a dialogue between character and narrator' (200).

52 The specifically male narrator was, as mentioned, abandoned in Eliot's later novels, but was replaced by what Susan Sniader Lanser calls the 'Male of Authority' which, she claims, is 'all the more powerful for being invisible and impersonal rather than particularised and sexualized'; *Fictions of Authority: Women Writers and Narrative Voice* (Ithaca: Cornell University Press, 1992), p. 96.

53 Susan Sniader Lanser discusses the prevalence of male pseudonyms among female authors in the Victorian period, arguing that the practice increased after 1860 when 'narrative status is authorized diegetically according to the social identity of the (presumed) author rather than, as in earlier periods, mimetically according to the truth claims made for the narrative itself' (88-89). The same applied to narrative strategies which indicated male

and by employing the male pseudonym, Eliot circumvented the risk of having her novels interpreted on the strength (or rather weakness) of the author's gender.[54] Part of the narrative strategy in chapter 17 builds on a tension between the male narrator and the female narratee. By taking advantage of gendered power structures in Victorian society at large, the narrator emphasises his authority and fortifies his argument, partly at the expense of a female narratee.

To the extent that chapter 17 can be considered Eliot's aesthetic manifesto, it should be regarded both as a part of the novel *Adam Bede* and as an independent entity which, together with Eliot's critical essays and aesthetic aims expressed elsewhere, contribute to an ongoing discussion on representation, morality and art which Eliot conducted throughout her career. Indeed, chapter 17 introduces several issues which would come to form significant thematic concerns in Eliot's later novels. The principal argument, of course, pertains to the representation of the 'realistic' versus the ideal; but within this discussion and as a consequence of it, several other matters are broached. For example, the narrator is concerned with eliciting compassion in his readers. His pleas for interest in and sympathy for 'stupid, inconsistent people' relate back to Eliot's essay 'The Natural History of German Life', which she wrote for the *Westminster Review* in 1856. Inspired by Wilhelm Heinrich von Riehl, who had performed sociological analyses of the German peasantry, Eliot's essay sketches what Valentine Cunningham calls 'a programme of sociological research into the life of ordinary England'.[55] The Riehl essay, as it is commonly known, expresses the importance of attention to ordinary people as a reaction to the lofty and idealistic works of the past. Eliot wanted literature to make readers feel, claiming that 'Art is the nearest thing to life; it is a mode of

---

narrators within texts. Lanser claims that these strategies were commonly employed among female authors in the period such as George Sand, Mrs Gaskell, the Brontës and Harriet Beecher Stowe. Sand, Lanser claims, was Eliot's greatest influence. Her use of the male narrator as well as Eliot's, Lanser continues, 'allows the text to partake of the professional authority that, in mid-nineteenth-century France even more than in England, was resoundingly masculine' (93).

54 Regarding Eliot's use of pseudonym, George Henry Lewes wrote to Harriet Beecher Stowe: 'the object of anonymity was to get the book judged on its own merits, and not prejudged as the work of a woman, or of a particular woman. It is quite clear that people would have sniffed at it if the had known the writer to be a woman but they can't now unsay their admiration'; *Letters*, iii, 106. Ironically, Lanser notes, reviewers did in fact 'unsay their admiration' (94).

55 George Eliot, *Adam Bede*, introduction by Valentine Cunningham, p. x.

amplifying experience and extending our contact with our fellow-men beyond the bounds of our personal lot'.[56]

The narrator is also concerned with the complexity of 'true' representation, acknowledging the inevitability of subjective perspectives as well as the limitations and insufficiencies of language.[57] The difficulties of language are juxtaposed with those of painted art. Commenting on an aesthetics of the sublime, the narrator opposes an art which portrays religious, mythological or heroic ideals, arguing that it is morally useless.[58] Religious matters are further discussed through the medium of Adam, who voices the narrator's arguments in the second part of the chapter. Rejecting the notion of morality as a set of rules and principles regulated by religious

56 *Essays*, p. 271. Eliot's essay shows that she regarded the artist's task as 'sacred' (271). This conception has an obvious connection with the notion of the artist's inspired insight, a prevailing idea among philosophers and intellectuals in the Victorian era. Part of literary tradition involved the assumption that the author was an inspired genius whose dogmatic 'truths' could pass for inevitable law. Ruskin perceived his role as an artist in this fashion, stating: 'Until people are ready to receive all I say about art as unquestionable [...] I don't consider myself to have any reputation at all worth caring about'; see *Works*, ed. by E. T. Cook and A. D. O. Wedderburn, 39 vols (London, 1902-1912), xxxvi, p. 169. Thomas Carlyle invested Art with a social function, claiming that it was the responsibility of the artist to reinterpret 'reality' and going so far as to consider writers an actual priesthood. See Valerie Dodd, *George Eliot: An Intellectual Life* (London: The Macmillan Press, 1990), p. 62. Furthermore, Robert Browning announced, before embarking on his writing career, that he would be a 'priest and prophet as of old'; see Walter E. Houghton, *The Victorian Frame of Mind, 1830-1870* (New Haven: Yale University Press, 1985), p. 153 (first published in 1957). These notions were opposed by, among others, John Stuart Mill, who found the writers 'conceited of their function and of themselves, however unworthy of it'; *The Victorian Frame of Mind*, p. 154.

57 Several of Eliot's novels are concerned with epistemology and in particular with the problems of subjective and objective knowledge, with knowing the world and with understanding other minds. Like August Comte, who in his later work acknowledged that some forms of knowledge could be attained through other means than the empirical, Eliot struggled with the problems of reconciling subjective and objective perspectives. Feeling, Eliot believed, played a crucial part in the reconciliation: as discussed above, feeling is a basis for morality; and in Eliot's epistemology morality is an essential requirement for full knowledge. Suzy Anger describes Eliot's position as a belief that 'only a sympathetic disposition will allow one to escape subjective bias, to see from other viewpoints, and so attain a sort of impartiality'. Eliot's epistemology, then, allowed for knowledge which originated in feeling and was not necessarily attached to absolute experience. See Suzy Anger, 'George Eliot and Philosophy', in *The Cambridge Companion to George Eliot*, ed. by George Levine (Cambridge: Cambridge University Press, 2001), pp. 76-97 (p. 86).

58 The excursus which constitutes chapter 17 has often been compared to Wordsworth's preface to the *Lyrical Ballads* in which Wordsworth, like Eliot, asserts what could be considered an artistic manifesto. For further discussion of the Wordsworthian elements in *Adam Bede* and for parallels between Eliot's rejection of an aesthetics of the sublime and Wordsworthian thought-patterns, see Stephen Gill, *Wordsworth and the Victorians* (Oxford: Clarendon Press, 1998), and Jay Clayton, 'Visionary Power and Narrative Form: Wordsworth and *Adam Bede*', *ELH*, 46 (1979), 645-672.

decrees, Adam praises Mr Irwine's ability to stir 'feeling' as the key to the elicitation of human sympathy and morality.

Consequently, chapter 17 constitutes a narrative excursus which aims to establish and vindicate the principles on which the narrative is constructed. Within this hiatus in the tale, the narrator nevertheless continually endeavours to shape the reader's reaction to diegetic properties through methods attributable to narratorial commentary. Hence, while the chapter forms a pause in the story, it does not leave off attempting to affect the reader's response, not only to the argument put forward in the chapter but to the characters in the diegesis, to the narrator himself and, significantly, to the notion of an ideal reader – that is, one who dissociates himself or herself from the specified narratee and goes along with the narrator's position with regard to representation, art and morality.

Women, Men and Rustics

The technical-narratological aspects of narratorial commentary in *Adam Bede* are complemented by an array of thematic concerns. Among these certain recurrent issues stand out, suggesting a particular preoccupation on the narrator's part. The predominant thematic concerns which surface through narratorial commentary in *Adam Bede* involve class and gender issues, aspects of history, matters of the heart and religious and ideological interests. The remainder of this chapter examines how these concerns are considered in the novel's commentary.

In view of the arguments put forward in chapter 17, it may be a little surprising to find that the depictions of landscape and scenery in *Adam Bede* are seemingly eternally pastoral and sun-drenched.[59] Rural folk are generally depicted in a favourable light. Even so, the novel includes a number of comments which highlight less than flattering idiosyncrasies thought to be specific to bucolic characters. Introducing the villagers into the novel as they come to see Dinah preach on the green, the narrator offers his opinion on the nature of rustic folk considered as a collective group:

---

59 It is significant to the effect of the ensuing tragedies, however, that they are set against the backdrop of this beauty in nature. See, for example, the comment on pp. 363-364 in chapter 35, which illustrates this very point by evoking an image of the Cross at the roadside.

But do not imagine them gathered in a knot. Villagers never swarm: a whisper is
unknown among them, and they seem almost as incapable of an undertone as a cow
or stag. Your true rustic turns his back on his interlocutor, throwing a question over
his shoulder as if he meant to run away from the answer, and walking a step or two
farther off when the interest of the dialogue culminates (ii, 19).

The quotation forms an early indication of the narrator's idea of his audience. The rustics are characterised as 'other', and the seeming peculiarities
of their otherness serve to give the reader and narrator cause for shared
amusement. Simon Dentith identifies two different readerships for Eliot's
novels: a sophisticated elite and a middle-class majority.[60] Eliot was eager
for acceptance with both, and the comment gives the impression that the
narrator is pandering to the public at the expense of farmers and arti-
sans. This indulgence seems a far cry from Eliot's dedication in chapter 17
to 'tolerate, pity and love [...] these more or less ugly, stupid, inconsistent people, whose movements of goodness you should be able to admire'
(xvii, 176), as well as from her plea for social and political reform in 'The
Natural History of German Life'. Dentith argues that there is a paradox
inherent in Eliot's treatment of character in that groups of characters can
be depicted as representing the 'typical' in certain classes, while individual
characters with special status are seen to distinguish themselves within that
class. Adam and Dinah are examples of this paradox: they belong to the
group of rustics referred to in the quotation, but are treated differently in
the narrative. Their prominence is, however, no societally-orientated coin-
cidence, but a manifestation of their rich and gifted personalities.[61]

The narrator's implicit comparison between rustics and animals in the
quotation above suggests a disdain for the group which strikes a discordant
note when placed beside the attention given to the old women scraping
carrots in chapter 17. The discrepancy is relevant to the ambiguity commonly attached to Eliot's standing as a 'critical realist'.[62] The narrator's

---

60 Simon Dentith, *George Eliot* (Brighton: Harvester Press, 1986).
61 Dentith's criticism echoes Raymond Williams's observation concerning a collective voice
   of rustics who are, in contrast to the central protagonists, denied the opportunity of
   communicating ideas or developing a higher consciousness. The status of these rustics
   is distinguished from the prominence of the protagonists chiefly through different
   speech patterns. While the rural characters speak in broad local dialect in which they
   express simply constructed ideas, the protagonists regularly voice complex concepts and
   distinctive opinions in eloquent and coherent standard English. Distinctive to Eliot's
   early novels, Williams claims, is a kind of affection for the lower classes which easily slips
   into condescension. See *The Country and the City* (London: The Hogarth Press, 1985),
   pp. 165-181.
62 Although deeply critical of her society, her work, according to Arnold Kettle, remains
   essentially attached to the conventions of that society; see *An Introduction to the English
   Novel*, 2 vols (London: Hutchinson & Co., 1951), i, pp. 160-177. As *Felix Holt* will

comment on rustics serves to establish a mutual understanding between reader and narrator, based on the assumption that both adhere to particular views on social and political issues. However, this understanding is established at the expense of the ideological persuasions promoted in chapter 17.[63] The comment thus indicates not only a narratorial ambiguity, but also a narratorial anxiety as to the reader's response. In its own small-scale context, the comment bespeaks authority and ironic presence; but in its larger context and compared to other comments, it signals the narrator's continuous concern with winning the reader over.

A number of comments pertaining to gender solicit the same type of understanding between narrator and reader as the ones discussed above. Highlighting what the narrator holds up as gender-specific idiosyncrasies, some of these comments seek to reduce the distance between a male reader and a male narrator by regarding women in general as 'other'.[64] Several such comments are associated with Lisbeth Bede. In chapter 4, she is referred to in connection with Adam's annoyance at his father. Realising that he will have to stay up all night in order to do the work his father has

---

show, Eliot's espousal of social reform was combined with a nineteenth-century dread of a wild outbreak amongst the lower classes which would disrupt the established order and possibly lead to revolution.

63 It should be noted that the narrator's tendency to categorise a social group in this fashion is unusual in Eliot, who demonstrates no such inclination in her later novels. In fact, Eliot's treatment of the 'commonplace' has been compared to Thomas Hardy's ability to excite feeling for rustic characters, providing his rustic characters with distinct and complex personalities rather than regarding them as figures belonging to a homogeneous social group. See Jane Mattisson, *Knowledge and Survival in the Novels of Thomas Hardy* (Lund: Lund Studies in English, 2002).

64 Eliot has come in for much criticism for what has been considered un-feminist portrayals of female characters and plots. The first wave of feminist criticism in the 1970s expressed a sense of betrayal, protesting against Eliot's manner of having her female characters resign themselves to conventions. For example, Dinah gives up preaching and marries, Maggie's insubordination is punished with death, Dorothea resigns an independent life for marriage and Gwendolen's passionate nature is eventually subdued. The second wave of feminist criticism, however, heralded by Zelda Austen's article 'Why Feminist Critics are Angry with George Eliot', *College English*, 37 (1976), 549-561 and Elaine Showalter's article 'The Greening of Sister George', *Nineteenth-Century Fiction*, 35 (1980), 292-311, regarded Eliot's female portraits as heroines who stimulate visions of revolt and who steer the unfolding of the plot from disadvantageous positions. These articles exemplified a new critical approach which discerned the complexities incorporated in Eliot's women. See also Sandra M. Gilbert and Susan Gubar, *The Madwoman in the Attic: The Woman Writer and the Nineteenth-Century Literary Imagination* (New Haven: Yale University Press, 1979), pp. 443-535, and Gillian Beer, *George Eliot* (Brighton: Harvester Press, 1986). However, most feminist criticism focuses on Eliot's characters, and relatively scant attention has been devoted to those comments in Eliot's novels which directly remark on gender issues. In the case of *Adam Bede*, this is possibly due to critics' feeling that Eliot's narrator is not yet the mature authoritative persona who would develop in the later novels.

neglected, Adam becomes irritated with his mother's wailing. But he soon notices that Gyp, his dog, is affected by his temper and so immediately mellows, whereupon the narrator remarks: 'We are apt to be kinder to the brutes that love us than to the women that love us. Is it because the brutes are dumb?' The 'we', seemingly deriving from a male narrator, at first gives the impression of being limited to a male readership. Assuming that the reader is male, the narrator endeavours to reduce the distance between himself and the reader by referring to an experience which the male reader is expected to recognise. Women are regarded as 'other', and the recognition of their alleged tendency to be garrulous serves as a humorous element by which the male reader and narrator are bonded.

However, it is possible to read the comment as a general reflection without out a humorous dimension, a statement acknowledging a universal phenomenon which the narrator considers peculiar. It is true that the male voice regards women as 'other', as a distinct and homogeneous group; but the narrator's attitude regarding the male tendency to treat animals more kindly than human beings is ambiguous. Seen in the context of Adam Bede's behaviour, the comment could be read as criticism of a character who lacks patience with his fellow human beings, considers himself superior and, not least, treats his dog more kindly than he does his mother. The comment forms part of a passage which depicts the imbalanced relation of power between Adam and his mother – an imbalance to which the narrator returns by revealing more of Lisbeth's character.

As if qualifying the depiction of Lisbeth, the narrator remarks on her nature a few lines further down, partly in order to show what causes her disharmonious relationship with Adam and partly to reveal the loving emotions which underlie her cantankerousness:

> Women who are never bitter and resentful are often the most querulous; and if Solomon was as wise as he is reputed to be, I feel sure that when he compared a contentious woman to a continual dropping on a very rainy day, he had not a vixen in his eye [...] Depend upon it, he meant a good creature, who had no joy but in the happiness of the loved ones whom she contributed to make uncomfortable, putting by all the tid-bits for them, and spending nothing on herself (iv, 42-43).

There is no hint of male superiority here and no suggestion that the address is aimed at a male readership only. Rather, the comment assumes an authoritative and impersonal tone (despite the 'I'). By commenting on women in general, the narrator presents a perspective on Lisbeth which adds depth to her character. Emphasising her maternal instinct, the comment encourages the reader to sympathise with Lisbeth's resignation and to understand the origin of her laments.[65] The reference to the Book of Proverbs, furthermore, serves to add authority not only to the argument, but to the narrator himself. By elaborating and adapting Solomon's analogy, the narrator assumes a sage-like status and hence authenticates the credibility of his contention as well as the authority of his narrative role.

A further example showing yet another narratorial attitude with regard to men and women appears in chapter 15, in connection with the long passage on Hetty's beauty. Discussing the tendency to equate beauty with impeccable morals, the male narrator offers his own experiences:

> I find it impossible not to expect some depth of soul behind a deep grey eye with a long dark eyelash, in spite of an experience which has shown me that they may go along with deceit, peculation, and stupidity. But if, in the reaction of disgust, I have betaken myself to a fishy eye, there has been a surprising similarity of result. One begins to suspect at length that there is no direct correlation between eyelashes and morals (xv, 154).

The long passage into which this obviously ironic comment is incorporated discusses male appreciation of female beauty in general and Adam's fascination with Hetty's beauty in particular. The narrative pattern of the comment is similar to the remark above about women and dogs. Initially it seems to address a male audience, appealing to male readers with reflections they are assumed to recognise; but underneath this recognition the irony undermines its very basis. The irony and the context reverse the perspective so that it is the narrator himself, as a representative of an erroneous masculine tendency, who is satirised.

The narrator's position with regard to gender issues in *Adam Bede* is consequently unstable. Moving from attitudes which seem to indulge male audiences to impersonal proverb-like approaches and self-irony, narratorial positions with regard to gender issues as manifested in commentary are erratic. These ambiguities affect the reader's position in relation to the text, a position which is in constant flux in accordance with the narrator's shifting attitudes not only to the text but also to the reader. By alternating

---

65 The self-sacrificing woman is a common character in Eliot's novels. Her most famous heroines, Dinah, Maggie and Dorothea, are all recast secular versions of suffering martyrs and all subject to criticism from feminist quarters. Kate Flint attempts to explain Eliot's concern with the subject of female resignation by attaching it to her rejection of idealistic representation. See 'George Eliot and Gender', in *The Cambridge Companion to George Eliot*, ed. by George Levine (Cambridge: Cambridge University Press, 2001), pp. 159-180. But it is possible to interpret renunciation and resignation in the later novels as formative processes by which the characters endure experiences which lead them to moral maturity. Lisbeth's self-sacrifice described above, however, has more to do with her parental impulses than with a hypothetical expectation of female resignation.

between addressing a female narratee, a male narratee and an unspecified 'you', the narrator continually modifies the reader's relation to both the diegesis and to himself, undermining the notion of a constant and connecting consciousness. In Eliot's later novels, gender issues continue to form significant themes in narratorial commentary; but the narrator's attitude gradually becomes more coherent and the comments increasingly mature and serious in nature.

Love and Fellow-feeling

A major theme in *Adam Bede* concerns Adam's personal development from harsh self-righteousness to humble compassion. Learning through suffering the difference between the love for an exterior ideal and the love which derives from sympathy and fellow-feeling, Adam illustrates the Feuerbachian idea of the individual's progress towards a 'religion of humanity'. Love as experienced between lovers and love defined as the compassionate empathy felt by one human being for another are thus significant ideas in the novel, and they figure as important themes in narratorial commentary as well as in the running narrative. Perceiving the close connection between these two modes of love, the narrator remarks about Seth's feelings for Dinah:

> He was but three-and-twenty, and had only just learned what it is to love – to love with that adoration which a young man gives to a woman whom he feels to be greater and better than himself. Love of this sort is hardly distinguishable from religious feeling. What deep and worthy love is so? (iii, 37).

The statement indicates Eliot's indebtedness to Feuerbach, who contends that God is the idea of human perfection. In essence, the notion of God, according to Feuerbach, is comprised of human ideals, rendering the worship of God a veneration of what are actually humankind's highest attributes. The divine love of Christ, self-sacrificing, suffering and forgiving, is, according to Feuerbach, the most supreme form of human love. To follow Christ's example, to love humans the way God does, is, he argues, to understand the highest principle of Christianity. In other words, religion for Feuerbach consists in the love between humans, and this is the theory which the comment above adheres to.[66] Suggesting that Seth's love for Dinah involves much more than just sexual attraction, the narrator indicates the profundity of his feelings. For Seth, Dinah embodies divine qualities and thereby becomes an object of worship. But Seth's love does not arise independently of Dinah's character; her beauty of soul activates his love, as it will Adam's towards the end of the novel. This is the significant contrast between Dinah's and Hetty's beauty. Hetty's beauty cannot excite the type of love which appropriates 'religious feeling', and her narcissism prevents her from achieving that highest form of love herself.[67]

The positioning of the comment quoted above is important to an understanding of its function. Situated prior to a discussion of Methodism, it precedes a direct solicitation for the reader's sympathy. Expecting the reader to have views on Methodism, even commenting ironically on his or her potential preconceived notions, the narrator devotes a long passage to discussing how a dedication to 'erroneous theories' (iii, 38) need not entail the individual's lack of 'sublime feelings' (iii, 38). The comment hence introduces the reader to those 'sublime feelings' by way of preparation for the ensuing discussion of Methodism, encouraging the reader to understand the sincerity and intensity of the love Seth feels for Dinah and inviting him or her to recognise the emotion.[68] Besides, the comment introduces the reader to a philosophy of love which is significant to his or her understanding of the novel as a whole, that is, the Feuerbachian philosophy on love and fellow-feeling which serves as a guiding principle in the narrative.

---

66 Feuerbach states: 'The relations of child and parent, of husband and wife, of brother and friend – in general, of man to man, – in short, all the moral relations are *per se* religious' (271). One principal argument in Feuerbach's *Das Wesen des Christenthums* is that Christianity is essentially a religion of Man rather than a religion of God. Man projects his own being and feelings into an entity outside himself – God – and so objectifies as religion that which is fundamentally human in content. See also Bernard Paris, *Experiments in Life*; 'George Eliot's Religion of Humanity', *ELH*, 29 (1962), 418-443; and U. C. Knoepflmacher, 'George Eliot, Feuerbach and the Question of Criticism', in *George Eliot: A Collection of Essays*, ed. by George R. Creeger (London: Prentice-Hall, 1970), pp. 79-85.

67 Peter C. Hodgson claims that this is the quintessence of Eliot's aesthetic theory: 'beauty is a matter not simply of harmony and proportion, as in classical views, but of ethical self-transcendence, the capacity to share in the pathos of another'. See *The Mystery beneath the Real: Theology in the Fiction of George Eliot* (Minneapolis: Fortress Press, 2000), pp. 49-50.

68 The passage as a whole can be regarded as a preliminary to chapter 17; the narrator anticipates the reader's derision not only of the characters' religious affiliation, but also of their humble circumstances. Towards the end of the chapter the narrator states: 'Considering these things, we can hardly think Dinah and Seth beneath our sympathy, accustomed as we may be to weep over the loftier sorrows of heroines in satin boots and crinoline, and of heroes riding fiery horses, themselves ridden by still more fiery passions' (iii, 38).

The novel's preoccupation with fellow-feeling is connected to notions of how that emotion is achieved. Suffering, Eliot believed, is a necessary part of the individual's personal development and the crucial experience which conducts humans from their innate subjectivities to an awareness of others.[69] This notion of suffering plays a vital role in Adam's personal maturity; it is a determining factor for his ability to forgive Arthur and Hetty, for his understanding of their suffering and for his falling in love with Dinah. In order for the reader to understand this development in Adam, he or she must acknowledge the significance that suffering possesses. Hence, the narrator devotes a number of comments to the notion of acquiring and incorporating fellow-feeling through the experience of suffering. In chapter 19, before the element of suffering has emerged, the narrator comments on Adam's hardness and his lack of fellow-feeling for the weaknesses and errors of others:

> Without this fellow-feeling, how are we to get enough patience and charity towards our stumbling, falling companions in the long and changeful journey? And there is but one way in which a strong determined soul can learn it – by getting his heart strings bound round the weak and erring, so that he must share not only the outward consequence of their error, but their inward suffering (xix, 209).

The comment appears just after a passage where Adam has been daydreaming about his future with Hetty and serves as a premonition of the emotional pain he will eventually suffer. The reader is aware of a flirtation between Arthur and Hetty and may read the comment as a revelation of their romance. But in retrospect he or she will understand that the comment involves much more, that it requires of Adam that he empathise with Hetty's and Arthur's imminent suffering although he must share in 'the outward consequence of their error'. By indicating that it is through empathising with the 'weak and erring', through incorporating and understanding their torment, that Adam will proceed towards fellow-feeling, the comment encapsulates the moral essence of the story.

Moving into narration now and addressing the reader, the comment converts Adam's lack of empathy into a general reflection on fellow-feeling in which the reader is invited to participate. Employing the first-person

---

69 Almost all Eliot's major characters progress from some form of egoism or self-centredness through suffering to perceiving and empathising with the interior lives of others. Bernard Paris has elaborated a three-stage process of moral development from this progress, arguing that Eliot's characters are shocked out of a first stage of self-centredness into a second stage of harsh reality where the world is perceived as alien and the self becomes unimportant. If the character is amenable to the experiences this suffering occasions, he or she will eventually reach the third stage, which entails understanding of others and moral maturity. See *Experiments in Life*, p. 128 *et passim*.

pronoun 'we', and introducing the reflection in the form of a question, the comment draws the reader into the consideration. The first part of the comment, i.e. the question, encourages the reader's participation, implying his or her active role in the interpretative process. Although the question is rhetorical, it nevertheless signals an awareness of a responding and participating reader. The 'we', moreover, makes assumptions about the reader's agreement, taking it for granted that he or she places as much importance on the individual's 'charity towards our stumbling, falling companions' as the narrator does. The first part of the comment thus endeavours to inspire the reader's appreciation of fellow-feeling, signalling its importance in the narrative. The second part of the comment, after the question-mark, refers to Adam but discusses him in general terms, still in narration now. This second sentence insinuates the particular although remaining in the general and thereby serves all the more forcefully as a premonitory indication.

Adam Bede includes several comments concerned with the link between suffering and fellow-feeling like the one quoted above. Although most of them concern Adam's moral development, some also reflect on Hetty's suffering. What all these statements have in common, apart from subject matter, is that they emanate from an authoritarian narrative voice. Unlike the narrative voice discussing gender issues, these comments demonstrate a coherent and consistent narrative voice which maintains the same tone of authority and distance to the text throughout. Hence, the narrator's attitude shows a respect for the discussions contained in these comments which testifies not only to their sensitive nature and to the importance the narrator places on them, but also to the significance they have for the reader's sympathy and overall understanding of the novel.[70]

Love as manifested between lovers constitutes another major theme in narratorial commentary. Indeed, anything else would be surprising, as the novel tells the complicated love stories of its five main protagonists. This is a subject of which the narrator seems to presuppose the reader's personal experience, repeatedly referring to his or her recognition as if to corroborate the credibility of the narrative. In chapter 50, the reader is addressed directly, and his or her expected response to the preceding scene is challenged. Adam's and Dinah's tentative encounters before either understands the feelings of the other are commented on as the narrator approaches the reader: 'That is a simple scene, reader. But it is almost certain

---

70 That is not to say that gender issues are not important or of a sensitive nature, but in *Adam Bede* the subjects are treated differently. In Eliot's later novels, however, the narrator's attitude changes, and gender issues are discussed with the same respect and severity as other important matters.

that you, too, have been in love – perhaps, even, more than once, though you may not choose to say so to all your lady friends' (1, 493). Love of a romantic and even erotic nature is hence also venerated, not as a contrast to fellow-feeling but as a complement to it. The beginning of Adam's and Dinah's romantic love, however, does not generate scenes of ardent passion but consists in 'the timid looks, the tremulous touches, by which two human souls approach each other gradually' (1, 493). These are the aspects of Adam's and Dinah's wooing which the narrator identifies as 'simple', asking the reader to recognise them from his or her own experience rather than comparing them with other love scenes.[71] The reader's personal life is thus drawn into the reflection, and he or she is warned not to judge the scene harshly.

Several comments pertaining to romantic love make the same point: that 'we are all very much alike when we are in our first love' (xxvi, 285). Throughout the novel, romantic love serves as a point of reference by which the narrator assumes that the reader can relate to the emotion described. However, although the novel contains several love stories and lovers – Seth, Adam, Arthur, Hetty and Dinah – only Adam's love features in narratorial commentary. Seth's love for Dinah is remarked on once, as is Arthur's for Hetty and Hetty's for Arthur; but otherwise narratorial commentary is exclusively concerned with Adam's love life. Studying the commentary in isolation thus reveals a narrative strategy geared to inclining the reader to sympathise and identify with Adam. Although this realisation is unsurprising (he does after all give his name to the novel), it demonstrates how important narratorial commentary is in *Adam Bede* as a narrative strategy towards shaping the reader's response.

References to History

All Eliot's novels except *Daniel Deronda* are historical narratives, taking place during, or some decades prior to, the time of the author's childhood. In *Adam Bede* the time of the narrative is proclaimed at the very outset. Set in 1799 and some years forward, the story takes place approximately sixty

---

71 In one sense the passage can be regarded as part of the narrator's vindication of trivial scenes, commonplace characters and rustic settings. See Sarah Gates, pp. 30-31.

years before the narrating.[72] The narrator hence has the advantage of hindsight, a privilege which he repeatedly remarks on. Several comments refer to the differences between the narrator's 'now' and the narrative 'then', taking the form of informative pieces which 'enlighten' the reader as to a historical period with which he or she is assumed to be unfamiliar. A number of these comments are introduced by phrases such as 'for in those days', or 'for those were times'. In chapter 9, for example, the narrator gives a reason as to why it is possible for Hetty and Adam to marry: 'For those were times when there was no rigid demarcation of rank between the farmer and the respectable artisan' (ix, 97). The conjunction introducing these statements signals their explanatory purpose. Positioning himself as a mediator between the time and world of the narrative and those of the reader, the narrator indicates his privileged access to the narrative as well as his explicatory role. Here the reader is situated well outside the time and world of the diegesis, as if those instances of metalepsis when he or she was imagined to partake in the diegesis had never happened. The time and world of the novel is, in these instances, assumed to be alien to the reader, the narrator serving as mediator between him or her and the time of the narrative.

The historical reference also lends credibility to the narrative, as well as to the authority of the narrator. Consolidating narrative elements on historical 'facts', these references give the impression of an 'authentic' story and of a narrator knowledgeable about the time and world in which it takes place. Although these statements remain in story-time now, not constituting proper narratorial commentary, they are nevertheless significant to the investigation of communication between narrator and reader and as preliminaries to Eliot's later novels, where references to the narrator's role as historian more frequently form part of narration now.

Some historical references express evaluations, condemning particular characteristics on the basis of their being anachronistic. Commenting on Hetty's daydreams of Arthur, the narrator exclaims: 'Foolish thoughts! you see; having nothing at all to do with the love felt by sweet girls of eighteen in our days; but all this happened, you must remember, nearly sixty years ago' (ix, 100). The indication of anachronism is of course ironic, the implication being that eighteen-year-old girls of any era are preoccupied with 'foolish thoughts' of a gentleman as 'dazzling as an Olympian God' (ix, 100).[73] The comment nevertheless emphasises the temporal distance

---

72 For a detailed time-scheme, see Maurice Hussey, 'Structure and Imagery in *Adam Bede*', *Nineteenth-Century Fiction*, 10 (1955), 115-129.

73 Charles Palliser regards the comment as an example of Eliot's deliberate ambivalence as to historical objectivity. He argues that *Adam Bede* is about 'the shaping of expectations

between the reader and the diegesis. The reader must 'see' and 'remember', indications which suggest his or her unfamiliarity with the period as well as the narrator's superior status.

Although the narrator poses as a chronicling historian, direct references to this role are only sporadic. As if refraining from the label, the narrator often indicates his chronicling task but rarely uses the word 'historian'. Examples do occur, however, and one appears as a meta-narrative comment in chapter 12. Having been resolved to ride to Windsor, Arthur is exceedingly annoyed to hear that his horse has been lamed. His reaction to the news causes the narrator to remark: 'The judicious historian abstains from narrating precisely what ensued. You understand that there was a great deal of strong language' (xii, 127). By referring to himself as a historian, the narrator attempts to reinforce the impression of the narrative being an authentic story. The epithet indicates the recording of actual events, implying that this is what the events and characters in the narrative are, i.e. 'actual'.[74] In these instances the narrator rejects omniscience in the sense of being invested with god-like powers. By suggesting that the narrator is a historian accounting for 'real' people and events, the comment indicates that the narrator's knowledge of characters' minds derives from his interpretation and reconstruction of their natures, rather than from some sort of metaphysical access to their consciousnesses. The narrator's role as historian hence signals to the reader that his account of events is an interpretation necessarily based on a subjective perspective. Consequently, while authenticating the veracity of the narrative, and underpinning narratorial control, references to the narrator's role as historian also emphasise the subjective interpretation of the account.[75]

---

in life as well as in fiction' and that the narrator's ambivalent attitude with regard to the past in the novel is part of a design which aims to disturb expectation. The irony in the comment, then, Palliser maintains, 'works both against the past and against any assumption of superiority on behalf of the present' (62).

74 Referring to Eliot's essay 'Notes on Form in Art', K. M. Newton argues that Eliot was concerned with the inevitable form that narration imposes on the world in its attempt to represent or describe it, and that her view was that narrative can only ever be a construction of the world. In order to come to terms with this construction, Newton states, Eliot created the illusion of a narrator who is writing about real events and characters. Through the medium of this narrator, Eliot demonstrates that the way in which the novel forms and shapes 'reality' does not represent a mirroring of an order which is immanent in the world, but rather demonstrates the narrator's own subjective 'take' on the world. The conclusion is that Eliot, through the use of this historical novelist, arrives at a justification for the form that a narrative imposes on 'reality'. See 'The Role of the Narrator', p. 100.

75 See Nünning, pp. 163-164.

Historical references in narratorial commentary thus possess a number of different functions: controlling the reader's distance to the diegetic world, reinforcing the authenticity of the text, emphasising the subjective perspective by showing that the events are told 'as they have mirrored themselves in [the narrator's] mind' (xvii, 175) and demonstrating the narrator's status as director. All these functions, however, serve one final end – to shape the reader's response in order to have him or her reach the 'right' interpretation.

* * *

In *Adam Bede*, consequently, narratorial commentary presents a narrator concerned with the reader's response, but also a narrator trying to find his own distance to and role in the narrative. Not least chapter 17 reveals an insecure narrator, concerned not only with the reader's response but with subject matter, mode of representation and with his own part in the diegesis. Still, narratorial commentary in *Adam Bede* operates in ways which will recur in all Eliot's novels. In this sense, it would be fair to say that the *Adam Bede* narrator sets a pattern for subsequent narrators.

3. *The Mill on the Floss*

The Mill on the Floss is considered the most autobiographical of George Eliot's novels. Its action set at the time of Eliot's own childhood, *The Mill* tells the story of a young woman's personal development in an environment where an individual character grapples with rigid societal conventions. Combining Wordsworthian acknowledgment of the powerful inspiration of the past with dramatic presentations of the numbing constraints which that past can entail, *The Mill* presents a complex picture of the conflicts in Maggie Tulliver's character, conflicts between her passionate intellect, her yearning for love and her inability to break away from the past.[1] *The Mill* is not only Maggie's story, though; it is also the story of a family caught up in the tension between past and present. In addition, like all Eliot's novels, it considers issues such as religion, aesthetics and philosophy. The thematic emphases in *The Mill* rest on the interplay between past and present and on the consequences of patriarchal traditions for a young woman's personal development.[2]

The Mill was published in three volumes in 1860 and sold 6,000 copies in seven weeks. Nevertheless, the novel was not as favourably received as *Adam Bede*, critics pointing to the absence of rural charm and religious essence as qualities which rendered it inferior to the first novel.[3] Although

---

1   The novel brims with Wordsworthian thought patterns, from the merging of intellect and feeling and the connections between past and present to the veneration of childhood memories and the healing capacities of nature. For a comprehensive account of Eliot's indebtedness to Wordsworth, see Stephen Gill, pp. 157-161.

2   In her introduction to the World's Classics edition, Dinah Birch points to the qualities which make *The Mill* 'a novel of extraordinarily diverse achievement', arguing that '[w]hat combines them into a single narrative is Eliot's steady insistence that our human identity [...] is deeply rooted in the past' (xxix).

3   George Henry Lewes speculated as to the different responses to *Adam Bede* and *The Mill*, reasoning that the revelation of George Eliot's identity and the fact that *The Mill* was a follow-up novel had much to do with its reception. Admitting to a third reason

several contemporary reviewers admired Eliot's depiction of childhood as well as her portrayal of realistic characters, most criticism was concerned with what was considered the major flaw of the third volume. Outraged with what they saw as unacceptable and uncharacteristic behaviour in a character whom they did not recognise from the earlier volumes, contemporary reviewers regarded the third volume as a sudden and morally reprehensible disruption.[4] Later critics have also had trouble with Eliot's third volume, primarily with its ending and with the narrator's reminiscences of blissful childhood. The ending, often considered abrupt and badly prepared for, is said to disagree with the careful depictions in the early books of the novel. Moreover, critics have argued that the general Wordsworthian reverence for childhood strikes a discordant note in relation to the particularities of Maggie's early days.[5]

Regardless of these criticisms, however, *The Mill* is a literary achievement on a par with Eliot's earlier and later novels. It combines sympathy and pathos with satire and criticism, displays sensitivity to general social movements as well as to individual emotions and juxtaposes comic and tragic elements, doing full justice to the complexities of both. Most importantly, however, *The Mill* is as compelling an exploration of an individual's personal growth in the face of harsh reality as Eliot ever wrote.

This chapter begins by discussing instances of commentary which move between the general and the particular as well as commentary involving the narrator's references and addresses to the reader and then proceeds to examine metalepsis in *The Mill*. Subsequent sections investigate the appearance of two distinct narratorial attitudes in the novel. Having considered these narratological/technical aspects of commentary, this chapter

---

in his journal, however, Lewes wrote: 'I doubt whether it is intrinsically so interesting as *Adam*. Neither the story nor the characters take so profound a hold of the sympathies'; as quoted in *George Eliot: The Critical Heritage*, ed. by David Carroll (London: Routledge, 1971), p. 12.

4 See, for example, an unsigned review in the *Guardian*, which states that 'the actual course of human things is not necessarily the pattern for a work of art'; *The Critical Heritage*, p. 130 (first publ. in *The Guardian* (25 April, 1860), 377-378).

5 In an introduction to the novel, Gordon Haight states that 'dissatisfaction with the catastrophic ending is almost universal'; *The Mill on the Floss* (Boston: Houghton-Mifflin, 1961), p. xix. See also Graham Martin, '*The Mill on the Floss* and the Unreliable Narrator', in *George Eliot: Centenary Essays and an Unpublished Fragment*, ed. by Anne Smith (London: Vision Press, 1980), pp. 36-54 and Barbara Hardy, '*The Mill on the Floss*', in *Critical Essays on George Eliot*, ed. by Barbara Hardy (London: Routledge & Kegan Paul, 1970), pp. 42-58, in which Hardy argues that the reconciliation of Maggie and Tom contradicts the novel's emphasis on renunciation and refraining from wish-fulfilment.

goes on to analyse central thematic concerns in *The Mill*, including child-hood, the tension between past and present and gender issues.

Particular-General-Particular

Like all Eliot's novels, *The Mill* contains a large number of comments which progress from story-time now to narration now by moving between the general and the particular. By fitting particular feelings or events into a general perspective, these comments serve to authenticate the particular as well as to encourage the reader's recognition.[6] An example appears in Book Second, where Tom is sent off to King's Lorton for tutoring. Commenting on Tom's confusion as to his new environment and as to Mr Stelling's character, the narrator's image situates Tom's particular state within a wider context:

> If there were anything that was not thoroughly genuine about Mr Stelling, it lay quite beyond Tom's power to detect it: it is only by a wide comparison of facts that the wisest full-grown man can distinguish well-rolled barrels from more supernal thunder (II, i, 134).

The colon demarcates the narrator's transfer from story-time now to nar-ration now, as if typographically signalling the advent of a generalisation which applies to the reader as well as to the fictional character. It reflects on Tom's particular ignorance, not only by situating it as a phenomenon in a larger universal context but also by locating it within an adult world. Tom is, of course, a child, and his awkwardness and insecurity at King's Lorton are primarily accounted for within the framework of childhood. But the comment locates his situation within a world which adult readers can recognise as theirs. By such means, the narrator encourages the reader

---

6 Elizabeth Ermarth regards the movement between particular and general from another perspective. She claims that '[t]he very fact that the narrator must resort to generalizations and patterns merely testifies to the human limitation of the narrator, not to his omniscience. A really omniscient mind would require none of the categories which weaker minds require'; see 'Method and Moral in George Eliot's Narrative', *Victorian Newsletter*, 47 (1975), 4-8 (p. 5). It could be argued against Ermarth that the narrator's 'resorting to generalizations' is for the reader's benefit – that is, the generalisations are there not because the *narrator* is restricted by human limitations but because the *reader* is.

to identify with Tom's bewilderment, although he or she may not identify with Tom.

The use of imagery for generalisations is common in Eliot's commentary, and it is telling that a comment pertaining to Tom should involve images of 'full-grown men' and 'well-rolled barrels'.[7] The imagery also invests the narrator with sage-like status, establishing his authority and emphasising the weight of wisdom and experience.

Structurally, the comment facilitates a change of focaliser. In the first statement, Mr Stelling is considered through Tom's eyes; but the second 'it is only…' introduces the narrator's perspective, thereby turning the narrator into the focaliser. The statement hence not only emphasises the narrator's authority in a general sense; it also acts as a preliminary to the narrator's particular description of Mr Stelling.

Comments that move from the particular to the general serve other functions as well. For instance, by elaborating on feelings and by drawing the reader into the context the narrator intensifies the reader's sympathy and understanding. These types of comment are especially prevalent in the latter part of *The Mill*. As the little sister stands before her brother, facing him for the first time after her lapse with Stephen Guest, the narrator comments:

> Her brother was the human being of whom she had been most afraid, from her childhood upwards: afraid with that fear which springs in us when we love one who is inexorable, unbending, unmodifiable – with a mind that we can never mould ourselves upon, and yet that we cannot endure to alienate from us (VII, i, 483).

The comment reflects on Maggie's particular predicament, placing it in a universal context and reinforcing the impact of the emotion by elaboration. The narrator's emotional involvement is deliberately exposed, and the personal pronouns presuppose the reader's recognition and experience.[8] The sage-like, authoritative narrator who reflects on and calls attention to the nature of human kind from a distance is replaced by an emotionally engaged narrator who assumes the reader's personal experience of the particular phenomenon described, but who nonetheless approaches the reader in narration now attempting to elicit his or her empathy for Maggie.[9]

---

7 Cf. imagery used in comments pertaining to Hetty. She is, for example, compared to a rootless plant and various types of animals.

8 It is this type of affective involvement on the narrator's part which has prompted speculation into the biographical content of *The Mill*, and considering what is known of the relationship between George Eliot and her elder brother it is speculation which seems impossible to disregard.

9 Jane McDonnell observes that Tom's contempt for Maggie's actions, the severity of his rebuke and Maggie's fear of his refusal are expressions of Maggie's own conscience. See

Because of the narrator's intense involvement, the shift from story-time now to narration now and back again becomes almost imperceptible, the comment never really shifting focus from Maggie but merely serving as clarification of her feelings.

As in *Adam Bede* and Eliot's later novels, the transfer between general and particular is repeatedly initiated by the conjunctions 'for' and 'but'. The causal 'for'-clause often serves an explicatory function, whereas the 'but'-clause, naturally enough, suggests opposition or a change of perspective. Unlike *Adam Bede*, however, *The Mill* only contains four 'for'-clauses, and one of those instances appears in combination with an ensuing 'but'-clause. The example occurs in Book Sixth, 'The Great Temptation', and refers to Maggie's destiny:

> [Y]ou have known Maggie a long while, and need to be told, not her characteristics, but her history, which is a thing hardly to be predicted even from the completest knowledge of characteristics. For the tragedy of our lives is not created entirely from within. "Character," says Novalis, in one of his questionable aphorisms – "character is destiny." But not the whole of our destiny (VI, vi, 401).

By introducing an argument through the causal conjunction, the narrator adopts a tone of authority, communicating a line of reasoning which is presumed to be evident. The 'for'-clause appears as an explanation and elaboration on the particular mechanisms shaping Maggie's life. It also opens up a philosophical discussion, involving complex matters such as tragedy, destiny and determinism. Proceeding from the 'for'-clause, the comment continues the argument by stating Novalis's dictum and then employing a 'but'-clause to challenge his claim. Both the 'for'- and the 'but'-clause thus operate in collaboration, conveying the narrator's argument and establishing his sage-like authority. The passage continues with a reference to *Hamlet*, linking Hamlet's destiny – which, the narrator suggests, is conditioned by circumstances, contexts and the intricate web of human activities – to Maggie's approaching tragedy.[10]

' "Perfect Goodness" or "The Wider Life": *The Mill on the Floss* as Bildungsroman', *Genre: A Quarterly Devoted to Generic Criticism*, 15 (1982), 379-401 (p. 396).

10 About this particular comment, Felicia Bonaparte remarks that 'Eliot does not attempt to identify Maggie's tragedy with Hamlet [...] but rather [...] she restates Hamlet's tragedy in the same terms as Maggie's' (165-166). About the *Hamlet* reference, John Hagan maintains that it suggests that Maggie's tragedy is determined by circumstances which are 'comprised in the characters and actions of her close relations – her father and her brother'. Hagan also identifies two groups of critics: those who regard Maggie's attempts at renunciation as damaging to her character and those who regard her renunciations as stages of spiritual development; see 'A Reinterpretation of *The Mill on the Floss*', *PMLA*, 87 (1972), 53-63 (p. 55). See also George Levine, 'Determinism and

The first sentence in the quotation above is significant to the standard set for the relationship between narrator and reader, as well as between reader and character. Insisting, with a hint of flattery, that the reader 'knows' Maggie rather than 'knowing of' her, the narrator implies an intimate and unmediated relationship between the reader and Maggie. However, the direct acknowledgment of what the reader '[needs] to be told' counteracts that notion. Indicating not only the narrator's superior knowledge but also his pedagogical aim, the statement suggests that the narrative is designed for an audience and that the narrator adjusts his information accordingly. In this sense, the comment accentuates the respective roles of narrator and reader in the narrative process while invoking the reader's intimate familiarity with Maggie. The passage thus demonstrates the narrator's attempts to facilitate the reader's sympathy for Maggie by reducing the distance between the two while retaining his position as mediator between the reader's world and the world of the diegesis.

Three chapters in *The Mill* are introduced by narratorial commentary, whereas twelve are concluded in narration now.[11] Introductory comments often serve as preliminaries, operating almost as forewords in the form of general reflections concerning some phenomenon that will be particularised in the chapter. One example appears in chapter 2 of 'The Valley of Humiliation'. Mr Tulliver has not only lost his lawsuit against Mr Wakem, he has lost his pride and his zest for life, and as a family the Tullivers have lost spirit. Introducing the chapter in which the family's new life is depicted, the narrator reflects on 'the agitation that accompanies the first shocks of trouble' (IV, ii, 275) in relation to 'the time when sorrow has become stale, and has no longer an emotive intensity that counteracts its pain' (IV, ii, 275). It is when this latter type of grief sets in, the narrator maintains, that 'despair threatens' (IV, ii, 276). The comment appears as an introduction to the new circumstances that the Tulliver family finds itself in, both in terms of material assets and in terms of mental states. Up to this point, Mr Tulliver's anger and determination have led to proactive deeds and have kept emotions running high. The comment, however, introduces a changed attitude. Its strategic positioning is important for the reader's understanding of the time lapsed between Tom's oath of vengeance in the last chapter of Book Third and the dull monotony of a debased life

---

Responsibility in the Works of George Eliot', *PMLA*, 77 (1962), 268-279; and George Levine, 'Intelligence as Deception: *The Mill on the Floss*', *PMLA*, 80 (1965), 402-409.

11 Seven chapters are introduced by passages in which the narrator crosses diegetic levels in a metaleptic fashion, presupposing the reader's presence in or access to the scene. These types of comment are dealt with below.

which weighs heavily on the family in chapter 2 of Book Fourth.[12] As with other narratorial comments, the statement encourages the reader's sympathy through general analysis of processes involving human suffering and so invites the reader to participate through his or her sense of recognition.

Comments which conclude chapters often leave the reader in narration now. By avoiding the circular movement back to story-time now, these statements are given extra weight, encouraging the reader, by way of structural positioning, to remain with the comment a little longer. These concluding remarks often express the narrator's thoughts on what has been related, or they convey information, through general analogy, that sheds light on particularities in the chapter. In chapter 10 of Book Sixth, this type of elucidating remark verifies what the reader has probably suspected all along – Philip's jealousy of Stephen Guest. Having asked Maggie if it is only her ties to the past that hinders their union, Philip finds himself unhappy with her affirmative answer, and the narrator comments: 'Jealousy is never satisfied with anything short of an omniscience that would detect the subtlest fold of the heart' (VI, x, 444). This comment conveys information which has only been hinted at until now: so far, Philip's sexual feelings for Maggie and his resentment of Stephen have only been insinuated. Here, however, by acknowledging Philip's jealousy in a proverb-like comment as well as ending the entire chapter on that note, the narrator not only confirms Philip's feelings but also highlights their significance for his relations with Maggie and Stephen. Furthermore, the comment concludes the chapter in which Stephen has recognised an attachment between Maggie and Philip and has become overwhelmed with passion, throwing himself at Maggie. The chapter thus comprises an explosion of emotions which have long lingered latently. Concluding the chapter in narration now therefore opens up the possibility of attaching the veracity of the final comment not just to Philip's particular state, but to any of the characters depicted in the chapter.

The comment could also be interpreted as a premonition of what may be expected from Philip. Premonitory narratorial comments are infrequent in *The Mill* and rarely present any surprises; but when they do occur, they corroborate or verify discussions conducted in story-time now. With regard to Tom's and Philip's relationship as children, the narrator remarks: 'If boys and men are to be welded together in the glow of transient feeling, they must be made of metal that will mix, else they inevitably fall asunder

---

12 It is possible to regard the issue discussed in this comment – that 'true' deprivation involves the monotony and dreariness of everyday life and lacks any element of sensationalism – as indirectly juxtaposed to Maggie's voluntary renunciation of literature and culture.

when the heat dies out' (II, vi, 185). The descriptive passages preceding this comment illustrate the frosty relations between the two boys, so the statement does not raise any unforeseen perspective. However, the fact that it concludes the entire chapter, that it emanates from the extradiegetic narrator in narration now and that it involves universal notions regarding the relations between men, signals that this comment embodies important information about Tom and Philip's relationship.

Comments which introduce and conclude chapters may seem to differ from other particular-general-particular commentary in that they do not form part of a circular movement in the reading process. While, for structural reasons, this may be true of the *introductory* comment, it need not be true of the *concluding* statement, which can often be – and is indeed sometimes obviously intended to be – related back to particular aspects of the preceding chapter. In the same manner as other instances of movement between general and particular, then, these comments form part of a reading process which encourages the reader to recognise certain phenomena in his or her world and to return to the particular situation of the diegesis with the experience of that recognition.

As in *Adam Bede*, the movement between particular and general in *The Mill* is regularly signalled through various typographical means. Also, as in the earlier novel, these movements serve to authenticate diegetic particularities by situating the reader's recognition and understanding of general phenomena within the confines of the narrative.

References and Addresses to the Reader

As in all Eliot's novels, a number of comments appear as direct references and addresses to the reader, often anticipating and remarking on possible reader responses which the narrator endeavours to modify. These instances of commentary explicitly acknowledge the reader's part in the interpretative process as well as reveal the narrator's concern with 'right' interpretation. In *The Mill* the narrator frequently approaches the reader, involving him or her in an imagined dialogue and establishing a close relationship between the two. For example, in chapter 1 of Book Fifth where Philip pressures Maggie into maintaining a relationship with him in defiance of her family loyalties, the narrator approaches the reader: 'You can hardly help blaming him severely [...] But you must not suppose that he was capable of a gross selfishness, or that he could have been satisfied with-out persuading himself that he was seeking to infuse some happiness into Maggie's life' (V, i, 308). Expecting the reader to respond unfavourably to Philip's insistence, the narrator acknowledges the soundness of such a reaction but endeavours to qualify it by adding depth to Philip's motives. Although Philip has egoistic reasons for wanting to maintain a friendship with Maggie, he is also the only character who recognises the injury her vow of renunciation is doing her. By changing the perspective, focusing on the benefits of Philip's friendship, the comment serves to vindicate Philip by showing how his motives are not entirely selfish.[13]

This comment expects and seemingly accepts the reader's potential dis-approval of Philip before adding information which serves to explain his actions further. However, in another similar comment, also with regard to Philip, the narrator's tone is more pleading. Maggie has once again at-tempted to break off their communication, and Philip has resisted. This time, however, the focus is on Philip's need for love and affection, the narrator imploring the reader: 'Do not think too hardly of Philip' (V, iii, 331). The appeal is followed by a reflection which entreats the reader to understand how Philip's needs, desires and aspirations are the same as they would be, had he not been deformed. His deformity excludes him 'from what was a matter of course with others' (V, iii, 330-331), rendering him melancholy and lonely. Therefore, the narrator suggests, his insistence on Maggie's friendship derives not so much from egoism as from a vital need for attention and affection. This address, however, although endeavouring to explicate Philip's emotional state, does not serve to vindicate his actions; rather, it directly appeals to the reader's compassion, inviting him or her to consider Philip's circumstances before judging him.

With regard to the reader's response to Philip, the narrator's emotional engagement is intense and active. He reveals a sense of concern both for Philip as a character and for the reader's appreciation of him. In respect of Stephen Guest, however, a sterner tone is adopted. Having stated that Stephen's increased penchant for singing was instigated by a 'not distinctly conscious' desire to intensify Maggie's feelings for him, despite their renun-ciation of each other, the narrator admonishes: 'Watch your own speech,

---

13 June Skye Szirotny's remark about this passage shows how differently readers interpret narratorial commentary. She argues that the statement 'discredits Philip as selfish' and 'suggests criticism that would hardly have occurred to us'; 'Maggie Tulliver's Sad Sacrifice: Confusing But Not Confused', *Studies in the Novel*, 28 (1996), 178-199 (p. 185). Elizabeth Ermarth points out that Philip's egoistic reasons for sustaining a friendship with Maggie in no way invalidate the accuracy of his perception that Maggie's renunciation forms one long suicide; see 'Maggie Tulliver's Long Suicide', *Studies in English Literature, 1500-1900*, 14 (1974), 587-601 (p. 595).

and notice how it is guided by your less conscious purposes, and you will understand that contradiction in Stephen' (VI, xiii, 459). Again, as with Philip, the narrator requests the reader to excuse a lover whose desire for Maggie's attention causes her anguish. Both Philip and Stephen, through expressions of love, manipulate Maggie's sense of propriety and challenge the principles she has adopted. Neither beau acknowledges the fact that it is at least in part for his own sake that he brings pressure to bear on her.[14]

The statement concerning Stephen employs a tone of reproof, urging the reader to examine his or her own emotional processes before censuring Stephen's. Here, the reader is divested of any sense of superiority in relation to the character, the narrator pointing to aspects which the reader and Stephen have in common. The statement thus incorporates the reader's personal experience into his or her interpretation of the narrative. It does so not by way of general reference but by targeting the reader's own self, thereby encouraging the reader to identify with Stephen. This identification, in turn, lends authenticity to the narrative, implying that the mechanisms operating in Stephen's unconscious mind are as authentic as the reader's own.

As always in Eliot's novels, the narrator continually shifts the reader's distance to the diegesis, alternately locating him or her on a level superior to the characters and alternately attacking his or her sense of superiority, as

---

14 In this sense, both Stephen and Philip resemble Eliot's other egoists, who make their visions of 'reality' fit in with their subjective desires. One of the principal themes in *The Mill* is Maggie's conflict between interior desire and exterior conventions. She is the passionate and intelligent young girl who has to learn to stifle those characteristics in a society which cannot accept brilliant women unless their brilliance is of a conventionally feminine kind. Accordingly, Maggie is burdened with a constant inner conflict between a bright young person's natural desire for experiencing the world and her craving for love and acceptance in a world where those natural aspirations offend and upset her domestic sphere. It is important to notice, however, that Maggie's ties to the past, her strong bond to the family unit and her almost frantic craving for acceptance, love and affection, particularly from her family, constitute a strong hold on her character. These are the essentials of her character which win in the end, i.e. which bring her back to St Ogg's after the 'elopement'. Both Philip and Stephen, however, through persistent argument, activate Maggie's passion and curiosity, influencing her to temporarily abandon her more sensible nature and to give in to the temptations created by her passionate temperament. Maggie's inner turmoil is therefore not only instigated from within as a result of an innate oscillation between her two natures, but also from without by Philip's and Stephen's unrelenting appeals to her more sensual nature. Neither of them appreciates the anguish such an appeal causes Maggie, neither accepts that she cannot break free from the restraints of the past, and neither can see far beyond his own needs and desires. In fact, the requirements both men place on Maggie reveal an astounding selfishness which has received relatively scant attention in Eliot criticism. For more on the egoists in Eliot's novels, see Bernard Paris, *Experiments in Life, passim*, and K. M. Newton, *George Eliot: Romantic Humanist* (London: Macmillan, 1981), *passim*.

in the comment quoted above. Referring to Tom's severity with Maggie in the last book of the novel, the narrator remarks on what he believes might be the reader's perception of Tom:

> Tom, like every one of us, was imprisoned within the limits of his own nature, and his education had simply glided over him, leaving a slight deposit of polish: if you are inclined to be severe on his severity, remember that the responsibility of toler-ance lies with those who have the wider vision (VII, iii, 500).

This comment invites sympathy by two methods of persuasion. First, by employing the first-person pronoun it associates Tom with the reader and human nature in general. As with Stephen in the comment above, the reader is stimulated to relate Tom's circumstances to his or her own experi-ences. In this way the comment attempts to elicit sympathy on the basis of a shared sense of human imperfection. The reader's recognition, and his or her anticipated adherence to the phrase 'like every one of us', join Tom, the narrator, the reader and human nature in general within similar confines – that is, character and reader are considered equals. By the sec-ond method, however, the reader is situated on a higher level in relation to Tom. Referring to the reader's potential response, the narrator indicates the reader's intellectual superiority, suggesting that he or she is no victim of nature's, but a person of 'wider vision' who, it is implied, has control of his or her feelings and can rise above personal inclination, unlike Tom. Far from levelling the differences between Tom and the reader, the comment reinforces those differences, flattering the reader's ego in order to have him or her feel sorry for Tom.[15]

The comment above refers to the reader as a person of 'wider vision'. *The Mill* comprises several similar statements which imply a specific type of audience. As in *Adam Bede*, some comments suggest communication between a male narrator and a male audience and in some comments the narrator addresses a specific narratee. In *Adam Bede* these specified narra-tees are predominantly female, but in *The Mill*, the narrator approaches a male narratee. One example, which appears in chapter 4 of Book Second, is

---

15 Mary Ellen Doyle observes that passages like the one quoted above are the only means by which the reader can comprehend Tom in the last books of the novel, as he is never judged or analysed by any other character. Although Mrs Glegg condemns his severity towards Maggie, Doyle contends, she does not understand it, and so it can only be explained through the narrator; p. 80. It is noteworthy that several appeals to the reader's interpretative ability attempt to evoke sympathy for characters that afflict Maggie with inner turmoil. Stephen and Philip are excused for activating Maggie's passions and causing her to break her loyalties with her family, and Tom is excused for judging her when she has failed to resist acting on feelings which Philip and Stephen have set in motion.

another remark concerning Tom. Describing his plans to astonish Maggie with his borrowed sword, the narrator addresses the supposedly disbelieving narratee:

> If you think a lad of fourteen would not have been so childish, you must be an exceptionally wise man, who, although you are devoted to a civil calling, requiring you to look bland rather than formidable, yet never, since you had a beard, threw yourself into a martial attitude, and frowned before the looking-glass (II, iv, 175-176).

The comment addresses a particular narratee – a man who, the narrator suspects, takes issue with the veracity of the story. But instead of contending with the anticipated objection, the narrator contends with the objector, ridiculing him as a line of defence rather than counteracting his expected response. Of course, the ridicule operates as a counter-argument, implying that the narratee is no better than Tom, secretly indulging in boyish play-fighting despite his mature age and 'civil calling'. Again, the comment challenges the reader's sense of superiority, here represented by the narratee; but in this particular example the concern is primarily with authenticity. By exposing the narratee to scrutiny, suggesting the connection between him and Tom, the narrator authenticates Tom's behaviour.

It should be noted that this type of argument – that is, the type that refutes a potential response by scoffing at the responder – requires a specified narratee. The narrator's irony would not be appreciated by a reader who is the butt of the joke, so the comment addresses a textually constructed addressee instead. In this manner, the tone of the comment can be caustic and persuasive without running the risk of offending the reader.

The most common way of shaping reader response, however, is by bringing the reader into a particular experience, often by including him or her in the first-person pronoun. By generalising particular situations, the narrator's reference to 'we' connects the reader, narrator and diegetic character with human nature in general, thus creating a sense of solidarity which preconditions the reader to sympathise with characters. The first- and second-person pronouns are employed throughout the novel, but it is in the last book of *The Mill* that references to 'we' are at their most intense. When Maggie receives Stephen's letter, the narrator describes her reaction in the following manner:

> At the entrance of the chill dark cavern, we turn with unworn courage from the warm light; but how, when we have trodden far in the damp darkness, and have begun to be faint and weary – how, if there is a sudden opening above us, and we are invited back again to the life-nourishing day? The leap of natural longing from

under the pressure of pain is so strong, that all less immediate motives are likely to be forgotten – till the pain has been escaped from (VII, v, 514).

Stephen's letter appears as another trial for Maggie, tempting her with a life which could satisfy her yearning for love and affection. Presenting a concrete image of the conflict between temptation and duty in Maggie's mind – a conflict which she has been faced with several times before in the novel – the comment invites the reader into the analogy.[16] Hence, whether or not the reader understands or recognises Maggie's circumstances, he or she can enter into the image described. However, the image does not only serve to explain Maggie's feelings in order for the reader to understand, but actually induces the reader to feel.[17] By living the part of an individual entering a 'chill dark cavern', the reader is encouraged to imagine Maggie's conflict. The comment hence guides the reader through the cavern, employing the 'we' to indicate that the metaphor applies universally.

The image lends poignancy to the episode but also, more importantly, to the reader's engagement with the narrative. Whenever the first- or second-person pronoun is used, the reader's active participation in the narrative is called upon. In the comment above, the level of intensity is increased not just by including the reader in 'we' but also by encouraging him or her to become a participant in the image. As a preparation for Maggie's imminent drowning, which occurs in the same chapter, the narrator endeavours to increase the reader's degree of sympathy for her. The passage serves not merely to deepen the reader's engagement with the diegesis, but also as a narratological device intensifying the effect of the tragic ending.[18]

---

16 Peter Hodgson identifies two forms of religion in the novel: one is the religion of the Tullivers and Dodsons – a half-hearted, spiritually barren form of religion – and the other is Maggie's religion. Inspired by Thomas à Kempis's theory on renunciation and suffering, Maggie throws herself into a value-system by which she seeks to make sense of the tragic aspects of the human condition. However, Hodgson notes, as does the narrator, that Maggie does not at first understand that renunciation requires sorrow; pp. 71-72. In this passage above, though, she does suffer, and her renunciation of Stephen stems from her adherence to principle rather than from a whim. Here she truly feels what renunciation entails and realises, as the narrator comments, that the pain is only genuinely felt once it has enfeebled character and turned the temptation of another 'reality' into an aching longing.

17 Laurence Lerner, however, considers the image too melodramatic to be convincing, contending that the only value it embodies consists in its corroboration of Stephen's plea. See *The Truthtellers: Jane Austen, George Eliot, D. H. Lawrence* (London: Chatto & Windus, 1967), p. 274.

18 The ending of *The Mill* is, as mentioned, considered its major weakness. Henry James, for example, argued that 'the chief defect – indeed, the only serious one – in *The Mill on the Floss* is its conclusion'; 'The Novels of George Eliot', in *A Century of George Eliot Criticism*, ed. by Gordon S. Haight (London: Methuen & Co, 1965), pp. 43-54 (p. 52), first publ. in the *Atlantic Monthly*, 18 (October, 1866), 479-492. In fact, George

The narrator's engagement in the narrative is more conspicuous in *The Mill* than in any other Eliot novel. Maggie's story is told with pathos, and the narrator shows obvious concern with the reader's 'right' interpretation. This emotional involvement in the narrative is partly revealed through the narrator's use of the first-person pronoun 'I'. Indicating a manifest presence in the narrative, the 'I' conveys the impression of personalisation, providing the narrator with a persona in spite of his extradiegetic status. Most of the narrator's references to himself in *The Mill* appear in a borderland between story-time now and narration now. Remaining with the particularities of the story rather than stepping outside the diegesis, the narrator's 'I' seems included in story-time now. However, most of these instances suggest some sort of communication with the reader, expressing the narrator's remarks on the diegesis although remaining within the particular. For example, in chapter 7 of Book First, the 'I' appears in a description of Maggie's basted frock and bonnet: 'I must urge in excuse for Maggie, that Tom had laughed at her in the bonnet, and said she looked like an old Judy' (I, vii, 60). Although this 'I' implies the presence of an audience and accentuates the narrator's role as story-teller, it does not leave the sphere of the particular. The reader is not alerted to another 'now' in which his or her own experiences are brought in. Accordingly, although the narrator comments on the story, this comment does not constitute narratorial commentary as such.

The personal 'I' appears in narratorial commentary as well, though, albeit not as frequently. Remarking on Maggie's fascination with *The Imitation of Christ*, the narrator evinces a contemplative mood: 'I suppose that is the reason why the small old-fashioned book [...] works miracles to this day, turning bitter waters into sweetness [...] It was written down by a hand that waited for the heart's prompting' (IV, iii, 291). Rather than explaining why Maggie is impressed with the book in a matter-of-fact fashion, this comment is of a philosophical nature, revealing a less controlling aspect of the narrator's persona. In this context, the 'I' expresses a degree of modesty, thereby reducing the distance between reader and narrator: the 'supposing' gives the impression of a narrator temporarily relaxing his

---

Eliot herself, in response to Sir Edward Bulwer-Lytton's criticism, admitted that 'the tragedy is not adequately prepared'; *The Critical Heritage*, p. 123. As a response to all the criticism of the ending, Kerry McSweeney sets out to show that it is 'in fact grounded in the body of the text' (56), and one of McSweeney's points of departure is the contention that the ending is not a tragedy but what the narrator calls a 'supreme moment' (VII, v, 521). See 'The Ending of *The Mill on the Floss*', *English Studies in Canada*, 12 (1986), 55-68 (p. 58). For more on tragedy in Eliot's novels, see Barbara Hardy, *The Novels of George Eliot*, and Darrell Mansell Jr., 'George Eliot's Conception of Tragedy', *Nineteenth-Century Fiction*, 22 (1967), 155-171.

authoritative hold on the narrative. However, like all comments, this reflection explains a particular aspect of the narrative, accordingly lending greater depth to Maggie's adoption of Thomas à Kempis's ideas.

As often happens with Eliot's narrators, however, tone and attitude continually shift, so that the 'I' which communicates modesty in one instance can connote complacency in the next. In Book Sixth, for example, the narrator prides himself on depicting an action which, he believes, some readers will recognise. Describing how Tom, after absolving Maggie of her promise about Philip, pulls the bell on his watch, flinging it across the room, the narrator comments on the act as 'a touch of human experience which I flatter myself will come home to the bosoms of not a few substantial or distinguished men who were once at an early stage of their rise in the world' (VI, iv, 395). This 'I' forms part of a meta-narrative element which remarks on the narrative act, emphasising the narrator's role as the creator of a drama, the ultimate aim of which is to present fiction which accords with recognisable 'reality'. The narrator's presence in this example accentuates his role as story-teller while endeavouring to authenticate the narrative by drawing attention to the resemblance between Tom and a specific type of reader. Here, then, the narrator's role as director of the story is sustained, but he nevertheless attempts to bolster the authenticity of the story by appealing to a particular reader's recognition.

Consequently, the narrator's references to himself in *The Mill* express several dissimilar attitudes with regard to his relation to the story and to the reader. But like the narrator's direct remarks on an anticipated reaction, his references to a specified narratee and the inclusion of the reader in 'we', the comments which include the narrator's 'I' serve to shape the reader's response by lending greater depth to diegetic phenomena and by substantiating the veracity of the narrative.

Metalepses

The opening chapter of *The Mill* is particularly well known for the narratorial ambiguities it presents. It introduces the narrator as a first-person 'I', through whose focalisation the reader is presented with the environs of Dorlcote Mill. Giving the impression that the narrator has come back to the area of St Ogg's after having been away for some time, the passage emphasises remembrance as an important element in his return.[19] Nostalgically reminiscing, the narrator wanders along the river Floss, eventually fixing his gaze on a small girl standing by the tributary Ripple. Having studied the girl for a little while from a nearby bridge, the narrator takes notice of the dusk setting, thinking to himself that the girl should be heading home. Indeed, he too has to pick himself up from his musings on the bridge where he has rested his arms on the cold stone. Here, a sudden shift occurs in the text. Illusion and 'reality' are unexpectedly severed as the narrator discloses that it has all been a dream. The whole scene turns out to be part of the narrator's reverie about 'one February afternoon many years ago' (I, i, 9).

> It is time the little playfellow went in, I think; and there is a very bright fire to tempt her: the red light shines out under the deepening grey of the sky. It is time, too, for me to leave off resting my arms on the cold stone of this bridge. . . . .
>
> Ah, my arms are really benumbed. I have been pressing my elbows on the arms of my chair, and dreaming that I was standing on the bridge in front of Dorlcote Mill, as it looked one February afternoon many years ago. Before I dozed off, I was going to tell you what Mr and Mrs Tulliver were talking about, as they sat by the bright fire in the left-hand parlour, on that very afternoon I have been dreaming of (I, i, 8-9).

This first chapter presents an intradiegetic narrator who takes part as a character in the narrative he tells, but who does not tell his own story. At this early stage, the chapter does not contain any example of narratorial metalepsis, the narrator not crossing any diegetic levels. He is introduced on an intradiegetic level, and as far as the reader knows, this is where he remains until the end of the chapter. This first notion of the narrator's intradiegetic status sets the tone for the narrator's relation to the diegesis in the rest of the novel. Reflecting on memories in an emotional mood, in a manner that verges on Romantic self-exploration, the intradiegetic narrator establishes a familiarity and intimacy with the narrative, conveying the

---

19 Several critics have pointed out the literary analogies in this first chapter, the most evident being the Wordsworthian ideal poet attempting to achieve and represent emotion recollected in tranquillity. See Stephen Gill, pp. 157-161. In addition, the dream vision in this first chapter is connected with the classic idea of a dreamer-narrator falling asleep and the narrative being enacted in his dream. In 'The Narrator of *The Mill on the Floss*', *Sydney Studies in English*, 3 (1977-1978), 32-46, Margaret Harris discusses analogies to dream-narratives of an allegorical kind dealing with the notion of ideal states. Although Harris admits that *The Mill* does not present a dream vision of an ideal world, it still, she argues, concerns itself with the discrepancies between an illusory and desired ideal and the limitations of the 'real'. This dream-vision, Harris contends, forms part of Eliot's attempt to fashion her 'religion of humanity' in the same way as medieval allegorical works shaped their own perspectives on Christian beliefs.

impression that the image of an idyllic and blissful past which he presents is part of his own memory.[20] The first-person pronoun emphasises the narrator's involvement in the diegesis.[21] The intimate and intense relationship that he establishes to the diegesis thus largely derives from the impression which this first chapter presents. Of course, his emotional involvement with characters is maintained throughout the novel; but it is this first impression of having personal remembrance of the story which establishes the narrator's relation to it.[22]

Consequently, in chapter 1 the narrator's participation in the diegesis does not constitute an instance of metalepsis, as he is not leaving one diegetic sphere for another. The intradiegetic level is the one on which he starts out, as it were. However, the narrator's exhortations to the reader to 'look' and 'see' constitute instances of metalepsis on the part of the reader. Observing a wagon coming from the mill over the bridge, the narrator pays special attention to its horses, inviting the reader to '[s]ee how they stretch their shoulders up the slope towards the bridge, with all the more energy because they are so near home. Look at their grand shaggy feet that seem to grasp the firm earth' (I, i, 8). Here, the narrator presupposes the reader's actual visual access to the diegesis, encouraging him or her to 'see' and 'look' as if there were no ontological divide between the world of the diegesis and the reader's world. By drawing the reader into the diegetic

---

20 Gill claims that 'the most important association between Wordsworth and *The Mill on the Floss* is in their use of memory' (158).

21 According to Monika Fludernik, a major effect of employing a first-person narrator is that it provides the narrative with a ' "realistic" justification for the omniscient author convention, pretending that the narrative is a mere fireside dream by a none too well defined authorial "I" '(168). Indeed, Fludernik argues, the 'dreamer-narrator' creates the illusion that the narrator is not so much a narrator as an existing person dreaming in an armchair, an illusion which unites the narrator and reader as they seem to enter into the dream together. The most significant purpose of this personalised narrator, and of the intimacy he initiates with the reader already in this first chapter, Fludernik maintains, is to establish a basis of trust between narrator and reader – a basis of trust which, evoked regularly throughout the novel in the form of narratorial commentary, escorts the reader through the narrative, 'providing a level of understanding on which narrator and narratee can find themselves in agreement' (171); Monika Fludernik, 'Subversive Irony: Reflectorization, Trustworthy Narration and Dead-Pan Narrative in *The Mill on the Floss*', *REAL: Yearbook of Research in English and American Literature*, 8 (1991-1992), 157-182.

22 Some reviewers of *The Mill* have complained that Eliot was too close to the narrative, meaning that the narrator's emotional involvement in the story disturbs the reading experience. F. R. Leavis claimed that 'in George Eliot's presentment of Maggie there is an element of self-idealization'; *The Great Tradition* (Harmondsworth: Penguin, 1962), p. 54 (first published in 1948). However, it is possible to regard the degree of the narrator's engagement with diegetic characters as grounded in the first chapter, without necessarily having to bring in biographical aspects.

world, this instance of reader metalepsis strengthens the impression of authenticity, suggesting that the properties of the story are 'real' enough for the reader to see. It also reduces the distance between the diegetic world and the world of the reader, initiating an intimate relation between reader and fiction.

However, the narrator in chapter 1 'wakes up' from his intradiegetic level. By maintaining that the depicted scene was merely part of a dream and by purporting to embark on a historical narrative, the narrator subverts the impression of a narrative told in the 'here and now' and presages his own extradiegetic status.[23] Still, although the reader has been introduced to the world of Dorlcote Mill under false pretences, the narrator's initial intradiegetic status and the metaleptic instances in the first chapter ensure that the intimate relation between the reader and the diegetic world remains.

The illusion of the reader's capacity to 'see' fictional characters and environments is occasionally resumed. For example, chapter 3 of Book First begins: 'The gentleman in the ample white cravat and shirt-frill, taking his brandy-and-water so pleasantly with his good friend Tulliver, is Mr Riley' (I, iii, 14). Sustaining the assumption that both reader and narrator are part of the diegesis, figuring as invisible spectators, the passage resembles several similar examples in *Adam Bede*. This inclusion into the narrative initiates an intimacy between narrator and reader without the narrator's stepping out of story-time now. Chapter 12 of the same book is introduced in a similar manner: 'In order to see Mr and Mrs Glegg at home, we must enter the town of St Ogg's – that venerable town with the red-fluted roofs and the broad warehouse gables' (I, xii, 115). Here, the narrator not only presupposes the reader's ability to 'see' Mr and Mrs Glegg, but also assumes that he or she can 'enter' St Ogg's. Since this introduction to chapter 12 also forms part of the narrator's historical account of St Ogg's, the reader is invited not just into the town itself, but also into its history.[24]

Similarly, Maggie's meetings with Philip in the Red Deeps are repeatedly described with reference to the reader's ability to 'see' diegetic scenes. As Maggie enters the woods, the reader is addressed: 'You may see her now, as she walks down the favourite turning, and enters the Deeps by a narrow path through a group of Scotch firs' (V, i, 299). This exact entrance into

---

23 R. P. Draper discusses temporality in this first chapter, arguing that although it is written in the present tense it is not the ' "historic present" […] since it has the effect of suspending the novel in an aesthetic timelessness until the last paragraph, when the narrator suddenly awakens to the reader-writer present'; 'The Fictional Perspective: *The Mill on the Floss* and *Silas Marner*', in *Eliot: The Mill on the Floss and Silas Marner*, ed. by R. P. Draper (London: Macmillan, 1977), pp. 234-251 (p. 237).
24 See Harris, pp. 40-42.

the woods is returned to in chapter 4 of the same book, again indicating the reader's visual access to the scene.[25] Again, although these metaleptic references remain within story-time now, not forming part of narratorial commentary *per se*, they nevertheless serve to shape the reader's response to the narrative, reducing the distance between him or her and diegetic properties by transgressing the ontological divide which separates the reader's world from the world of the fiction.

The narrator of *The Mill*, however, like the narrator of *Adam Bede*, continually shifts the reader's distance and relation to the text, at times pulling him or her into the diegesis (as in the examples above) but at other times excluding him or her from it. By recognising the reader's inability to experience the narrative in other ways than through the medium of the narrator and through his or her own imagination, the narrator vacillates between readerly levels, alternately presupposing the reader's part in the diegesis and acknowledging the infeasibility of such a notion. In chapter 1 of Book Fifth, only one page before the reference to Maggie in the Red Deeps mentioned above, the narrator asks the reader to use his or her imagination:

> [T]here may come moments when Nature makes a mere bank a means towards a fateful result, and that is why I ask you to imagine this high bank crowned with trees, making an uneven wall for some quarter of a mile along the left side of Dorlcote Mill and the pleasant fields behind it, bounded by the murmuring Ripple (V, i, 298).

Here, the reader's position is regarded as outside the diegesis, the narrator's request taking it for granted that the reader can only access the scene through his or her imagination. Consequently, only one page prior to 'you may see her now', the narrator acknowledges the discrete universes in which reader and fictional character exist. It could be argued that this preceding recognition of the reader's location outside the narrative world affects the interpretation of 'see' in the following passage, divesting it of actual visual meaning and transferring it to the operation of the mind's eye. By signalling the importance of the scene, the narrator attempts to motivate the reader to imagine it vividly in preparation for several passages to come. Significantly, all applications to the reader to 'see' following the 'imagine' passage above refer to Maggie's and Philip's meetings in the Red Deeps. In a sense, the reader's image of the Red Deeps, evoked by the narrator's request, operates as a window on the narrative through which the

---

25 Arguing that *The Mill* comprises numerous clues which signal witchery in Maggie, Nina Auerbach maintains that Maggie's alliance with the Scotch fir trees connotes witchcraft. See 'The Power of Hunger: Demonism and Maggie Tulliver', *Nineteenth-Century Fiction*, 30 (1975), 150-171 (p. 162).

reader can 'see' Maggie and Philip. However, the understanding of 'see' as a mode of visualising is qualified by the narrator's reference in chapter 4 of Book Fifth to what the reader has 'witnessed' (V, iv, 331), a word which explicitly signals sensory powers. Nevertheless, whether or not the word 'see', when referred to after Book Fifth, should be interpreted as denoting an actual sensory ability or a mechanism of the imagination, the passages quoted above constitute metaleptic instances which serve to give the impression that the story and its characters are somehow 'real'.

As the preceding discussions have shown, the narrator's status as intradiegetic or extradiegetic is not always straightforward in *The Mill*. Occasionally he seems to figure as a character in the narrative, but it is by no means always clear that this narrative is in fact the same as Tom's and Maggie's. For example, the concluding discussion of childhood and remembrance in chapter 5 of Book First includes the narrator's references to his own 'here and now':

> The wood I walk in on this mild May day, with the young yellow-brown foliage of the oaks between me and the blue sky [...] what grove of tropic palms, what strange ferns or splendid broad-petalled blossoms, could ever thrill such deep and delicate fibres within me as this home-scene [...] such things as these are the mother tongue of our imagination, the language that is laden with all the subtle inextricable associations the fleeting hours of our childhood left behind them (I, v, 41-42).

The passage at first gives the impression of an intradiegetic narrator in the process of describing a scene which he is currently immersed in. But the contents of the discussion challenge that notion. When regarded from a Wordsworthian standpoint, imagining that the narrator is himself in the process of conjuring up childhood scenes through memories recollected in tranquillity, this passage points to the dreamer-narrator in chapter 1, rendering the 'actuality' of the scene ambiguous.[26] The passage could also be interpreted as emanating from an extradiegetic level, the present tense serving as part of an example. In this sense, the 'wood I walk in on this May day' would not signify that the narrator is actually walking in a wood,

---

26 Mary Ann Kelly notes that in this passage the narrator speaks from a vantage point which resembles that of Wordsworth in *The Prelude*; 'The Narrative Emphasis on the Power of the Imagination in *The Mill on the Floss*', *The George Eliot Fellowship Review*, 14 (1983), 86-93 (p. 87). John Rignall regards the whole passage as providing 'a means of understanding the closing image of the two children with hands clasped in love' by its bringing together 'nature, childhood, the metaphor of language, and the language of metaphor in a meditative moment of harmony which unites past and present, man and nature, the estranged adult and the familiar countryside of home'; 'Metaphor, Truth and the Mobile Imagination in *The Mill on the Floss*', *The George Eliot Review: Journal of The George Eliot Fellowship*, 24 (1993), 36-40 (p. 39).

but would constitute an example which serves to illustrate the narrator's argument. There are thus three possible interpretations of this passage: as deriving from an intradiegetic narrator actually present in the diegetic scene; as emanating from the intradiegetic dreamer-narrator absorbed in memory; or as stemming from the extradiegetic narrator employing the present tense to illustrate a point.

Given the nature of the *Mill* narrator's relation to the diegesis, the first two alternatives seem more probable. Both interpretations would entail narratorial metalepsis. Read in this way, the passage animates the diegetic world for the reader, giving the impression that it is 'real' because the narrator is 'in it'. By implication, these 'real' scenes serve to authenticate the narrative as a whole. The reader's metalepsis in *The Mill*, however, is not as clear-cut as the narrator's, as visionary images can be understood differently in various contexts. As in *Adam Bede*, the reader is continually pulled in and out of the diegesis, but with the difference that these occurrences of fewer and less explicitly metaleptic than in the first novel.

Two Narratorial Attitudes

By introducing the novel through an intradiegetic narrator who subsequently exists on an extradiegetic level but occasionally takes part in the diegesis, Eliot presents the idea of a narrator who can alternate between diegetic levels – that is, a narrator who does not transgress diegetic boundaries as defined by metalepsis, but who involves himself on both levels. On the intradiegetic level the narrator's relation to the text is intimate, the contents of the story suggesting themselves as reveries recollected from a time past. On the extradiegetic level, the narrator's distance to the text is remote, accentuating the story-teller's superior authority. It could be argued that *The Mill* simply incorporates two narrators, one intradiegetic and the other extradiegetic; but two aspects of the novel refute this notion: one is the narrator's contention in the last passage of chapter 1: 'Before I dozed off, I was going to tell you what Mr and Mrs Tulliver were talking about' (I, i, 9), suggesting that it is this dreamer-narrator who tells the story; the second aspect pertains to narratorial attitudes in the novel.

Throughout the book, the emotional bond which the dreamer-narrator establishes with the diegesis is reinforced and substantiated by narrative description and commentary. The narrator's concern for characters and

his implied personal ties with the time and setting of the narrative suggest a nostalgic and unconditionally sympathetic relation to scenes and
characters. However, there are passages in the novel which seem to derive
from a very different source. Analytical and ironical comments reveal a
narrative voice which commands authority not only over the text but also
over the reader. This voice has no personal tie to the narrative but exists
at a level above the diegetic, which of course indicates an extradiegetic
narrator. But these two distinct narratorial attitudes do not correspond
to the extradiegetic and intradiegetic narrative levels, as the extradiegetic
narrator frequently expresses the same type of concern and sympathy for
characters as the dreamer-narrator.[27] The differences in attitude thus appear to take place in another dimension, rendering it impossible to speak
of one intradiegetic, intimate and sympathetic narrative voice and another
extradiegetic, remote and sarcastic one.

In chapter 2 of Book First, for example, the extradiegetic narrator articulates a sarcastic remark about Mrs Tulliver: 'I have often wondered whether
those early Madonnas of Raphael, with the blond faces and somewhat stupid expression, kept their placidity undisturbed when their strong-limbed,
strong-willed boys got a little too old to do without clothing' (I, ii, 14).
The comment considers society's regard for Mrs Tulliver's good-tempered-
ness, not through an analogy which conveys sympathy but through one
which criticises her character. On the other hand, when Maggie is rejected
by Tom after her boating with Stephen, the narrator has this to say about
Mrs Tulliver's open arms: 'More helpful than all wisdom is one draught
of simple human pity that will not forsake us' (VII, i, 485). The novel
hence presents two narratorial attitudes towards the diegetic world: one is
an emotionally and personally engaged attitude towards characters, concerned with memory and the past, allowing the reader full intimacy; the
other is a detached and shrewd attitude, frequently resorting to irony, even
sarcasm, and keeping the narrative world at a distance.

One need not be surprised to find in Eliot's novels a narrator revealing himself through conflicting voices; all Eliot's novels contain narrators
whose relations to the text are contradictory to some extent.[28] However,
The Mill distinguishes itself by the narrator's exceptionally intimate rela-

---

27 Several critics have commented on the two narratorial attitudes in *The Mill*. Monika
Fludernik identifies what she regards as three kinds of narrator in the novel: an embodied
narrator, a 'generalizing trustworthy narrator' and what Fludernik calls a 'dead-pan
narrator', that is, an ironic narrator 'who pretends to concur with the views of the
fictional characters while at the same time exposing them more radically than moral
diatribe could have done' (173). See also Graham Martin, p. 41.

28 Felicia Bonaparte discusses two narrative voices which, she argues, appear in all Eliot's
novels. One is analytical, objective and non-partisan, and the other is subjective both in

tionship to the narrative, established in chapter 1. It is the striking contrast between this emotionally engaged attitude and the narrator's ironical attitude which characterises the narrator in *The Mill*.[29] It is, however, possible to see these two seemingly contradictory stances coexisting in the novel. Indeed, in the well-known chapter 'A Variation of Protestantism Unknown to Bossuet' the narrator moves seamlessly from the one attitude to the other, demonstrating how both approaches can be traced to the one narrator.

The chapter considers the connection between past and present as experienced by and represented in characters. Similarly to chapter 17 in *Adam Bede*, it suspends the course of events in the story in order to discuss and confirm with the reader the credibility of the narrative and the significance of 'realistic' content. As the narrator steps out of the world of St Ogg's and enters the surroundings of the Rhône, he addresses the reader: 'Journeying down the Rhône on a summer's day, you have perhaps felt the sunshine made dreary by those ruined villages which stud the banks in certain parts of its course' (IV, i, 271). Appearing to be in conversation with the reader, the narrator metaphorically contrasts two orders of 'reality'. The landscape of the Rhine, the narrator contends, symbolises a life of confidence, fervour, adventure and romance, which generates lasting achievements as well as progress. In contrast, the landscape of the Rhône symbolises a life of oppressiveness, apathy and 'a narrow, ugly, grovelling existence' which 'will be swept into the same oblivion with the generations of ants and beavers' (IV, i, 271-272). The passage argues that the order of 'reality' represented by the Rhône corresponds to life by the river Floss and consequently to the type of 'reality' Maggie and her family are immersed in. It is a world of small ambitions and simple minds, in which change and modernisation are regarded with suspicion. The chapter conveys the ideals and mindset of this world at length, connecting general patterns of belief to the Dodson and Tulliver families.[30] This account of contrasting worlds displays a sharp,

---

terms of accessing all characters' internal consciousnesses and in terms of understanding 'the final and unquestionable validity of the egocentric view' (163).

29 Monika Fludernik suggests a useful idea on the relationship between these two conflicting attitudes. Arguing that both approaches are necessary for the narrative to steer clear of a consistent and overbearing moralisation of the fictional world, Fludernik says that by complementing moralising narratorial comments with irony and sarcasm the narrative avoids promoting maxims rather than advocating understanding. In her own words, the narrative 'enacts what it implicitly propounds – it sympathises with erring humanity and refrains from clear-cut incontrovertible moral judgement' (182).

30 The chapter is well known, and several critics have examined the parallel set up between the worlds of the Rhine and the Rhône and life by the river Floss. See, for example, U. C. Knoepflmacher, *George Eliot's Early Novels*, pp. 178-179; and Renata R. Mautner

analytical tone. Including the reader's anticipated reaction, the narrator reveals his own attitude:

> Perhaps something akin to this oppressive feeling may have weighed upon you in watching this old-fashioned family life on the banks of the Floss [...] You could not live among such people; you are stifled for want of an outlet towards something beautiful, great or noble [...] I share with you this sense of oppressive narrowness (IV, i, 272).

By attributing a less than flattering view of the Dodson-Tulliver world to the reader, the narrator implies his own.[31] Admitting to sharing in the view he has elaborated for the reader, these first passages explain how the narrator can be sarcastic towards the characters in this narrow world. The narrator's confession, however, is immediately followed by a 'but'-clause: 'but it is necessary that we should feel it, if we care to understand how it acted on the lives of Tom and Maggie' (IV, i, 272).[32] The statement signals the emotionally engaged aspect of the narrator who, proceeding to argue that it is necessary to represent those 'petty minds', changes the perspective and meta-narratively regards the importance of this type of representation from a historical standpoint. Here the narrator expresses what is to be considered his genuine attitude towards the represented world. However, the narrator cannot be consistently compassionate towards this world if the reader is to believe in its 'oppressive narrowness'. His sharing in that sense with the reader therefore occasionally surfaces in the form of ironical commentary. Consequently, the narrator's attitude to the diegetic world is predominantly sympathetic, but now and then he returns with sharp acerbity to elements which remind the reader of the pettiness of Dodson-Tulliver mentalities. This is how empathy and irony need not be mutually exclusive, but incorporated in the one narrator whose relation to the narrative is multifaceted.

As was suggested above, 'A Variation of Protestantism Unknown to Bossuet' could be regarded as a counterpart to chapter 17 in *Adam Bede*. Constituting a pause in the unfolding of events, the chapter stops to explicate the type of religiosity adopted by the Dodsons and Tullivers in order for the reader to understand Mr Tulliver's act of pledging a vow of venge-

---

Wasserman, 'Narrative Logic and the Form of Tradition in *The Mill on the Floss*', *Studies in the Novel*, 14 (1982), 266-279.

31 See David Carroll's *Conflict of Interpretations*, pp. 106-139 for an exhaustive account of the differences in Dodson and Tulliver mentalities.

32 Mary Ellen Doyle notes that this statement reveals that Eliot was concerned with depicting Tom's fate as much as Maggie's, arguing that 'her purpose is the revelation of two protagonists, one a martyr and one a victim' (57).

ance on the inside leaf of the family Bible. But it also, like *Adam Bede's* chapter 17, meta-narratively reflects on the aesthetics of representation. *The Mill*, however, includes few meta-narrative comments. As if refraining from emphasising the fictionality of the text by calling attention to the narrative act, the narrator understates his role as story-teller; and those instances of meta-narration that do occur are subtle references which highlight the veracity of the text rather than accentuating artificiality. When Maggie discovers Thomas à Kempis in chapter 3 of Book Fourth, the narrator elaborates a social criticism which simultaneously serves as a clarification of Maggie's ready adoption of Thomas's ideas. The discussion is introduced by a reference to the act of narrating: 'In writing the history of unfashionable families, one is apt to fall into a tone of emphasis which is very far from being the tone of good society' (IV, iii, 291). Although he refers to his role as 'writer', the narrator's mention of a 'history' suggests that the story is not fictional, but that the events and characters are somehow historical and that the narrator is a chronicler presenting a historical account. Like many meta-narrative comments in Eliot's novels, this statement serves to underpin the authenticity of the text rather than point to its merit as fictional construct. *The Mill*, however, differs from the other novels in that it contains so few meta-narrative comments, a circumstance which results from the narrator's semi-adopted persona as dreamer-reminiscer – a persona incompatible with the idea of an authoritative director who is in control of narrative content and distanced enough to comment on the narrating act.

Similarly to instances of metalepsis, the narrator's disparate attitudes in *The Mill* continually affect the reader's distance to both narrator and characters as he or she is subject to constant shifts in relation to the diegesis. In a sense, the narrator's contradictory attitudes are what sets *The Mill* apart from the rest of Eliot's fiction. This element of contradiction goes some way towards accounting for the difficulties some critics have with this novel, difficulties often ascribed to its allegedly inconsistent handling of characters. However, like the characters he depicts, the *Mill* narrator's make-up is complex in that he is at once intradiegetic and extradiegetic. Consequently, as the narrator's relation to the diegesis is multifaceted, so must the reader's be.

Husbands, Wives and the 'World's Wife'

Although *The Mill* is a novel which embodies a number of themes, its narratorial commentary engages with relatively few concerns. The lines of reasoning which feature as principal interests in the novel's commentary deal with gender-related matters, memories of childhood and references to history and literature. Other concerns, related to such areas as education, religion and society, form major themes in the novel but do not appear as recurring topics in narration now. For instance, while Maggie's personal adherence to a theory of renunciation forms a significant concern in the novel, this theme does not occur repeatedly in commentary. Nor does the topic of Maggie's restricted education or the concept of tragedy. Although the latter occasionally appears in the narrator's comments, it does not leave a significant impression on narratorial commentary in the novel as a whole.

Issues involving gender in *The Mill* have been subject to a great deal of scholarly criticism, a large part of it dealing with Maggie's entrapment within socially confined structures, with her eventual fate, and with her complex relationships to Philip, Stephen, Tom and her father.[33] The novel is certainly intensely concerned with patriarchal conventions and the restrictions these place on women's personal development. Addressing such gender-specific problems through Maggie's story, the novel itself constitutes a critique of women's situation in the nineteenth century. Therefore, it is surprising that these serious concerns occasion little discussion in narration now. Only one comment in the novel approaches gender issues from a critical perspective. Appearing in connection with Philip's and Maggie's meetings in the woods and Tom's embarking on a career in business, this comment considers the differences between Maggie and Tom from a historically gendered perspective. Describing Maggie's inward struggles as compared to Tom's outward actions, the comment illuminates and contextualises their differences by means of historical analogy:

> So it has been since the days of Hecuba, and of Hector, Tamer of horses: inside the gates, the women with streaming hair and uplifted hands offering prayers, watching the world's combat from afar, filling their long, empty days with memories and fears: outside, the men, in fierce struggle with things divine and human, quench-

---

33 See for example David Smith, 'Incest Patterns in Two Victorian Novels', *Literature and Psychology*, 15, (1965), 135-162; Elaine Showalter, *A Literature of Their Own: British Women Novelists from Brontë to Lessing* (Princeton: Princeton University Press, 1977); and Deirdre David, *Intellectual Women and Victorian Patriarchy: Harriet Martineau, Elizabeth Barrett Browning, George Eliot* (Ithaca: Cornell University Press, 1987).

ing memory in the stronger light of purpose, losing the sense of dread and even of wounds in the hurrying ardour of action (V, ii, 308-309).

Tom's and Maggie's roles, the comment implies, are predetermined by history. Their characters are defined by their separate spheres of experience, which are governed by historical and social conventions. Maggie's restriction from an active life and a 'stronger light of purpose' leaves her introverted and anxious, her mind occupied with fighting the armies 'within her own soul' (V, ii, 308). This is the one proper narration-now comment in the novel to present Maggie's circumstances as resulting from gendered politics and historically conditioned structures. By perceiving Maggie's situation from a historical perspective, the comment situates her within a larger context, indicating that Maggie's story is not only hers but that of numerous women throughout history. The indication is subtle, though, the narrator's high-flown language and romantic associations veiling its underlying criticism. Still, the implication is plain, and the author's caustic views on gender and injustice become increasingly obvious in the later novels.

However, most comments related to gender in *The Mill* are humorous in kind, often ridiculing either particular characters or idiosyncrasies connected to the relations between the sexes. Mr and Mrs Tulliver and Mr and Mrs Glegg in particular are the objects of these types of comments. In chapter 12 of Book First, for instance, the narrator reflects on the mechanisms governing the marriage between Mr and Mrs Glegg:

> The economizing of a gardener's wages might perhaps have induced Mrs Glegg to wink at this folly, if it were possible for a healthy female mind even to simulate respect for a husband's hobby. But it is well known that this conjugal complacency belongs only to the weaker portion of the sex, who are scarcely alive to the responsibilities of a wife as a constituted check on her husband's pleasures, which are hardly ever of a rational or commendable kind (I, xii, 120).

Chapter 12, entitled 'Mr and Mrs Glegg at home', gives the first detailed introduction into this couple's home environment. Alternating between perspectives, the chapter regards the Glegg marriage from the point of view of each spouse. As the quotation above shows, these perspectives smack of narratorial irony. The passage (of which only the second sentence belongs to narration now proper) is redolent of free indirect discourse (FID), adapted to Mrs Glegg's character. Her values seem to shine through the narrator's comment; but the irony, diction and vocabulary derive from him alone.[34] By half mimicking Mrs Glegg, the narrator pokes fun at her, encouraging the reader to recognise a phenomenon which the narrator claims is 'well known'. Concerned with the dynamics between spouses, the comment actually serves to reveal the processes inherent in Mrs Glegg's mind. While attaching its ridicule to a general reflection on husbands and wives, the comment is not so much about gender as about Mrs Glegg's character.

Mrs Tulliver is the object of similar narratorial remarks. However, unlike the statements above, where the narrator's irony emerges from mimicry, comments pertaining to Mrs Tulliver convey sarcasm through animal analogy. With regard to her determination to discuss business with Mr Wakem, the narrator remarks on her resolve:

> Imagine a truly respectable and amiable hen, by some portentous anomaly, taking to reflection and inventing combinations by which she might prevail on Hodge not to wring her neck, or send her and her chicks to market: the result could hardly be other than much cackling and fluttering (III, vii, 245).

Here, Mrs Tulliver is mocked by the narrator even before the actual scene begins, the comment serving as a premonition of her failure. Indeed, even the chapter heading, 'How a Hen Takes to Stratagem', derides her character by analogy while acknowledging her initiative.[35] Like the comments discussed above, this illustration is less a reflection on gender than a statement on character. Employing metaphor, the comment takes advantage of and reinforces gendered language, ridiculing Mrs Tulliver by associating her with a typically low-standing animal.

The relationship between Mr and Mrs Tulliver is one of the tragicomic elements in the first part of the novel. On Mrs Tulliver's objection to her husband's going to court, the narrator comments: 'Mrs Tulliver, as we have

---

34 Monika Fludernik contends that while the passage describes Mrs Glegg's moralism and her tendency to pass judgement on others, the reader in turn passes judgement on Mrs Glegg; p.173. Fludernik discusses this passage extensively on pages 159-163 and comments that although the segment resembles FID, it does not contain syntactic markers such as exclamations, progressive tenses or root transformations characteristic of FID. For more on FID in *The Mill*, see W. Siward Atkins, 'Free Indirect Style and the Rhetoric of Sympathy in *The Mill on the Floss*', in *Perspectives on Self and Community in George Eliot: Dorothea's Window*, ed. by Patricia Gately *et al.* (Lewiston, NY: The Edwin Mellen Press, 1997), pp. 163-192.

35 See Janet K. Gezari, '*Romola* and the Myth of Apocalypse', *George Eliot: Centenary Essays and an Unpublished Fragment*, ed. by Anne Smith (London: Vision Press, 1980), pp. 77-102; and Barbro Almqvist Norbelie, *"Oppressive Narrowness": A Study of the Female Community in George Eliot's Early Writings* (Uppsala: Almqvist & Wiksell International, 1992) for discussions on Mrs Tulliver's guilt in the downfall of her husband and family.

seen, was not without influence over her husband. No woman is; she can always incline him to do either what she wishes, or the reverse' (II, ii, 157). The tragicomic dimension of this statement is, of course, that Mrs Tulliver's influence over her husband in this instance is precisely the reverse of what she wishes, and that the consequences lead to Mr Tulliver's downfall. Here, however, the narrator's tone is less mocking than in the examples above. The irony is coupled with a tone of quiet wisdom. There is no mimicking of character and no sense of a narrator trying to connect with a particular type of reader at the expense of characters. Instead, it is the perceptive narrator, observing the sometimes amusing interactions between couples, who recognises the human elements in personal relationships.

Consequently, the instances of commentary discussed in this subsection demonstrate how a novel greatly concerned with the notion of oppressor and oppressed, as well as with the encroachment of patriarchal conventions on the personal development of its main protagonist, can involve very little commentary in the way of feminist argument. Although gender issues are broached in the comments above, they mostly serve as facilitators for the narrator's humorous explication of characters.

However, the novel does include a passage of free indirect discourse which could be read as a comment on gender from the perspective of social criticism. In chapter 2 of Book Seventh, the reader is introduced to the 'world's wife', whose perspective on Stephen's and Maggie's elopement betrays severity and prejudice. Before proceeding into the FID of this public persona, the narrator argues that 'public opinion, in these cases, is always of the feminine gender – not the world, but the world's wife' (VII, ii, 490). The 'world's wife', the reader learns, is a community chorus, fascinated with gossip, ruthlessly judgemental and significantly more lenient in its verdict of Stephen than it is of Maggie. It is a female community which condemns Maggie for violating the rules of female conduct and transgressing the boundaries of societal ideology. The narrator's FID mimicry of this female public persona reveals her as vicious and narrow-minded, emphasising the hypocrisy which pervades the argument conducted by the community chorus.[36]

But narrow-mindedness is not attributed exclusively to the female gender. Concluding the same chapter, the narrator refers to the 'man of maxims' (VII, ii, 498). The conclusion pertains to Dr Kenn's contemplation of Maggie's circumstances. As he attempts to find the best solution for all involved, he realises that he must give up the effort of 'balancing conse-

---

36 For an extensive analysis of the 'world's wife' in *The Mill*, see Norbelie, pp. 135-139.

quences' (VII, ii, 497), as well as of trying to conquer Maggie's conscience with fixed principles. With regard to Dr Kenn's line of reasoning, the narrator comments:

> All people of broad, strong sense have an instinctive repugnance to the man of maxims; because such people early discern that the mysterious complexity of our life is not to be embraced by maxims, and that to lace ourselves up in formulas of that sort is to repress all the divine promptings and inspirations that spring from growing insight and sympathy. And the man of maxims is the popular representative of the minds that are guided in their moral judgement solely by general rules, thinking that these will lead them to justice by ready-made patent method (VII, ii, 498). [37]

The passage demonstrates how the 'world's wife' and the 'man of maxims' resemble each other in terms of prejudice. Both are completely dependent on established and static principles which they cannot see beyond, and both are deficient in imagination and independent thought.[38] They are governed by rules which they fail to rise above and by which they understand and classify the world around them.[39] In its entirety, the chapter is less concerned with attaching prejudices or tendencies to a particular gender than with subjecting fundamentalism and rigidity of principle to socially orientated criticism. Again, the narrator's overt references to gender serve other purposes.

Still, the general criticism of over-reliance on principle does not veil the fact that the 'world's wife' is a specifically female community chorus, responsible for administering reproof and spreading rumours. In this sense the epithet must be understood as an implicit accusation against the female gender in the social sphere. Besides reproaching a gendered community voice, however, the narrator's lengthy account of the 'world's wife' serves the purpose of placing Maggie's anguish in relief against the finger-pointing chorus, thereby intensifying the reader's involvement in Maggie's humiliation. By collaborating to depict an unbearable public arena into which Maggie must enter, the 'world's wife' FID and narratorial commen-

---

37 In an essay on the German philosopher Gruppe (*Leader*, 28 July 1855, p. 723-724) George Eliot reveals her dislike of dogma and general systems and commends Gruppe for not partaking in German system-making.

38 For discussions on George Eliot's own use of maxims, see Susan Sniader Lanser, pp. 81-101, and Mary Jacobus, 'The Question of Language: Men of Maxims and *The Mill on the Floss*', *Critical Inquiry*, 8 (1981), 207-222.

39 Nancy K. Miller recognises the kinship of the two epithets, arguing that the chapter does not demonstrate an 'inadequacy of received social ideas in gender *per se*' but that the argument is with the notion of 'a master-key that will fit all cases' and directed at the man of maxims. See 'Emphasis Added: Plots and Plausibilities in Women's Fiction', *PMLA*, 96 (1981), 36-48 (pp. 45-46). For a critique of Miller's claim, see Norbelie, p. 138.

tary elicit the reader's sympathy and pity for Maggie. Effectively, the representation of a community incapable of expressing compassion towards Maggie summons a reader who is.

Childhood

It is not surprising that *The Mill*, which is a novel largely dealing with the connection between past and present and with the impact of childhood experiences, should include a considerable number of comments pertaining to youth and memories of childhood. Nostalgic reminiscences, especially in the latter part of the novel, have, however, occasioned some debate, critics claiming that reminiscences in this latter section conflict with the particulars of Maggie's childhood. The first two books of the novel, some critics maintain, relate a rather difficult childhood on Maggie's part, full of conflict, scolding and oppression. Maggie defiantly cuts her hair, she hammers nails into a rag doll, she pushes Lucy into a puddle of mud and she runs away to join a group of gypsies. These are clearly the actions of a troubled child. The latter books of the novel, on the other hand, melancholically reminisce over this childhood as if it were an Eden full of warmth, love and compassion. Indeed, already in the conclusion to Book Second after Mr Tulliver has lost the mill to lawyer Wakem, the narrator looks back on Tom's and Maggie's lives, contrasting their future with their past and stating: 'They had entered the thorny wilderness, and the golden gates of their childhood had for ever closed behind them' (II, vii, 191).

The 'golden gates' referred to here do not adequately correspond to the upheavals and disappointments which Maggie's passionate nature continually causes in the first two books. This conflict of interpretation causes Graham Martin to argue that 'we have to conclude that the narrator's final formulation for [Tom's and Maggie's] childhood belongs to a different novel than the one we have been reading'.[40] Martin's comment is, of course, somewhat flippant, but it raises the notion of a collision between ideas about childhood expressed by the narrator and the actuality of Maggie's childhood as presented in the novel.[41] Because of this collision, it

---

40 Martin, p. 44.
41 Martin touches upon this notion himself when he argues that 'the narrator who dreams of an ideal childhood seems not to know what his wide-awake *alter ego* has remembered in such convincing wealth of detail' (44).

is worth investigating the ways in which childhood memories are treated in the novel's commentary. In view of the alleged discrepancy between the respective images of childhood in the early and late books of *The Mill*, it is interesting that there are no narratorial comments pertaining to childhood in the last three books of the novel. Instead, all narration-now remarks on childhood occur in the depiction of Maggie's and Tom's early days. Furthermore, these comments meditate not only on the joys of childhood, but also on suffering as a part of growing up. For example, when Maggie cuts her hair and realises her mistake, the narrator contemplates the gravity of her misery as compared to adult griefs:

> We have all of us sobbed so piteously, standing with tiny bare legs above our little socks, when we lost sight of our mother or nurse in some strange place; but we can no longer recall the poignancy of that moment and weep over it, as we do over the remembered sufferings of five or ten years ago. Every one of those keen moments has left its trace, and lives in us still, but such traces have blent themselves irrecoverably with the firmer texture of our youth and manhood; and so it comes that we can look on at the troubles of our children with a smiling disbelief in the reality of their pain (I, vii, 65-66).

In the spirit of Wordsworth, the comment acknowledges the hidden traces of childhood anguish within each adult and appeals to the reader's experience of this as he or she regards and interprets Maggie's despair. Serving to prevent the reader from trivialising Maggie's anguish, the comment points out that the emotion is as severe on the child as any anxiety might be for an adult. Here, then, the gates of childhood are far from golden, and the comment sharpens the impression of emotional adversity and conflict within Maggie's nature. The voice is that of a poet-narrator, capable of recovering emotion and acting as mediator of that emotion. By anchoring those feelings in the reader, i.e. by evoking the memory of childhood distress, the comment shapes the reader's interpretation of Maggie's dilemma, promoting an acutely empathetic reading.

With regard to childhood as portrayed in the early and latter books, the novel distinguishes between emotions experienced at first hand and the emotions which 'remembered cares' elicit. The narrator argues that the intense feelings we experience in childhood live in us always, but that they are fused with more proximate emotions. It is those later emotions that we remember and recognise as 'real' and valid, forgetting that they partly originate in emotions which we learnt to feel in childhood. The authenticity of the emotions experienced in childhood and adulthood is consequently the same, but the difference is that the child experiences everything for the first time and so has no sorrows to dwell on. This absence of remembered sorrows is the essence of the 'golden gates'. However, the narrator also acknowledges that remembered sorrows are 'outlived' and that the adult's experience of recovering from grief is an advantage unavailable to the child. Before Maggie's visit to Garum Firs and her subsequent escape to the gypsies, the narrator states: 'Childhood has no forebodings; but then, it is soothed by no memories of outlived sorrow' (I, ix, 85). This point is emphasised again when the downfall of the Tulliver family is a fact and no help seems to be at hand: 'There is no hopelessness so sad as that of early youth, when the soul is made up of wants, and has no long memories, no superadded life in the life of others' (III, v, 235). Consequently, these comments argue that the relationship between actual childhood experiences and the memories of those experiences is complex. To accept and respond to this argument amounts to accepting that the particulars of Maggie's childhood as depicted in the first books of *The Mill* need not correspond to the memories of those particulars as depicted in the later books.

Accordingly, comments dealing with difficult aspects of childhood alternate with nostalgic tributes to a time of light-heartedness and joy. It is impossible to disregard the fact that *The Mill* is a Victorian work and that its author is very much in tune with, if not at the forefront of, contemporary aesthetics. In the mid-nineteenth century, that aesthetics embraced a nostalgia for rural life and countryside childhood as contrasts to the industrialisation of the modern cities. The childhood home symbolised warmth, affection and kinship, an image which the Tulliver household lives up to in the depiction of Tom's coming home for Christmas:

> There is no sense of ease like the ease we felt in those scenes where we were born, where objects became dear to us before we had known the labour of choice, and where the outer world seemed only an extension of our personality [...] And there is no better reason for preferring this elderberry bush than that it stirs an early memory – that it is no novelty in my life, speaking to me merely through my present sensibilities to form and colour, but the long companion of my existence, that wove itself into my joys when joys were vivid (II, i, 151-152).[42]

By fortifying the 'golden gate' image, this comment challenges the notion of absolutes. Childhood memories, even Maggie's, consist of both good and bad. Importantly, however, the narrator emphasises the intensity of childhood impressions of which the adult may be poignantly reminded by the mere sight of, for example, an elderberry bush. These impressions, and the emotions they generate, stay with us and can be summoned as 'emotions recollected in tranquillity'.

42 The passage is a reference to Tom coming home, but it may also be applied to Maggie as it deals with childhood in general.

To recapitulate, narratorial commentary in *The Mill* broaches the subject of childhood in the first four books of the novel only. Some of these comments reminisce on the 'golden' years of childhood, voicing the type of nostalgia which critics have claimed dominate the latter part of the novel. Other comments regard childhood from a more analytical perspective, inviting the reader to consider Maggie's feelings of suffering and sorrow as seriously as if she were an adult. Together these comments represent the dual nature of Maggie's childhood, alternating the images of bliss with manifestations of sorrow and despair. Whichever image is presented, though, the reader is invited to remember and share the woes and joys of childhood.

References to History

The Mill is a novel preoccupied with the relations between past and present and with the processes of social as well as natural history. It examines questions of evolution and change on a public as well as a private level, demonstrating how the inability to adapt to and move forward with circumstances eventually leads to tragedy.[43] The narrator's historical perspective is an integral part of all Eliot's novels in which narrated time is posed against the narrator's, and by implication the reader's, present. In *The Mill*, however, this narratorial perspective differs from that of other novels owing to the dreamer-narrator's personal and immediate relation to the historical time of the narrative. As distinct from the situation in *Adam Bede*, where the narrator enters the novel from an extradiegetic level to comment 'objectively' on the historical setting by way of explaining it to the reader, the narrator in *The Mill* enters the narrative through reveries, immersing himself in its historical time.[44] Although chapter 2 approaches the story from an extradiegetic level, the narrator's intradiegetic relation to the story is not abandoned, as was pointed out above. There is a sense of the narrator's subjective and personal relation to the historical time of the

---

43 For discussions of references to scientific and Darwinian theories in *The Mill*, see Dinah Birch's introduction to the Oxford World's Classics edition and for scientific references in Eliot's novels in general, see Gillian Beer's *Darwin's Plots: Evolutionary Narrative in Darwin, George Eliot and Nineteenth-Century Fiction* (London: Routledge & Kegan Paul, 1983) and Sally Shuttleworth's *George Eliot and Nineteenth-Century Science: The Make-Believe of a Beginning* (Cambridge: Cambridge University Press, 1984).
44 Sally Shuttleworth also notices this distinction. See p. 51.

novel – a relation distinct from Eliot's earlier and later novels, where narrators aim to establish their roles as those of factual historians. *The Mill*, by contrast, only contains one comment that directly casts the narrator as historian. Rarely referring to the historical setting in narration now, *The Mill* perceives the past through narrative description and through the narrator's dreams. Accordingly, although historical references are scarce in the novel's commentary, a brief consideration of the narrator's relation to the narrative past is warranted, partly because this is such an important theme in the novel as a whole and partly because the narrator's historical perspective offers an interesting comparison with Eliot's other novels.

The historical setting of the novel is primarily described in chapter 12 of Book First, which is introduced by an invitation to the reader to 'see Mr and Mrs Glegg at home' (I, xii, 115). Proceeding from this intimation of reader metalepsis, the first part of the chapter digresses from the primary story to relate the history of the town of St Ogg's and its legendary patron saint. The account takes the form of narrative description, giving the impression that the narrator is a well-informed historian – an impression which he reinforces when introducing the legend of Saint Ogg, which forms yet another digression from the primary plot. As if emphasising that this is another digression, and a legend at that, the narrator takes care to exempt himself from any responsibility as to its 'truthfulness'. St Ogg, the narrator says, is 'the patron saint of this ancient town, of whose history I possess several manuscript versions. I incline to the briefest, since, if it should not be wholly true, it is at least likely to contain the least falsehood' (I, xii, 116). By referring to his own 'manuscript versions' and also to his 'private hagiographer' (I, xii, 116), the narrator separates the legend of St Ogg from his account of the town, indicating that the one is legendary fable, rendered in secondary material, whereas the other derives from the narrator's own historical knowledge.[45] This meta-narrative indication, while highlighting the fictionality of the legend, imparts authenticity to the narrator's historical account of the town. The whole historical excursus establishes the narrator's role as historian, in spite of his occasional dreamer-like status and despite the passage's remaining within story-time now.

The narrator's status as historian is reinforced throughout the novel, not least in another excursus: 'A Variation of Protestantism Unknown to

---

45 Renata R. Mautner Wasserman juxtaposes the tales of the witch and St Ogg, arguing that they 'occupy two extreme positions in a series of stories dealing with ways in which groups handle inherent contradictions within the system of values regulating their behavior' (271). Maggie, Wasserman contends, is 'balanced at a point midway between the two' throughout the novel (272).

Bossuet', discussed above, primarily elaborates on the Dodson-Tulliver versions of religiosity and argues for a particular mode of representation; but these discussions issue from the narrator's considerations of social evolution, which he regards from a historical perspective. Furthermore, the narrator occasionally addresses the reader, reminding him or her of the temporal and, by implication, cultural gap between the time of the narrative and the reader's time. With regard to the applicability of Mr Goodrich, for example, the narrator remarks: 'All this, you remember, happened in those dark ages when there were no schools of design' (II, iv, 167). Consequently, although *The Mill* introduces a dreamer-narrator who occasionally participates in the diegesis, this role nonetheless alternates with that of an extradiegetic historian.

The Mill is, however, not exempt from references to history in narration now.[46] For example, in one of the few comments pertaining to education, the narrator highlights the discrepancies between ancient times, the narrative past and his own present. With regard to Mr Stelling's teaching methods, the narrator refers to the ancients, stating:

> It was the practice of our venerable ancestors to apply that ingenious instrument the thumb-screw, and to tighten and tighten it in order to elicit non-existent facts; they had a fixed opinion to begin with, that the facts were existent, and what had they to do but to tighten the thumbscrew [*sic*]? (II, iv, 169).

In line with his attitude towards the 'narrow oppressiveness' of the Dodson-Tulliver families, the narrator regards Mr Stelling's teaching methods as another example of the process of degradation which is caused by resistance to progress. Like a community that crumbles because it cannot reconcile itself to social and historical changes, Mr Stelling's antiquated inferences about Tom's faculties serve to break the boy down rather than to build him up. In this comment, then, the narrator regards history and the narrative past in relief to his own present which is, the irony implies, more advanced. The comment adopts an attitude towards the historical past which contrasts with the dreamer-narrator's nostalgic reminiscences. Here, in critical mode, the narrator is detached from the time and setting of the narrative, regarding the past not merely from a historical distance but from another diegetic level.

However, the narrator's extradiegetic status does not always entail a critical attitude. When Bob Jakin gives Maggie a present of books (*The Imitation of Christ* among them), making her smile over his reasonings

---

46 See also the comment referring to 'the days of Hecuba, and of Hector, Tamer of horses' (V, ii, 308-309), discussed above.

about his thumb-trick, the narrator reflects on how some things never change:

> The days of chivalry are not gone, notwithstanding Burke's grand dirge over them:
> they live still in that far-off worship paid by many a youth and man to the woman
> of whom he never dreams that he shall touch so much as her little finger or the hem
> of her robe (IV, iii, 285).

The comment introduces a change of perspective in terms of historical consciousness. The days of chivalry, the narrative past and the narrator's present are all connected through the phenomenon described. There is no conflict between past and present here, no gap which requires explanation. Instead, the human impulse which inspires Bob's kindness subsists in all ages, connecting one generation with the next. Here, there is no suggestion of an oppressive past; rather, the past is the model by which the present is evaluated. The comment, moreover, attaches historical significance and grandeur to Bob's simple gesture. His worship of Maggie does not derive from some teenage infatuation; it is associated with that of chevaliers and maidens in literary romances. Investing Bob with peculiar earnestness, the comment makes an example of him, suggesting that his kindness to and regard for Maggie refute Edmund Burke's lament over the end of chivalry. The statement changes the perspective not only on history but also on Bob – a character who, immediately prior to the comment, admitted to Maggie that he cheats his customers when measuring out the flannel they buy. By regarding Bob in a historical context, situating him in an advantageous light, the comment lends depth to his person, encouraging the reader to regard him as more than merely a comic character.

* * *

Consequently, although *The Mill* contains few comments that refer to history, the ones that do appear regard the past from various perspectives. But as is the case with many important thematic concerns, the novel does not discuss its most pressing issues in narration now. Maggie's confinement within the constraints of the past, for instance, the patriarchal conventions which stifle her intellectual development, her desperate search for a higher meaning and the consequences of an ever-evolving society are all principal issues which the novel itself offers commentary on, but which are not discussed in narration now. *The Mill* thus differs from Eliot's other novels in two respects: it omits discussions of several significant thematic concerns in its narratorial commentary, and it presents a narrator who operates on both an intradiegetic and an extradiegetic level, assuming contrasting attitudes towards the text. Hence, *The Mill*, George Eliot's most autobiographical novel, is also her least characteristic in terms of narrator and commentary.

4. *Silas Marner*

Commonly referred to as the last of Eliot's early novels, *Silas Marner* remains close in spirit to the pastoral world of *Adam Bede* and to the preoccupation with history in *The Mill on the Floss*. In various ways these early novels all examine the conversion of 'traditional' societies into 'progressive' forms of social structures. However, the compact organisation of *Silas Marner* in conjunction with its double-stranded plot and its themes of chance, lineage and alienation distinguishes it from the earlier novels and anticipates the later works.[1] In *Silas Marner*, George Eliot downplays the narrator's intimacy with characters, crafting a story with a more focused narrative control and with a sense of narratorial command over character representation as well as flow.[2] The contrasting communities of Lantern Yard and Raveloe and the carefully structured convergence of Silas's and Godfrey's stories represent some of the many symmetries and connections, on a textual as well as a structural level, in a novel in which weaving constitutes a major metaphor. The carefully woven pattern of *Silas Marner* forms a tight narrative, but one which simultaneously provides scope for reflection and commentary from a narrator concerned with human relations and the nature of mankind.

---

1   F. R. Leavis described the novel as a 'moral fable' containing elements of the 'fairy tale', and critics generally concur with his labelling *Silas Marner* a 'minor masterpiece'; see *The Great Tradition*, p. 58. The novel certainly incorporates fairy-tale features such as Silas's mysterious trances and the replacement by a child of a treasure-hoard of gold; but it is the interweaving of these mythical elements with the novel's 'realistic' context and organisation which makes it worthy of being called a 'masterpiece'. See Jonathan R. Quick's article '*Silas Marner* as Romance: The Example of Hawthorne', *Nineteenth-Century Fiction*, 29 (1974), 287-298, for criticism of Leavis's labelling. Quick claims that 'moral fable' and 'fairy-tale' refer only to Silas's story and not to the 'realistic' account of Godfrey Cass. See also Joseph Wiesenfarth, 'Demythologizing *Silas Marner*', *ELH*, 37 (1970), 226-244, who claims that 'to be a modern novel and true to George Eliot's own time, it must depict the reality she believes in [...] *Silas Marner*, therefore, must perform the difficult task of using its legend to enhance its realism' (228).
2   F. R. Leavis argues that it is on account of the 'absence of personal immediacy' that *Silas Marner* is a masterpiece and *The Mill on the Floss* is not; see *The Great Tradition*, p. 58.

Following discussions of the movement between the particular and the general and of references and addresses to the reader, the narratological-technical section of this chapter is concluded by a short segment on metalepsis in the novel. The thematically orientated section is introduced by a discussion of the historical references in the novel, which are connected to religious references investigated in the subsequent subsection. This chapter on *Silas Marner* concludes by a discussion of 'Chance', which is the third major theme broached in narratorial commentary in the novel.

Particular-General-Particular

In terms of narratorial presence and commentary, *Silas Marner* differs considerably from *The Mill on the Floss*. The narrator is more consistently extradiegetic in *Silas Marner*, more emotionally restrained, and he appears to be in firmer control of the reader's distance to the narrative. *Silas Marner* contains practically no direct addresses or appeals to the reader's response and proportionally fewer instances of the narrator's 'I' and metalepsis. The novel nevertheless contains a large number of comments which move between the particular and the general in order to add perspectives and depth to specific phenomena.

For example, introducing Dunstan and Godfrey Cass in chapter 3 the narrator relates an argument between the brothers, an argument through which the reader learns about Godfrey's marriage to Molly Farren. After the argument Godfrey's thoughts on his predicament are intruded on by the narrator, who remarks: 'The yoke a man creates for himself by wrong-doing will breed hate in the kindliest nature; and the good-humoured, affectionate-hearted Godfrey Cass was fast becoming a bitter man' (iii, 31). The narration-now statement before the semi-colon takes on a proverb-like tone which is characteristic of commentary in this novel. It is succinct and exempt from elaborate rhetoric, emanating from an extradiegetic narrator who sets an emotional distance to the narrative.[3] By regarding Godfrey's situation from a general perspective, this narrator gives the impression of identifying a common human propensity from a sage-like

---

3   That is not to say that *Silas Marner* only comprises this type of comment. There are several long passages of commentary in the novel; but compared to *Adam Bede* and *The Mill*, commentary in *Silas Marner* is briefer and more emotionally restrained.

distance.[4] However, the transition into story-time now following the semi-colon prevents the statement as a whole from seeming impersonal or detached, Godfrey's particular situation being directly related to. Moreover, the sentence which these clauses lead up to is followed by Godfrey's free indirect discourse (FID), which brings narrator and reader even closer to this character. Within two sentences, then, the narrator shifts the reader's distance to Godfrey from a detached and generalised perspective to being drawn into his FID. Although the comment is proverb-like, it nonetheless elicits some compassion for Godfrey, demonstrating to the reader how his own contempt for his wrong-doing is projected onto his unfortunate wife.

Godfrey's brother Dunstan is also guilty of wrong-doing; but his is not the 'kindliest nature', and the narrator accordingly adopts a different tone. Describing how Dunstan persuades himself that Silas, being out of his cottage, is dead and his money there for the taking, the narrator comments on Dunstan's mental processes: 'A dull mind, once arriving at an inference that flatters a desire, is rarely able to retain the impression that the notion from which the inference started was purely problematic' (iv, 37). Again adopting a superior tone, the narrator identifies a 'truth' about human nature; but whereas the same type of proverb-like statement regarding Godfrey conveys an element of understanding, this comment is sarcastic. Inviting the reader onto a superior level shared with the narrator, the comment reduces the distance between narrator and reader by their likewise shared derision of 'dull minds'.[5]

It may seem self-evident that the two comments adopt dissimilar tones with regard to Dunstan and Godfrey. Dunstan is after all depicted as the entirely wicked, egoistic younger brother, serving as a pawn in the structure of the plot. But in comparison, the two statements show how narratorial commentary functions in conditioning reader response. These comments, although they only form a small part of the reader's reading, add subtly to his or her interpretative process. They present a context which the reader can recognise and which adds depth to his or her understanding of characters. In addition, they serve to shape the reader's attitude.

---

4 For more on the narrator's sage-like status in Eliot's novels, see John Holloway, *The Victorian Sage: Studies in Argument* (New York: W. W. Norton & Co, 1965).

5 Alexander Welsh examines Dunstan's role in the narrative, arguing that he is 'the narrator's cat's paw'. According to Welsh, Dunstan 'personifies the risk inherent in the religion of chance and in all concealment' and is moreover 'eminently expendable'; see Alexander Welsh, *George Eliot and Blackmail* (Cambridge, MA: Harvard University Press, 1985), pp. 166-167.

Generalisations frequently add new perspectives to discussions, encouraging the reader to regard particular matters from a variety of angles. However, *Silas Marner* contains a few comments which seem to work in the opposite direction, giving the impression that the narrator is arguing with earlier impressions rather than regarding them from alternative viewpoints. These instances occur in relation to Molly Farren's appearance in the story. Molly is introduced, through Godfrey's references, as early as chapter 3; but she does not actually appear until chapter 12, where she is depicted walking in the snow to confront Godfrey on New Year's Eve. As she makes her way toward the house, the narrator interrupts her thoughts: 'It is seldom that the miserable can help regarding their misery as a wrong inflicted by those who are less miserable' (xii, 105). Information about Molly's addiction to opium follows just after, the narrator indicating that Molly's 'dingy rags' are caused by her addiction rather than by Godfrey's neglect. Asserting that Molly is herself responsible for her deprived state, the narrator endeavours to focus attention away from Godfrey's wrongdoing onto Molly's own culpability in her miserable lot. Reinforcing this perspective, the narrator again comments in relation to Molly's thoughts of vengeance: 'Just and self-reproving thoughts do not come to us too thickly, even in the purest air, and with the best lessons of heaven and earth' (xii, 105). These two comments clearly aim to steer the reader's attitude, inducing him or her to regard Molly as a drug addict, ultimately responsible for her own degradation.[6]

Even so, the perspective that these two statements introduce runs counter to much that has been intimated about Molly up to this point. Godfrey's anguished conscience unmistakably reveals his responsibility; he has after all impregnated and married Molly, actions which inevitably make him responsible, at least in part, for her well-being, despite her addiction. Moreover, the account of Molly's walk to the Red House on New Year's Eve follows just after the depiction of Godfrey's flirtations with Nancy Lammeter. Hence Molly's tormented state is set against Godfrey's advances to another woman. These structural and contextual details, along with Molly's status as a working-class woman, somehow argue against the notion that she only has herself to blame. The narratorial comments thus – unusually for commentary in Eliot's novels – seem incompatible with the

---

6 Welsh observes the parallel between what he calls Dunstan Cass's expendability and Molly's death which, Welsh claims, is 'presumably acceptable because she is a drug addict and meditating "vengeance"'. Arguing that *Silas Marner* belongs to George Eliot's early experiments, Welsh says that 'one cannot imagine Mrs. Glasher in *Daniel Deronda* sinking down on the snow, though Mrs. Glasher is both an inconvenience and a blackmailer' (167).

particular details of the narrative. Rather than opening up new perspectives on Molly's situation, inviting the reader to regard her circumstances in a new light, these statements seem gratuitously harsh. One reason why the narrator exhibits such a hard attitude towards Molly might be that she dies in the same chapter. By suggesting that Molly dies because of her drug addiction, the narrator exempts Godfrey from culpability. His conscience and anxiety are easier for the reader to sympathise with if he or she does not believe that Godfrey's failure to recognise Molly leads straight to her death.

On the whole, however, Eliot's generalising comments express an extradiegetic narrative voice detached from fictive characters and situations, and with an overall control of the narrative. This controlled detachment is particularly manifest in the proverb-like statements where the narrator not only attempts to relate fictive phenomena to human nature in general, but also assumes a tone of sage-like wisdom.[7] For example: : 'A man falling into dark waters seeks a momentary footing even on sliding stones; and Silas, by acting as if he believed in false hopes, warded off the moment of despair' (v, 41). This statement claims to assert something 'true' and as with other proverb-like comments it could, in theory, be lifted out of its context and still make sense as a declaration on human kind in general.

Chapter 5 demonstrates how the narrator's sage-like, proverbial tone operates alongside his less distanced, more reasoning attitude. Although they interact with the narrative from different distances, both these types of commentary serve to elicit the reader's recognition by moving between the particular and the general. Inducing the reader to understand a specific phenomenon in the general sense, they invite him or her to apply this understanding to the particular situation in story-time now.

---

7 Henry Auster notices a connection between the narrator's distance and the theme of alienation in the novel, arguing: 'The detachment and generalizing perspective that the narrator consistently maintains are well suited to the story of alienation and readjustment. They reinforce the distance between Silas and the village society and make clear their mutual ignorance and fear'; see '*Silas Marner*: A Qualified Redemption of Ordinary and Fallible Humanity', in *Eliot: The Mill on the Floss and Silas Marner*, ed. by R. P. Draper (London: Macmillan, 1977), pp. 217-233 (p. 217).

References and Addresses to the Reader

Silas Marner is the only novel studied here which does not contain any direct references to the reader's response. The narrator does not address the reader directly, anticipating his or her reaction, nor does he make any assumptions as to the reader's interpretation. In this sense, the relation between the reader and the narrator is more distanced in *Silas Marner* than in earlier novels. One comment, however, refers to a potential reaction without directly acknowledging the reader's part in the interpretative process. As the congregation in Lantern Yard resolves to find out whether or not Silas is guilty of theft by 'drawing lots', the narrator remarks: 'This resolution can be a ground of surprise only to those who are unacquainted with that obscure religious life which has gone on in the alleys of our towns' (i, 12). The comment indirectly addresses the reader, remarking on his or her potential surprise at the way in which Silas's guilt is being determined. Suggesting that 'drawing lots' belongs to religious custom common in the back-alleys of cities and towns, the narrator refers to an idea of a divine providence which, he implies, should not be alien to the reader. By implication, the comment intimates that the reader's possible surprise indicates his or her unfamiliarity with certain religious practices. Subtly accusing the reader of ignorance, the comment reinforces the impression of authenticity in the story and underpins the narrator's authority.

References to the reader involving the use of the first-person pronoun are common in *Silas Marner*, however. By including the reader in 'we', narratorial commentary acknowledges his or her participation in the narrative while reducing the distance between reader, narrator and diegetic characters. When Silas rushes to the 'Rainbow Inn' for help and sits down to relate the story of his stolen money, the narrator remarks on the 'strangely novel situation' of Silas sitting among his neighbours asking them for assistance: 'Our consciousness rarely registers the beginning of a growth within us any more than without us: there have been many circulations of the sap before we detect the smallest sign of the bud' (vii, 54-55). By referring to human nature in general and drawing the reader into the reflection through the first-person pronoun, the narrator endeavours to elicit the reader's recognition, helping him or her to realise how the experience affects Silas. As with so many narratorial comments in the novel, the statement emanates from a sage-like, detached narrator who remarks on the particularities of the text in the manner of a proverb.

There are instances when the narrator is neither detached nor sage-like, however. In chapter 2, for example, the narrator seems anxious to justify Silas's money-hoarding. Having begun by posing a rhetorical question, the narrator goes on to explain how the question will help the reader understand:

> Do we not wile [*sic*] away moments of inanity or fatigued waiting by repeating some trivial movement or sound, until the repetition has bred a want, which is incipient habit? That will help us to understand how the love of accumulating money grows an absorbing passion in men whose imaginations, even in the very beginning of their hoard, showed them no purpose beyond it (ii, 18).

The explicit 'that will help us to understand' highlights the purpose of the question. The reader is urged to consider his or her own imperfections before making any hasty judgements about Silas's hoarding. Addressing the reader with a direct, albeit rhetorical, question, the passage invites him or her to take active part in an ostensible communication with the narrator. Appealing to the reader's recognition, the question urges the reader to respond 'truthfully'; and by way of the reader's recognition and his or her part in the 'we', the narrator downplays the aspects of financial greed or miserliness in Silas's hoarding, instead attempting to represent his behaviour as a natural response to his circumstances. Assuming the reader's agreement, the second part of the statement indicates how the reader's understanding of accumulation, habit and repetition may be applied to Silas's particular situation.[8] Here, the narrator is explicit about the purpose of the statement, explaining how it should be applied to the particularities of the narrative rather than letting the reader work it out.

Including the reader in the first-person pronoun does not always serve to elicit sympathy, though. Occasionally a character's mental processes are traced through commentary, highlighting a less than flattering predisposition. In relation to Godfrey's reaction to Molly's death, the narrator remarks on his reliance on chance: 'When we are treated well, we naturally begin to think that we are not altogether unmeritorious, and that it is only just we should treat ourselves well, and not mar our own good fortune' (xiii, 117). The 'we' involves human beings in general, including the reader. In this sense, it reduces the reader's distance to Godfrey. But whereas many other

---

8   Susan R. Cohen comments on this particular statement, arguing that it shows how hoarding creates meaning and order for Silas. Cohen argues that order and meaning are ends towards which the whole novel aspires, but the narrator, Cohen maintains, 'unlike the characters, remains conscious that this ideal cannot be realized'; see ' "A History and a Metamorphosis": Continuity and Discontinuity in *Silas Marner*', *Texas Studies in Literature and Language*, 25 (1983), 410-426 (p. 422).

references to 'we' encourage sympathy for a particular character through the reader's affinity with him or her, the comment above calls attention to an unflattering human inclination. The reader is drawn into the 'we' and induced to recognise the phenomenon. Recognition facilitates his or her ability to relate to Godfrey's thinking without necessarily identifying with him but instead observing Godfrey's reasoning from a distanced but non-judgmental vantage-point. The comment is preceded and followed by Godfrey's FID, which reveals his treacherous reliance on chance. Situated as an interruption in Godfrey's thinking, then, the comment contextual-ises and explains his mental processes, reminding the reader, as he or she is engaged in Godfrey's foolhardy thinking, of his or her own resemblance to him.

With regard to the narrator's presence in *Silas Marner*, this is less im-mediate than in any other Eliot novel. His controlled distance from the narrative is revealed not least by the rarity of references to the narrator as 'I' in this novel. However, the examples of 'I' which do occur often serve to reduce the distance between the narrator and the diegesis. The very first reference to 'I' introduces a narrator who takes part in the narrative, us-ing his own experiences to illustrate a point: ' "Is there anything you can fancy that you would like to eat?" I once said to an old labouring man' (i, 5). This 'I' is far from suggesting a distanced, sage-like observer; rather, it introduces the reader to a personal and immediately present narrator who inscribes his own story into the narrative. This is the only instance in the novel where the narrator draws directly on personal experiences. Other examples of 'I' yield an interesting pattern in relation to the narratorial attitudes in the novel, most of them indicating some kind of hesitation or humility. For example, with regard to Godfrey's longing for children, his inability to find contentment in married life and the burden of his secret, the narrator comments:

> I suppose it is the way with all men and women who reach middle age without the clear perception that life never *can* be thoroughly joyous: under the vague dullness of the grey hours, dissatisfaction seeks a definite object, and finds it in the privation of an untried good (xvii, 154).

The sentence has a tentative tone, giving the impression that the narrator is less than authoritative here; the 'I suppose' implies that there is room for doubt. Its meditating mode serves to entice the reader into responding to the suggestion, inviting him or her to engage actively in the question of why Godfrey cannot attain happiness.[9] Instead of inviting the reader into the narrator's sphere, placing him or her on a shared diegetic level, there is an impression that the narrator temporarily relaxes his hold on the narrative to meet the reader on a mutual level. His supposition renders him more 'approachable' and less sage-like. However, the ensuing sentence (not quoted) reinstates the narrator's characteristically authoritative tone, thus re-establishing his control of the narrative. This control is important, not just to authenticate historical features but also because this is a novel that in part rests on mythological structures while supposedly engaged with realistic representation. Still, the comment reveals the narrator's need to clarify. It conveys his own hypothesis, rendering him more accessible and motivating the reader to engage with the question of what underlying causes make Godfrey unhappy.

In the few passages which make up chapter 15 of *Silas Marner*, the narrator's 'I' is referred to twice, both times signalling his authoritative role in the narrative. It is significant that both instances appear in chapter 15, which is the last chapter of part one. Had the novel been serialised in its first publication, these references to the narrator might have been regarded as reminders to the reader of the narrator's authority in preparation for the next instalment; but *Silas Marner* was published in one volume. Still, the end of part one in the novel reinforces the narrator's significance as a preliminary to part two, which depicts Raveloe sixteen years later.

Metalepses

Part two of *Silas Marner* not only introduces Raveloe after the passing of sixteen years, it also contains the only instances of metalepsis in the novel. Describing the parishioners coming out from morning service, the narrator assumes the reader's visual access to the scene:

> Foremost among these advancing groups of well-clad people, there are some whom we shall recognise, in spite of Time, who has laid his hand on them all. The tall

---

9 David Sonstroem discusses this particular comment, arguing that Godfrey's good fortune has made him greedy for more and that the only way the novel allows him happiness is by letting him experience suffering. See 'The Breaks in *Silas Marner*', *Journal of English and Germanic Philology*, 97 (1998), 545-567. Sonstroem's reading corresponds well with Eliot's idea that suffering humanises and leads to sympathy. Compare, for example, Adam Bede, who cannot understand weakness and fallibility until he himself has undergone suffering.

blond man of forty is not much changed in feature from the Godfrey Cass of six-and-twenty (xvi, 132).

A little further on the narrator adds: 'We will not follow them now; for may there not be some others in this departing congregation whom we should like to see again' (xvi, 133) and still further on: 'you see how neatly her prayer-book is folded in her spotted handkerchief' (xvi, 133). For the first and only time in *Silas Marner*, the reader's actual visual access to the depicted fictional scene is postulated. This is particularly interesting in a novel which professes to take place in historical time, devoting its first two chapters to describing a remote period to a contemporary audience.[10] At the beginning of part two, however, there has been a lapse of sixteen years; and the narrator initially treats the narrative differently, pulling the reader into the frame of the scene as if the reduced temporal distance would allow him or her greater access to the story. In effect, the metalepsis draws the reader into story-time now – a practice recognisable from *Adam Bede* and *The Mill on the Floss*, where narrator and reader appear to be regarding a fictive scene together, as if simultaneously contemplating and commenting on a painting or performance.

As with these instances in the earlier novels, the reader's participation in story-time now suppresses the distinction between narration now and story-time now, closing the gap between narrated time and the reader's time and consequently condensing the distance between fictive characters and reader. Only when the narrator returns to the past tense is the balance restored and the reader re-situated outside the diegesis, spatially and temporally detached from the fiction. However, by locating the reader temporarily within the fictional sphere the narrator relinquishes some of his control as mediator, granting the reader direct access to the fictive scenes and to the characters, thus providing him or her with the prospect of establishing a personal bond to them seemingly 'independently' of the narrator's interpretation. This personal bond between reader and characters serves as a basis for sympathy, as the narrator's mediating presence is diminished and the distinction between fictive and 'real' is blurred.[11]

With only one chapter in which metalepsis occurs, *Silas Marner* demonstrates a movement away from the type of novel which transgresses diegetic boundaries. Developing towards a tighter control of narrative dis-

10 On temporal levels in relation to this comment, see Nünning, p. 194.
11 Janice Carlisle claims that present-tense narration became conventional at mid-century, often signalling 'an author's dependence on an aura of melodramatic intensity' (182-183). Although it is difficult to discern any melodrama in Eliot's use of the present tense in *Silas Marner*, Carlisle does have a point when she argues that Eliot employed 'present-tense narration to create rhetorical demands on the reader's attention' (183).

tances, the novel occupies an intermediate position between Eliot's early and late novels. Containing no direct references to the reader's anticipated responses, no meta-narrative comments, only a few references to the narrator as 'I' and isolated instances of metalepsis, *Silas Marner* is the Eliot novel that employs the fewest and least extensively applied methods by which narratorial commentary conditions the reactions of readers. Speculation as to why the novel differs so much from Eliot's other novels in terms of narratorial commentary has come up with the idea that criticism of the emotionally engaged narrator in *The Mill on the Floss* compelled Eliot to create a less 'involved' narrator in her next novel. But narratorial commentary in *Silas Marner*, although employing fewer narratologically definable devices, nevertheless involves an engaged narrator who obviously attempts to shape reader response. The difference between the narrator in *The Mill on the Floss* and *Silas Marner*, then, is that the latter disguises his active engagement by experimenting with narratorial distances.[12]

References to History

The principal thematic concerns dealt with in the novel's commentary generally correspond to the significant thematic issues of the novel as a whole. In his commentary the narrator discusses the differences between the narrative past and the narration present, differences in religiosity between the world of the narrative setting and the narrator's world and questions involving the notions of chance and providence. Chapter 1 introduces a major concern relating to history and historical change. The reader learns that the story of Silas's lonely linen-weaving takes place some time around 1800, and that he arrived from Lantern Yard to take up his weaving in Raveloe 15 years before, having been forced to leave under humiliating circumstances. This period of the Napoleonic wars sees a rural community enjoying a reasonably comfortable life, with a lack of agricultural competition from abroad and with an Industrial Revolution which, although it had started to change town life radically, had not yet reached the remote countryside with any significant force. This period is distinct

---

12 Suzanne Graver comments on the differences between *Silas Marner* and *The Mill*, arguing that while the narrator in the latter 'alienates the contemporary reader from the familiar', the narrator in *Silas Marner* makes familiar what at first seems alien. See Graver, p. 287.

from that of the narrator, who is writing retrospectively from the time of the novel's publication in the 1860s, and the narrator is eager to emphasise the differences in society and outlook between story-time now and the narrator's own time of writing. But the narrator also alludes to a history even more remote, beyond story-time. His concern with historical change and the differences between 'then' and 'now' is alluded to regularly in the form of commentary, and it is particularly this remote history which gives rise to extensive reflections. Describing the extent of Silas's sense of alienation, the narrator comments:

> In the early ages of the world, we know, it was believed that each territory was inhabited and ruled by its own divinities, so that a man could cross the bordering heights and be out of the reach of his native gods, whose presence was confined to the streams and the groves and the hills among which he had lived from his birth. And poor Silas was vaguely conscious of something not unlike the feeling of primitive men (ii, 15).

It is debateable whether the comment qualifies as belonging to narration now, as it does not detach itself entirely from the fictional sphere nor separate itself from the development of the story. But the presence of 'we know' suggests the acknowledgement of a reader with whom the narrator is on a similar level, distanced and detached from the events of the story. By jogging the reader's memory with information he or she is presumed to possess, the passage conveys a clever image of Silas's feelings of estrangement and establishes a bond between narrator and reader which situates them on a level above the diegesis.

Furthermore, the comment serves to authenticate the twofold sense of alienation that Silas experiences. He arrives in an environment where nothing is recognisable and has lost his own frames of reference, having been betrayed by the very ideology that he has lived by. As in *Adam Bede*, where George Eliot juxtaposes the pastoral world of Hayslope with the rural town of Stoniton, and in *The Mill on the Floss*, where the landscapes of the Rhine and the Rhône metaphorically represent two contrasting orders of 'reality', so the worlds of Lantern Yard and Raveloe are contrasted in *Silas Marner*. Silas loses not only his evangelical faith in Lantern Yard, but also the cultural and social certainties which are inseparable from that faith.[13] The two communities are contrasted but also linked by the non-

---

13 Jerome Thale explains Silas's problem as founded in a loss of 'a sense of the world' rather than a loss of creed. See *The Novels of George Eliot* (New York: Columbia University Press, 1959), p. 61. See also Fred C. Thomson's article 'The Theme of Alienation in *Silas Marner*', *Nineteenth-Century Fiction*, 20 (1965), 69-84, for a discussion of Silas's sense of estrangement.

sophistication of their beliefs. Both worlds are preoccupied with the supernatural and miraculous, and the novel examines these value-systems with a detached, almost anthropological, curiosity, suggesting that they originate in a fundamental need for human beings to make sense of their world. When those belief-patterns have collapsed, as in Silas's case, alienation ensues, and modern man's disorientation in the world is as palpable as that of the primitive man who wandered too far away from the 'streams and groves' which encompassed his gods.

Similarly to Silas, Godfrey Cass experiences a sense of alienation, although his isolation is concealed under the heavy burden of lies and secrets with which his conscience battles.[14] As Dunstan rides off to sell Godfrey's horse, he is left to contemplate his lot, with little to interrupt his anxious harping 'save by the excitement of sporting, drinking, card-playing, or the rarer and less oblivious pleasure of seeing Miss Nancy Lammeter' (iii, 28-29). In order to have the reader sympathise with Godfrey, for whose difficult circumstances only Godfrey himself is to blame, the narrator again directs attention to a history distanced from both story-time now and narrative time:

> The lives of those rural forefathers, whom we are apt to think very prosaic figures [...] had a certain pathos in them nevertheless. Calamities came to *them* too, and their early errors carried hard consequences [...] Assuredly, among these flushed and dull-eyed men there were some whom [...] even riot could never drive into brutality; men who, when their cheeks were fresh, had felt the keen point of sorrow or remorse [...] and under these sad circumstances, common to us all, their thoughts could find no resting-place outside the ever-trodden round of their own petty history (iii, 29).

By incorporating Godfrey's anxieties into a historical frame, the narrator suggests that his errors are no more than common human imperfections which man has characteristically struggled with in all ages. The sympathy which is solicited does not spring from this acknowledgement, though, but rather from Godfrey's innate 'human-kindness' which prevents him from ever forgetting the consequences of his youthful errors. This human kindness, it is important to note, does not emanate from any religious creed or value-system; it is inherent in Godfrey himself, and it is to this quality

---

14 The parallels between Silas's and Godfrey's plots and these characters' psychological struggles have been discussed extensively by several critics. See, for instance, Bruce K. Martin, 'Similarity Within Dissimilarity: The Dual Structure of *Silas Marner*', *Texas Studies in Literature and Language*, 14 (1972), 479-489; and David Carroll, '*Silas Marner*: Reversing the Oracles of Religion', *Literary Monographs*, vol.1, ed. by E. Rothstein and T. K. Dunseath (1967) (repr. in R. P. Draper, *Eliot: The Mill on the Floss and Silas Marner* (London: Macmillan, 1977), pp. 188-216).

the narrator appeals when petitioning for sympathy. Frames of reference, value-systems and principles all change with the passing of time; but as the narrator points out, the inner turmoil which can afflict a human being with the knowledge of having done wrong is conditioned by an instinctive bent towards goodness which is familiar to all men, regardless of the times they live in.[15] This humanity, rooted in mankind itself and independent of religious or political ideology, is an essential concern in the novel. It comprises a philosophical doctrine which regards human compassion as an elementary moral power in life and derives from the ideas of Ludwig Feuerbach, who honoured the best qualities in mankind as the only valid religion. The saving quality in both Silas's and Godfrey's lives is human love.[16] Consequently, the human kindness Godfrey displays, safeguarding him from ever being driven 'into brutality', is esteemed higher than any religion in the novel as it originates in humanity itself.

The narrator's references to the historical time of the story usually come across as brief, almost parenthetical, asides, which swiftly explain the differences between 'then' and 'now'. These asides emerge as small pieces of information which the narrator seems to deem necessary to the reader's understanding of the historical time and almost appear to be pushed in as if the narrator were impatient to carry on with the narrative. Describing Silas's thoughts about hiding his gold, the narrator states: 'Not that the idea of being robbed presented itself often or strongly to his mind: hoarding was common in country districts in those days' (ii, 18-19). This succinct, barely perceptible piece of information offers itself as a direct address to the reader, who is consequently alerted to the narrative as history and to the narrator's and reader's detachment and distance above it. In addition to acknowledging the presence of a reader and recognising his or her status in relation to the diegesis, the comment substantiates the authenticity of the fiction, maintaining the 'realistic' accuracy of the story.[17] The narrator

---

15 Commenting on the quotation above, Henry Auster argues that it is Godfrey's 'better instincts' which 'preserve him from utter degradation' and that the narratorial comment emphasises the 'pathos of his position' when describing the 'psychological corruption to which Godfrey, with all his admirable qualities, has made himself susceptible'; see *Local Habitations: Regionalism in the Early Novels of George Eliot* (Cambridge, MA: Harvard University Press, 1970), pp. 190-191.

16 David Carroll claims that the novel requires the reader to 'assess the various religious beliefs in the novel, the several "theologies" as they are called, by measuring their human content'; see 'Reversing the Oracles', p. 192.

17 Having largely accepted the definition of *Silas Marner* as a moral fable containing features of the fairy tale, critics have argued about whether or not *Silas Marner* is an example of realistic representation. George Eliot herself saw the novel as a realistic one, as she wrote to Blackwood: 'It came to me first of all, quite suddenly, as a sort of legendary tale, suggested by my recollection of having once, in early childhood, seen

is hence situating the story of Silas' treasure hoard – which is legendary in origin – into a 'realistic' and credible context, interweaving legendary elements with factual information in order to extenuate the impression of a mythological tale by stressing the authenticity of the story and its fidelity to actual historical data. Furthermore, the narrator is asserting his own reliability. By commenting in a factual tone, almost in passing, on circumstances in story-time now which are historical and so remote from the narrator's own time, the narrator implies his own expert knowledge and authority on matters concerning the period in which the story takes place. This information signals a narrator in control of his subject matter and accordingly underpins his reliability as a storyteller and historian.

The last long passage of chapter 2 ends: 'This is the history of Silas Marner until the fifteenth year after he came to Raveloe' (ii, 20). The *history* of Silas further promotes the idea that reader and narrator are engaged in a historical rendering rather than in a fictional story. This literary phenomenon is not of course a novelty in Eliot's writing: all the earlier works, *Scenes of Clerical Life*, *Adam Bede* and *The Mill on the Floss*, feature attempts to stifle the notion of fictionality by introducing a narrator-historian who is familiar with essential facts of the historical period. However, the narratorial presence in the first three books implies a narrator who is remembering a historical past which he himself has been part of, albeit only peripherally. In *Silas Marner* the narrator is principally extradiegetic and only touches on his own part in the diegesis twice. The distinction between the respective sets of historical data in the novels, then, is that the information submitted by the narrator in *Silas Marner* is acquired through external knowledge about a bygone era, whereas in the earlier novels this knowledge is combined with the narrator's alleged experiences of that particular era.[18]

---

a linen-weaver with a bag on his back; but as my mind dwelt on the subject, I became inclined to a more realistic treatment'; see *Letters*, iii, 382.

18 In 'Narrative and History', *ELH*, 41, (1974), 455-473, J. Hillis Miller argues that '[b]y calling a novel a history its author at one stroke covers over all the implications of gratuitousness, of baseless creativity and lie, involved in the word "fiction." At the same time he affirms for his novel that verisimilitude, that solid basis in pre-existing fact, which is associated with the idea of history' (457). Miller also discusses Henry James's interesting criticism of Trollope's penchant for reminding his reader, in a meta-narrative fashion, that the story he or she is reading is indeed a fiction and that the author himself has full control of it. In *The Art of Fiction and Other Essays* (New York: Oxford University Press, 1948), James claims that 'it is impossible to imagine what a novelist takes himself to be unless he regards himself as an historian and his narrative as history. It is only as an historian that he has the smallest *locus standi*. As a narrator of fictitious events he is nowhere; to insert into his attempt a back-bone of logic, he must relate events that are assumed to be real' (59-60).

References to Religion

References to history are closely connected to reflections on superstition and religion in the two communities of the novel. Although the parallels and dichotomies between the creeds of Lantern Yard and Raveloe constitute a major theme in *Silas Marner*, the specific differences or similarities between them are expressed in dialogue and descriptive narrative rather than through narratorial commentary. However, *Silas Marner* does contain religious references in the form of commentary which serve to illuminate and develop particular phenomena. Describing Eppie as Silas's 'new-found treasure', replacing and surpassing the value of the gold he lost, the narrator comments:

> In old days there were angels who came and took men by the hand and led them away from the city of destruction. We see no white-winged angels now. But yet men are led away from threatening destruction: a hand is put into theirs, which leads them forth gently towards a calm and bright land, so that they look no more backward; and the hand may be the little child's (xiv. 130).

The comment, which ends chapter 14 depicting Silas's new-found life with the arrival of Eppie, refers to Genesis. It equates Eppie with the angels who led Lot and his family away from the destruction of the doomed cities, Sodom and Gomorrah, as well as recalling the book of Isaiah which anticipates the arrival of the Messiah on earth and reads: 'The wolf shall live with the lamb, the leopard shall lie down with the kid, the calf and the lion and the fatling together, and a little child shall lead them' (Isa 11. 6). In Eliot's interpretation, the child-Messiah who brings salvation does so by liberating man from self-centredness and backward-looking harping. Eppie, the child, saves Silas from his human suffering, not by sacrificing herself but by redirecting his focus, by making him feel and become indispensable through her vulnerability and dependence and by stirring his emotions.[19]

By integrating legend with 'realistic treatment' (*Letters*, iii, 382), i.e. by interpreting the myth as a symbol of 'realistic' phenomena, Eliot demythologises the narrative, according to several critics.[20] Although the idea of demythologisation is relevant to *Silas Marner* and to George Eliot's belief

---

19 See Peter C. Hodgson, pp. 74-81, for a more detailed account of religious and Biblical references in *Silas Marner*.
20 See Joseph Wiesenfarth and Peter C. Hodgson, who both argue that Eliot stripped legendary material of its mysticism in the effort to show that everything originates in human emotions and actions.

in a religion of humanity, it is possible to reverse the idea – to see the narrator's references to legendary material as a reinforcement of the mythological associations in the plot. Unquestionably, the stories of Silas's gold and Eppie's arrival originate in tradition and it is incontestable that the novel offers 'realistic' solutions to these events, attempting to demonstrate that all events stem from human effort and human motivation. Only through human relations, and through the love germinated in these, is salvation attainable. This is a major theme in the novel.[21] However, with the Biblical reference quoted above, the narrator emphasises the spiritual and divine within the 'realistic', rather than the reverse. The fact that Eliot, following in the footsteps of David Friedrich Strauss, interpreted the Bible as a historical document rather than as a sacred text telling incontrovertible truths does not necessarily imply that she experienced Biblical stories as bereft of mysticism and spirituality. Hence, the reader can agree that there are no actual 'white-winged angels'. But the child who acts as saviour, who gives new life and purpose to humanity, represents the angel – and it is only by understanding the elevation of the reference, by rising above and beyond the 'realistic', that the reader can appreciate what Eppie means. Thus, in this case, by offering an intertextual reference the spiritual quintessence of which readers can recognise, the comment mythologises rather than demythologises the advent of the child into Silas's life.[22]

The comment quoted above also refers back to the initial novel epigraph taken from Wordsworth's *Michael*:

> A child, more than all other gifts
> That earth can offer to declining man,
> Brings hope with it, and forward-looking thoughts (ll.146-148).

In Wordsworth's pastoral, Michael's son Luke falls into dishonour, shaming his father who ends his life with no 'forward-looking thoughts'.[23] But it is primarily the significance that the child brings to the life of the adult

---

21 A general theme, presumably influenced by Feuerbach's concept of religion. See David Carroll's '*Silas Marner*: Reversing the Oracles of Religion'.

22 It is important to note that this mythologisation does not jeopardise the theory of a general demythologisation in the novel espoused by Wiesenfarth.

23 Stephen Gill argues that readers familiar with Wordsworth's poem would read the novel in anticipation of a different ending; see Gill, p. 163. However, Eliot herself wrote to Blackwood concerning the motto: 'Do you think it indicates the story too distinctly?', implying that she did not expect readers to assume that the novel would follow Wordsworth's pastoral from beginning to end, but that her audience might disregard the context and interpret the extract in isolation. See *Letters*, iii, 385. Gill recognises the discrepancy but does not problematise beyond considering Eliot's question 'strange' (163).

which is underlined in the epigraph, a notion which – although it is extracted from a particular context – is relevant as an isolated idea independent of its original source. The narratorial comment above, then, serves as a rendering of the Wordsworthian motto, reminding the reader of the significance of the child as well as further invoking the story's close relation to Wordsworthian language, patterns and themes. It situates Eppie's and Silas's relationship within a legendary tradition, but also within the Wordsworthian materials in the form of language, structure, themes and metaphors which constitute such an important substratum in the novel.[24]

Some narratorial comments carry more general reflections on religion which are not necessarily directly associated to Biblical texts or legend. As Silas loses the drawing of lots, the narrator remarks:

> To people accustomed to reason about the forms in which their religious feeling has incorporated itself, it is difficult to enter into that simple, untaught state of mind in which the form and the feeling have never been severed by an act of reflection. We are apt to think it inevitable that a man in Marner's position should have begun to question the validity of an appeal to the divine judgment by drawing lots [...] If there is an angel who records the sorrows of men as well as their sins, he knows how many and deep are the sorrows that spring from false ideas for which no man is culpable (i, 12-13).

R. P. Draper discusses this comment extensively, arguing that it serves 'to bridge the gap between the naïve consciousness of Silas, with its fundamentalist assumption that lots, since mentioned in the Bible, must be the voice of a just God, and the more sophisticated awareness of Victorian readers that guilt needs to be established by valid evidence and testimony.'[25] But Draper also acknowledges that the statement is double-edged, as the majority of Victorian readers would also be practising Christians

---

24 For further reading on Wordsworthian affinities in the novel, see Robert H. Dunham, 'Silas Marner and the Wordsworthian Child', Studies in English Literature, 1500-1900, 16 (1976), 645-659; Lilian Haddakin, 'Silas Marner', in Critical Essays on George Eliot, ed. by Barbara Hardy (London: Routledge & Kegan Paul, 1970), pp. 59-77; and Peter Simpson, 'Crisis and Recovery: Wordsworth, George Eliot and Silas Marner', University of Toronto Quarterly, 48 (1978-1979), 95-114. See also Eliot's early essay 'The Wisdom of the Child', which she applauds 'that purity and simplicity which characterizes early youth'; Essays, p. 20. Commenting on the novel herself, Eliot wrote to Blackwood: 'I should not have believed that any one would have been interested in it but myself (since William Wordsworth is dead) if Mr. Lewes had not been strongly arrested by it'; see Letters, iii, 382. For a discussion of common elements between Silas Marner and Shakespeare's The Winter's Tale, see Ian Milner, 'Structure and Quality in Silas Marner', Studies in English Literature, 1500-1900, 6 (1966), 717-729.
25 R. P. Draper, 'The Fictional Perspective: The Mill on the Floss and Silas Marner', in Eliot: The Mill on the Floss and Silas Marner, ed. by R. P. Draper (London: Macmillan, 1977), pp. 234-251 (p. 239). Cf. also Nünning, pp. 195-196.

who would protest against a rationale that queried Christian doctrine and instead promoted the Feuerbachian idea that all religion emanates from and resides within man himself. Accordingly, the narrator is remarking not only on Silas's inability to think independently, but also on the reader whose possible adherence to religious belief similarly deprives him or her of the power to think outside the parameters of that specific belief. It is important to note, however, that this 'nudge', as Draper calls it, given to the reader, is subtly concealed under the assumption that the reader is *not* incapable of independent thought, but on the contrary, like the narrator, accustomed to questioning his or her own forms of religious expression. The narrator thus expects a reader who has made reason his or her prioritised form of attaining conviction. In addition, the narrator presents this assumption as such a self-evident fact that readers might find it difficult to disagree, insofar as they even realise that their incorporation of religious doctrine is being condemned. By the use of 'we', the reader is included into a select group; and by seemingly neglecting to acknowledge that the reader's own faith may control him or her similarly to the manner in which Silas's does him, the narrator indirectly offers his disapproval of this type of religious conviction.

The *Silas Marner* narrator examines not only the ways in which religion manifests itself, but also how various kinds of unorthodox convictions integrate with doctrine and become part of a community's religious belief. Both in the evangelical Lantern Yard and in the orthodox Raveloe, the narrator observes tendencies to explain events by way of the supernatural, including inclinations to hold the devil, witches or ghosts responsible for that which cannot be immediately explained. These manifestations of heterodox belief constitute some of the novel's 'fairy-tale' elements and are investigated by a narrator who is interested in them historically and anthropologically, rather than disparagingly.

Following August Comte's theory of an evolution of religious response in three stages, the novel serves as an illustration of how some of these stages may be manifested. Comte argues that in the first phase – the 'Fetishist- and Theistic-stage' – man is initially driven by animist beliefs, attaching significance to inanimate objects, which he eventually abandons to end the first phase in the belief in a comprehensive, monotheistic higher power. In the second phase the objects and gods have been replaced by a belief in metaphysics, where humankind worships 'Reason' in the form of philosophy, science and politics. In the final 'Positive' stage, humankind has managed to liberate itself from preconceived assumptions in order to base its beliefs on empirical knowledge. In this final phase, humankind has reached a degree of religious susceptibility capable of acknowledging the human feelings concealed within earlier forms of belief and is able to find 'true' expression for them. This 'new discovery' of belief constitutes a 'religion of humanity'.

The third stage, then, allows earlier manifestations of belief, such as Fetishism, to persist, indicating that the development of religious response in history signifies a transformation and variation of expression rather than replacing belief with something new. This notion is important to *Silas Marner*, where the narrator comments on Silas's love for his 'old brick hearth' and his 'brown pot': 'The gods of the hearth exist for us still; and let all new faith be tolerant of that fetishism, lest it bruise its own roots' (xvi. 137). The 'gods of the hearth' refer to domestic gods in the shape of small figures which would be kept on the hearth in Roman times, thus, in the context of the novel, signifying the first fetishist stage of religious development according to a Positivistic view. Hence, the comment demonstrates the manner in which the old beliefs of the first stage reappear in the final positivistic stage, recognising how the old and original is transformed and recycled in the new. Terence Cave argues that the quoted comment alters the narrator's rather unfavourable appraisal of religious expression in the old days displayed in the early pages of the novel, so that the reader is very nearly tricked into one perspective in the beginning of the novel only to be made to pass judgment on that very belief as the story progresses.[26] By qualifying the initial sentiment, however, the comment still acknowledges the primitiveness of fetishism, but more importantly identifies the history of human emotion which it encompasses. This religious origin, or – as the narrator terms it – root, is crucial to the advancement of humanity, a notion which is consistent with Eliot's view of history in general.[27]

Moreover, the comment is consistent with the narrator's overall attempt to bring the reader into the narrative experience, closing the gap between fictional character and reader in order to have the reader recognise particular phenomena.[28] Here, the narrator curbs possible attitudes of superiority

---

26 George Eliot, *Silas Marner*, ed. by Terence Cave, Oxford World's Classics (Oxford: Oxford University Press, 1996), p. xiv. In his introduction to the novel, Cave discusses the comment extensively from a Comtean perspective and touches on several points which are of importance to my discussion above.

27 The rooted-plant metaphor is one which Eliot uses in all her novels. It may have been inspired by Wordsworth; the symbolism is the same for both authors. See Robert H. Dunham, 648-651 and Thomas Pinney, 'The Authority of the Past in George Eliot's Novels', *Nineteenth-Century Fiction*, 21 (1966), 131-147.

28 Cave argues that the comment 'modifies the crude value-judgement, the implication of superiority and historical distance that seems to follow from the early reference to the "superstition" of that "far-off time"' (xiv).

in the reader's response to Silas's attachment to his hearth and pot, reminding him or her not only of the continued existence of 'primitive' religious manifestations in contemporary culture, but also of the incorporation of these into more 'sophisticated' and modern patterns of belief.

Chance

The plot in *Silas Marner* relies on a great many chance incidents taking place. Godfrey's first wife, Molly, dies in the snow before she can reveal his big secret; the child makes her way into Silas's cottage just as he is having a cataleptic seizure; Dunstan steals Silas's money and then falls into the pit; and before all this happens Silas has been forced to leave Lantern Yard as a result of the drawing of lots. The large number of coincidences in the novel makes up part of its fairy-tale character, although most events spring from logical origins.[29] Still, chance and providence constitute an important feature in the novel, and it is evident that the narrator's attitude toward these phenomena alters considering which character is involved. Regarding Silas, chance constitutes a redeeming force, exchanging his selfish adherence to material objects for a profound, altruistic and reciprocated love for another human being. For him, chance arrives as a series of events which eventually lead to a happy ending. For Godfrey, however, chance is something relied upon and expected, the last resort in which he places his faith in order that his hidden, humiliating past may not be revealed. The chance phenomenon remains the same regarding both characters, but their attitudes to it differ – a difference which the narrator observes and comments on. Relating to Godfrey's failure to speak the whole truth to his

---

29 Joseph Wiesenfarth explains that events in *Silas Marner* which seem to happen by chance actually stem from human character and action. For example, Molly dies in the snow because she is addicted to opium, and Eppie finds light and warmth in Silas's cottage because it is New Year's Eve and Silas has let the door open in keeping with 'the traditional vigil, which he hopes will bring him good luck and the restoration of his money' (243, n41). Efraim Sicher argues that the plot 'depends on chance at the same time as it denies the role of the supernatural in true belief', claiming that the 'authorial voice appears to deny the supernatural at the same time as exploiting it to confirm the authority of symbolic pattern'; see 'George Eliot's Rescripting of Scripture: The "Ethics of Reading" in *Silas Marner*', *Semeia: An Experimental Journal for Biblical Criticism*, 77 (1997), 243-270. See also Thomas Vargish, *The Providential Aesthetic in Victorian Fiction* (Charlottesville: University of Virginia Press, 1985), pp. 196-205, for a discussion of Silas's reliance on providence.

father, and to his hopes of winning Nancy Lammeter despite already being married to Molly, the narrator muses:

> Favourable Chance, I fancy, is the god of all men who follow their own devices instead of obeying a law they believe in. Let even a polished man of these days get into a position he is ashamed to avow, and his mind will be bent on all the possible issues that may deliver him from the calculable results of that position [...] Let him forsake a decent craft that he may pursue the gentilities of a profession to which nature never called him, and his religion will infallibly be the worship of blessed Chance, which he will believe in as the mighty creator of success. The evil principle deprecated in that religion, is the orderly sequence by which the seed brings forth a crop after its kind (ix, 71-72).

It is important to distinguish between the belief in a Providence by which Dolly Winthrop, with the benefit of hindsight, explains Silas's good luck, and a reliance on chance to which Godfrey, and also his brother, adhere.[30] Passively waiting around for situations to solve themselves, frantically hoping that they will, depending on chance to act in his stead, Godfrey demonstrates the cowardice of a man who, having violated his own principles, futilely resorts to a false belief – a belief which anxiously rejects the notion of actions eventually leading to consequences which will render 'a crop after its kind'.[31] Concluding the chapter in which Godfrey fails to tell his father the truth about his marriage to Molly but instead manages to get himself further entangled in lies and evasions, the narrator's rather censorious comment serves as a premonition of the consequences that Godfrey's blind reliance on chance will eventually have. Alluding to the idea that all men shall reap the consequences of their actions, the narrator is 'planting a seed' in the reader's mind, causing him or her to anticipate the revelation of Godfrey's secret.

However, as all readers of *Silas Marner* know, chance is good to Godfrey, rewarding rather than punishing him. The only reason his secret is disclosed is because he chooses to reveal it himself; and his revelation turns out to be

---

30 In 'Chance in *Silas Marner*', *English: The Journal of the English Association*, 31 (1982), 213-218, Donald Hawes argues that the novel offers contradictory attitudes toward Chance, reproving Godfrey for relying upon it and in comparison offering no criticism as to the impact it has on Silas's life. Hawes himself remarks that the difference involves Godfrey's conscious anticipation that Chance will rule in his favour versus Silas's complete inattention to Chance. But as Peter New observes in 'Chance, Providence and Destiny in George Eliot's Fiction', *English: The Journal of the English Association*, 34 (1985), 191-208, Hawes does not seem to recognise the degree of importance attached to this brief remark.

31 There are several Biblical parables to which the last sentence could be a reference, the most quoted being Matthew 13 and Paul's statement in Galatians 6. 7-10 that man shall reap what he sows.

a blessing for him, drawing him closer to Nancy and allowing him access to Eppie. The generalising comment thus misleads the reader into false expectations, expectations which are corroborated by the notion that the novel must carry some 'moral message'. David Sonstroem explains this 'deception' by arguing that *Silas Marner* deviates from conventional novels by refraining from endorsing morality in spite of its being, in essence, a novel concerned with morality.[32] Even so, it is difficult to neglect the morality implicated in the death of the wicked Dunstan, or in the eventual happiness of Silas and Eppie, or in Godfrey's eventual decision to reveal the truth about his first marriage to Molly, who died alone and abandoned in the snow and whose child he renounced. Indeed, the comment could be interpreted as misleadingly indicating that Godfrey will eventually reap what he has sown, that his dependence on chance will turn against him and that he will have to learn his moral lesson. But the imagined eruptive climax serving to disclose his hidden past, to disgrace him and his family and to cause Nancy to distance herself from him, never materialises in the novel. The continuous anxiety Godfrey suffers from, however, his incessant 'harping' and feelings of guilt, are all consequences of his restless reliance on capricious chance. Godfrey's reaping consists in this psychological distress. Unlike Dunstan, who similarly expects fortune to turn in his favour, Godfrey's punishment or moral lesson does not amount to public humiliation or death, for the very reason that his own inner turmoil is wreaking havoc on his soul. Therefore, considering Godfrey's constant anxieties, the comment is not misleading. The 'evil principle' which his 'religion' is attempting to ward off nonetheless manages to strike its claws into him and prevent him from ever achieving inner harmony.

The generalising nature of the 'Favourable Chance' comment detracts attention from the particularities of Godfrey's predicament to emphasise a character trait which he has in common with many others. By rebuking this characteristic generally, the narrator not only makes an ideological statement, implying that reliance on chance emanates from a failure to adhere to one's own principles, but also situates Godfrey's weakness within a larger perspective which renders it a way of reasoning that is common but nonetheless, the narrator insists, deplorable. Hence, the reader is invited to recognise a type of character but in this case, interestingly, discouraged from sympathising. The comment instead serves to extract and condense those elements which prevent Godfrey from being a decent, upstanding

---

32 Sonstroem, p. 563. Sonstroem also argues that *Silas Marner* differs from conventional novels by not promoting continuous causal systems which imply that character determines destiny, instead demonstrating how 'random events deform and reform character and belie the very concept of destiny' (563).

individual, urging the reader to repudiate these without withdrawing his or her sympathy for Godfrey as a whole character.

* * *

Although *Silas Marner* contains fewer direct addresses to the reader than other Eliot novels, no meta-narrative instances, a very small number of references to the narrator as 'I' and only a few instances of metalepsis, narratorial commentary in the novel nevertheless strives towards eliciting the reader's understanding. By moving between the general and the particular and by involving the reader in narrative experiences through the first-person pronoun, the novel establishes a closeness between the reader and the diegesis although its narrator is primarily distanced and sage-like. In terms of narratorial commentary and the narrator's position, the novel constitutes a definite change of direction from *The Mill on the Floss*. Notwithstanding their differences, however, narratorial commentary in both novels serves the same end – to influence the reader's interpretation of narrative events and characters and to shape his or her response in the direction of sympathy and understanding.

Romola

As early as 1860, even before writing *Silas Marner*, George Eliot had plans to write a historical novel about Girolamo Savonarola, to be set in fifteenth-century Florence. Begun in July 1862, *Romola* was published in fourteen monthly parts, all of which received disappointing reviews from critics and general public alike. The novel was a bold experiment in which George Eliot shifted her milieu from the English Midlands to a scene remote in time as well as place. Although many contemporary critics expressed admiration for the ambition and erudition of the novel, most found it difficult to grasp and criticised its cumbersome explorations of moral questions, its relentless accounts of details and its failure to make the reader fully engaged with the fate of the characters. On the whole, *Romola* was and still is regarded as an artistic failure.[33]

---

33 Almost all contemporary reviews of *Romola* express serious reservations about it. A selection of favourable reviews can, however, be found in David Carroll's *George Eliot: The Critical Heritage*, pp. 195-250. George Eliot herself was troubled during its composition, being obliged to deal with the problems caused by the writing itself as well as with publishing matters (the novel was first serialised in the *Cornhill Magazine*

Romola differs from Eliot's other novels in several ways. Settings in time and place have been mentioned, as the novel, depicting a far-off time and place, calls attention to differences between the world of the narrative and the contemporary reader's world. *Romola* also draws specifically on historical events, as well as on unfamiliar cultures and modes of belief. Accordingly, *Romola* includes an array of historical signposts which are unknown to most readers and which need to be explained in order for the reader to obtain the full experience of the novel. These particulars have naturally limited *Romola's* readership, but George Eliot herself seems to have been untroubled by this detail, commenting in a letter to Sara Hennell: 'Of necessity, the book is addressed to fewer readers than my previous works, and I myself have never expected – I might rather say *intended* – that the book should be as "popular" in the same sense as the others' (*Letters*, iv, 49).

With regard to narratorial commentary, however, *Romola* has a great deal in common with Eliot's earlier and later novels. The comments traverse the boundaries between general and particular in the same manner as in the other novels, and typographical indicators are used in a similar fashion, as are first-person pronouns and direct addresses to the reader. A typical example of commentary in *Romola* appears in chapter 61, where Romola's loss of faith in Savonarola is expressed:

> With the sinking of high human trust, the dignity of life sinks too; we cease to believe in our own better self, since that also is part of the common nature which is degraded in our thought; and all the finer impulses of the soul are dulled (lxi, 473).

Drawing the reader into narration now, the sage-like narrator explains Romola's feelings by way of a profound 'wisdom' intended to emphasise the similarity between the character and the reader, encouraging the reader to employ his or her own recognition in order to understand Romola. In this way, narratorial commentary in *Romola* functions in the same manner as it does in Eliot's other novels, i.e. to stimulate the reader's recognition in order for him or her to sympathise with characters. Significantly, however, *Romola* is the one Eliot novel in respect of which critical debate has spoken of an *in*ability to elicit sympathy for characters. Mary Wilson Carpenter, for instance, claims that readers are 'troubled with their lack of

---

and then published as a book in 1865, at great loss to the publishers), and with physical illness, too. The novel marked a transition in her life, as she remarked to John Walter Cross: 'I began it a young woman – I finished it an old woman'; see *George Eliot's Life as Related in Her Letters and Journals*, ed. by John W. Cross, 3 vols (New York, 1885), ii, p. 352.

sympathy for Romola' owing to conflicting voices in the narrative.[34] These conflicting voices, Carpenter argues, emanate from a difference between what Carpenter understands as the maternal voice and the 'writer' in the narrative.[35]

Along with the complexities which the distance in time and space present in the novel, these seemingly conflicting voices in the narrative are what invests the analysis of narratorial commentary in that work with an intricacy beyond the scope of the present investigation. *Romola* certainly includes narratorial commentary; but the convoluted manner with which these comments interact with the voices in the narrative would require a separate in-depth investigation.

---

34 Mary Wilson Carpenter, 'The Trouble with Romola' in *Victorian Sages and Cultural Discourse: Renegotiating Gender and Power*, ed. by Thaïs Morgan (London: Rutgers University Press, 1990), pp. 105-128 (105).

35 Carpenter, p. 128.

5. *Felix Holt*

Succeeding *Romola*, *Felix Holt, the Radical* sees a return to nineteenth-century English provincial life and the familiar, accessible matters which had made the early novels such successes with contemporary audiences. However, *Felix Holt* differs from the earlier works in terms of the author's treatment of issues and themes. Taking place during the months before and after the 1832 election on the First Reform Bill and published a year before the election on the second, *Felix Holt* is Eliot's most political novel, functioning not merely as commentary on the morals of human kind but also as a contribution to the political debate of the 1860s.[1] Also, by depicting characters and settings on a higher social plane than in the earlier novels, by compacting the action to take place within a mere six months and by introducing a decidedly forward-looking community, the novel constitutes a distinct departure from the earlier novels. This departure, however, although signifying a recovery from *Romola*, was not tantamount to artistic success on the part of Eliot who, according to several critics, had devised a legal plot too ambitious and intricate for readers to comprehend fully and a hero too uninteresting to attract any lasting attention. Generally speaking, critics tend to classify the political matrix and the downright pompous hero as the unsatisfactory parts of the novel, while the Transome and Lyon sections are considered examples of the author's genius for dramatic representation and psychological investigation.[2] Notwithstanding these classifi-

---

1 However, although the title and plot of *Felix Holt, the Radical* suggest a political novel, Fred C. Thomson, in his introduction to the Oxford World Classic's edition, argues that it does not belong to the political-novel genre *per se*, as it does not attempt to promulgate doctrines belonging to a particular party, nor is the author using the novel to convey frustrations at and criticisms of social and economical injustices in her own age; see *The Mill on the Floss*, p. viii.

2 See, for example, F. R. Leavis, *The Great Tradition*, pp. 63-74; Arnold Kettle, '*Felix Holt, the Radical*', in *Critical Essays on George Eliot*, ed. Barbara Hardy (London: Routledge & Kegan Paul, 1970), pp. 99-115; and Mary Ellen Doyle, *The Sympathetic Response*. It should be noted, however, that the novel was favourably received by a contemporary audience, so favourably in fact that Henry James in his first piece of criticism on George Eliot in an unsigned review in *The Nation*, August 1866, felt the need to dispute the

cations, *Felix Holt* marks an advance in its attempts to fuse character and society.[3] Although this fusion cannot be deemed a complete success, the novel nevertheless makes a contribution to the debate on the individual's part in society and so constitutes a sort of dress-rehearsal in its treatment of the relation between character and society which Eliot would come to perfect in *Middlemarch*.[4]

This chapter begins, as usual, with an examination of the movement between particular and general in the novel. The following section deals with comments introducing and concluding chapters; it involves some discussion of epigraphy, which *Felix Holt* is the first novel analysed in this study to contain. The technical-narratological part of this chapter ends with an analysis of the narrator's references and addresses to the reader. The thematically orientated section deals with two separate concerns: first, gender issues as broached in narratorial commentary, and second, the narrator's references to social, political and historical matters.

Particular-General-Particular

The practice of approaching a particular matter by discussing it in general terms is the essence of most narratorial comments in Eliot's work. These transitions frequently involve a circular movement in which the narrative moves from story-time now to narration now and back again, in order to relate the reader's possible recognition directly back to the narrated instance.

At times the movement between particular and general works to intellectualise or deepen the processes in characters' minds in order for the reader to appreciate how individual thoughts can be part of a bigger picture, i.e.

---

adulation, arguing that '[b]etter, perhaps, than any of George Eliot's novels does "Felix Holt" illustrate her closely wedded talent and foibles'; see *The Critical Heritage*, p. 273. For more on Henry James's reactions to *Felix Holt*, see Christine Richards, 'Towards a Critical Reputation: Henry James on *Felix Holt, the Radical*', *The George Eliot Review: Journal of the George Eliot Fellowship*, 31 (2000), 47-54.

3 Influenced by Matthew Arnold and August Comte, Eliot's novel could be interpreted as commentary on the politics enveloping the Second Reform Bill, but it is her spin-off article 'Address to Working Men, by Felix Holt' that directly serves as political agitation.

4 For discussions on character and society in *Felix Holt* and Eliot's inability to fuse the two, see David Carroll's '*Felix Holt*: Society as Protagonist', *Nineteenth-Century Fiction*, 17 (1962), 237-252, and Jerome Thale, pp. 87-105.

how particular concerns can be components of philosophical debates held on a larger, more general scale. Describing the trouble Mr Lyon experiences when attempting to convince the community that Felix's actions in the riot were intended to prevent violence and not to stir it, the narrator attaches his deliberations to a larger discussion concerning signification: 'The enthusiasms of the world are not to be stimulated by a commentary in small and subtle characters which alone can tell the whole truth; and the picture-writing in Felix Holt's troubles was of an entirely puzzling kind' (xxxvii, 297-298).

The relationship between signs and their meanings is an issue to which Eliot's narrator returns in this novel, as well as in *Middlemarch*. Concerning Harold's mistaken ideas about Esther's feelings for Felix in chapter 49, the narrator states: 'But we interpret signs of emotions as we interpret other signs – often quite erroneously, unless we have the right key to what they signify' (xlix, 387); and in *Middlemarch* the narrator argues that 'signs are small measurable things, but interpretations are illimitable' (*Middlemarch*, iii, 23). The ambiguity of the world, then, the narrator claims, does not allow for any easy ways to separate good from bad, and each individual interprets signs according to his or her particular context. The transfer from story-time now to narration now and back in the quoted comment stimulates the reader's understanding of how large philosophical concerns are manifested in private worlds. Of course, realising that signs are unreliable and recognising the frustrations this unreliability gives rise to may stimulate the reader into emotionally sympathising with Mr Lyon, who is struggling to untangle the interpretations Felix's actions have generated.[5] The reader's rational comprehension of the more general, theoretical concern facilitates his or her understanding of Mr Lyon's particular predicament on an intellectual level as well as on an emotional one.

The novel's concern with signs and interpretations is closely linked with the matter of perspectives. The movement between general and particular often serves to alter perspectives, reminding the reader of the dangers of adhering to absolutes. The narrator's emphasis on the existence of several perspectives is gradually increased with each subsequent novel. In *Felix*

---

5 In 'The Failure of Realism: *Felix Holt*', *Nineteenth-Century Fiction*, 35 (1980), 372-384, Catherine Gallagher claims (382) that the narrator is criticising the minister for not realising that signs and meanings have no absolute correlation, but I do not agree that the comment involves a criticism. On the contrary, it acknowledges a fact that is only possible to appreciate retrospectively or from an outside point of view. Situated within a particular circumstance it is impossible to refrain from interpreting signs, no matter how intellectual the character. Thus, the comment reflects on a phenomenon which is natural to all human kind, simultaneously calling attention to the shortcomings inherent in this phenomenon.

Holt the issue of multiple perspectives is raised several times in narratorial commentary. One instance appears in chapter 6, where Esther and Rufus Lyon's relationship is described. With regard to the father's subjection to his daughter's will, the narrator reflects:

> The stronger will always rule, say some, with an air of confidence which is like a lawyer's flourish, forbidding exceptions or additions. But what is strength? Is it blind wilfulness that sees no terrors, no many-linked consequences, no bruises and wounds of those whose cords it tightens? [...] There is a sort of subjection which is the peculiar heritage of largeness and of love; and strength is often only another name for willing bondage to irremediable weakness (vi, 66).

The comment problematises the notion of strength, at first disparaging a particular attitude and then questioning the whole idea of what the concept constitutes. By so doing, the narrator guides the reader through his own line of reasoning towards an understanding which alters the perspective on Mr Lyon's relation to his daughter. Instead of reading his subjection to Esther's wishes as an expression of weakness on his part, the comment encourages the reader to regard Mr Lyon's acquiescence as a manifestation of strength deriving from an innate feeling of love. By criticising a conventional notion, continuing the comment by questioning the definition of strength and then making his own reflection, the narrator steers the reader towards the 'right' understanding of the relationship between father and daughter. This generalisation does not attempt to elicit a latent recognition; rather, it guides the reader through a line of reasoning which serves to adjust his or her perspective on the particular circumstances in the narrative.

The adjustment of perspectives is often facilitated by the conjunction 'but'.[6] Functioning as a co-ordinating conjunction, 'but' expresses a re-directing or contrasting general reflection which offers new angles on a particular discussion. Referring to Matthew Jermyn's relationship to Johnson, the narrator states:

> Jermyn was aware of Johnson's weaknesses, and thought he had flattered them sufficiently. But on the point of knowing when we are disagreeable, our human nature is fallible. Our lavender-water, our smiles, our compliments, and other polite falsities, are constantly offensive, when in the very nature of them they can only be meant to attract admiration and regard. Jermyn had often been unconsciously disagreeable to Johnson, over and above the constant offence of being an ostentatious patron (xxix, 236-237).

---

6 As many as fourteen narratorial comments in *Felix Holt* are introduced with 'but', but none, apart from in the introduction to the novel, are begun by the causal conjunction 'for'.

This type of 'but' frequently introduces comments which alter or extend particular perspectives in an attempt to offer readers a comprehensive view of specific relationships and situations. In the example quoted above, the narrator explains the complexities inherent in the Jermyn-Johnson relationship by including the reader in a reflection on behaviour typical of human nature, thus encouraging him or her to appreciate both Jermyn's misinterpretation of Johnson and Johnson's indignation. The comment forms part of Eliot's larger theme of shifting perspectives, incorporated in all her novels, but it does not compassionately urge the reader to sympathise with either Jermyn or Johnson; rather, it endeavours to elicit recognition in order for the reader to understand the intricate details of the relationship between the two men. As with other comments regarding Lawyer Jermyn, the reflection stimulates the reader's recognition, not so much in order for him or her to sympathise with the character – as this would entail an element of excuse for him – but simply to understand his conduct, without necessarily condoning it.

A significant number of statements in story-time now which follow and particularise a general narratorial comment begin with the phrase 'so it was' or 'thus it was'.[7] The inverted phrase emphasises the link between the generalisation and the continuing fiction in story-time now. These linking phrases frequently refer to a particular figure's characteristics, introducing the reader to mind-processes or emotions which he or she is invited to recognise before actually ascribing them to a particular character.[8] Referring to the fashion in which Lawyer Jermyn has had to compromise his morals in order to satisfy his greed, the narrator links the phrase: 'So it was with Matthew Jermyn' (ix, 99) to an account communicating the human propensity for giving in to temptation. Even more interesting, however, is that this account is expressed in the form of a parable.[9] By telling a story about a German poet, the narrator makes an analogy to the way in which Jermyn has become successful in satisfying his material wants:

> A German poet was intrusted with a particularly fine sausage, which he was to convey to the donor's friend at Paris. In the course of a long journey he smelt the sausage; he got hungry, and desired to taste it; he pared a morsel off, then another, and

---

7 Four comments in the novel are followed by 'so/thus it was' and two are followed by a single 'so'.

8 Cf. the narratorial comment ending the novel's introduction, which presents the reader with Mrs Transome's emotional situation in general terms before introducing the character herself.

9 *Felix Holt* incorporates several comments which make allegorical comparisons, but the comment above and the parable in the introduction are the only examples that can be considered full parables.

another, in successive moments of temptation, till at last the sausage was, humanly speaking, at an end. The offence had not been premeditated. The poet had never loved meanness, but he loved sausage; and the result was undeniably awkward.

So it was with Matthew Jermyn (ix, 99).

Contrary to the parable in the novel's introduction, this comment hovers between story-time now and narration now. It is clearly a statement which operates to arrest the reader's attention by looking beyond story-time now. Yet, it is not necessarily a comment which meets the reader in narration now, since it embarks on another story intended to symbolise and parallel a specific phenomenon in story-time now. Consequently, it does not acknowledge or 'meet' the reader on a mutual, narration-now level, but instead maintains the established roles adopted by narrator and reader without altering the distance between the two. However, the comment does temporarily shift the reader's focus away from the narrated story, as well as giving him or her a taste of the narrator's humour. The comical analogy to Lawyer Jermyn's insatiability for social influence and material gain at the expense of his own morality somewhat diminishes the culpability of his conduct and invites the reader not only to smile in recognition at the poor German poet who suddenly realises that he is sausageless on arrival in Paris, but accordingly to understand how Jermyn could have 'nibbled' at his own principles for the sake of gaining influence in his community. Therefore, in the sense that the comment undermines the gravity of Jermyn's immorality by encouraging the reader to understand how easily temptation may overpower principles, it serves the same function as most comments in narration now, that is, to increase the reader's understanding by relating the particular diegetic instance to a sphere beyond the narrative.

Introductions and Conclusions

Unlike the earlier novels, *Felix Holt* contains a general introduction in which the narrator presents a multifaceted survey of English life in 1831 in order to establish a historical, political and social context in which the ensuing story will take place.[10] The introduction takes the reader on a stage-coach journey through the English Midlands, travelling spatially from ru-

---

10 *Romola* was the first of Eliot's novels to be introduced by a 'proem'. For further discussion on the contents of the introduction in *Felix Holt*, see David Carroll, *Conflict of Interpretations*, pp. 201-205.

ral landscapes to villages to towns as well as travelling temporally through the contrasts made between past and present, symbolised in the juxtapositions of coach and railway as modes of transport. Edging the reader closer and closer towards Treby Magna, the introduction ends in the manner of a long narratorial comment which serves first as a prophesy and then, in the narrator's own words, as a parable which reads:

> The poets have told us of a dolorous enchanted forest in the under world. The thorn-bushes there, and the thick-barked stems, have human histories hidden in them; the power of unuttered cries dwells in the passionless-seeming branches, and the red warm blood is darkly feeding the quivering nerves of a sleepless memory that watches through all dreams. These things are a parable (Introduction, 11).[11]

The poets referred to are Virgil and Dante. In Book III of the *Aeneid*, Aeneas, after escaping from Troy, prepares to offer sacrifices by tearing at the roots and branches of a tree. As he tears the tree, dark blood soaks the ground under him and the tree begins to speak, imploring him to stop. The second allusion is to Dante's 'Wood of the Suicides' in Canto XIII of *Inferno*, where Dante breaks off a branch from a tree which begins to wail in pain.[12] These classical works serve as intertexts preparing the reader for Mrs Transome's tragic fate, living as a 'passionless-seeming branch' filled to the brim with 'unuttered cries' in the hell that is Transome Court. The introduction thus begins with a wide perspective which gradually narrows until it takes on the form of narration now and ends in an intimate reflection on human misery, in particular referring to Mrs Transome's silent suffering.

The parable foreshadows Mrs Transome's agonised character, the details of which follow in chapter 1; but it also somewhat misleadingly suggests itself as a premonition to the novel. The introduction which slowly but steadily leads up to Mrs Transome's story gives the impression that her story constitutes a major theme in the novel, that Mrs Transome's pain is somehow what the novel is 'about', despite its title.[13] Her story is of

---

11 In '*Felix Holt*: Language, the Bible and the Problematic of Meaning', *Nineteenth-Century Fiction*, 37 (1982), 146-169, Robin Sheets argues that George Eliot encourages the reader to consider two possible meanings of the term 'parable'. First, it could have a straightforward meaning – a simple story which conveys some type of moral example – but additionally the term could suggest that the author 'has written something enigmatic, a dark saying that would align her with Johnson, Antiochus, and other devious agents of obscurity' (169).

12 For a detailed account of Dantean influences in *Felix Holt*, see Andrew Thompson's article 'George Eliot, Dante and Moral Choice in *Felix Holt, the Radical*', *Modern Language Review*, 86 (1991), 553-566.

13 In *Vocation and Desire: George Eliot's Heroines* (London: Routledge, 1989) Dorothea Barrett makes a similar point, arguing that 'the author's introduction suggests that this novel will be, in some way, a guided tour of hell' (p. 119).

course only a small part of the novel, but the possible misunderstanding the introduction gives rise to may not be entirely erroneous in view of the important theme of public versus private in the book. The most famous quotation from *Felix Holt* deals with this topic, stating that 'there is no private life which has not been determined by a wider public life' (iii, 43).

The introduction presents the public lives of shepherds, manufacturers, dissenters and eventually the public life of the Transomes. Towards the end of these accounts, it adjusts the perspective to show how public life is related to the most private of worlds presented in the novel, namely the tragic life of Mrs Transome. Not only does this process from public to private signal a major theme; it also demonstrates the narrator's ability to move between 'public matters' and the 'private lot of a few men and women' (iii, 43), a movement which resembles the function of so many narratorial comments in George Eliot's novels, i.e. the movement between general and particular. The concluding comment in the introduction thus adopts a tone of premonition on two separate levels. On the one hand, it serves as a preparation for the reader's 'meeting' with Mrs Transome. Significantly, the analysis of the type of torment Mrs Transome undergoes precedes the introduction of the character herself. As if anxious about of the reader's response to her sin, the narrator attempts to elicit sympathy for her situation before depicting the causes behind it. Hence, apart from the coachman's brief account, Mrs Transome is initially introduced to the reader through his or her recognition of silent suffering and repressed emotions. On the other hand, the comment, in conjunction with the whole introduction, indicates a major theme, preparing the reader for a narrative which vacillates between public and private, illustrating how these are ultimately interwoven.

Felix Holt is the first novel discussed here to include chapter epigraphs. It is questionable whether prose epigraphs deriving from the author should be considered narratorial commentary or should be treated separately, as they are deliberately disconnected from the actual text. In effect, the narrative voice in the epigraph presents a narrator on a different structural level and operating outside the framework of the story. Furthermore, it is possible to discern a distinction between the language employed by the epigraphic voice and the narratorial commentator's language. Introducing chapter 8, the epigraphic tone seems more formal, declaring, for example, that 'then *happeneth* a time' (viii, 89, my italics). The inverted word-order and old-fashioned conjugation of the verb reinforces the impression of ceremony, distinguishing the epigraphic voice from the voice or voices communicating narratorial comments. Therefore, although epigraphs re-

semble narratorial comments in supplying the reader with reflections, premonitions and analyses, they cannot be considered part of the narratorial
commentary in narration now because of the differences in language, tone,
structural level and, of course, for most of the epigraphs in Eliot's later
novels, genre.[14]

Still, it is impossible to disregard the epigraph to chapter 8, particularly
when considering introductory narratorial comments. Chapter 8 is in fact
preceded by two epigraphs; the first is taken from Shakespeare's *Henry
IV* and relates directly to the discussion of 'Rumour' in the introductory
passage. The Shakespearian intertext reads: 'Rumour doth double like the
voice and echo' (viii, 89). The second epigraph is one that Eliot presumably wrote herself, and it serves as a reflection on the chapter as a whole.
The epigraph compares the 'mind of a man' to a 'country which was once
open to squatters' (viii, 89) and continues:

> But then happeneth a time when new and hungry comers dispute the land; and
> there is trial of strength, and the stronger wins. Nevertheless the first squatters be
> they who have prepared the ground, and the crops to the end will be sequent [...]
> somewhat on the primal labour and sowing (viii, 89).

Of course, the reader cannot know to which characters the epigraph refers
until he or she has read the chapter. In this sense it constitutes a premonition of what will take place in the chapter, as well as an advance reflection on the psychological processes at work in one or several characters'
minds. But by regarding the epigraphic voice as separate from the voice(s)
of narratorial commentary, the reader's transition from one to the other is
actually facilitated as the two pull in different directions, each introducing
a particular discussion. At first the prose epigraph seems entirely uncon-
nected to the introductory passage; this particular epigraph may in fact
seem most relevant after the reader has read the chapter, at which point he
or she understands that the reflection relates to both Harold Transome and
his mother. Nevertheless, the introductory narratorial comment in this example must be read as an independent introduction to the chapter despite
the preceding motto, not only because of the differences between the two
forms of narrative mentioned above, but also because the epigraph relates

---

14 See my article 'Influential Voices in George Eliot's Epigraphs', *Vetenskapssocietetens Årsbok
of 2005* (Lund: Vetenskapssocieteten i Lund/The New Society of Letters at Lund, 2005),
pp. 5-18. See also J. R. Tye, 'George Eliot's Unascribed Mottoes', *Nineteenth-Century
Fiction*, 22 (1967), 235-249, and David Leon Higdon's interesting article 'George Eliot
and the Art of the Epigraph', *Nineteenth-Century Fiction*, 25 (1970), 127-151, in which
Higdon discusses the literary functions of epigraphs in Eliot's novels.

to the chapter as a whole, while the introductory comment merely serves as a general reflection relating to the ensuing particularities.

Discussing 'Rumour' allegorically as 'that talkative maiden' who is really nothing more than 'a very old maid' and who 'does no more than chirp a wrong guess or a lame story into the ear of a fellow-gossip' (viii, 89), the comment alerts the reader's attention to a general social phenomenon before relating it to the particular situation in the narrative, where the rumour about Harold's fortune spreads like wildfire in Treby Magna. But besides serving as a general introduction to a particular issue, the comment also, albeit humorously, criticises this common social phenomenon, asserting that rumours and gossip spread 'with the help of a plentiful stupidity against which we have never yet had any authorized form of prayer' (viii, 89). Although it is impossible to disregard the glint in the narrator's eye in this statement, it forms yet another interesting example of a comment in which the narrator is scathingly critical of human imperfectability rather than sympathetic, as is the common practice in Eliot's narratorial comments. Again, the narrator is cynical as to what can be expected of humankind, and it is evident that the 'stupidity' referred to here is very different from the qualities of those 'ugly, stupid, inconsistent people' whom the narrator in *Adam Bede* asks the reader to 'tolerate, pity and love' (*Adam Bede*, xvii, 176). *Felix Holt* hence reveals a narratorial attitude which has few reservations about acknowledging and condemning blemishes on humankind. On the contrary, the entire second volume of the novel, in which the riot scenes are described, demonstrates the hazardous situation that Harold Transome's Radical campaign has created by inciting the masses with drink and false promises.[15] Accordingly, caustic remarks like the one above corroborate the notion of an existence of 'plentiful stupidity' which in this novel, in contrast to *Adam Bede*, the reader is not asked to pity and love but rather to condemn and fear.

---

15 Several critics ascribe these rioting scenes to George Eliot's (and many others' in the nineteenth century) fears of a revolutionary mob. Indeed, the fear of revolution was very real, as Walter E. Houghton states in *The Victorian Frame of Mind, 1830-1870*: 'For all its solid and imposing strength, Victorian society, particularly in the period before 1850, was shot through, from top to bottom, with the dread of some wild outbreak of the masses that would overthrow the established order and confiscate private property' (54-55). Raymond Williams also discusses *Felix Holt* as the expression of a fear of revolution and sees in Eliot and her contemporaries a dread of democracy founded on distrust of the uneducated classes. Williams claims that Eliot's 'view of the common people is uncomfortably close to that of Carlyle in *Shooting Niagara*' in which Carlyle describes the lower classes in unrestrained words: ' "blockheadism, gullibility, bribeability, amenability to beer and balderdash" ', *Culture and Society, 1780-1950* (London: Chatto & Windus, 1958), p. 105.

Six chapters in *Felix Holt* end in a narratorial comment (three in a row from chapter 16 to 18), and three of these include the narrator's referring to himself as 'I'. While not purporting to be personally included within the fiction, the narrator's 'I' suggests a special engagement with a particular matter and comes across as an eager attempt to influence the reader's response. Besides, the 'I' implies a presence on a level closer to the reader's, bringing reader and narrator together, but at the expense of the narrator's reliability as the voice of the extradiegetic sage is replaced by that of a personally involved persona. The significance of an engaged narrator who concludes passages *in propria persona*, as it were, is that the closeness between reader and narrator is emphasised at a crucial point in the narrative, and so remains with the reader a little bit longer. For example, in chapter 37, the narrator refers to his own opinions in relation to how Mr Johnson came to be working both for and against Jermyn in the matter of Esther's claim to Transome Court:

> Mr Johnson's character was not much more exceptional than his double chin.
>
> No system, religious or political, I believe, has laid it down as a principle that all men are alike virtuous, or even that all people rated for £80 houses are an honour to their species (xxxvii, 301).

Unusually for commentary in Eliot's work, the statement plainly asserts that all humans are not equally honourable, implying that Mr Johnson belongs to those who are less so. The narrator is not counteracting the reader's possible prejudices against a dubious character but instead reinforcing such prejudice under the claim that it would be unreasonable to assume that all individuals are equally righteous. The comment therefore differs considerably from other comments in respect of attitude. Although it gives the impression of expressing a general truth it also conveys a sense of resignation on the part of the narrator. Given its position in the conclusion to chapter 37, the comment carries particular weight. Additionally, the narrator's communication of a personal opinion – the presence of 'I believe' – brings reader and narrator closer together, as discussed above. Taken together, these factors unveil a frankness far removed from high-flying ideals. Instead the statement expresses a candid acknowledgement of what can be expected of the world and its inhabitants, an acknowledgement which temporarily 'humanises' the sage-like, high-flown narrator.

As in Eliot's early novels, the narrator gives the impression that the characters and events presented in the narrative are renderings of actual history, that the characters have existed and the events taken place. However, in *Felix Holt* the author devotes less space to the creation of this illusion. The quotation above is the first example of a comment in which the narrator implies a personal relation to the presumably non-fictive characters. In *Adam Bede*, the reader learns that the narrator is someone to whom Adam tells his story in his old age; in *The Mill on the Floss*, the narrator gives the impression of having come back to the community of St Ogg's, of which he has childhood memories; and in *Silas Marner*, the story is dated too far back for the narrator to have any part in it. In *Felix Holt*, however, as mentioned above, the narrator has no evident relation to the fictive characters and events, and apart from the epilogue the quotation above constitutes the only comment in which he hints at having personal relations to fictive figures. Consequently, *Silas Marner* and *Felix Holt* seem to mark a gradual movement away from the personally involved narrator.[16]

The conclusion of the long last passage in chapter 16 is articulated by the narrator who reflects on the events of a particular day, depicted as if he had been there:

> At present, looking back on that day at Treby, it seems to me that the sadder illusion lay with Harold Transome, who was trusting in his own skill to shape the success of his own morrows, ignorant of what many yesterdays had determined for him beforehand (xvi, 157).

The narrator modifies his previous argument by contrasting Mr Lyon's illusions – which originate in ideology – with Harold's, which stem from an overestimation of his own capabilities and a lack of awareness of what has happened in the past. The juxtaposition between Harold's illusions and Mr Lyon's epitomises a significant concern intrinsic to all Eliot's novels – the moral disparity between one character reaching for self-serving goals and another character striving after altruistic ones.[17] Yet, the comment expresses a modest sympathy for the complacent Harold who, the narrator realises in retrospect, is ignorant of the humiliations awaiting him. By inviting the reader to share in this hindsight, the narrator attempts to conjure up some sympathy for Harold, indicating that as a character he

---

16 Although not referring to narratorial commentary, and speaking of Eliot's treatment of Mrs Transome in particular, F. R. Leavis early on acknowledged a parallel development, arguing that the 'beneficent relation between the artist and intellectual is to be seen in the new impersonality of the Transome theme [...] the directly personal engagement of the novelist – that we feel in Maggie Tulliver's intensities even at their most valid is absent here' (67-68).

17 David Carroll also discusses this distinction and makes a comparison between Harold and Felix who, he argues, are both characters with 'a "too confident self-reliance," but whereas the latter's is directed towards an altruistic object, Harold's is egoistic'; see 'Society as Protagonist', p. 247.

may not be the best of Christians, but that the sins for which he will have to pay will not have been his own.

Consequently, some concluding narratorial comments in *Felix Holt* act as premonitions to forthcoming chapters while others serve as comments on the chapter at hand. What these conclusions have in common is that they wrap the chapter up, as it were, by reinforcing the narrator's presence or authoritative status. This narratorial manifestation also draws the reader in, reducing his or her distance to the narrator at a structurally crucial point in the narrative. *Felix Holt* also introduces the chapter epigraph which expresses commentary on the chapter at hand but which cannot be defined as narratorial commentary *per se*. Although epigraphs can serve the same functions as comments, they nevertheless emanate from voices detached from the narratorial persona.

References and Addresses to the Reader

Felix Holt makes references to the reader and to his or her response to characters and events, but less frequently than *Adam Bede* and *The Mill on the Floss*. Furthermore, when these instances do occur they seem to acknowledge the reader's possible part in, or relation to, the text more subtly than corresponding passages in the earlier books. Still, some comments candidly recognise the reader's presence by addressing him or her directly. Having described Harold Transome, the narrator concludes his portrayal, stating:

> If Harold Transome had been among your acquaintances, and you had observed his qualities through the   medium of his agreeable person, bright smile, and a certain easy charm which accompanies sensuousness when unsullied by coarseness – through the medium also of the many opportunities in which he would have made himself useful or pleasant to you – you would have thought him a good fellow, highly acceptable as a guest, a colleague, or a brother-in-law. Whether all mothers would have liked him as a son, is another question (viii. 93-94).

Previous to this statement the reader has to a large extent observed Harold through the eyes of his mother, which has inevitably left the reader with some prejudice towards his character. The comment, however, without attempting to alter the reader's perception of Harold, situates him in the reader's sphere; that is, the reader is made to imagine the fictive character in his or her own non-fictive world. By encouraging the reader to disregard his or her prior knowledge of Harold's character and merely visualise him as the delightful candidate that he can be, the narrator promotes the reader's understanding of how Harold is received outside his domestic sphere in the community of Treby Magna. Besides, by inspiring the reader to conceive of Harold as an actual acquaintance, the narrator reduces the distance between fictive character and reader, and Harold becomes more than merely a fictitious construct. In this example, the narrator hence diminishes the distance between the fictive and non-fictive – not, as in many other instances, by inviting the reader into the fictitious scenes, but instead by pulling a character out of the narrative. By encouraging the reader to consider a character as part of the reader's 'real' world, the statement downplays the aspect of fictionality in the novel.

However, the comment quoted above conveys a sense of ambiguity as to the pleasantness of Harold's personality. The 'medium of his agreeable person' of course implies that there is another medium of the not-so-agreeable person, and that the 'easy charm' is not at all times 'unsullied by coarseness'. Moreover, by insinuating that Harold is often highly regarded as a guest or a colleague, but not always as a son, the narrator places doubt in the reader's mind as to the genuine agreeableness of Harold's character. Mrs Transome, of course, is implicitly accused of being disappointed with her son at his return; but the comment indicates that in this case Mrs Transome's expectations have not been too high. In fact, it goes even further, questioning whether other mothers would have liked him for a son.[18] The comment is therefore ambiguous, as it serves to commend and disparage Harold at the same time. In a sense it seems both to reveal and to conceal something about Harold's character, which might make the reader as mystified when considering his experiences abroad as the characters surrounding him in Treby Magna are.

An indirect reference to the reader's anticipated response appears in chapter 6. With regard to Mr Lyon's relationship with Annette Ledru and its consequences for his sense of spirituality, the narrator reveals some anxiety as to the impression Mr Lyon is making on the reader: 'Mr Lyon will perhaps seem a very simple personage, with pitiably narrow theories; but none of our theories are quite large enough for all the disclosures of time' (vi, 73). By including the reader in the reflection through the use of the first-person pronoun, the narrator checks the reader's possible sense of su-

---

18 The continuation of the comment implies that even though Harold is kind to his mother, she is afraid of him. This fear, ascribed to nothing tangible, infects the relationship between the two and consequently affects the reader's interpretation of Harold.

periority in relation to Mr Lyon, arguing that few world views stand the test of time and suggesting that eventually the reader's philosophies will also seem antiquated and narrow. However, this curb on the reader's potential sense of superiority is less explicit than similar instances in Eliot's first two novels. After discontinuing the practice in *Silas Marner*, *Felix Holt* sees a resumption of references to the reader's response, but here expected reactions are commented on with more subtlety and finesse than in the earlier novels. In this example, by bringing the reader into the general reflection, associating him or her with the character, with the narrator himself and with human nature in general, the comment reduces the distance between the reader and Mr Lyon and so endeavours to prevent the reader from censuring the character.

As with references to the reader in earlier books, the first-person pronoun is used extensively to reduce the distance between characters, narrator and reader. Suspecting Felix of being an electioneering agent in chapter 11, Mr Chubb, the publican, attempts to impress him by excessive self-promotion. Blowing his own trumpet, Mr Chubb claims: 'And in the way of hacting for any man, them are fools that don't employ me' (xi, 111). The narrator comments:

> We mortals sometimes cut a pitiable figure in our attempts at display. We may be sure of our own merits, yet fatally ignorant of the point of view from which we are regarded by our neighbour. Our fine patterns in tattooing may be far from throwing him into a swoon of admiration, though we turn ourselves all round to show them. Thus it was with Mr Chubb (xi, 111).

Rather than relating to Felix, who in this scene is acting the part of the 'straight character', the reader is asked to acknowledge his or her own resemblance to Mr Chubb, implying that he or she – together with the narrator – is really no better than the boasting publican. This attitude towards Mr Chubb differs from the approach adopted in the introduction to chapter 8, where the narrator speaks of 'a plentiful stupidity'. In the sense that comments in *Felix Holt* sometimes express diverging attitudes to characters, the novel bears some resemblance to *The Mill on the Floss*, where two narratorial attitudes are patently felt.[19] However, these diverging attitudes

---

19 In 'George Eliot and Arnold: The Narrator's Voice and Ideology in *Felix Holt: the Radical*', *Literature and History*, 11 (1985), 229-240, Lyn Pykett acknowledges the presence of inconsistent attitudes in *Felix Holt* and discusses two distinct narratorial voices. One, she remarks, is the voice of 'mellow wisdom' (229), which is a voice inspired by moral sympathy seeking to communicate 'a unified set of values' (234); the other, Pykett argues, is a sharply incisive voice which employs irony 'to proclaim [the narrator's] superiority to, and distance from, the class-divided world he describes' (232). Although Pykett does not discuss narratorial comments in particular, her classifications work well in relation

are much less pronounced in *Felix Holt*, and are more symptomatic of a narrator regarding his characters from various angles than of the manifestation of two distinct narratorial stances.

Some instances of the narrator's 'I' have been mentioned above in relation to introductory and concluding commentary. However, a number of 'I's which do not belong in narration now should be mentioned, too. These references to the narrator's presence take place in story-time now, but nevertheless convey an impression of narratorial control. In chapter 6, for example, the narrator refers to his knowledge of Esther's psyche when remarking on the satisfaction she gets out of spending her earnings on clothes and accessories: 'I cannot say that she had any pangs of conscience on this score' (vi, 66). Although this statement is not a narratorial comment as such, it establishes the narrator's omniscience, demonstrating his familiarity with a character's mind. By emphasising the narrator's omniscient status, this type of 'I'-statement actually reinforces the fictionality of the narrative.

Another instance appears in the epilogue to the novel, but here the reverse effect is solicited. Commenting on the fates of the novel's main protagonists, the narrator states: 'As to the town in which Felix Holt now resides, I will keep that a secret, lest he should be troubled by any visitor having the insufferable motive of curiosity' (Epilogue, 398). This statement both suggests the authenticity of the narrative and highlights the narrator's exclusive knowledge, demonstrating that the narrator's privileged access to information need not spoil the validity of the narrative.[20]

---

to the different attitudes in the novel's commentary. Arguing that the sudden shifts in tone and attitude are part of the novel's Arnoldian strategy, Pykett maintains that the narrator's incisive voice serves to reveal the blemishes existing in all parts of society and to undermine the reader's preconceived notions about class or convention which, she states, were notions which Arnold also criticised in *Culture and Anarchy*. Pykett's point is that the shifting narratorial voice in *Felix Holt*, on the one hand, by the use of irony, uncovers the 'limitations of the ordinary self' (238) but, on the other hand, is eventually replaced by a sympathetic voice of wisdom, which expresses a 'positive social vision of the best self' (238). What is interesting about Pykett's article is that she recognises that Eliot's ironic, incisive voice makes no distinction between classes, i.e. that it approaches all classes represented in the novel in a similar manner. Her point somewhat challenges the idea that *Felix Holt* is a novel in which Eliot expresses personal prejudices towards the uneducated classes. Rather, Pykett's article suggests that *Felix Holt* unfolds a vision of culture and of every individual's power to strive for a 'best self' (234), regardless of social class. This argument is, however, based on Pykett's opinion that Felix himself has received too much attention as Eliot's mouthpiece, and that Rufus Lyon and Esther figure as representatives of the author's opinions.

20 Elizabeth Starr also notices that in this passage 'the narrator both reminds readers of her superior knowledge and retains the prerogative to be the only one in possession of it'; see ' "Influencing the Moral Taste": Literary Work, Aesthetics, and Social Change in *Felix Holt, the Radical*', *Nineteenth-Century Literature*, 56 (2001-2002), 52-75 (p. 74).

Moreover, the statement is preceded by a further underpinning of authenticity through the narrator's admission that he has had no correspondence with anyone in Treby Magna after Felix's and Esther's departure, arguing that whether anything can be said about the area on the basis of its not producing 'a Radical candidate, I leave to the all-wise – I mean the newspapers' (Epilogue, 398). The irony of this statement further establishes the narrator's authority and reduces his distance to the reader, who is expected to share in the wry bow to the press.

Accordingly, the Epilogue attempts to establish the events of the narrative as though they had actually happened by means of addressing the reader directly. These addresses are resumed in *Felix Holt* after having been abandoned in *Silas Marner*. However, although these references and addresses serve the same end as in the earlier books, i.e. to elicit the reader's recognition and active participation in the narrative, these instances in *Felix Holt* are fewer and more subtly expressed than in *Adam Bede* and *The Mill on the Floss*.

Gender Issues

The thematically orientated section of this chapter deals with gender issues and with socio-political and historical references. *Felix Holt* is the first Eliot novel to discuss gender issues in an earnest manner without resorting to ridicule of idiosyncratic behaviour. Consequently, this is the first section in the present study to be titled 'gender issues', although both *Adam Bede* and *The Mill on the Floss* are also concerned with gender. Furthermore, *Felix Holt* is the only Eliot novel to foreground social and political issues as part of a novelistic concern. Therefore the last section of this chapter will investigate how, and to what degree, these concerns are dealt with in narratorial commentary.

At the time when *Felix Holt* was written the question of female enfranchisement had become a critical issue in political debates, as feminist groups stressed the connection between developing the franchise to include working-class men and offering it to women. In 1866 John Stuart Mill presented Parliament with a petition for female suffrage signed by, among others, Harriet Martineau and Barbara Bodichon. Together with the Reform Bill of 1867, although the Bill still refused women the right to vote, the petition roused a political awareness which stimulated the movement towards female suffrage. Viewed in this context *Felix Holt* is a highly topical novel not only about the politics of the first Reform Bill, and by extension the second, but also about sexual politics directly prior to the organisation of the feminist movement.

Even so, George Eliot was more ambivalent than some of her feminist friends; expressing mixed feelings towards women's suffrage, she viewed it in relation to larger issues of social and political change.[21] Bonnie Zimmerman claims that *Felix Holt* aligns parliamentary politics with sexual politics in that it maintains that the uneducated masses in the electoral sphere, who endanger social order and create chaos and unrest, are analogous to the threat to the security of the domestic sphere caused by the egoistic and shallow individual woman.[22] According to Zimmerman, Mrs Transome, whose selfishness makes domestic harmony impossible, is hence contrasted to Esther Lyon, who learns to subdue selfish ends in order to be educated in the art of resignation and love. Whether or not one agrees that Mrs Transome's resistance to oppression and bitterness at her loss of sexual power can be compared to the oppression felt by the working classes, it is clear that the narrator in *Felix Holt* invests a large number of comments in Mrs Transome's particular plight.

Mrs Transome's dilemma consists in her entrapment within society's conventional ideas about the responsibilities and abilities of women. The restrictions these ideas impose on her are the subject of a number of elucidating comments. Introducing the complex relationship between the adult Harold and his mother, the narrator discusses motherhood:

> The mother's love is at first an absorbing delight, blunting all other sensibilities; it is an expansion of the animal existence; it enlarges the imagined range for self to move in; but in after years it can only continue to be joy on the same terms as other

---

21 In 1853 George Eliot wrote to Clementia Taylor: ' "Enfranchisement of women" only makes creeping progress; and that is best, for woman does not yet deserve a much better lot than man gives her'; see *Letters*, ii, 86. By 1867, however, Eliot had modified her views, writing to Mrs Taylor that 'on the whole I am inclined to hope for much good from the serious presentation of women's claims before Parliament' (*Letters*, iv, 366); but only four weeks later she criticised Sara Hennell for campaigning 'for an extremely doubtful good'; see *Letters*, iv, 390. But George Eliot was painfully aware of her own ambivalence, as she admitted to Jane Elizabeth Senior: 'There is no subject on which I am more inclined to hold my peace and learn, than on the "Women Question". It seems to me to overhang abysses, of which even prostitution is not the worst. Conclusions seem easy so long as we keep large blinkers on and look in the direction of our own private path'; see *Letters*, v, 58.

22 Bonnie Zimmerman, '*Felix Holt* and the True Power of Womanhood', *ELH*, 46 (1979), 432-451. Zimmerman contends that Eliot was greatly influenced by the ideas espoused in *Woman's Mission* (Boston: Wm. Crosby & Co., 1840), which viewed women's moral influence as being rooted in resignation and love.

long-lived love – that is, by much suppression of self, and power of living in the experience of another (i, 22).

According to Zimmerman, the comment conveys a favourable view of motherhood and reinforces the idea of deep love emanating from the suppression of selfish wants which, she argues, is the type of love that Eliot herself proposed as the basis for woman's influence.[23] However, the continuation of the comment reads: 'Mrs Transome had darkly felt the pressure of that unchangeable fact' (i, 22). For Mrs Transome, then, the suppression of self is a pressure which she cannot escape. Rather than expressing an idealisation of motherhood, the comment makes it clear that even a mother's love must make some kind of commitment outside the self, that her love does not spring automatically from her own self but rather from the suppression of that self.[24] Zimmerman acknowledges that the supposed idealisation of motherhood in the comment quoted above is contradicted in other comments, most expressly in the comment following the narrator's analysis of the type of character Harold is in chapter 8:

> It is a fact perhaps kept a little too much in the background, that mothers have a self larger than their maternity, and that when their sons have become taller than themselves, and are gone from them to college or into the world, there are wide spaces of their time which are not filled with praying for their boys, reading old letters, and envying yet blessing those who are attending to their shirt-buttons (viii, 94).

Situated beside each other and in isolation from their contexts, the comments seem to embody conflicting views about the nature of motherhood. However, considering the first comment in context it becomes apparent

---

23 See Zimmerman, p. 442. Cf. also Nünning, p. 232.

24 Zimmerman and I read the passage differently. Zimmerman argues that 'Mrs Transome's stubborn egoism prevents her from making this maternal redefinition of power' and that 'she rejects motherhood, and in doing so, rejects her womanliness' (442-443). But judging from the commentary in context, the narrator is not implying that Mrs Transome's egoism hinders her from suppressing her own wants in order to live through Harold. Indeed, she very much attempts to do this. The reason she fails, however, and the reason for her bitterness, is that a total suppression of self is not, of course, the means through which love and harmony are attained. Also, Mrs Transome is much more than a wife and mother; but in the eyes of the community in which she lives, any qualities she may offer which exceed the roles of mother and wife are unwanted. Thus, her bitterness emanates from a frustration at only having had the opportunity to develop an identity as wife and mother, and at being without an identity once she finds that she is not needed in those roles. It is understandable that the comments may be interpreted differently in view of Eliot's own ideas about female resignation and influence as evinced in her correspondence, but independently of this information the comments in the text do not subscribe to any ideas about female resignation being the only source of a mother's love for her child.

that the love emanating from a mother's resignation of self depends on the fulfilment of certain conditions, the most important being that the 'experience of another' is one which the mother respects and approves of. Of course, Harold has disappointed his family by taking up banking at Smyrna instead of embarking on a diplomatic career in Constantinople; but more importantly, Harold has disappointed his mother by failing to express interest in the lives of his family back home. His vulgar existence and his indifference to his family in England, in addition to the temporal distance between meetings, make it almost impossible for Mrs Transome to live through the experiences of her son.[25] She must attempt to find a meaningful existence elsewhere, as she does with the management of the estate.

Accordingly, the narrator modifies the first comment, stating that Mrs Transome had 'clung to the belief that somehow the possession of this son was the best thing she had lived for; to believe otherwise would have made her memory too ghastly a companion' (i, 22). The statement indicates that the suppression of self, the phenomenon of a love fostered by the experiences of another, is not a natural fact but a theory which Mrs Transome has to convince herself of; that is, it surfaces as a belief which she can choose either to adopt or discard, not as an instinct which appears automatically and naturally with maternity. Therefore, the first comment, which initially seems to idealise motherhood, actually depicts the suppression of self as a pressure which Mrs Transome must force herself to submit to – in other words, loving Harold by living through his experiences does not automatically emerge as a natural feeling because she is his mother. Instead, Mrs Transome needs to 'cling to the belief' that through Harold her cup of happiness will be filled. Rather than contradicting the first comment, then, the second quotation further reinforces and reformulates the first, expressing the fact that mothers are women whose identities encompass a great deal more besides that which forms part of their roles as mothers.

Undoubtedly, Mrs Transome is an egoistic character. However, her egoism is not a primary issue in the comments quoted above through which the reader is invited to participate in her crises, but also, in more general terms, to appreciate the constraints women could be imprisoned in.

---

25 Besides, Mrs Transome is bitter as it is the hated eldest son Durfey who is heir to the Transome estate, giving her little opportunity to rejoice in the experiences of Harold as he must make a career of his own. The death of Durfey changes the situation and Mrs Transome sees some hope, but Harold's return to England turns out to be a disappointment. For similarities between the Transome plot and classic tragedy, see Fred C. Thomson, 'Felix Holt as Classic Tragedy', Nineteenth-Century Fiction, 16 (1961), 47-58.

Mrs Transome's predicament, and the narrator's commentary regarding it, clearly underlines the impossible situation of suppressing self within a confined role only to find that once the role is made redundant, there is no self to fall back on, which leaves the subject in a crisis of identity which may, as in Mrs Transome's case, result in bitterness and heartbreak.

K. M. Newton considers Mrs Transome the novel's foremost egoist, but admits that her selfishness is not wholly condemned by a narrator who states that '[t]here is heroism even in the circles of hell for fellow-sinners who cling to each other in the fiery whirlwind and never recriminate' (xlii, 337).[26] However, there is another side to Mrs Transome which bespeaks something other than a preoccupation with self. Her stifled suffering signifies a troubled soul who recognises the powerlessness of her will and experiences the dread of an impending humiliation. Her silence is not only based on the fear of disclosure, however, but also on the realisation that any speech on her part would be useless. As she is an old woman and a mother made redundant, her opinions seem no longer to count. Candid displays of emotion and personal will become instances of humiliation, as she realises when confronting Harold about his Radicalism, occasioning the narrator to comment: 'But half the sorrows of women would be averted if they could repress the speech they know to be useless; nay, the speech they have resolved not to utter' (ii, 35).[27] The statement implies that a part of women's sorrows derives from the realisation that their speech is futile, that women are incapable of influencing any situation and accordingly powerless in society as a whole.[28] Revealing a narrator who is concerned

26 K. M. Newton, *George Eliot: Romantic Humanist, A Study of the Philosophical Structures of her Novels* (London: Macmillan, 1981), p. 42. Newton also acknowledges that the novel shows Mrs Transome's egoism as 'socially determined', that is, it rests on the deterioration of the social class to which she belongs. Newton argues that 'Mrs Transome's determination to find satisfaction for her will is in part a response to this social alienation, and her belief in the primacy of her will is only a transformation into personal terms of the aristocratic values she has been brought up to believe in' (p. 43). See also Andrew Thompson, who identifies the Dantean allusion in the comment, arguing that the love affair between Jermyn and Mrs Transome is a parallel to the romance between Francesca da Rimini and Paolo Malatesta, whose souls Dante meets in the 'circle of the lustful' in Canto V of the *Inferno* (p. 554).

27 Dorothea Barrett discusses speech in the novel as a phenomenon which is at once forceful and terrifying as it reaches beyond the characters' control. To Mrs Transome language rises within her as a compelling urge to express, but she at once suffocates it for fear of exposing herself. See, pp. 119-120.

28 The comment can also be read as characterising *some* speech as useless, i.e. that women's sorrows would be averted if they refrained from trying to exert influence where minds have already been made up. But this interpretation does not cancel out my main point, which is that the narrator is highlighting the ineffectiveness of Mrs Transome's speech and, by way of continuation, applying her situation to the powerlessness of speech for women in general.

with what happens to women when society no longer deems them necessary as mothers or as sexual beings, the comment serves as a wider, social criticism which both illuminates the restrictions Mrs Transome finds herself under and invites the reader to recognise the injustices committed against women on a general level. Hence, Mrs Transome may be showing signs of the egoist by being unable to repress her opinions, but it is an egoism which the reader is encouraged to understand.

In another instance the narrator refers to women's power to influence. In relation to Harold and his mother, the following observation is made: 'In this way poor women, whose power lies solely in their influence, make themselves like music out of tune, and only move men to run away' (xxxiv, 277). As stated in *The Mill on the Floss*, women's power is restricted to their influence on the men around them; but in *Felix Holt* this influence is negative, as there is an acknowledgment of oppression here.[29] In Mrs Transome's case, her attempts to influence both Jermyn and Harold miscarry, leaving her completely helpless.[30] The reader is reminded of the hopelessness of her situation and encouraged to relate her predicament to the situation of women in general.

Regarding Esther Lyon, however, the narrator returns to the matter of female influence in a more optimistic tone. As Esther prepares to speak up for Felix towards the end of his trial, the narrator reviews the psychological processes which have triggered her initiative to speak:

> When a woman feels purely and nobly, that ardour of hers which breaks through formulas too rigorously urged on men by daily practical needs, makes one of her most precious influences: she is the added impulse that shatters the stiffening crust of cautious experience. Her inspired ignorance gives a sublimity to actions so incongruously simple, that otherwise they would make men smile (xlvi, 373).

---

29 The passage in *The Mill* reads: 'Mrs Tulliver, as we have seen, was not without influence over her husband. No woman is; she can always incline him to do either what she wishes, or the reverse' (II, ii, 157).

30 As mentioned above, Bonnie Zimmerman argues that George Eliot was affected by the ideology of 'Female Influence' as it was outlined in *Woman's Mission*. In Zimmerman's words, this female conduct guide regarded women's influence as 'heightened by submission to oppression, not rebellion against it' (p. 434). A consideration of the narrator's comments in relation to this detail, however, demonstrates the dangers of having biographical material colour the interpretation of a text. If Eliot herself was in favour of women's influence being restricted to a 'submission to oppression', then why does the narratorial comment above regard women as 'poor', and why the use of 'solely'? Again, considering the text as independent of Eliot's personal conviction (which on the particular matter of women's issues was continuously in flux and ambivalent) becomes essential in making a fair assessment as to what the text is actually communicating.

Esther's guiltless ignorance invests her with the confidence to speak as well as to trust in the positive influence of her speech. Thanks to her being temporarily ignorant of gendered restrictions, Esther disables the limitations placed on women and makes her voice heard. Although Esther's panegyric has little effect on Felix's fate and although her efforts are primarily regarded in terms of her youth and beauty, the comment nevertheless acknowledges her potential for independent initiative and for claiming her space in a forum which is predominantly occupied by men. Here, then, Esther's inability to repress speech is regarded as positive, not only by the narrator but also by the other characters involved in the scene. It is significant, however, that Esther is regarded in sexual terms – that is, she is young, delicate and beautiful – and that her speech is considered with these qualities in mind. The difference between Mrs Transome's and Esther's capacity to affect any situation lies in this very essential circumstance.[31]

Most narratorial comments in *Felix Holt* which broach the subject of women concern Mrs Transome. By way of general reflection, they serve to bring the reader into her mental processes in order to have him or her sympathise with a character who could be regarded as egoistic, bitter and callous. Comments pertaining to Mrs Transome's experiences of being trapped within restricting gender roles, together with what she herself expresses regarding the relations between men and women, combine to form an attitude towards gender issues which challenges the idea that Esther Lyon is the heroine who triumphs as a moral ideal through conscious submission to the supposedly superior Felix. The novel thus demonstrates how differently two women are forced to subject themselves to rigid rules about how they should appear and behave on social and domestic levels. It also shows how such rules, while favourable for some individuals – such as young, attractive women who can afford to be selfless – oppress others who become completely invisible when their roles as sexual beings or mothers have run their course. Hence, these narratorial comments function as reminders of the complex situations in which Esther and Mrs Transome

31 Mary Ellen Doyle regards this particular comment as a gaffe in George Eliot's handling of narratorial commentary, criticising it for incorporating 'trite, formulaic diction' and taking on the form of 'sentimentalized peroration' (p. 106-107). Bonnie Zimmerman considers the contrast between Esther and Mrs Transome a close parallel to the political distinctions in the novel and argues that Esther exemplifies the ideology which finds power through submission. Zimmerman contends that the 'new, submissive Esther Lyon offers as a corrective to Mrs Transome's partisan view of power the wider social vision of helping a great man meliorate society through the power of opinion' (p. 445). However, Zimmerman also concedes that the comment quoted above, in which one notices the rhetoric of 'Female Influence', had been deleted in the Cabinet edition by George Eliot herself.

exist, calling attention to perspectives of their characters that cannot be rendered through descriptive passages alone.

Socio-Political and Historical Commentary

Given that *Felix Holt* is George Eliot's most political piece of work, it would be natural to expect this novel to contain a large quantity of commentary dealing with the social and political debates that accompanied the passing of the Reform Bill in 1832, and in continuation the passing of the second Bill in 1867. Surprisingly, however, the novel only contains a relatively small number of comments (less than ten) which relate directly to social or political affairs.[32] The introduction to the novel, of course, constitutes a historical survey of life in 1832; but this introduction cannot be considered narratorial commentary on historical, social or political issues, as it serves a descriptive and contextualising function in story-time now rather than functioning as commentary in narration now. The first expression of a social concern in the form of commentary appears in chapter 3 and has been mentioned above. It is the famous comment relating to public and private life which maintains that 'there is no private life which has not been determined by a wider public life' (iii, 43).

Similarly to *Adam Bede's* chapter 17, the narrator in *Felix Holt* assures the reader of the humble circumstances under which his characters exist and refers to them as if they are or were actual people whose histories the narrator, in his assumed role as historian, is retelling. Continuing his comment about public and private, the narrator argues that 'the lives we are about to look back upon [...] are rooted in the common earth, having

---

32 Several critics discuss *Felix Holt* as an expression of George Eliot's own contribution to the political debate of 1867 concerning the Second Reform Bill. See, for example, Jerome Thale, pp. 92-98, and F. B. Pinion, pp. 164-166. Regarding the political 'message' in the novel, Felix himself has often been understood to be Eliot's mouthpiece particularly with regard to his adamant opposition to enfranchisement. Judging from letters and articles George Eliot wrote, especially her 'Address to Working Men, by Felix Holt', it is clear that Eliot herself resisted the idea of enfranchisement specifically on the grounds that an uneducated 'mob' might be swayed, bribed or otherwise taken advantage of by the governing classes and that such a trend would inexorably lead to social disorder and eventually to chaos and anarchy. Should one choose to believe that *Felix Holt* incorporates the author's own personal agenda concerning her political present, the comment above might serve to support the idea that Eliot's personal anxiety about a disrupted social order is expressed in the novel.

to endure all the ordinary chances of past and present weather' (iii, 43). The 'present weather' of 1832, the reader learns, was sufficiently ignited to 'produce unusual perturbations in organic existence' (iii, 43).

The passage from chapter 3 in *Felix Holt* calls attention to two significant matters with regard to narratorial commentary. To begin with it introduces the idea of how organic societies are formed by a mass of components, claiming that these components and the whole, public and private, are interdependent. This idea constitutes a theme in the novel, besides forming an important part of 'Felix's' argument in Eliot's 'Address to Working Men, by Felix Holt'.[33] That essay is interesting as it expresses, in concentrated form, the discussions and arguments concerning enfranchisement which are represented by Felix and to some extent by Rufus Lyon in the novel. However, apart from the analogy just mentioned, the essay rarely parallels ideas formulated in the novel's commentary. In other words, the essay – often said to express George Eliot's own views on enfranchisement – reinforces the notion that discussions on politics in the novel are primarily mediated through characters and not through the narrator.

Secondly, the comment reiterates the narrator's status as historian and the fates of the characters as actual. Although *Felix Holt* contains attempts to endorse the authenticity of the story, the narrator does not imply that he has had first-hand contact with the characters. As in *Silas Marner*, the narrator remains detached in relation to the diegesis. Still, one striking example of the narrator's attempts to place his characters in the 'actual' world reveals his determination to authenticate the narrative. With regard to Philip Debarry, who is about to read out his letter of reply to Mr Lyon, the narrator intervenes, informing the reader that '[t]here is a portrait of Mr Philip Debarry still to be seen at Treby Manor, and a very fine bust of him at Rome, where he died fifteen years later, a convert to Catholicism' (xiv, 132-133). As in chapter 8, in which the reader is encouraged to im-

---

33 Concerned with how the working classes would use the franchise in 1867, the essay admonishes the working man to regard the franchise as a responsibility which should be handled with care. The speaker, Felix, urges the reader to consider the general good before his own needs and to promote change without upsetting order and tranquillity. As a part of his argument, he points to the responsibility of each individual by equating society with the human body. His argument, which is directly analogous to the discussion held in *Felix Holt*, is formulated as follows: 'We all know how many diseases the human body is apt to suffer from, and how difficult it is even for the doctors to find out exactly where the seat or beginning of the disorder is. That is because the body is made up of so many various parts, all related to each other, or likely all to feel the effect if any of them goes wrong. It is somewhat the same with our old nations or societies'; see *Essays*, p. 420. See also Ian Milner's 'The Genesis of George Eliot's Address to Working Men and Its Relation to *Felix Holt, the Radical*', *Philologica 1: Prague Studies in English*, 10 (1963), 49-54.

agine Harold Transome as one of his or her acquaintances, this intervention situates Philip Debarry within the reader's actual world, pulling the
character out of the diegesis rather than inviting the reader into it; and
although the statement does not belong to narratorial commentary, it emphasises the notion of authenticity in the narrative.

Yet, *Felix Holt* does include one instance where the reader is if not invited into the narrative scene, then at least inspired to imagine himself
or herself as part of it. Introducing Sir Maximus and Lady Debarry, the
narrator addresses the reader, stating: 'If you had looked down on them
from the box of Sampson's coach, he would have said, after lifting his hat,
"Sir Maximus and his lady – did you see?" thinking it needless to add the
surname' (vii, 77). Here the narrator does not assume that the reader can
take part in the diegesis as in *Adam Bede* and *The Mill on the Floss*, but
instead kindles his or her imagination in order to illustrate the status of the
Debarrys in Treby Magna. The reader's oscillating relation to the narrative
sustains a continuous movement which not only serves to keep the reader
alert to his or her active part in the narrative, but also supports the impression of historical authenticity.

As in the earlier works, the narrator in *Felix Holt* refers to the historical time of the novel as if it needs explication, describing the social and
political atmosphere to a reader who is assumed to be unfamiliar with the
period. This is how the narrator explains how Mr Lyon could be opposed
to the idea of the ballot-box, when his fellow Liberals were in favour:[34]

> At that time, when faith in the efficacy of political change was at fever-heat in ardent
> Reformers, many measures which men are still discussing with little confidence on
> either side, were then talked about and disposed of like property in near reversion.
> Crying abuses – "bloated paupers," "bloated pluralists," and other corruptions hin-
> dering men from being wise and happy – had to be fought against and slain. Such
> a time is a time of hope. Afterwards, when the corpses of those monsters have been
> held up to the public wonder and abhorrence, and yet wisdom and happiness do
> not follow, but rather a more abundant breeding of the foolish and unhappy, comes
> a time of doubt and despondency. But in the great Reform-year Hope was mighty
> (xvi, 153).

The passage not only informs the reader of the political atmosphere at
the time of the passing of the Bill in 1832; it also serves as a comment on
reform politics. Even though it is not disengaged from the narrative proper
and thus not part of narration now, it nevertheless addresses the reader in

---

34 Mr Lyon's character demonstrates how intricately religion and politics are interwoven
   in the novel, a subject which A. G. van der Broek discusses in 'The Politics of Religion
   in *Felix Holt*', *The George Eliot Review: Journal of the George Eliot Fellowship*, 30 (1999),
   38-48.

the manner of commentary as well as offering indirect opinions which take on the form of reflections, derived from experience, on the nature of reform and political change. Again, the passage recalls Eliot's 'Address to Working Men, by Felix Holt', which also raises the idea of dreadful consequences in a community where reform politics have been allowed to run rampant.[35] Consequently, the details concerning the historical period do not only supply information for the reader's benefit; they also serve as an outlet for the narrator's semi-veiled attitudes towards the powers of reformation. Here, the narrator's presence is tangible and much more explicit than in *Silas Marner*.

* * *

With regard to narratorial commentary, *Felix Holt*, nevertheless, shares many features with *Silas Marner*: it contains no elaborate examples of metalepsis and meta-narration, and it presents a narrator who is less emotionally involved in the narrative than the narrators in *Adam Bede* and *The Mill on the Floss*. However, *Felix Holt* also demonstrates a gradual return to the characteristics of the earlier novels by way of its references to the reader's response and to the narrator as 'I', which are narrative devices resumed with greater subtlety than in the first two novels.[36] In this sense, *Felix Holt* serves as an intermediary between the early experiments in the first three novels and the perfection of narratorial skills which would come to characterise Eliot's last two novels.

---

35 Addressing his fellow working-men, 'Felix' argues: 'We have reason to be discontented with many things, and, looking back either through the history of England to much earlier generations or to the legislation and administrations of later times, we are justified in saying that many of the evils under which our country now suffers are the consequences of folly, ignorance, neglect, or self-seeking in those who, at different times have wielded the powers of rank, office, and money. But the more bitterly we feel this, the more loudly we utter it, the stronger is the obligation we lay on ourselves to beware, lest we also, by a too hasty wresting of measures which seem to promise an immediate partial relief, make a worse time of it for our own generation, and leave a bad inheritance to our children. The deepest curse of wrong doing, whether of the foolish, or wicked sort, is that its effects are difficult to be undone'. *Essays of George Eliot*, p. 418.

36 See L. R. Leavis, 'George Eliot's Creative Mind: *Felix Holt* as the Turning-Point of Her Art', *English Studies: A Journal of English Language and Literature*, 67 (1986), 311-326.

6. *Middlemarch*

In her journal from 1 January 1869, George Eliot noted the composition of a novel to be called 'Middlemarch' among the tasks to be undertaken in the coming year.[1] In September, after the completion of an introduction and three chapters, the work seems to have been abandoned, and on 31 December 1870 Eliot's journal records that she has completed 100 pages of a different story called 'Miss Brooke'.[2] At some point during the winter of 1871, these separate projects were combined into one: on 19 March of that year, Eliot wrote that 236 pages of her novel were finished.[3] *Middlemarch: A Study of Provincial Life* was published in eight parts from December 1871 to December 1872.

In 'Notes on Form in Art' written in 1868, Eliot, possibly without conscious reference to her own projected work, presented an illuminating outline of *Middlemarch*: her discussion of a 'conception of wholes composed of parts more and more multiplied and highly differenced, yet more and more absolutely bound together by various conditions of common likeness or mutual dependence' forms an apt description of the novel.[4] It is a complex and multifaceted work which incorporates a number of plots, all separate but interwoven to form a composite whole.[5] Art, religion and science are central concerns in the novel which demonstrates how intricately these phenomena are integrated within society, within individual

---

1   See *Letters*, v, 3.
2   See *The Journals of George Eliot*, ed. by Margaret Harris and Judith Johnston (Cambridge: Cambridge University Press, 1998), p. 142.
3   In *Middlemarch from Notebook to Novel* (Urbana, University of Illinois Press, 1960), Jerome Beaty attempts to reconstruct the historical composition and fusion of Eliot's two separate beginnings 'Middlemarch' and 'Miss Brooke'.
4   *Essays*, pp. 431-436 (p. 433).
5   Henry James characterised the novel as a 'treasure-house of details' but 'an indifferent whole' in *A Century of George Eliot Criticism*, ed. Gordon S. Haight, pp. 80-87 (p. 81), first publ. in *Galaxy*, 15 (March, 1873), 424-428. The unity or wholeness of the novel has been challenged by post-structuralist critics, who argue that several images in the novel counteract readings geared towards 'wholeness'. See, for example, J. Hillis Miller's famous deconstructive reading in 'Optic and Semiotic', p. 128.

lives and within historical processes of change. Like *Felix Holt* the novel is set at the time of the first Reform Bill in 1832, and the same themes of political unrest and public opinion are staged, albeit more subtly, in *Middlemarch*. The novel's foremost concern lies with the interweaving of human lives and the intricate pattern of relations which form between characters. Difference and disparity are as prominent as connectedness, and the oscillation between unity and disjointedness is manifested primarily in the narrator's voice(s) and in the use of images. Still, the range and scope of this book's engagement with fundamental aspects of human life impart universal relevance to its account of a particular phase in the history of modern England.

Before investigating the movements between particular and general in *Middlemarch*, this chapter provides a brief summary of some twentieth-century critical responses to the novel's narrator. Because *Middlemarch* is the Eliot novel which has received by far the most critical attention, it seems appropriate to situate discussions of narratorial commentary in this particular novel in relation to previous critical views on the narratorial dimension. The narratological-technical analyses of particular and general are followed by discussions of comments which introduce and conclude chapters. Subsequent sections review references and addresses to the reader, meta-narrative statements and comments within parentheses. Being the multifaceted novel that *Middlemarch* is, it incorporates a large number of thematic concerns. The themes which have been singled out here as the ones frequently recurring in narratorial commentary involve egoism, references to science, history, literature and religion, problems of interpretation and gender issues. Finally, this chapter is brought to a close by a discussion of the novel's Prelude and Finale.

Critical responses to the narrator

All narrators in Eliot's novels display some degree of control and omniscience, and all intrude on the narratives in various ways; but the narrator in *Middlemarch* has intrigued critics especially. This may be due to the richly varied voice of the *Middlemarch* narrator: a voice continually moving between sympathy and sarcasm, combining ridicule with understanding in its presentation of character and adjusting its own as well as the reader's distance to the text. It is this notion of a controlling, authoritative narrative voice which has given rise to most of the critical debate. Marxist critics reacted to an omniscient narrative stance which, they believed, imposed a specific ideological position on the text. As early as 1951, Arnold Kettle criticised Eliot for operating within a restricted ideological position and neglecting larger historical processes of change.[6] This criticism was elaborated on by, among others, Terry Eagleton, who argued that Eliot attempted to recast 'historical contradictions into ideologically resolvable form' and when failing to do so displaced history into 'ethical, and so "timeless", terms'.[7] Eagleton disliked what he saw as larger social and political concerns being relegated to a personal level and imbued with the narrator's moral discourse. However, favourable arguments were also expressed in the 60s and 70s. For example, Barbara Hardy saw the narrator's voice as a 'formal constituent' serving several functions in the text, such as providing context and situating the reader inside experiences rather than above or outside them.[8] Additionally, Isobel Armstrong argued that the narrator's addresses to the reader 'invoke a general body of moral and psychological knowledge or, rather, *experience*, which can be the corporate possession of both writer and reader'.[9] Nevertheless, many critics of *Middlemarch* objected to the idea of one omniscient, dominating voice. An important response to this criticism was voiced by David Lodge who, influenced by Bakhtin, interpreted the narrative voice not as controlled and authoritative, but as ambiguous and capricious. Lodge maintained that the narrative voice in *Middlemarch* displays an indistinctness which benefits the reading: 'it is precisely because the narrator's discourse is never entirely unambiguous, predictable, and in total interpretative control of the other discourses in *Middlemarch* that the novel survives, to be read and re-read, without ever being finally closed or exhausted'.[10]

Ambiguity is also emphasised in J. Hillis Miller's deconstructive reading of *Middlemarch*, which juxtaposes images of connectedness with contra-

---

6 Arnold Kettle, *An Introduction to the English Novel*, pp. 160-177.

7 Terry Eagleton, *Criticism and Ideology: A Study in Marxist Literary Theory* (London: Verso, 1976), pp. 114-121.

8 Hardy, *The Novels of George Eliot*, p. 155.

9 Armstrong, p. 120.

10 David Lodge, '*Middlemarch* and the Idea of the Classic Realist Text', in *The Nineteenth Century Novel: Critical Essays and Documents*, ed. by Arnold Kettle (London: The Open University, 1981), pp. 218-238 (p. 236). Lodge's article serves as a rejoinder to Colin MacCabe's *James Joyce and the Revolution of the Word*, in which MacCabe views the narrator of *Middlemarch* as one dominating voice serving to promote one single ideological purpose to which all individuals should subscribe. Lodge acknowledges the paradox, remarking that his own rejoinder 'follows inevitably from the post-Saussurian theories about language and discourse to which Colin MacCabe, and other critics of the same persuasion, subscribe' (236).

dictory images of disparity. Miller takes issue with the notion of a narrator engaged in endorsing a totalising vision, contending that the text incessantly undermines its own position, rendering the notion of one dominating voice unacceptable.[11] Another Miller, D. A., appreciates the novel's indeterminacy but maintains that the idea of coherence and unity should not be lost. Resorting to imagery, D. A. Miller argues that both approaches to the novel are possible and indeed compatible: 'Like one of those optical drawings that won't resolve once for all into five cubes or six, a vase or two human profiles, *Middlemarch* seems to be traditional and to be beyond its limit, to subvert and to reconfirm the value of its traditional status'.[12] Miller's image is not only relevant to the interpretation of narrative voice or voices in *Middlemarch* but also to literary criticism in general. Allowing different critical readings to open up the text in various ways, it shows how disagreement and uniformity need not be mutually exclusive. Instead, recognising interpretations from diverse literary camps, the reader of *Middlemarch* is made aware of a text which is inconsistent, open-ended and variable at the same time as it incorporates an ideological position and moves towards coherence and wholeness. Rosemary Clark-Beattie's analysis of the narrator's style in *Middlemarch* amounts to a similar claim. Clark-Beattie identifies two narratorial voices which interact with all the other voices in the novel. These two narrative voices – one empiricist and the other idealist – are placed in contradiction to each other, but at the same time neither is 'seen as adequate unless qualified by its opposite'.[13]

Consequently, critical debate concerning the narrator's voice in *Middlemarch* has to a large degree focused on the tension between unity and contradiction. Regardless of coherence or diversity, however, narratorial commentary in *Middlemarch*, as in the earlier novels, serves the function of modifying the reader's distance to the text and influencing his or her response. By moving between the general and the particular, by addressing the reader directly and by including him or her into the text and making the reader an active participant, narratorial comments in *Middlemarch* – as in all Eliot's novels – communicate with the reader, shaping his or her interpretation of the text.

---

11 J. Hillis Miller, 'Optic and Semiotic', p. 144.

12 D. A. Miller, *Narrative and Its Discontents: Problems of Closure in the Traditional Novel* (Princeton: Princeton University Press, 1981), p. 108.

13 Rosemary Clark-Beattie, '*Middlemarch's* Dialogic Style', *The Journal of Narrative Technique*, 15 (1985), 199-218 (p. 201).

Particular-General-Particular

The circular transfer from particular to general and back is the character-istic feature of the textual movement between story-time now and narration now. Lending greater depth and adding new dimensions to particular instances, these movements serve to make the reader aware of the complexities inherent in human emotions. As in the earlier novels, they can materialise as distinct shifts in narrative tone. Such a shift occurs in relation to, for example Mrs Waule: Depicted as disagreeable and spiteful, Mrs Waule's character represents the greedy relative who eagerly awaits the death of a wealthy kinsman. She is introduced through the unsympathetic perspectives of Rosamond and Fred, and in dialogue with her brother she displays a propensity for spreading vicious rumours to benefit her self-interest. Adding to an already unfavourable portrayal, Mrs Waule's free indirect discourse (FID) oozes with the narrator's satirical tone.[14]

However, Mrs Waule's FID is followed by a narratorial comment which immediately qualifies that impression: 'The human mind has at no period accepted a moral chaos; and so preposterous a result was not strictly con-ceivable. But we are frightened at much that is not strictly conceivable' (xii, 100-101). Constituting a distinct shift from Mrs Waule's FID, the narrator's address abandons the humorous tone and situates Mrs Waule's circumstances within a larger context. Approaching her character from another perspective, the comment shows how Mrs Waule, despite be-ing greedy and envious, also possesses a conviction of what she considers 'morally right'. Suggesting that Mrs Waule's reasoning with regard to her brother's legacy is not engendered by self-interest only, but also by an idea of propriety, the transfer from particular to general entails a change in nar-ratorial tone which redirects focus from Mrs Waule's greed to a notion of morality. Hence, the reader's relation to Mrs Waule's character is at once transported from one extreme to the other: from being encouraged to join in the narrator's ridicule in story-time now to being induced to understand and recognise in narration now.

This shift in narratorial tone is a good example of the *Middlemarch* nar-rator's inconsistent attitude. By moving deftly between satire and sympa-thy, the narrator imposes a palpable and immediate presence, signalling an authority which occupies a commanding position in relation to the text. It is a shift which influences the reader's perception of the narrative, mak-

---

14 Roy Pascal argues that FID frequently mimics the idiom and voice of a character. The degree of mimicry, he maintains, gives 'a fair indication of the author's sympathies', often serving a 'humorous or satirical function'; see pp. 81-82.

ing him or her attentive to continual changes of direction. Although such shifts are not as abrupt and obvious in Eliot's other novels, they do occur there too, rooted in an all-pervading tendency to change tacks.

The movement from story-time now to narration now in the comment above forms a palpable shift, alerting the reader to a change of direction in narrative voice and perspective.[15] However, as seen in the earlier novels, such transfers may also evolve as subtle, almost imperceptible developments from the particular perspective to the general. One such understated shift appears in chapter 20, which depicts the turbulent emotions that Dorothea experiences in her sixth week of married life. Confused and despondent, Dorothea finds herself in a state of unhappiness, and the narrator remarks:

> Not that this inward amazement of Dorothea's was anything very exceptional [...] Nor can I suppose that when Mrs Casaubon is discovered in a fit of weeping six weeks after her wedding, the situation will be regarded as tragic. Some discouragement, some faintness of heart at the new real future which replaces the imaginary, is not unusual, and we do not expect people to be deeply moved by what is not unusual. That element of tragedy which lies in the very fact of frequency, has not yet wrought itself into the coarse emotion of mankind; and perhaps our frames could hardly bear much of it. If we had a keen vision and feeling of all ordinary human life, it would be like hearing the grass grow and the squirrel's heart beat, and we should die of that roar which lies on the other side of silence. As it is, the quickest of us walk about well wadded with stupidity. However, Dorothea was crying (xx, 182).

Here, the transfer from particular to general is accomplished through the use of a bridging sentence in which the narrator appears in the first-person plural to make conjectures about the reader's response to Dorothea's situation. Notwithstanding the narrator's evident concern with the reader's reaction, the sentence remains partly fixed within story-time now, primarily acting as narrative description. In the ensuing sentence, however, narration now is entered, the narrator turning to the reader by way of relating Dorothea's particular circumstances to general phenomena. What

---

15 The devices employed to create FID can be so similar to those employed for narratorial commentary that it can be difficult to distinguish the two. These instances of confusion which render the distinction between voices blurred are, however, infrequent in *Middlemarch*. See my discussion of FID and narratorial commentary in *Daniel Deronda*, in which confusion between the two is more frequent. Roy Pascal claims that FID is used less frequently in *Daniel Deronda* than in the earlier novels (78), but the instances of confusion as to whether a statement is FID or narratorial commentary is more common in this book.

follows is a much quoted and discussed passage.[16] It begins with a supposition about the reader's response to Dorothea, which initially seems to be a response compatible with the narrator's. Tragic experience, the narrator argues, is common among individuals whose illusions are replaced with reality. But these everyday tragedies cannot be felt by others, or life would become unbearable – stupidity thus serves as a mechanism for survival. Consequently, the narrator seems to assume and accept the reader's possibly tepid response to Dorothea's tragedy, arguing that frequency neutralises feeling.

However, as is usual with Eliot's commentary, and especially with comments in *Middlemarch*, the passage is double-edged. Argument and imagery conflict when the narrator maintains that Dorothea's situation is unexceptional, but simultaneously depicts her feelings of tragedy as a smothered 'roar' – an image which spotlights the very core of Dorothea's frustration. Additionally, the passage strips the reader of his or her 'stupid padding' by imparting that very 'vision' of tragedy which cannot be seen or heard. The essence of the argument thus conflicts with the devices employed to build it.[17] The conflict functions as a kind of reverse psychology, indirectly encouraging the reader to sympathise with Dorothea's situation.[18] By mov-

---

16 In 'The Roar on the Other Side of Silence: Otherness in *Middlemarch*', in *Rereading Texts / Rethinking Critical Presuppositions: Essays in Honour of H. M. Daleski*, ed. by Shlomith Rimmon-Kenan *et al.* (Frankfurt am Main: Peter Lang, 1997), J. Hillis Miller discusses this passage, arguing that the type of insight which 'lies on the other side of silence' is actually demonstrated in Eliot's 'The Lifted Veil'. That 'keen vision and feeling' of course causes a catastrophe in the novella, much as the passage suggests. Moreover, Miller acknowledges a parallel argument in Joseph Conrad's *Heart of Darkness* when Marlow says: 'The inner truth is hidden – luckily, luckily' (143). Peter Garrett observes that the passage brings to mind episodes in earlier novels where the reader is invited to 'see the possibility of tragedy beneath the surface of undistinguished lives'. As an example, Garrett points to the introduction of chapter 5 in *Amos Barton* where the narrator turns to the reader, arguing: 'Depend upon it, you would gain unspeakably if you would learn with me to see some of the poetry and the pathos, the tragedy and the comedy, lying in the experience of a human soul that looks out through dull grey eyes, and that speaks in a voice of quite ordinary tones' (*Scenes of Clerical Life*, 'Amos Barton', v, 37); see *Scene and Symbol from George Eliot to James Joyce* (London: Yale University Press, 1969), p. 60.

17 Rosemary Clark-Beattie makes a similar observation with reference to this passage, arguing that 'whenever common sense would dictate a response of indifference to the intensity of another's suffering or of hostility to noble aspirations, the voices of moral fervour and genial worldliness come into conflict' (204).

18 Carol Howe Spady claims that the intention of comments in *Middlemarch* is to 'humanize the reader' and that this is achieved primarily through metaphor. With reservation for the idea of an explicit authorial intention in this context, Howe Spady's argument is closely related to mine as she also discusses sympathy as elicited through appeals to the reader's recognition. Howe Spady says that 'by making a widely applicable metaphor, the narrator creates an intersection between the world of the characters and

ing from the particular to the general, by employing the first-person pronoun and so inviting the reader into the example, the narrator solicits the reader's recognition of private, muted and unacknowledged suffering. In effect, the narrator turns up the volume on Dorothea's roar for the reader to hear.

Although the narrator's voice in *Middlemarch* can be ambiguous, it is by no means always so. Most of the images used are fairly straightforward, and the movement from the particular to the general usually serves to lend further depth to the specifics of the text without necessarily involving shifting and contradictory attitudes. Still, it is impossible to disregard the erratic nature of the *Middlemarch* narrator. The technique of bridging the particular with the general through subtle means is repeatedly discontinued. Instead, comments frequently occur as abrupt interventions, taking arguments in new directions and offering opinions on particular episodes, occasionally aided by the narrator's manifest presence in the form of the first-person pronoun. As Lydgate and Rosamond fall further into debt, the narrator's depiction moves from the particular to the general by way of an exclamation:

> It is true Lydgate was constantly visiting the homes of the poor and adjusting his prescriptions of diet to their small means; but, dear me! has it not by this time ceased to be remarkable – is it not rather what we expect in men, that they should have numerous strands of experience lying side by side and never compare them with each other? Expenditure – like ugliness and errors – becomes a totally new thing when we attach our own personality to it, and measure it by that wide difference which is manifest (in our own sensation) between ourselves and others (lviii, 552).

The whole passage demonstrates the shifts in tone and attitude emanating from the narrator, who not only imposes his judgment on the text, but also draws the reader into a common lot by way of assuming mutual agreement to his rhetorical question. As such, the first part of the comment serves as an act of communication between narrator and reader, enforcing the reader's active engagement with the text. By addressing the reader directly and suddenly, the comment not only constitutes a striking break in the narrative, catching the reader's attention; it also creates an ironic distance to Lydgate, whose failure to compare notes with himself induces the narrator's sarcasm.

The first part of the comment, then, presents a personal narrator offering opinions in the form of irony, establishing a connection between himself and the reader on the basis of that irony and hence distancing both

the world of the reader. When the two worlds cross, the reader recognizes himself in the character' (64-65).

himself and the reader from the character. However, the second part of the comment introduces a new tone and attitude with regard to Lydgate's circumstances. Here the narrator reverts to a detached and wholly extradiegetic position, offering no personal opinions other than applying Lydgate's particular situation to larger, more general phenomena in order to inform the reader of the process of change taking place in his character. Here is a balanced voice, familiar with the 'real' world and free from irrational excesses of emotion. This voice seems trustworthy and open to a more liberal attitude with regard to the imperfections of humans.[19] The narrator's detachment and the way in which he unfolds a notion of the general by which the particular can be interpreted actually diminish the distance between Lydgate and the reader. Moreover, the comment serves to prepare the reader for Lydgate's imminent experience. The reader is thus influenced to recognise and sympathise with Lydgate, even before he is hit by 'reality' himself.[20]

The quotation demonstrates the versatility of the narrative voice in *Middlemarch*, which continuously repositions itself in relation to the reader and to the characters in the text.[21] But it also shows how the reader's stance vis-à-vis the narrator and the characters is determined by these shifts, in the one instance being drawn into the experience of characters and encouraged to sympathise and in the other made to regard them from a distance with the help of irony.[22] Furthermore, the passage shows that the

---

19 These two narrative voices are interesting to compare with narratorial attitudes in *The Mill on the Floss*, in which it is possible to discern a similar distinction in narratorial tone and attitude. But whereas these attitudes are more or less consistent throughout the earlier novel, the narrative voices in *Middlemarch* remain in continuous flux.

20 Suzanne Graver comments on this particular passage, arguing that it illustrates George Eliot's attempts to enrich the reader's understanding of human complexities by 'bringing the power of comparison to bear on the fictional worlds she has created' (68). Graver maintains that the comment serves as social criticism, urging the reader to see that 'what the characters take to be desirable marks of social difference' are really 'signs of a damaging conventionality' (69).

21 Derek Oldfield has also discussed the shifting nature of the narrative voice, maintaining that 'George Eliot makes her point by zigzagging. We oscillate between an emotional identification with a character and an obliquely judicious response to their situation'; 'The Language of the Novel: The Character of Dorothea' in *Middlemarch*: *Critical Approaches to the Novel*, ed. Barbara Hardy (London: Athlone Press, 1967), pp. 63-86 (p. 81).

22 Jane S. Smith recognises the reader's alternating position with regard to the text and connects it to psychological processes contained in any reading experience, contending that '[t]he shifting role accorded to the reader in *Middlemarch*, sometimes detached and superior, sometimes deeply implicated in the events of the story, is also a paradigm for the actual reader's position in any experience of reading and provides the continual changes in perspective which enable us to understand the text both intellectually and emotionally' (200).

practice of moving between the particular and the general need not always involve the narrator's appeal to the reader's sympathy; it may also serve the reverse effect of establishing ironic distance. However, it is significant – and characteristic of the types of commentary which involve more than one narratorial attitude – that prior to returning to story-time now, the general statement is concluded not in the ironical voice but by the speaker engaged in eliciting the reader's sympathetic understanding.

As in the earlier novels, the transition between the general and the particular, separating story-time now from narration now, is often signalled by typographical or rhetorical devices such as, for instance, semi-colons and conjunctions. The two diegetic levels hence converge in the same sentence, moving from one to the other, smoothly and subtly, yet directing the reader's focus away from the specifics of the text. An example appears in chapter 10, where the narrator comments on Casaubon's failure to conjure up genuine delight at the prospect of being married:

> Poor Mr Casaubon had imagined that his long studious bachelorhood had stored up for him a compound interest of enjoyment, and that large drafts on his affections would not fail to be honoured; for we all of us, grave or light, get our thoughts entangled in metaphors, and act fatally on the strength of them (x, 79).

Functioning as a causal conjunction, 'for' suggests the explicatory element of the secondary clause, advertising its direct relation to what has gone before. The reader is invited to comprehend the mechanisms involved in Casaubon's misconceptions and to abstain from censure. While the reader is drawn into the assertion, the address does not so much serve to elicit recognition as to draw the reader's attention to an observable 'truth'. The comment hence discourages derision of Casaubon by pointing to the common processes by which 'we all' interpret the world. The causal conjunction characteristically refers the comment back to whatever particularity it is in immediate propinquity to, but the statement also relates to one of the most significant thematic concerns in the novel, that is, the crisis which erupts when illusions conflict with reality.[23] Several characters, for example

---

23 George Eliot was aware of the complexities of figurative language and of the problematic relationship between language and 'reality'. In 'Narrative and History', *ELH*, 41 (1974), 455-473, J. Hillis Miller broaches this theme, noting that every major character in the novel makes the mistake of 'taking a figure of speech literally, of assuming that because two things are similar they are equivalent' (464) and follows up this idea by accounting for each character's error. Some twenty years later, Miller returns to the metaphor comment in *Middlemarch*, arguing that it forms part of Eliot's theories on the human habit of misreading signs. Miller states that Eliot's passage shows that humans have a 'habit of thinking by analogy, that is, by figurative displacements', which 'lead us to see one person as like some other person and then to literalize that similarity'; 'The

Dorothea and Bulstrode, are 'entangled in metaphors', heading for disaster when acting on them. Consequently, the comment works on three levels at once. Initially, the causal conjunction refers back to the primary clause, elucidating the processes which have instigated Casaubon's misapprehensions; then the reader is reminded of his or her own subjection to these mechanisms; and finally the closing sentence remarks on the problematic relationship between illusion and 'reality' which runs as a thematic concern throughout the novel.

Comments beginning with 'for' are characteristically explicatory, presupposing an authoritative and convincing narratorial tone. They are rarely ambiguous or ironical, but rather articulated in a matter-of-fact way in order to reinforce the narrator's trustworthiness. Elaborating on particular instances, they underpin the reader's reliance on a narrator whose protean relationship to both text and reader can easily confuse the reader's understanding of the narrator's relation to the text. Towards the latter part of *Middlemarch*, the narrator's authoritative, unambiguous voice takes precedence, and in the last book of the novel the narrator has ceased referring to himself in the first person. With the unfolding of tragic events, the narrator restrains his ironical and personal voice in the interest of dignity and reliability.

In contrast to 'for', the conjunction 'but' denotes a degree of opposition or signals a discussion or argument taking a new direction. 'But' initiates both primary and secondary clauses and, similarly to 'for', operates to separate narration now from story-time now. Analysing particular instances from a general perspective, the 'but'-clause introduces oppositions or developments of perspective which examine and qualify details presented in story-time now. An example of how the 'but'-conjunction bridges the two diegetic stages appears in connection with Mr Bulstrode's purchase of Stone Court. The acquisition of Mr Featherstone's old land has elevated Bulstrode to unusually high spirits, but the narrator voices a caution:

> He was doctrinally convinced that there was a total absence of merit in himself; but that doctrinal conviction may be held without pain when the sense of demerit does not take a distinct shape in memory and revive the tingling of shame or the pang of remorse. Nay, it may be held with intense satisfaction when the depth of our sinning is but a measure for the depth of forgiveness, and a clenching proof that we are peculiar instruments of the divine intention. The memory has as many moods as the temper, and shifts its scenery like a diorama (liii, 490).

Roar on the Other Side of Silence', p. 138. Bernard Paris contends that almost all Eliot's principal characters experience the intrusion of 'harsh reality' on nurtured illusions. See *Experiments in Life*, p. 146.

Bulstrode believes that he is chosen to exalt God's cause and that part of serving God entails profit being placed in the hands of his servants, i.e. Bulstrode himself. He is equally convinced that all good which comes to him comes through the grace of God, and that he himself is without 'merit'. Embodying an opposition, the passage formulates, in general terms, an argument which qualifies the reader's understanding of Bulstrode. The comment rotates the perspective on his morality, suggesting that there are dubious aspects to his character. Working as an advance mention, the argument simultaneously creates expectations of Bulstrode's future and curiosity about his past. The comment is particularly effectual for three reasons: as an element of surprise in the reading process, it indirectly suggests the hitherto undisclosed nature of an established character. Furthermore, its structural position creates tension, as it conveys an ominous premonition of Bulstrode's fate in between a description of his purchase of Stone Court and a passage of FID through which he expresses his trust in providence. Finally, it emanates from a narratorial voice which is atypically severe in tone and uninterested in the reader's sympathy. Emphasising the hypocrisy of Bulstrode's 'tortured Calvinist code', the comment condemns his conduct even before revealing to the reader the details of what he has done.[24] Consequently, the comment provides the reader with information which reaches both forward and back in the narrative, and which serves to influence the reader's interpretation of actions of which he or she is as yet ignorant.

Only four pages after the passage above, when Bulstrode is referred to again, the narrator's attitude has mellowed. Raffles has emerged on the scene, and as a result so has Bulstrode's anguish. Bulstrode habitually justifies self-serving acts by adjusting his interpretation of them to agree with what he believes is divine providence.[25] With Raffles's appearance, however, Bulstrode becomes painfully confused, and the narrator remarks:

> In his closest meditations the life-long habit of Mr Bulstrode's mind clad his most egoistic terrors in doctrinal references to super-human ends. But even while we are talking and meditating about the earth's orbit and the solar system, what we feel and adjust our movements to is the stable earth and the changing day. And now within all the automatic succession of theoretic phrases [...] was the forecast of disgrace

24 See Hodgson, p. 123.

25 Bernard Paris sees a comparison between Bulstrode's character and the criticism George Eliot levelled against Dr John Cumming in her essay 'Evangelical Teaching: Dr Cumming', published in the *Westminster Review*, LXIV in October, 1855. Paris contends that '[l]ike Bulstrode in *Middlemarch*, Cumming treats external facts in a subjective way, rationalizing, twisting them about to make them fit into a preconceived notion of God's plan'; *Experiments in Life*, p. 82.

in the presence of his neighbours and of his own wife. For the pain, as well as the public estimate of disgrace, depends on the amount of previous profession. To men who only aim at escaping felony, nothing short of the prisoner's dock is disgrace. But Mr Bulstrode had aimed at being an eminent Christian (liii, 494).

Chapter 53 is pivotal in the Bulstrode plot, as it not only reveals a scandalous past and introduces the element of blackmail into the narrative but also describes a reversal in Bulstrode's character.[26] From the reader's point of view, this reversal is chiefly understood through the increased amount of FID through which his fears and anxieties are expressed. By increasing the reader's direct access to Bulstrode's thoughts and at the same time revealing his past through his own mental processes, the narrator attempts to assuage the reader's possible judgment of him. Moreover, with Bulstrode's increasing pain, the narrator's severity is subdued and his appeals to the reader's recognition intensified. In the quotation above, the text moves in and out of narration now, oscillating between Bulstrode's mental processes and the narrator's comments. Interestingly, the passage includes both a 'but'-clause qualifying Bulstrode's 'life-long habit' and a 'for'-clause which explicates the impending threat of humiliation. With both these comments, a changing narratorial attitude towards Bulstrode can be discerned: with the first comment through the use of the first-person pronoun, which indicates an analogy between the character and the reader, and with the second by the use of the causal conjunction which introduces a general analysis intended to elucidate the conditions Bulstrode finds himself in. Consequently, chapter 53 demonstrates a gradually growing narratorial leniency towards Bulstrode in proportion to his increasing anxieties.

Apart from typographical and syntactic devices such as semi-colons and conjunctions, *Middlemarch* includes parentheses, which similarly function to bridge the gap between story-time now and narration now. The parenthesis operates as a separate sphere where the narrator and reader can meet openly, as it signals a narratorial level which is exclusive to the reader and the narrator. An example of such an exclusive space appears in chapter 39, where Mr Brooke is given a dressing-down by the drunken Mr Dagley, causing the narrator to comment parenthetically on Mr Brooke's view of himself as 'a general favourite' (xxxix, 372): '(we are all apt to do so, when we think of our own amiability more than of what other people are likely to want of us)' (xxxix, 372-373). Mr Brooke is one of those characters who provide comic relief in the novel. Generally jovial and with muddled opinions on most things, he frequently occasions ironical commentary. Here, however, the parenthetical aside abates the reader's possible sense

---

26 For more on the blackmailing of Bulstrode, see Alexander Welsh, pp. 230-258.

of superiority over Mr Brooke by drawing him or her into the general reflection. Unusually, then, the comment downplays the humorous element connected with Mr Brooke by stimulating the reader to identify with the confusion which can transpire when exterior attitudes conflict with a firmly held self-image. The narrative thereby challenges its own previously established conception of Mr Brooke and encourages the reader to regard him differently from that select perspective which the parenthesis constitutes.[27] Hence, the parenthesis signifies a narration-now sphere which facilitates the reader's and narrator's meeting on what gives the impression of being a shared equal level.

Subsequently, the movements between particular and general in *Middlemarch* are manifested in a variety of ways, at one instance appearing as subtle, almost undetectable, modifications to perspective and at another emerging as abrupt shifts of narratorial tone. However, regardless of whether these transfers are signalled delicately or by means of sharp indicators, they all serve to situate the reader in relation to the text and to affect his or her interpretation, drawing it towards what the narrator considers the 'correct' understanding of characters and events.

Introductions and Conclusions

Like *Romola* and *Felix Holt*, *Middlemarch* is preceded by a fairly long introduction which works as an initial narratorial commentary on the narrative.[28] This is where the narrator establishes contact with both reader and narrative, presenting thematic concerns and indicating his position vis-à-vis the text. *Middlemarch* also includes chapter epigraphs to all its 86 chapters. Operating as commentary on each chapter, the epigraphs function on different levels, simultaneously prophesying about impending events and situating them within wider literary contexts.[29] In addition, several chapters in *Middlemarch* are introduced through narratorial

---

27 For a discussion of how the narrator becomes the genuine avuncular figure that Mr Brooke cannot be, see U. C. Knoepflmacher, '*Middlemarch*: An Avuncular View', *Nineteenth-Century Fiction*, 30 (1975), 53-81.

28 The Prelude and Finale to *Middlemarch* are discussed separately below.

29 *Middlemarch* includes only one prose epigraph (interestingly, the one preceding chapter 53) which has no literary source. Therefore epigraphs will only be discussed when they have specific impact on an introduction, as they operate outside the framework of the story and present a voice on a separate narrative level.

commentary.[30] To continue with the topic of Bulstrode, further narratorial commentary on his mental and spiritual crisis introduces chapter 85. The chapter is preceded by an excerpt from the *Pilgrim's Progress*, depicting the scene in 'Vanity Fair' where Faithful is condemned to death. As a direct reference to the epigraph, the narrator introduces the chapter in the following manner:

> When immortal Bunyan makes his picture of the persecuting passions bringing in their verdict of guilty, who pities Faithful? That is a rare and blessed lot which some greatest men have not attained, to know ourselves guiltless before a condemning crowd – to be sure that what we are denounced for is solely the good in us. The pitiable lot is that of the man who could not call himself a martyr even though he were to persuade himself that the men who stoned him were but ugly passions incarnate – who knows that he is stoned, not for professing the Right, but for not being the man he professed to be (lxxxv, 772).

The passage introduces Bulstrode's preparation for exile, redefining established notions of martyrdom so as to have them apply to human imperfections.[31] The direct reference to the epigraph, which comes across almost as a reminder, is an unusual feature in the novel. Epigraphs generally exist as autonomous entities which, although referring to the chapter at hand, are rarely acknowledged within the diegesis. Here, however, the narrator 'prepares' the introductory comment by ensuring that the evoked literary context is fresh in the reader's mind. In this sense, the epigraph works as a preliminary to the introductory passage rather than – or at least as well as – as a commentary on the chapter.

The reference to Bunyan invites the reader onto a separate narrative level where he or she is encouraged to revisit the original context. In a second phase, the reader is stimulated to apply the relevance of Bunyan's text to the particular scene in the diegesis. But in the quoted passage, the narrator modifies his understanding of the original context, challenging the reader to revise his or her reading of the original as well. Proceeding from this altered understanding of a well-known literary text, then, the narrator presents an argument for sympathy which serves to influence the reader's

---

30 Two of the most famous introductory passages are the narrator's references to Fielding, introducing chapter 15, and to the metaphor of a 'pier-glass or extensive surface of polished steel' (xxvii, 248), introducing chapter 27; but these passages involve so many interesting aspects of the narratorial comment that they are discussed in my section on themes.

31 David Carroll interprets the epigraph and introductory comment as a 'Puritan counterpoint to [Bulstrode's] ambiguous situation', but nonetheless contends that 'George Eliot won't allow her fictions to be allegorised in this way and, as a result, the presence of his wife remains, despite her compassion, "a tribunal before which he shrank from confession and desired advocacy" '; *Conflict of Interpretations*, p. 263.

understanding of Bulstrode. Juxtaposing his character with 'Faithful' and emphasising the fundamental distinction between being rightfully and wrongfully condemned, the narrator appeals to the reader's recognition of the imperfections of fallible humans. 'Faithful', the narrator reasons, needs no sympathy – he has been condemned by a body of inverted values, his conscience is clear and his martyrdom ascertained. Fallible man, i.e. Bulstrode, on the other hand, has been condemned by his own values – unlike 'Faithful', he knows that he is wrong, accepts the condemnation and endures the humiliation. According to the narrator, his is the pitiful fate. By extending the reference to an argument on the imperfections of human beings in general, reminding the reader of the exceptionality of guiltlessness, the narrator draws an analogy between the reader and Bulstrode. Consequently, recognising that he or she has more in common with the imperfect Bulstrode than with infallible 'Faithful', the reader is inspired to sympathise with his situation.

Another type of introductory passage appears in chapter 29, when Dorothea and Casaubon have returned from their honeymoon:

> One morning some weeks after her arrival at Lowick, Dorothea – but why always Dorothea? Was her point of view the only possible one with regard to this marriage? I protest against all our interests, all our effort at understanding being given to the young skins that look blooming in spite of trouble; for these too will get faded, and will know the older and more eating griefs which we are helping to neglect (xxix, 261).

This unexpected outburst succeeds an epigraph from *The Vicar of Wakefield*, which has obvious reference to Casaubon.[32] The epigraph signals that the focus of the chapter will be on Casaubon; but the comment still startles, drawing the reader's attention to the narrator's presence and to matters of perspective and interpretation. It emphasises the human propensity for making connections between exteriors and interiors, broaching the theme of deceptive appearances that permeates all Eliot's novels. Heralding the possibility of other perspectives, the comment prepares the reader for his or her imminent partaking of Casaubon's point of view, but it is especially interesting with regard to the relationship between the reader and the narrator.

Questions interwoven in direct addresses are generally rhetorical. They chiefly serve to elicit agreement in order to establish a bond between reader and narrator on a diegetic level above the characters and events of the text.

---

32 The epigraph reads: ' "I found that no genius in another could please me. My unfortunate paradoxes had entirely dried up that source of comfort". – Goldsmith' (xxix, 261).

In the passage above, however, the questions raised are not of the general type. Instead they concern specific matters in the text, begging the question whom they are aimed at. Of course, these questions are not necessarily aimed at anyone: they fill the technical and narratological function of effectually switching attention from Dorothea to Casaubon, challenging the reader to extend his or her sympathy to a character who may not deserve it. Still, the fact that these are questions that only the narrator can answer, and furthermore questions that express objections to limited perspectives which only the narrator himself can be responsible for – insistent as he is on eliciting sympathy for Dorothea and using powerful rhetoric to her advantage – constitutes yet another example of the shifting narratorial voice in *Middlemarch*. Giving the impression of not being in control of the narrative, of being subject – like the reader – to perspectives given by the text, the statement conflicts with other commentary which emphasises authoritative control and omniscience.

Regardless of the narrator's position, however, the passage serves to draw an analogy between the reader and Mr Casaubon, which it does through the general reflection. As if uncertain that this analogy suffices, though, the narrator stresses Casaubon's vulnerability a few lines further down, remarking that he is 'spiritually a-hungered like the rest of us' (xxix, 261). Consequently, although the introductory sentences demonstrate narratorial unpredictability, the passage as a whole diminishes the distance between narrator, reader and character in order to prepare the reader for added dimensions to Casaubon's make-up.[33]

Only six chapters in *Middlemarch* are concluded by narratorial commentary. None of these comments constitutes a definite premonition as to the unfolding of events. Most serve as general commentary on a preceding scene, closing chapters with general reflections which weigh heavily on the particularities of the text. Chapter 6, the first chapter following Dorothea's engagement to Mr Casaubon, depicts Mrs Cadwallader's and Sir James's reactions to the match. To Sir James, who of course wished to marry Dorothea himself, the news of her engagement is particularly upsetting. He is in no position to reveal his emotions, though, as the narrator comments:

> We mortals, men and women, devour many a disappointment between breakfast and dinner-time; keep back the tears and look a little pale about the lips, and in

---

33 It is significant that the narrator's commentary regarding Casaubon escalates in chapter 29, in which he has a minor coronary resulting from a small quarrel with Dorothea. In anticipation of his approaching death, appeals to the reader's understanding and sympathy are gradually intensified.

answer to inquiries say, 'Oh, nothing!' Pride helps us; and pride is not a bad thing
when it only urges us to hide our own hurts – not to hurt others (vi, 57-58).

The generalisation encourages the reader to explore personal experiences
and to activate a sense of recognition. That recognition, in turn, elicits
sympathy for Sir James's situation.[34] But it is important to note that the
reader's sense of recognition does not necessarily derive from actual experiences. Instead recognition may be based on a consciousness which is able to
inhabit the feelings of others. With regard to the circular reading process,
this consciousness is fundamental to the narrator's solicitations for sympathy. Only when the reader relates his or her personal recognition back to
the particularities of the text is sympathy for character or events evoked.
In the example above, the narrator additionally reinforces the notion of a
connection between character and reader through the use of first-person
pronouns. The 'we' presupposes a universal experience which unites the
diegetic sphere with that of the reader: all three agents, character, narrator
and reader, are thus assumed to exist within one shared sphere of experience in which understanding is made possible.

It is significant that this reflective comment concludes a chapter which
is predominantly humorous in its account of responses to Dorothea's engagement. Depicting Mrs Cadwallader's reaction in particular – describing how she immediately, in turncoat fashion, decides that Celia is the
better match for Chettam – the chapter initially makes light of the effects of Dorothea's engagement. But in the closing statement the attitude
has changed and the reader's understanding is invoked. Consequently, the
chapter gradually moves from a humorous perspective to a more serious
one, eventually closing in on Sir James's subconscious reaction and drawing the reader into his psychological processes.

References and Addresses to the Reader

In a sense all narratorial comments could be considered to be references
and addresses to the reader, as their fundamental effect is to influence his

---

34 Isobel Armstrong discusses this comment, arguing that it provides an example of an
erroneous narratorial comment as it is 'simply not wise'. Armstrong finds the comment
irritating because, she claims, the instinct to complain about disappointments is
more natural than to endure them quietly. Armstrong contends that the comment is
'moralizing and preachy' and that it serves as a pointer to the reader 'suggesting that we
should swallow disappointment, not that we *do*' (119).

or her interpretation of the text. However, some comments deal more directly than others with the reader's response, either assuming that he or she will react in a specific way or remarking on how a particular phenomenon should be understood. These direct addresses frequently purport to authenticate fictional events and characters in addition to conditioning the reader's understanding of the text. In *Middlemarch*, the narrator, often conspicuously present, is not only concerned with the characters in the text, but also with the reader and with how he or she relates to the particulars of the diegesis. By drawing attention to the reader's interpretation, the narrator emphasises the reader's active part and raises the level of awareness as to the idea of active communication between diegetic properties, narrator and reader. Besides, the narrator reveals his own concern with the precise depiction of certain characters and phenomena, indicating a consciousness of self as well as an awareness of a responding reader.

In chapter 15, which is unique in its detailed account of Lydgate's personal history, the narrator repeatedly reflects on the presence of a reader and on his or her impression of Lydgate. The first comment pertains to Lydgate's professional ambitions:

> Does it seem incongruous to you that a Middlemarch surgeon should dream of himself as a discoverer? Most of us, indeed, know little of the great originators until they have been lifted up among the constellations and already rule our fates (xv, 137).

With its extensive character analysis, chapter 15 ensures that the reader receives more background information about Lydgate than about any other character in *Middlemarch*, including Dorothea.[35] In the form of FID, it outlines his ambitions for a professional future, and analyses and interprets him through narrative description.[36] The reader learns that Lydgate views his part in the medical profession as constituting a combination of roles: he is rural doctor, medical scientist and groundbreaking discoverer all in one, wishing 'to do good small work for Middlemarch, and great work for

---

35 In effect, little is revealed about Dorothea's life before the beginning of the narrative. The reader learns that she is orphaned at the age of twelve and has been to school in Switzerland, but little else. With regard to chapter 15, David Carroll observes how well George Eliot's commentary interweaves the 'hermeneutic language and perspective of the character under discussion', causing interpretation and representation to become one. See *Conflict of Interpretations*, p. 267.

36 Chapter 15 not only depicts Lydgate as the ambitious scientist but also as the jilted lover whose passion strikes as 'the sudden impulse of a madman' (xv, 143). Insinuating that 'he had two selves within him' (xv, 143), the narrator emphasises the complexities of Lydgate's character. Bernard Paris maintains that it is this other, passionate self, vaguely delineated by the narrator, which is to blame for his eventual ruin. See *Rereading Eliot: Changing Responses to Her Experiments in Life* (Albany: State University of New York Press, 2003), p. 63.

the world' (xv, 139). It is Lydgate's professional aspirations that occasion questions to the reader, questions that imply that the narrator has misgivings about the reader's acceptance of Lydgate's plans. It is unclear in the quoted comment above, however, whether the narrator's query concerns the authenticity of the narrative or the viability of Lydgate's ambitions. The one interpretation would suggest distrust of the narrative, and the other distrust of Lydgate.

If the address is regarded as an assumption that the reader may have reservations concerning the authenticity of the text, an element of meta-narration comes into play. In this interpretation the narrator imagines a disapproving reader who questions the degree of 'realism' in the text. The purpose of the second sentence ('Most of us…') is to convince the reader of the legitimacy of the narrative, assuring him or her that the notion of a highly ambitious provincial doctor need not conflict with the idea of realistic representation. The continuation of the comment, which mentions the eighteenth-century astronomer Sir William Herschel, reinforces the presumption of realistic representation by reference to an incontestable fact. In this sense, the focus of the comment is on the relationship between the reader and the narrator, the narrator's assumption of the reader's scepticism increasing the distance between the two – at the same time as communication between narrator and reader is particularly direct and palpable here.

On the other hand, the narrator could be taken to suppose that the reader is critical of Lydgate as a character, that he or she regards his aspirations as naïve and excessively idealistic. In this sense, the generalisation serves to defend Lydgate, convincing the reader that his ambitions, albeit high, are nonetheless reasonable. In this interpretation, focus is on the reader's relation to Lydgate, the narrator functioning as an intercessor between the two. However, an ironical element surfaces here as well. As events unfold, it becomes evident that Lydgate's plans prove to *be* unrealistic and that he *does* fail, not necessarily because his ambitions are too high but because his calculations do not allow for the interference of social claims – that is, his lack of success rests on a failure to balance professional plans against the realities of a workaday world.[37] Read in this way, the comment presupposes a reader reservation which in fact turns out to be well-founded.

---

37 Suzanne Graver makes this observation, too, maintaining that '[o]nce the novel begins to test Lydgate's dream […] the inexactness of relation he brings to his own intellectual and social life becomes increasingly more apparent'. Graver argues that Lydgate 'thinks to unify the prosaic and the poetic, but this thoroughly conventional and false poetic cannot but debase the life it transforms' (141).

Chapter 15 continues to analyse Lydgate's character and weaves in and out of FID, narrative description and narratorial commentary. A few pages further on from the first example, the narrator is again concerned with the reader's evaluation of him:

> The faults will not, I hope, be a reason for the withdrawal of your interest in him. Among our valued friends is there not some one or other who is a little too self-confident and disdainful; whose distinguished mind is a little spotted with commonness; who is a little pinched here and protuberant there with native prejudices (xv, 140).

There are several possible reasons for the narrator's devoting so much space to the analysis of Lydgate. As a newcomer in Middlemarch, he is as unknown to the members of the community as he is to the reader.[38] Besides, he is an outsider and so must be understood differently from characters who are products of Middlemarch society. What is more, Lydgate's desire to combine the prosaic with the poetic reflects the pervading theme of unity and disparity in the novel, and his passion for scientific discovery stands out in sharp relief to Casaubon's painstaking but futile research. Hence, the reader's understanding of his character is vital to his or her discernment of significant themes in the novel, but also – and perhaps more importantly – to his or her appreciation of the tragedy which will eventually transpire.

Having established Lydgate's medical excellence and noble ambitions, the novel must also provide the reader with a human and fallible character. But before Lydgate's flaws are depicted, the reader is addressed in the quotation above. The narrator's tone has become more circumspect, expressing uncertainty as to the reader's reaction. By carefully including the reader in the example, drawing on his or her recognition, the quotation serves to establish a favourable evaluation of Lydgate before his mistakes are described.[39] In contrast to previous addresses regarding Lydgate,

---

38 Bulstrode is another character who enters into the community from the outside. Accordingly, he is the only other character, apart from Lydgate, whose personal history is accounted for in the narrative. The difference, however, is that the reader sees Bulstrode as an established member of the Middlemarch community before his personal history is revealed, whereas Lydgate's personal history in chapter 15 serves as an introduction to his character. Jerome Beaty suggests that chapter 15 in fact constitutes the original introduction to 'Middlemarch', the separate novel which Eliot commenced after abandoning 'Miss Brooke'. See Beaty, p. 24.

39 Eliot's commentary is sometimes said to express the author's anxiety about characters being misunderstood. Karl Kroeber argues that 'Eliot assumes again and again that her reader will misunderstand or misjudge her characters and their actions'; *Styles in Fictional Structure: The Art of Jane Austen, Charlotte Brontë, George Eliot* (Princeton: Princeton University Press, 1971), p. 59. As mentioned, however, I regard the address to

the comment here attempts to bring all three parties together, reducing the distance between narrator and reader as well as between character and reader.[40]

The narrator's tone with regard to Lydgate is predominantly compassionate and earnest. Other characters are not so lucky, for example Rosamond.[41] In chapter 16 she has met with Lydgate, and her considerations regarding him reveal much about her character. The narrator reports that she thinks the 'piquant fact about Lydgate' is 'his good birth' (xvi, 156) whereupon he turns to the reader, remarking:

> If you think it incredible that to imagine Lydgate as a man of family could cause thrills of satisfaction which had anything to do with the sense that she was in love with him, I will ask you to use your power of comparison a little more effectively, and consider whether red cloth and epaulets have never had an influence of that sort (xvi, 156).

Commenting on the relation between Rosamond's obsession with 'family' and her fascination with Lydgate, the sceptical reader is approached again. Here, however, the narrator's tone is ironical, as if responding in the affirmative to the reader's question: 'Can she really be that bad?' In this example, the reader is called upon to participate actively in the interpretation of the narrative, even more forcefully than in previous examples.[42] The

---

the reader's response above as part of the narratological structure of the novel, ensuring the reader's understanding of a character, so that he or she has a full comprehension of the eventual tragedy. Regarding the narrator as a 'licensed trespasser', Eugene Goodheart argues the paradox that omniscient narration is a necessity in a world riven by opposing perspectives, claiming that the narrative voice in *Middlemarch* is not the voice of the ego but the voice of the other; see ' "The Licensed Trespasser": The Omniscient Narrator in *Middlemarch*', *The Sewanee Review*, 107 (1999), 555-569.

40 Carol Howe Spady examines the relationship between narrator and reader in this passage and arrives at a similar conclusion. She argues that the metaphors in the passage alternately elevate the reader to a superior level and remind the reader that he/she is no different from the characters. 'Only after we have been gently puffed up and deflated several times', she claims, 'are we adequately prepared to hear about Lydgate's particular "conceit"' (68). Cicely Palser Havely maintains that the novel 'makes children of its readers' by the 'author's thumb in the scale'; see 'Authorization in Middlemarch', *Essays in Criticism*, 40 (1990), 303-321 (p. 318). It should be noted that the narrator refers to the reader's response in connection with Lydgate and Casaubon more than with any other characters. In Lydgate's case, the narrator addresses the reader again in chapter 64 to comment on his ruin: 'His troubles will perhaps appear miserably sordid, and beneath the attention of lofty persons who can know nothing of debt except on a magnificent scale' (lxiv, 609).

41 The narrator's commentary regarding Rosamond can be oblique. Compare for example his entreaty to the reader to '[t]hink no *unfair* evil of her' (xxvii, 252, my italics), an appeal which implies that there is justified 'evil' to be thought of Rosamond.

42 Jane Smith points out an important distinction when analysing these types of reader addresses. She argues that their function is not merely 'to help us understand the events

purpose here is not to elicit sympathy, however, but rather to extend the reader's vision so that Rosamond's rationale can be understood. But implicit in that understanding is also an appreciation of the narrator's irony: the reader is requested to expand his or her horizons in order to recognise the type of logic Rosamond epitomises, but also to comprehend the narrator's disapproval of it. At the same time, the reader is warned against indulging in complacency: the sharply censorious exhortation is followed by an invitation to remember times when outward marks of distinction evoked similar 'thrills' in the reader's own mind.[43]

The passage surfaces neither in story-time now nor in narration now. Directing his attention to the reader, the narrator of course proceeds into narration now, but the comment nevertheless focuses on the particularities of the diegesis, i.e. proper narration now is not fully effective until the narrator completes the transfer from the particular to the general, which has not taken place in the quotation above. The narrator and the reader thus meet in a narrative sphere which suspends both narration now and story-time now. In this twilight zone the narrator candidly acknowledges the presence of a reader in the narrative, addressing him or her without the aid of generalities. The reader consequently becomes part of the narrative process, but without the occurrence of metalepsis.

Instances of metalepsis are virtually absent from *Middlemarch*, but there are nevertheless allusions to the reader's ability to visualise. In a comment on Mary Garth, the narrator acknowledges the fact that the reader belongs to a different sphere, but attempts to facilitate the reader's notion of Mary's appearance: [44]

> If you want to know more particularly how Mary looked, ten to one you will see a face like hers in the crowded street to-morrow, if you are there on the watch [...] fix your eyes on some small plump brownish person of firm but quiet carriage, who looks about her, but does not suppose that anybody is looking at her (xl, 382).

---

of the novel' but also to help 'us understand our own involvement in those events' (198). Incidentally, Smith discusses the types of commentary which begin with 'Do not suppose' or 'If you think', like the one above, maintaining that they have 'the same effect of implicit accusation' (198).

43 Suzanne Graver considers this passage another example of George Eliot's social criticism and argues that by employing 'the most prosaic of activities – social climbing and financial extravagance', Eliot encourages 'her readers to comparisons important precisely because they involve commonplace experiences' (68).

44 Scenes of seeing and images of vision occur throughout the novel. Cf. the pier-glass analogy in chapter 27, the red drapery hung for Christmas in St Peter's in Rome which affects Dorothea like a 'disease of the retina' (xx, 182) and, in chapter 28, the feeling of oppression she experiences when gazing out on the dreary Lowick landscape which reflects the misery of her own dismal state back to her.

Having abandoned metalepsis, this narratorial comment firmly establishes the reader's position outside the narrative. It moreover disregards the reader's capacity for imagining what Mary looks like, instead proposing that he or she distinguish a 'Mary' in his or her own 'world'. Counteracting the impression of fictionality, this method of situating diegetic elements within the actual reader's 'world' serves to enhance the impression that the novel is telling a 'real' story. By emphasising parallels between the fictional world and the 'real', the comment lends authenticity to the narrative. In addition, approaching the idea of a contradiction between the exceptional and the commonplace, the passage seems to suggest that there are 'Marys' everywhere, in all worlds, at all times; so that someone like her is easy to spot even in the reader's order of 'reality'. Again, the narrator is engaging *with* the reader as well as engaging him or her *in* the narrative process.[45] An important distinction, however, which sets this passage apart from other comments, is that it turns the reader's visual field away from the diegesis and not onto a general, philosophical idea but onto his or her actual, tangible 'world'. Consequently, the recognition which the narrator expects to take place is visual rather than ideological and shaped according to the narrator's careful instructions rather than elicited from previous experience.

References are also signalled by the first-person pronoun, as seen in the earlier books, and in *Middlemarch* 'we' is used in two senses. It can signify an alliance between the narrator and the reader which excludes the characters in the text, but most often it denotes human nature in general, including diegetic characters. In this latter sense the engaging 'we' serves as a link between the diegetic world and the reader's world, positioning the narrator as mediator between the two. As seen in quotations above, *Middlemarch* is permeated with references to 'we' which serve to include characters and readers into a shared body of experiences. In chapter 47, the reader's understanding of Will Ladislaw is appealed to in this fashion. Remarking on his adoration for Dorothea, the narrator relates his emotions to general phenomena:

> Do we not shun the street version of a fine melody? – or shrink from the news that the rarity – some bit of chiselling or engraving perhaps – which we have dwelt on even with exultation in the trouble it has cost us to snatch glimpses of it, is really not an uncommon thing, and may be obtained as an everyday possession? (xlvii, 441).

---

45 There are several shorter references to the reader's estimation of characters which do not belong in narration now but which nonetheless engage the reader in the same way. See, for example, the introduction of Mr Farebrother's mother: 'Pray think no ill of Miss Noble' (xvii, 158), and referring to Mr Brooke: 'Pray pity him' (li, 473), and the already mentioned remark on Rosamond: 'Think no unfair evil of her, pray' (xxvii, 252).

The rhetoric of the question, 'do we not', not only incorporates the reader into the example but also obliges him or her to agree with the argument. Will's feeling for Dorothea is explained through metaphorical representation in such a way as to situate the reader within the metaphor. Stimulating the reader's recognition, the narrator justifies Will's standpoint on the grounds that his idolisation is a recognisable human idiosyncrasy. By associating Will's attitude with phenomena the reader can recognise, the comment urges him or her to sympathise with Will while simultaneously revealing the extent and nature of his feelings for Dorothea.[46]

Furthermore, the question, albeit rhetorical, is significant to the reader's involvement in the text. Reader addresses in the form of questions are frequent in *Middlemarch* and operate in distinct ways. As mentioned above, direct references to the reader's expected response can appear as questions to the reader; but queries also appear in a more general sense, to reinforce a mutual understanding between the narrator and the reader or to present suppositions on which arguments are based. These types of questions appear throughout the novel but are more frequent in the first half of the book, especially in Book 1. Here, regarding Casaubon's reaction to Dorothea's acceptance of his marriage proposal, the narrator approaches the reader, asking:

> Would it not be rash to conclude that there was no passion behind those sonnets to Delia which strike us as the thin music of a mandolin? Dorothea's faith supplied all that Mr Casaubon's words seemed to leave unsaid: what believer sees a disturbing omission or infelicity? The text, whether of prophet or of poet, expands for whatever we can put into it, and even his bad grammar is sublime (v, 46).

Casaubon has expressed his happiness to Dorothea, but his declaration of affection is stilted rather than heartfelt. The first question could be regarded as a remark on the reader's expected response but is so only in an indirect sense, as it is preceded by an insistence on the sincerity of Casaubon's speech. Rather than making assumptions as to the reader's reaction, then, the question reinforces the narrator's assertion by relating it to a literary reference. Again, the analogy serves to curb the reader's possible censure, reminding him or her, by way of a recognisable literary reference, of the possibility of incongruence between emotions and language.[47] The second

---

46 Cf. chapter 54, where Dorothea's feelings for Will are communicated through the narrator's use of imagery – the princess and the horse 'in the days of enchantment' (liv, 507).

47 Otice C. Sircy analyses this reference, claiming that the reader is asked to inspect Casaubon's sincerity 'against three standards: the amorous rook, the bark of a dog [...] and the sonnet-lover's ardour which is closely identified with the idealized language of

question elaborates the preceding sentence, associating Dorothea's particular frame of mind with a general phenomenon common to human nature. Here, there is no implicit reference to the reader's expected response; rather, the question serves rhetorically to situate the particular within the general and to facilitate the reader's understanding of Dorothea's biased perspective. The question which temporarily arrests the reading process, inducing the reader to see the connection between particular and general, is elaborated further in the ensuing sentence, which illustrates how Dorothea's subconscious compensates for Casaubon's inept declaration of love.[48] Aptly, Casaubon is likened to a text for Dorothea to interpret, and as her mind is already made up as to its excellence she subconsciously fills in the gaps.[49]

Dorothea's narrow view of Casaubon is comparable to Will's notion of her perfection. Both characters are convinced of another individual's pre-eminence, and both comments explicate their biased perspectives to the reader. But while Will recalls Dorothea's distinction merely by 'thinking of her just as she was' (xlvii, 441) at a particular moment in time, Dorothea continuously interprets Casaubon as something he is *not*. Therefore, while the narrator frequently insinuates that Dorothea's interpretation of Casaubon is inaccurate, Will's subjective adoration is not only excused on the grounds of his being in love but also reinforced by the narrator. Still, the phenomenon of constructing idealised images of another individual is

---

passionate love and rhetorical heat'. These three standards, Sircy contends, offer 'criteria for judging the evidence of Casaubon's "passion" '. See ' "The Fashion of Sentiment": Allusive Technique and the Sonnets of *Middlemarch*', *Studies in Philology*, 84 (1987), 219-244 (p. 228).

48 Compare this comment with a passage in chapter 9, where Dorothea visits Lowick for the first time: 'She filled up all blanks with unmanifested perfections, interpreting him as she interpreted the works of Providence, and accounting for seeming discords by her own deafness to the higher harmonies' (ix, 68). Of course, both passages are relevant to the idea of ambiguous interpretation which is an important theme in the novel and which will be discussed below.

49 Observing this point, J. Hillis Miller argues that Dorothea 'misreads' Casaubon and that this misreading 'exemplifies the way we misinterpret signs by projecting on them a coherence born of our own egoistic desires'; 'The Roar on the Other Side of Silence', p. 140. However, it is possible to argue against Miller's idea of *mis*reading as it implies that there is an absolute reading, which stems from an objective, 'true' perspective. Comparing Casaubon to a text, Dorothea approaches him with a certain set of expectations and attempts to meet those expectations by filling in the gaps (Iser) which Casaubon's character and contradictions lay open to interpretation. Rather than *mis*reading Casaubon, then, Dorothea reads him through the subjective perspective which is available to her. Gradually, this perspective will change and her reading will be a different one, but that does not imply that her first reading was necessarily a *mis*reading; rather, it was her reading at the time.

the same for both characters; it is only the narrator's attitude that makes them seem distinct.[50]

The first-person pronoun is abundantly used in *Middlemarch*. Not only 'we' is employed; the narrator's 'I' is prominent too. To a greater extent than in, for example, *Silas Marner*, *Felix Holt* and *Daniel Deronda*, the *Middlemarch* narrator appears as an immediate and perceptible presence, proffering his own opinions on the text and attempting to shape the reader's. However, as opposed to narratorial presences in *The Mill on the Floss* and *Adam Bede*, the *Middlemarch* narrator remains firmly fixed within an extradiegetic-heterodiegetic sphere and does not indicate that he plays any personal role in the diegetic world. Instead, his omniscience alternates with an engaged voice which stands close to characters and events but which is nevertheless positioned above and beyond the properties of the diegesis. In fact, this position outside the story is repeatedly emphasised through the narrator's use of the first-person pronoun.

Occasionally the 'I' is assertive, but the personal pronoun also often indicates a degree of prudence which undermines the idea of omniscience and authoritative control. As in earlier novels, these instances embody a rhetoric which temporarily relaxes the narrator's hierarchical hold on the narrative, seeming to allow him subjective opinions by which he can meet the reader on a shared level. The phrase 'I suppose' indicates this type of suspension of narratorial authority; it appears, for example, in connection with Lydgate's new, and in a Middlemarch context radical, way of practis-

---

50 In her analysis of reader response in *Middlemarch*, Carol Howe Spady argues that the typical structure of commentary in the novel is tripartite. Using the quotation above to illustrate her point, Howe Spady maintains that the first part conveys a general assessment of the character's mental status. Through descriptive narration the omniscient narrator communicates a particular character's psychological processes. In the passage above, Howe Spady argues, this is expressed in the sentence about Dorothea's faith. In the second part of the comment, Howe Spady continues, the question about what believers see repositions the narrator onto a new sphere which exists between the characters in the diegesis and the reader. Finally, the narrator secures the reader's participation in the text by the use of a metaphor which includes all of human nature into its symbolism. Although Howe Spady's analysis of this particular quotation is illuminating and her notion of a tripartite structure interesting, there is little in *Middlemarch* to suggest that comments are generally restricted to this threefold system. For example, Howe Spady does not include the narrator's question about Samuel Daniel's sonnets into her analysis. Immediately preceding the description of Dorothea, this reader address, which has already situated the reader in narration now, undermines Howe Spady's tripartite structure by its mere presence as a fourth dimension. Nevertheless, Howe Spady's structure does suggest itself as an interesting matrix for the organisation of narratorial commentary and supports the idea of the narrator's movement between particular and general. See Howe Spady, p. 65.

ing medicine.[51] The narrator comments: 'I suppose no doctor ever came newly to a place without making cures that surprised somebody' (xlv, 421). The supposition reveals a narrative voice which is less 'sage-like' than, for example, the voice of proverb-like comments, and which presents a more personalised attitude.[52] Waiving the previous assertive tone, the comment draws nearer the reader, approaching his or her level rather than pulling him or her onto the narrator's.

A similar reduction of distance between narrator and reader occurs through the use of the phrase 'I think'. For example, after an interview with Mary Garth, Mr Farebrother is deep in contemplation on his walk home and shrugs to himself at the folly of his own thoughts. This particular manifestation of body language causes the narrator to remark:

> I think that the rare Englishmen who have this gesture are never of the heavy type – for fear of any lumbering instances to the contrary, I will say, hardly ever; they have usually a fine temperament and much tolerance towards the smaller errors of men (themselves inclusive) (xl, 383).

The comment attaches several reservations to its own assertion, displaying an unusual degree of hesitance. First, the phrase 'I think' signals the narrator's subjective stance and indicates his awareness of the possibility of other perspectives. This awareness is emphasised, secondly, by an intimation of 'fear' and a modification of the assertion. Finally, the contention is qualified by the presence of 'usually' which adds further vagueness to it, serving almost as a precautionary measure should the narrator be accused of being categorical.[53] In view of the fact that most of Eliot's novels contain considerations of two principal themes, the idea of deceptive appearances and the notion of limitless interpretation, it seems reasonable that the narrator should add reservations to contestable assertions. But it is atypical for commentary in Eliot's novels to reflect on particularities which might not be recognised as universal phenomena. However, as stated in the comment

---

51 Ironically, Lydgate's radicalism is here represented by his reluctance to prescribe unnecessary medicines and by this treatment of Nancy Nash's 'tumour', which he diagnoses as a bout of cramp. He cannot set Nancy right in her amazement at his medical 'genius', as that 'would only have added to his breaches of medical propriety' (xlv, 423).

52 Coincidentally, the same chapter includes an address to the reader, instructing him or her to *not* suppose: 'And let it not be supposed that opinion at the Tankard in Slaughter Lane was unimportant to the medical profession' (xlv, 415).

53 Just a few passages prior to this quotation, the narrator displays a similar type of diffidence when commenting on Mary's judgment of Fred and Mr Farebrother: 'These irregularities of judgment, *I imagine*, are found even in riper minds than Mary Garth's' (xl, 382, my italics).

itself, the type of Englishman referred to is 'rare' and therefore, according to the assertion, possibly not accessible to the reader's frame of reference. The statement thus suggests that Mr Farebrother's unusual character is understood not through general phenomena, but through the reader's readiness to be alerted to this original cleric's exceptionality.

'I think' in the example above not only demonstrates the narrator's easing of authority, bringing him closer to the reader; it also invites the reader's active engagement into the text, encouraging him or her to consider the contention advanced by the narrator. Unlike most narratorial commentary, especially comments which include the plural first-person pronoun, 'I think' signals a suggestion rather than an assertion. The reader's concurrence is in this instance not a prerequisite for his or her understanding of characters or events, nor is it imperative for his or her comprehension of a pervading narratorial attitude. Consequently, in this example, 'I think' temporarily relaxes the narrator's control not merely of the text, but also of the reader.[54]

'I think' involves several nuances, however, and can be employed contrastingly to establish opinions which reinforce narratorial authority rather than relaxing it. Again referring to Casaubon and to the reader's understanding of him, the narrator admonishes an anticipated response:

> Instead of wondering at this result of misery in Mr Casaubon, I think it quite ordinary. Will not a tiny speck very close to our vision blot out the glory of the world, and leave only a margin by which we see the blot? I know no speck so troublesome as self (xlii, 392).

Responding to an expected objection, the use of 'I think' here serves to fortify the authenticity of the preceding description of Casaubon's mental state. The rhetorical difference between this 'I think' and the phrase above is that the latter quotation employs it to assert an opinion rather than to state a potentially refutable belief. Hence, there is a difference in confidence and conviction attached to the two uses of the phrase. Besides, in this example the narrator's tone of authority is reinforced by an ensuing rhetorical question and by an additional narratorial assertion which relies on experience for veracity.[55] In its context, the phrase privileges the narrator's power of interpretation. Here, contrary to the former quotation, 'I think' is supported by a general reflection. Asking and expecting the

---

54 Cf. Nünning, p. 247.

55 Carol Howe Spady maintains that this comment demonstrates a narratorial tactic by which the reader is gradually led to sympathise with Casaubon. The 'I' leading into the 'we' and then back to 'I' again, she suggests, prompts the reader to follow 'the lead of the more compassionate narrator' (70).

reader to confirm the accuracy of this general observation, the narrator manipulates the reader to recognise the authenticity of Casaubon's psyche.[56] Interestingly, this relatively short comment includes both the narrator's personalised first-person pronoun and the plural first-person. The distance between reader and narrator should, accordingly, be diminished, as the narrator not only appears as an individual presence in the comment but also involves the reader in the argument by the use of 'we' and by reshaping the observation into a question. However, the defensive tone counteracts a diminution of distance between the reader and narrator, as the comment somewhat testily responds to an assumed objection. Hence, although the two examples of 'I think' convey the narrator's presence and reveal his view of the text, they operate in contrasting ways.

Typically, comments which include the personalised 'I' reveal the narrator's attitude to characters or events in a conspicuous manner. The 'I' frequently appears where the narrator is candid about the 'right' interpretation of diegetic elements, as observed in the examples above where the 'I' makes assumptions about the reader's reaction. But in some cases the reader's solidarity with the narrator's attitude towards particular characters is taken for granted. For example, with regard to Dorothea's misery in Rome, the narrator starts by stating: 'I am sorry to add that she was sobbing bitterly' (xx, 180). Concerning Fred Vincy's unsuccessful horse-dealings, a similar approach is adopted: 'I am sorry to say that only the third day after the propitious events at Houndsley Fred Vincy had fallen into worse spirits' (xxiv, 226). These expressions of regret not only display the narrator's attitude to the situation of characters, they also presuppose the reader's absolute concurrence with that attitude. Here, then, there is no anxiety as to how the reader might interpret particular episodes but rather the reverse, as the reader is assumed to share in the narrator's stance. Moreover, these explicit statements generally appear prior to the depiction of the respective situations, thereby predisposing the reader to adopt a distinct attitude before he or she is acquainted with the details of each particular episode.

Consequently, regardless of how the first-person pronoun appears in narratorial commentary, it continuously operates to shape the reader's understanding of the text by offering personal opinions, seeming to relax the narrator's superior hold on the narrative and drawing the reader closer to the narrator's level. But although the narrator's personified presence seems

---

56 P. Di Pasquale argues that this passage serves as an example of the novel's theme of vision or rather the lack of vision. The passage shows, says Di Pasquale, that Casaubon is not only weak-sighted but also 'spiritually blind'; see 'The Imagery and Structure of *Middlemarch*', *English Studies: A Journal of English Letters and Philology*, 52 (1971), 425-435 (p. 431).

much on a level with the reader, it remains within an extradiegetic-hetero-diegetic paradigm, constantly in control of the text and generally endeavouring also to be in control of the reader.

Meta-Narrative Comments

Meta-narrative comments in *Middlemarch* are usually linked to the narrator's 'I'. By drawing attention to the narrator's presence and to the act of narrating, meta-narrative comments often serve as reminders of fictionality and narratorial control.[57] One of the most famous passages in *Middlemarch* is the introduction to chapter 15, where the narrator refers to Henry Fielding and the type of narration which prevailed in his day, 'when summer afternoons were spacious, and the clock ticked slowly in the winter evenings' (xv, 132) and when there was time for 'copious remarks and digressions' (xv, 132). Commenting on his own narrating task after having introduced the chapter with a fairly long discussion of history and narration, the *Middlemarch* narrator ironically claims to have no time for digression:

> I at least have so much to do in unravelling certain human lots, and seeing how they were woven and interwoven, that all the light I can command must be concentrated on this particular web, and not dispersed over that tempting range of relevancies called the universe. At present I have to make the new settler Lydgate better known to any one interested in him (xv, 132).

Purporting to be a 'belated historian' (xv, 132), the narrator makes claims as to the 'actuality' of diegetic characters, intimating that his task consists in structuring history into an intelligible and coherent whole. By claiming to be unfolding actual historical events, the narrator directs the reader's attention to the act of narration, but he does so without acknowledging any element of artificiality in the text. On the contrary, by modifying preconceived ideas about what the narrative act entails – that is, by defining the narrative as a historical account rather than a work of the imagination – the narrator endeavours to reinforce the impression of veracity. By assuming the role of historian, moreover, the narrator preserves his exclusive position vis-à-vis the text, reminding the reader of his privileged power of

---

57 Obvious examples of meta-narration in *Middlemarch* can be compared with meta-narrative comments in *Daniel Deronda* which are subtle and restricted, corresponding to the narrator's understated presence in the text.

interpretation. This assumed role can be seen almost as a performance on the part of the narrator, who self-consciously enacts the part of historian and continually draws the reader's attention to this assumed role. In this sense, the narrator enhances the notion of artificiality as he not only creates the text but also himself.

This narratorial display of control is further enhanced by the comment's attention to the narrator's management and structuring of the narrative. Including obviously meta-narrative signs which emphasise the narrator's authority over the text, the introduction to chapter 15 nevertheless reinforces an impression of authenticity, as the entire passage promotes the narrative as a historical account.[58] The narrator's alleged dissociation from an earlier type of historian (Fielding) further accentuates the task of narrating. Regarded as work, a duty to be performed which cannot be interrupted by subjective irrelevancies, the narrating task, the comment suggests, should be focused; the narrator must not fly off on tangents. As opposed to Fielding's narrating, which is regarded as a performance in which the story-teller brings 'his arm-chair to the proscenium' (xv, 132), the *Middlemarch* narrator claims that the unfolding of 'actual' events is his sole concern. Consequently, the whole passage is meta-narrative in that it discusses the act of narration and intimates the narrator's authority over it; but by stressing the narrator's role as historian, the comment nevertheless serves to reinforce the impression of authenticity in the diegesis.[59]

This connection between the narrator's alleged function as historian and meta-narrative commentary occurs repeatedly in *Middlemarch*, stress-

---

58 Colin MacCabe maintains that the narrator's digression in chapter 15 is 'no real digression because, situated in the middle of the narrative, its function is merely to efface itself; to testify to the reality of the story in which it is held' (19). Furthermore, MacCabe argues, the passage persuades the reader 'that language and form have disappeared, allowing light to shine on the previously obscured world' (20). I cannot agree with MacCabe's claim that the passage effaces itself. It is situated as an introduction, thus structurally drawing attention to itself, and furthermore it serves an ironical function which would be lost if the passage were self-effacing. Making a similar criticism, David Lodge states that MacCabe's argument 'seems a very stubborn refusal to credit George Eliot with ironic selfconsciousness' (234). Nor can I agree with MacCabe's second contention. The meta-narrative aspect of the passage, the narrator's emphasis on his structuring and organising task, undeniably highlights language and form as constituents in the 'unravelling'. Indeed, the narrator's indication of authority over the narrating act implies a firm control of language and form.

59 In 'Having the Whip-Hand in *Middlemarch*' in *Rereading Victorian Fiction*, ed. by Alice Jenkins and Juliet John (Basingstoke: Macmillan, 2000), pp. 29-43, Daniel Karlin claims that the 'task of unravelling [certain human lots] is given to the novelist, who forgets to mention that she has done the original weaving and interweaving with her own hands' (43). Appealing as Karlin's image is, it provides a good example of how many critics disregard the meta-narrative element which actually accentuates the narrator's role as director and arranger of the 'unravelling'.

ing the point of historical authenticity. Apropos of Mr Brooke's optimism as regards Casaubon's prospects of becoming a bishop, the narrator comments:

> And here I must vindicate a claim to philosophical reflectiveness, by remarking that Mr Brooke on this occasion little thought of the Radical speech which, at a later period, he was led to make on the incomes of the bishops. What elegant historian would neglect a striking opportunity for pointing out that his heroes did not foresee the history of the world, or even their own actions? (vii, 61).

The idea of the narrative as a rendering of historical events is emphasised in the comment and reinforced by its continuation, which juxtaposes Mr Brooke with actual historical figures such as Henry of Navarre and Alfred the Great. The comment serves to underpin the notion of veracity in the text, suggesting that Mr Brooke is as 'real' as these two historical figures. Additionally, by assuming the role of historian, the narrator promotes the impression of a mediated authentic history. But here, ironically, the meta-narrative element challenges the essence of the statement. As Mr Brooke's forthcoming 'Radical speech' (vii, 61) is anticipated, the historian-narrator reveals his exclusive control of forthcoming developments. This indication of control and authority exists on two levels. The first is the advance notice, which signals the narrator's omniscience. Of course, it could be argued that a historian 40 years after the fact has access to the same information about events as an omniscient narrator, therefore rendering the challenge futile. But the statement 'Mr Brooke on this occasion little thought of' (vii, 61) counteracts the notion of a chronicling historian, instead promoting the impression of an omniscient entity with access to characters' internal thoughts. Secondly, the comment draws attention to the narrator's management of the text, adumbrating his function as supervisor, positioned to alternately highlight and obfuscate narrative details at will. The meta-narrative comment thus reinforces the narrator's authoritative position in the text while reducing the impression of fictionality by stressing his role as historian.[60]

Upholding a position of authority, the narrator controls not only the structure, form and contents of the narrative, but also the mode of representation through which it is mediated. Choice of words, nuance and

---

60 In his analysis of meta-narration in John Fowles' *The French Lieutenant's Woman*, Frederick M. Holmes identifies a similar phenomenon, an author who is 'able to create the paradoxical effect of a narrative at once credible on a realistic plane and self-consciously artificial'; see 'The Novel, Illusion and Reality: The Paradox of Omniscience in *The French Lieutenant's Woman*' in *Metafiction*, ed. by Mark Currie (London: Longman, 1995), pp. 206-220 (p. 208).

tone all work together to shape the reader's understanding of the text. Although meta-narrative commentary draws attention to the narrating act, it rarely involves the narrator's making self-conscious references to the relevant mode of representation. Exceptions occur, however, as in chapter 42 where the narrator interrupts and qualifies his own description of Casaubon: 'This is a very bare and therefore a very incomplete way of putting the case' (xlii, 394). After acknowledging the inadequacy of the way in which the case is presented here, the narrator elaborates on his analysis. Atypically, this comment downplays the narrator's confidence, instead drawing attention to the fallibility of representation and to the problem of reliable interpretation. The concern of the comment is not with authority, authenticity or artificiality, but with the reader's response to Casaubon. By admitting that the rendering is deficient and facile, the comment arrests the reader's potential censure of Casaubon, by extension eliciting his or her understanding. It is important to note that it is only the reader's understanding that is solicited, not his or her compassion. The passage relates Casaubon's feelings of jealousy and vindictiveness, which he obscures in his codicil under an illusory concern for Dorothea's safety. In this case, the meta-narrative comment serves to affect the reader's interpretation of a particular character while inviting him or her to recognise the limitations which a certain chosen mode of representation entails.

Another deliberate reference to the mode of representation in connection with the reader's appraisal of character appears in chapter 23, where Fred receives Caleb Garth's signature to his bill of debt. The chapter forms an extensive introduction to the Garth family and includes a good deal of detail as to Caleb Garth's character and appearance. With regard to the meticulous account of Mr Garth's physical aspects, the narrator apologises to the reader in a parenthetical aside: '(pardon these details for once – you would have learned to love them if you had known Caleb Garth)' (xxiii, 219).

There are several functions at work in this comment. First, it is meta-narrative in the sense that it draws attention to diegetic constituents. Remarking on the narrating act, the comment emphasises the narrator's jurisdiction over what goes into the story and what does not.[61] Secondly, the comment addresses the reader directly, speculating on what he or she might have felt about Caleb Garth had he or she known him. *Middlemarch* is practically exempt from examples of metalepsis, but this comment sug-

---

61 Cf. a similar comment in *Daniel Deronda*: 'Contemptible details these, to make part of a history; yet the turn of most lives is hardly to be accounted for without them' (xxi, 195).

gests that diegetic levels can be overcome. The reader is invited to imagine himself or herself as part of the diegetic sphere, and this imagined breaking down of diegetic barriers reduces the distance between the reader and the character and enhances the reader's sympathy for Caleb Garth. Besides, the comment insinuates that the narrator is personally acquainted with Mr Garth and that he has learnt to love those details of which he speaks. This is the only instance in the novel where the narrator seems to leave the extradiegetic-heterodiegetic sphere by implying a personal and 'real' contact with the diegetic world, and it serves to authenticate Mr Garth's 'realness' in order for the reader to sympathise with his character. Finally, the parenthesised comment interjects a descriptive element, creating a sense of a dialogue with the reader. This brief and parenthetic meta-narrative address hence demonstrates the narrator's awareness of a responding and ubiquitous reader, whose possible objections and questions are met in narration now and whose presence as an active agent impels the narrator to appraise the credibility of his own story.

Egoism

It seems natural to begin the thematically orientated section of this chapter by discussing egoism. Egoism is *the* major theme which drives the narrative of *Middlemarch* forward and affects each principal character in one way or another. Dorothea's progress from an adolescence of ardent egoism to a maturity of altruism and compassion in many ways sets the pattern for the analysis of self-absorption in the novel.[62] But the manifestations and effects of egoism are presented in various ways by various characters. Casaubon, for instance, demonstrates a selfishness which exerts its will, psychological and legal, both in life and from beyond the grave, and the same applies to Peter Featherstone. Bulstrode represents the egoist who translates personal desire into providence and the execution of divine will, and Rosamond – perhaps the most self-absorbed character in the novel

---

62 K. M. Newton suggests that Dorothea 'possesses the same strength of feeling and potentially dangerous egotistic energies as Maggie Tulliver, Romola and Esther Lyon'; *George Eliot*, p. 124. This seems a just estimate but for one thing: the claim that Esther Lyon belongs to this group. It should be remembered that Esther is not trapped between a strong intellect and societal convention; she does not provoke the way Maggie does, or embody the type of ardent feeling that Romola and Dorothea do. Her altruism and self-abnegation are prompted and shaped by Felix, who becomes the most significant influence on her life.

– exists solely within her own ego.[63] But *Middlemarch* also presents characters who resign personal will to circumstance, and who incorporate a measure of self-abnegation which is not occasioned by ideological persuasion but by acquiescence in the conditions given. Mr Farebrother, for example, chooses not to compete with Fred for Mary's love, instead operating as a mediator between the two; Fred, in turn, eventually reconciles himself to his disappointment over Mr Featherstone's will and finds a purposeful profession; Mrs Bulstrode, unlike Rosamond, accepts the humiliation her husband has brought upon her and moves towards him in sympathy; and Lydgate, finally, accepts the failure of his high-flying plans and acquiesces in becoming one 'in the multitude of middle-aged men who go about their vocation in a daily course determined for them' (xv, 135).

One of the most famous comments in the novel pertains to Casaubon's egoism, but it is equally applicable to other characters: 'We are all of us born in moral stupidity, taking the world as an udder to feed our supreme selves' (xxi, 198).[64] The comment appears as Dorothea begins to discern Casaubon's self-centredness, and its continuation gives an early indication of Dorothea's gradual shedding of that stupidity which she too 'had early begun to emerge from' (xxi, 198).[65] It constitutes a significant distinction

---

63 Will's harsh words to Rosamond, after Dorothea has walked in on what seemed to her a compromising situation, drastically deflate her egoistic conceit: 'Rosamond [...] was almost losing the sense of her identity, and seemed to be waking into some new terrible existence' (lxxviii, 732-733).

64 Bernard Paris has shown that this comment, and the treatment of egoism in *Middlemarch* as a whole, demonstrates Eliot's adoption of a positivist epistemology which distinguishes between a subjective, metaphysical approach to reality and an objective, empirical approach. The subjective approach, Paris contends, translates interior experience into actual fact, thereby rendering subjective and objective orders of reality indistinguishable. Therefore, there is no separation between the self and the non-self; the ego is projected onto the world. Eliot's egoists, Paris argues, are fashioned after this idea as '[t]he egoist tends to presume that the order of things corresponds to the desires of the mind; and instead of cultivating a true vision of causal sequences, he delights in imaginatively shaping the future into accord with present wishes'; *Experiments in Life*, p. 129. See also Bernard Paris, *Rereading George Eliot*, pp. 81-82, and Nünning, pp. 254-255.

65 T. R. Wright argues that it is Dorothea's perception of Casaubon's selfishness that 'helps her to escape the worst form of egoism, which is "moral stupidity", of the sort displayed by Rosamond Vincy' (140); see '*Middlemarch* as a Religious Novel, or Life without God' in *Images of Belief in Literature*, ed. by David Jasper (London: Macmillan, 1984), pp. 138-152. The notion that Dorothea 'escapes' being like Rosamond is problematic, though. The egoism displayed by these two female characters is dissimilar: Dorothea's early ardour and exertion of will are constituents in a desire for a higher cause, whereas Rosamond's egoism is purely narcissistic. Furthermore, although Dorothea gradually comes to experience the nature and degree of Casaubon's egoism, it is primarily her suffering which moves her towards abandoning her own selfishness. Hence, Dorothea's personal development corresponds more with Feuerbach's ideas on suffering and fellow-feeling than with an epistemologically perceived understanding.

between the characters in *Middlemarch* whether they, like Dorothea, out-grow the notion that their subjective desires correspond to an objective order of reality or whether they, like Casaubon and Rosamond, are 'liable to think that others were providentially made for [them]' (x, 78).[66] Involving the reader in the reflection, the comment on 'moral stupidity' above implies that egoism is a natural starting-point for all humans; but for a successful improvement of character, the individual's self-centredness needs to be superseded by altruism and fellow-feeling. The comment is the first to broach the topic of egoism and appears one-quarter into the novel – a notably late occurrence, as the theme constitutes such an essential concern. But egoism has been dramatically presented from the beginning of the novel through narrative description, dialogue and FID. Interestingly, narratorial commentary engages directly with the subject only after Dorothea consciously perceives Casaubon's egocentricity, as if allowing the reader's awareness of egoism to grow gradually along with Dorothea's.[67] With regard to Dorothea's and Casaubon's dissimilar characters, the comment also evinces a repeated pattern as Dorothea's progress away from egoism is set off against Casaubon's increasing display of it.[68] Their disparate natures are frequently depicted in relation to each other, constituting juxtapositions which show how they gradually move towards respective extremes, Casaubon deep in feelings of pernicious jealousy and Dorothea in despairing self-effacement.

Several narratorial comments which broach the topic of egoism pertain to Bulstrode and depict the complex emotions that continuously beset him. His troubled psyche makes a good example of the intricate grey areas of interpretation and ethics, of a mind incessantly battling with morality, self-interest and a desire to comply with God's will.[69] Commenting on

---

66 It should be noted that the quotation in context refers to Casaubon only and that the narrator remarks that this is a tendency which is 'not quite alien to us, and, like the other mendicant hopes of mortals, claims some of our pity' (x, 78).

67 Carol Howe Spady makes a similar claim, arguing that 'by the time readers encounter this passage [...] we are aware of the thematic importance of egoism'. Discussing the reader's involvement, Howe Spady maintains that 'the passage is concerned with that very process which we readers are undergoing – the movement away from egoism' (67).

68 Bernard Paris analyses the rhetoric used for Dorothea in the novel and argues that Dorothea 'is championed from the beginning by the narrator, who employs a powerful rhetoric in her behalf'; *Rereading George Eliot*, p. 26.

69 An interesting difference between Bulstrode and Casaubon is that the banker finds strength and comfort in his religious faith whereas the theologically trained Reverend does not seem to find spiritual comfort anywhere. In an article contrasting Casaubon and Lydgate, W. J. Harvey also observes this point, maintaining that Casaubon's 'religious life [...] is even more non-existent than Mr Cadwallader's'; 'The Intellectual Background of the Novel: Casaubon and Lydgate' in *Middlemarch: Critical Approaches to the Novel*, ed. by Barbara Hardy (London: The Athlone Press, 1967), pp. 25-37 (p. 28).

Bulstrode's appeal to Lydgate's 'goodwill' (lxx, 665) by lending him the 1,000 pounds he once refused him, the narrator reflects on Bulstrode's uneasy sensibility:

> A man vows, and yet will not cast away the means of breaking his vow. Is it that he distinctly means to break it? Not at all; but the desires which tend to break it are at work in him dimly, and make their way into his imagination, and relax his muscles in the very moments when he is telling himself over again the reasons for his vow (lxx, 665).

Developing the idea of egoism, the comment shows how characters are rarely either egoistic or altruistic but incorporate conflicting qualities which continuously work in opposition to each other. Personal desire, the passage suggests, exists as a subconscious force within a character's mental processes, incessantly endeavouring to overthrow conscious morality. Bulstrode's 'diseased motive' (lxx, 665) runs like an 'irritating agent in his blood' (lxx, 665), but it is irritating because he will not own up to it. In Bulstrode's psyche, egoism survives as a subconscious energy with which his consciousness and conscience are in constant battle. Suggesting that Bulstrode's personal will exists almost as a demon over which his rational self has no control, the narrator again pardons Bulstrode's manipulative orchestrations. As if realising the sensitive nature of the inference, though, the narrator refrains from the more frequent use of 'we' and 'our', instead developing the argument in the third person, thereby assuming a general tone which involves human nature but does not implicate the reader directly.

In effect, most comments pertaining to egoism in Middlemarch serve one end, regardless of whether they refer to selfishness or selflessness, as they aim to 'take the reader by the hand' as it were, through the complex web of emotions that personal egoism emanates from and suffers through. By regarding these selfish and selfless characters not as 'good' or 'bad', but as representative strands of the reader's own multifaceted make-up, these comments typically solicit recognition and sympathetic understanding rather than scorn and derision.

Problems of Interpretation and References to Science

Comments concerning egoism are often closely related to matters of interpretation, as selfishness in *Middlemarch* is usually bound up with the individual's perception of the world.[70] As mentioned, egoistic characters in *Middlemarch* perceive the world as an extension of their own egos, situating themselves at a centre around which everything and everybody else revolves.[71] One of the most famous images in Eliot's oeuvre illustrates this very point:

> Your pier-glass or extensive surface of polished steel made to be rubbed by a house-maid, will be minutely and multitudinously scratched in all directions; but place now against it a lighted candle as a centre of illumination, and lo! the scratches will seem to arrange themselves in a fine series of concentric circles round that little sun. It is demonstrable that the scratches are going everywhere impartially, and it is only your candle which produces the flattering illusion of a concentric arrangement, its light falling with an exclusive optical selection. These things are a parable. The scratches are events, and the candle is the egoism of any person now absent – of Miss Vincy, for example (xxvii, 248).[72]

The comment introduces a chapter where Rosamond's vanity and craving for recognition are at a peak. Her flirtations with Lydgate during Fred's illness have a distinct purpose, and she is determined (long before he understands what is going on) that Lydgate will propose marriage. Unusually for commentary, it is remarkably direct in the sense that it includes an explicit reference to a character. The comment provides a good example

---

70 T. R. Wright states that *Middlemarch* is 'modern in its concern with the twin problems of perception and interpretation'; '*Middlemarch* as a Religious Novel', p. 140. It is fair to say, however, that all Eliot's novels are to some degree concerned with an epistemology which rests on the belief that morality is a prerequisite of knowledge and that it is through sympathy that the individual can escape subjective bias.

71 Reva Stump argues that the novel 'seems to be saying that the maturity of one's moral vision is in part defined by the nature of his expectations, since what he expects of the world about him is inseparable from the way he regards the world' (155).

72 The comment begins: 'An eminent philosopher among my friends [...] has shown me this pregnant little fact' (xxvii, 248). Imagining that this philosopher friend could be an actual acquaintance of Eliot's, T. R. Wright suggests that it could refer to John Tyndall, whose 'explanation of optical illusions makes him the most likely candidate for the role' (6). Another candidate, Wright proposes, is Herbert Spencer, 'who wrote in *The Study of Sociology* (1873) of standing by a lakeside in the moonlight and observing the bar of light created by the moon on the water appearing to follow him when he moved'; *George Eliot's Middlemarch*, p. 6. Considering the year of publication of Spencer's work, however, one would have to assume that Spencer had related this moonlight experience to Eliot prior to publication.

of the narrator's attitude to Rosamond. For every other principal egoist in the novel, the narrator curbs the reader's potential scorn with elicitations of his or her sympathy. Not so with Rosamond.[73] There are no extenuating perspectives by which Rosamond's egoism can be understood, nor does her suffering initiate a process towards selflessness.[74] In a sense, the narrator himself is holding up a candle to Rosamond's egoism, in this case producing an unflattering impression which is the only one the reader is invited to see.[75] By implication the narrator evinces an authority which derives from a position of privileged perspectives which in turn implies his power of interpretation.[76] The comment is thus an apt example of the narrator's general attitude to Rosamond: not only is it distinct from every other character in the novel, it also incorporates a double meaning. While demonstrating his attitude to Rosamond's biased perspective of the world, it shows that the narrator himself applies a one-dimensional perspective to Rosamond.

Problems of interpretation affect almost every aspect of *Middlemarch*, involving two interconnected, yet distinct, factors in the interpretative process.[77] The first, as in the example above, concerns the individual's inclination to read signs and situations so that they coincide with underlying subjective desires. The other concerns the equivocal nature of signs,

---

73 There is the appeal to 'think no unfair evil of her' which is ambiguous in itself, the narrator going on to remark that 'she never thought of money except as something necessary which other people would always provide' (xxvii, 252).

74 It is true that Rosamond is inspired to act selflessly after her meeting with Dorothea, but there is little to suggest that she has undergone any essential change of character.

75 Several critics have noted that the image refers as much to the narrator's project as it does to Rosamond's character. See, for example, Neil D. Isaacs, who argues that the parable reveals the 'author's method'. Eliot, he claims, 'holds up the pier-glass in many places and moves her light among them in order to illuminate the patterns in lives and in life'; '*Middlemarch*: Crescendo of Obligatory Drama', *Nineteenth-Century Fiction*, 18 (1963), 21-34 (p. 31). J. Hillis Miller juxtaposes the image with another narratorial comment from chapter 15: 'all the light I can command must be concentrated on this particular web' (xv, 132), arguing that 'with a slight change of formulation this could be seen as implying that the subjective source of light not only illuminates what is seen but also, as in the case of the candle held to the pier-glass, determines the structure of what is seen'; 'Optic and Semiotic', p. 140. In *The Language that Makes George Eliot's Fiction* (London: The Johns Hopkins University Press, 1983) Karen B. Mann sees a paradox at work in the image, stating that 'the very light that permits us to see is that which limits or even distorts what we do see' (44).

76 Isaacs maintains that the narrator's comments to the reader 'reveal her knowledge, not her power' (31). Surely there is a fine line between the two – indeed, a line which has occasioned the adage: 'knowledge *is* power'.

77 Peter Garrett claims that the 'bond between reader and character [is] formed by their participation in a common process of interpretation' and that it 'is only a short step beyond this observation to say that *Middlemarch* is "about" interpretation'; *The Victorian Multiplot Novel: Studies in Dialogical Form* (New Haven: Yale University Press, 1980), pp. 150-151.

which precludes constant and unambiguous meaning. As early as chapter 3, the problematic connection between 'signs' and 'interpretations' is illustrated in a reference to Dorothea's early appraisal of Casaubon: 'Signs are small measurable things, but interpretations are illimitable' (iii, 23). Here the two factors of interpretation are connected, indicating how signs may embody dissimilar meanings and how those meanings, in their turn, are liable to innumerable interpretations owing to the relative nature of the subjective point of view. The comment is a direct reference to Dorothea's misinterpretation of Casaubon's spiritual greatness, but it is applicable to several other characters in the novel as well.[78] For instance, Lydgate misinterprets Rosamond's character on the basis of her appearance and deportment; Bulstrode's imagination 'distorts' external signs of divine will to suit his own aims; and James Chettam misreads Dorothea's enthusiasm for his involvement in the building of new tenant homes as a sign of her affection for him.[79] Narratorial commentary frequently reminds the reader that the number and range of perspectives are vast, thereby encouraging the reader to keep revising his or her interpretation of characters; but this admission of unreliability, paradoxically, implicitly qualifies the narrator's own power of interpretation.

Thematic discussions in Eliot's commentary are seldom isolated; they usually link issues together. Just as discussions of egoism and interpretation are closely related, so are the subject of interpretation and the narrator's references to science. In *Middlemarch* scientific imagery is often connected with matters of perception and vision. By the use of scientific metaphors these comments take advantage of the potentiality for altered perceptions offered by science to concretise and examine problems of perspective and interpretation.[80] One of the most famous examples of scientific imagery in

---

78 It should be noted that at this stage the narrator does not directly state that Dorothea's interpretation of Casaubon is faulty. The only indication of misconstruction is made to Dorothea's 'hasty judgment', but of this the narrator states: 'Because Miss Brooke was hasty in her trust, it is not therefore clear that Mr Casaubon was unworthy of it' (iii, 24).

79 Thomas Vargish rightly points out that it is not only Bulstrode who relies on providence but also Casaubon, Lydgate and Fred Vincy, who 'each believes that he possesses a key whereby the secret of the order of things, the pattern that gives significance to the cosmos, can be unlocked and disclosed' (217). Of course, Bulstrode's egoism is closely related to his religiosity. For more on providentialism in connection with characters in *Middlemarch*, see also Peter Jones, *Philosophy and the Novel* (Oxford: Oxford University Press, 1975), pp. 36-40.

80 Some Victorian reviewers criticised Eliot's use of scientific language, finding it incompatible with artistic idiom. Henry James, for example, objected that *Middlemarch* was 'too often an echo of Messrs Darwin and Huxley'; *The Critical Heritage*, p. 359. With regard to such objections Gillian Beer notes that 'language that has now lost its

the novel concerns Mrs Cadwallader's match-making activities in chapter 6:

> Even with a microscope directed on a water-drop we find ourselves making interpretations which turn out to be rather coarse; for whereas under a weak lens you may seem to see a creature exhibiting an active voracity into which other smaller creatures actively play as if they were so many animated tax-pennies, a stronger lens reveals to you certain tiniest hairlets which make vortices for these victims while the swallower waits passively at his receipt of custom (vi, 55).

The passage juxtaposes the interpretation of Mrs Cadwallader's match-making with the analysis of a water-drop under a microscopic lens: with each new strength of lens, further minuscule causes are revealed, generating an altered image. The comment insinuates the impossibility of absolutes, suggesting that changes of perspective lead to differences in interpretation and that interpretation is therefore always relative.[81] Making the reader into a scientific experimenter along with the narrator, the image seems to concretise an argument which is otherwise philosophical in kind.[82] But like other scientific images, it detaches reader and narrator from the diegetic elements, increasing the distance between character and

---

scientific bearing still bore a freight of controversy and assertion for George Eliot and her first readers'; *Darwin's Plots*, p. 149.

81 Sally Shuttleworth maintains that 'George Eliot tries, through the structural organisation of her work, to reveal underlying organic unity beneath apparent surface disorder' (145-146) and claims that the characters in *Middlemarch* share this goal. Lydgate, Shuttleworth contends, 'searches for one primitive tissue, and Casaubon for the "Key to all Mythologies" ' (146). According to Shuttleworth, the characters mistakenly search for meaning in external form instead of looking 'beyond the details of external form to the underlying dynamic process', as 'each part only derives meaning from its position within the whole' (146). Although Shuttleworth's idea of disparate parts making up a whole applies to *Middlemarch*, it conflicts with the microscopic image above, which suggests that absolute meaning can never be arrived at because the constituents that make up the whole are in constant flux, altering their signification with each new interpretative viewpoint. The comment thus actually challenges the notion of an underlying organic whole, illustrating how a microscopic lens directed at what lies beneath demonstrates the complexities of the whole rather than its unity.

82 Considering many contemporary critics' opinions about Eliot's scientific language, one could well imagine that the scientific image which serves to illuminate specific phenomena and to elicit the reader's understanding would have alienated contemporary audiences rather than invited them into a shared and recognisable experience. Mark Wormald proposes that Eliot's 'fondness for Lewes's earlier studies in popularizing science led her to make her narrator an amateur microscopist, one who deploys the language of microscopy to similarly polemical social effect throughout the novel' (518) and continues to argue that Eliot's own scientific experience is 'reproduced […] in her narrative as acerbic commentaries on the nobler but fossilized strata of the mid-Victorian scientific community' (503); 'Microscopy and Semiotic in *Middlemarch*', *Nineteenth-Century Literature*, 50 (1996), 501-524.

narrator as well as between character and reader. Here, however, this detachment is of a humorous nature: its biological reference compares Mrs Cadwallader to a creature who waits passively, mouth open, to swallow the smaller creatures.[83] In a sense, the comment creates ironic distance to Mrs Cadwallader; but it simultaneously adds to the fascination of this character. That is significant, as the comment appears immediately prior to a long passage which describes Mrs Cadwallader and her role in the Middlemarch community.

Accordingly, scientific images regularly fortify the narrator's point regarding interpretation, namely that no absolutes can be arrived at as perspectives can be indefinitely altered. In this way, narratorial commentary reminds the reader to monitor his or her opinion of characters and events carefully and to adopt a generous view with regard to their seeming imperfections.

References to History and Literature

Middlemarch is the first Eliot novel to discuss science as a specific theme, and naturally, many of these discussions are conducted with reference to Lydgate.[84] In particular, chapter 15 examines the details of Lydgate's medical interests, situating them in relation to developments between the time when the action takes place and the time of the novel's composition.[85] Discussing scientific progress as an indication of historical distance, narra-

83 John L. Tucker seems to take the humour in the passage very seriously, as he objects that the comment conveys 'not objective science, but Swiftian satire, and as in Swift, the satire is double-edged. We may need to see the animal in man, but we lose some of our own humanity in the process' (781).

84 Shuttleworth, p. 143.

85 The connection between history and science is close in *Middlemarch*, where much of what is considered historical progress in the nineteenth century is defined in terms of scientific progress. T. R. Wright describes the impact of science in the period as the weaving of a 'web of previously unobserved connections, a labyrinth of explanations which attempted to make sense of a world for which conventional religious beliefs no longer seemed relevant, a world no longer to be seen as a stable, fixed reality but to be described in terms of complex patterns of relationship'. Wright refers to *Problems of Life and Mind*, in which George Henry Lewes expresses a new acknowledgment of the relativity of the world stating that '[w]hat we call laws of Nature are not objective existence, but subjective abstractions'; see *Problems of Life and Mind*, 2 vols (London: Trübner & Co., 1874-1879), i, p. 297. Not only Lewes but several other scientists and philosophers of the age, Wright argues, such as R. H. Huxley and Herbert Spencer, formed part of a discourse which pointed to 'a reality more complex than that which

tive description and narratorial commentary in chapter 15 serve not only to establish Lydgate's scientific prowess, but also to place his professional ambitions within a historical context:

> Perhaps that was a more cheerful time for observers and theorizers than the present; we are apt to think it the finest era of the world when America was beginning to be discovered, when a bold sailor, even if he were wrecked, might alight on a new kingdom; and about 1829 the dark territories of Pathology were a fine America for a spirited young adventurer (xv, 138).

The passage goes on to describe the scientific research which Lydgate is eager to conduct, following the French anatomist Bichat, and takes a favourable view both of the period and of Lydgate's aptitude.[86] The tone of the comment is unusual in its guardedness, however, the narrator seeming less confident than in other comments pertaining to history, avoiding the didactic tenor which presupposes the reader's unfamiliarity with the period. Instead, the 'perhaps' and the reference to what human nature is prone to think evince an unassuming attitude which solicits the reader's agreement rather than asserting an incontestable 'fact'. This attitude is also distinct from the historian-narrator's, who displays his authority over the text by claiming to have exclusive access to historical detail. Contrastingly, the comment reveals a narrative voice which can only speculate as to the general atmosphere of the narrative period and whose perspective on that period is situated in relation to his own present.[87]

A few passages earlier, however, the narrator employed a different tone, didactically and sardonically supplying the reader with information as to the historical period:

---

appears to the senses, a reality constructed of hypotheses rather than certainties'; *George Eliot's Middlemarch*, p. 7.

86 Going on to state how Lydgate desires to resume Bichat's research, the passage describes how 'he longed to demonstrate the more intimate relations of living structure, and help to define men's thought more accurately after the true order' (xv, 139). Di Pasquale suggests that this is precisely what Eliot attempts to do through the imagery in *Middlemarch*, claiming that it is in 'the pattern of imagery in *Middlemarch* that she makes a conscious attempt to discover the "common basis" from which "these structures" have all started' (435).

87 Commenting on the passage concluding chapter 35, which broaches the topics of 'low subjects' and 'historical parallels', W. J. Harvey argues that the comment 'enacts in miniature something which is basic to [Eliot's] view of the past: the idea that the present is equally vulnerable to time and change' and that Eliot's narrator confesses to 'feeling complacent about the superiority of the present and its comfortable pretensions to historical hindsight'; 'Idea and Image in the Novels of George Eliot', in *Critical Essays on George Eliot*, ed. by Barbara Hardy (London: Routledge & Kegan Paul, 1970), pp. 151-198 (p. 171). Although the passage above is not as explicit as the conclusion to chapter 35, it nevertheless suggests a similar approach to the past.

For it must be remembered that this was a dark period; and in spite of venerable colleges which used great efforts to secure purity of knowledge by making it scarce, and to exclude error by a rigid exclusiveness in relation to fees and appointments, it happened that very ignorant young gentlemen were promoted in town, and many more got a legal right to practise over large areas in the country (xv, 136).

Set in the years leading up to the First Reform Act in 1832, *Middlemarch* is to a great extent concerned with history, including discussions on politics, philosophy and science in terms of the differences that these fields of study present in relation to the time of the novel's composition.[88] But in narratorial commentary, references to history raise two concerns in particular: the first is the matter of intellectual and scientific enlightenment, and the other relates to the individual's sense of a personal history. Remarking on scientific progress, the comments quoted above demonstrate conflicting attitudes with regard to the historical past. The 'cheerful time' strikes a discordant note when considered against the 'dark period' mentioned shortly before, suggesting the narrator's complex perception of the historical past.[89] As the narrator's distance to the text fluctuates, so does his attitude towards the narrative period, shifting between appreciation and derision. As is common in *Middlemarch*, the comments in themselves are not unambiguous; for example, the term 'dark' may be interpreted as the opposite of 'enlightened', signalling that much was yet to be discovered which perhaps made the period 'a cheerful time for observers and theorizers' (xv, 138). Considering that chapter 15 locates Lydgate within a historical and intellectual context, the narrator's indeterminate position with regard to the historical past appears logical, as he needs to provide this young reformer with opportunity. The 'dark period' is therefore not whol-

---

88 Political events as well as intellectual problems of the nineteenth century are woven into the plot of *Middlemarch*. Set in the years between 1829 and 1832, the novel considers a period in which many great changes take place, for example the Roman Catholic Emancipation Act of 1829, growing fears of a working-class revolution and the eventual passing of the Reform Bill in 1832. Published only four years after the 1867 Reform Act, *Middlemarch* is clearly inspired by the parallels between the periods. Catherine Neale argues that 'after the furore surrounding the 1867 Reform Act it must have seemed to many observers that the schisms between the middle class and the working class, the social unrest, the pressure of reform, were all repetitions of a recent epoch'; *George Eliot: Middlemarch* (Harmondsworth: Penguin Books, 1989), p. 30. Michael York Mason agrees, saying that the 'two periods are comparable as times of crises' (423), but qualifies this observation by noting that 'the comparison of periods is more guarded, more implicit, in the case of *Middlemarch*' (424) than in *Felix Holt*; see 'Middlemarch and History', *Nineteenth Century Fiction*, 24 (1971), 417-431.

89 Mason makes a similar observation, stating that '[w]henever George Eliot explicitly adopts the perspective by looking back over forty years her remarks almost invariably express a puzzling mixture of approval and disapproval for the changes she can survey' (426).

ly dark: it incorporates potential for the likes of Lydgate, who can seize the opportunities presented to them and thereby contribute to scientific and historical progress.

Again philosophising on enlightenment, but this time in connection with Dorothea's unsettling encounter with classical and Christian art, the narrator assumes the position of privileged retrospection: 'In those days the world in general was more ignorant of good and evil by forty years than it is at present' (xix, 176). The narrative past is perceived in relation to the narrator's present, and his authority is reminiscent of narratorial comments on history in Eliot's earlier novels.[90] But there is no nostalgia involved in this statement, as the narrator regards the past from a superior perspective. Positioning the reader in a similarly superior relation vis-à-vis the narrative past, the comment suggests not only the reader's distance in time to the diegesis, but also his or her distance in culture.[91] In its continuation the comment mentions a general naïvety as regards the finer arts, as well as an unawareness of Romanticism which further accentuates the narrator's and reader's superiority.[92] The passage serves a further function too, though: situated prior to Dorothea's and Will's unexpected meeting in the Vatican, it emphasises not merely the period's naïvety of art, but in particular Dorothea's naïvety which is contrasted with Will's cultured experience.[93] The subsequent chapter deals in greater detail with the wide

90 Commenting on a generally complex relation to the past in much Victorian writing, Catherine Neale maintains that a lot of it conveys 'a confused mixture of representations: the present as advanced and positive, with the past as primitive and squalid, vie for attention with representations of the present as squalid and intolerable set against some golden age of the past' (25).

91 The idea of the reader's cultured distance derives from Jane Smith, who maintains that the narrator functions as 'the reader's interpreter, providing a gloss of the strange uses to which language was put in the special territory of 1830s Middlemarch' (196).

92 It is unclear how the narrator's reference to 'good and evil' should be interpreted. The argument in the passage as a whole contends with the naïvety of aesthetics rather than with the ignorance of 'good and evil'. This contention hence confuses the understanding of the passage as a whole. Is the narrator being ironic? Or is there an implied relation between aesthetics and ethics? Indeed, Eliot did adhere to a philosophy which saw a connection between art and morality; but is this really what the comment refers to? Consequently, the comment causes some confusion as to the understanding of the narrator's point, a consequence which is highly unusual for commentary in Eliot's novels. Hugh Witemeyer, however, is not confused. He cites the passage as an 'accurate and well-chosen [...] example of English ignorance', arguing that 'the scholarship inspired by Romanticism divided Dorothea's England of the first Reform Bill from George Eliot's of the second'; see *George Eliot and the Visual Arts* (New Haven: Yale University Press, 1979), pp. 84-85.

93 Analysing the narrator's attitude to a historical past in *Middlemarch*, Mason comments on the continuation of this passage, which remarks on 'travellers' who did not 'carry full information on Christian art either in their heads or their pockets' (xix, 176). Mason argues that it is sarcastic in tone, but that Eliot's 'sarcasm is a kind of rudimentary

difference in cultural experience not only between Dorothea and Will, but also between Dorothea and the reader:

> To those who have looked at Rome with the quickening power of a knowledge which breathes a growing soul into all historic shapes, and traces out the suppressed transitions which unite all contrasts, Rome may still be the spiritual centre and interpreter of the world. But let them conceive one more historical contrast: the gigantic broken revelations of that Imperial and Papal city thrust abruptly on the notions of a girl who had been brought up in English and Swiss Puritanism (xx, 181).

Rome represents a world which Dorothea cannot recognise. In a concrete sense, her illusions about the world clash with harsh reality as she is not intellectually or spiritually prepared to take in the paradoxes that the city offers. The comment suggests that her problem is of an epistemological nature, and that the confusion which Rome occasions is not necessarily connected to a historical point in time but to Dorothea's cultural and spiritual background. Culturally sophisticated and comprehensive knowledge, the comment suggests, serves as an interpreter by which 'reality' is understood, and without that knowledge the individual suffers feelings of loss, confusion and alienation. In this case it is the character, not the reader, who is distanced from the diegetic setting, i.e. Dorothea possesses no hermeneutic code by which she might have been able to understand Rome.[94] It is, however, important to note that it is the contrasts of Rome that perplex Dorothea; she cannot conceive of the idea that relics from a sacred historical past intermingle with the squalid features of everyday Rome: 'Ruins and basilicas, palaces and colossi, set in the midst of a sordid present, where all that was living and warm-blooded seemed sunk in the deep degeneracy of a superstition divorced from reverence' (xx, 181). Rome, then, is a new bewildering world which shatters her illusions not only about the place itself, but also about how the historical past may live in the present.

The comment introduces Dorothea's crisis in relation to Rome; but by extension her confrontation with that 'Papal city' is symbolic of her entry into the other new 'world' – that is, the realm of marriage. Her illusions

---

parody, usually relying on phrases [...] where the excessiveness of tone acquits the author of naïveté, but otherwise constitutes no more than an undirected sniping at optimism' (427).

94 Barbara Hardy claims that '[l]ike Dorothea, the reader is also forced out of the fiction into an awareness of history'. While both Dorothea and the reader are certainly forced into an awareness of history, it is a little difficult to see how Dorothea can be forced out of the fiction, or how history can be separated from the fiction. See 'Rome in Middlemarch: A Need for Foreignness', *George Eliot-George Henry Lewes Studies*, 24-25 (1993), 1-16 (p. 12).

about Casaubon's spiritual prominence are similar to those she has about Rome, and the degeneracy which she perceives there emerges gradually alongside her increasing insight into Casaubon's futile enterprise. The disillusionment Dorothea experiences with Rome thus figures as a representation of the despair she comes to undergo in her marriage to Casaubon.

While Dorothea's encounter with Rome rouses her historical consciousness, the idea of a consciousness of the past in *Middlemarch* refers to characters' personal histories as well as to a national, scholarly or antique precedent. Bulstrode, for example, represents the individual whose past catches up with his present.[95] With regard to the revelation of his past, the narrator comments on the manner in which his personal history constitutes an inescapable part of his present:

> With memory set smarting like a reopened wound, a man's past is not simply a dead history, an outworn preparation of the present: it is not a repented error shaken loose from the life: it is a still quivering part of himself, bringing shudders and bitter flavours and the tinglings of a merited shame (lxi, 577-578).

In a man's personal history, the comment suggests, there is no 'then' and 'now', as his 'then' continuously exists within the individual's remembrance.[96] Like Dorothea's Roman effigies, these memories survive in Bulstrode's subconscious as 'long vistas of white forms whose marble eyes seemed to hold the monotonous light of an alien world' (xx, 181). In the same way as the historical past manifests itself in society and culture, the individual's personal history is preserved in memory and can be triggered by the 'terror of being judged' (lxi, 577).[97] The impending threat of the past is, of course, a principal theme in the Bulstrode plot and thereby relevant as a theme primarily in connection with this character; but although he is the only character who must confront his own history directly, several other characters nevertheless live in the wake of their past. In *Middlemarch*, then, history, as treated in narratorial commentary, is discussed in terms of how fields of knowledge differ between the narrative past and the present of composition, but also in terms of how characters make sense of and fashion their respective 'realities'.

---

95 The narrator's references to Dorothea's historical precursor Theresa is pertinent here; it will be discussed below.

96 Cf. this passage to the epigraph preceding chapter 21 in *Felix Holt*: "Tis grievous, that with all amplification of travel both by sea and land, a man can never separate himself from his past history' (xxi, 182).

97 Sally Shuttleworth notices the physiological terms in this passage and argues that 'George Eliot uses physiology to suggest that for the individual, as much as for the society or culture, there is a vital interdependence in history' (154).

Significantly, the narrator often refers directly to the narrative as a 'history', arguing that the text presents an account of actual historical events. Assuming the role of historian, the narrator downplays the impression of artificiality and indicates his own relation to the text. Frequently appearing in combination with meta-narrative comments and the presence of the narrator as 'I', discussed above, these indications sometimes situate the narrator in a literary context, as he compares his own task to that of named predecessors. The reference to Fielding is, of course, the best-known of these references; but in the long passage on 'old provincial society' in chapter 11, which presents a broad vision of what can be found in the community of Middlemarch, the narrator compares himself with yet another literary giant: 'In fact, much the same sort of movement and mixture went on in old England as we find in older Herodotus, who also, in telling what had been, thought it well to take a woman's lot for his starting-point' (xi, 88-89). Comparing himself to the fifth century Greek historian – also called 'the father of history' – the narrator situates himself in a tradition of chroniclers. However, as Herodotus represents a type of historian whose veracity the narrator may not take for granted, the comment simultaneously serves as an acknowledgment of the problems of historical representation.[98] By purporting to reinforce the narrator's credibility as historian, then, the comparative element subverts the notion of an actual historical rendering, instead reinforcing the impression of ambiguity in the text.[99]

Connected to its concern with history is the novel's consciousness of literature – *Middlemarch* is a novel which abounds with literary references. The Prelude and Finale, the epigraphs to each chapter, indications of what characters read and what literary figures they are associated with – all function to explain people and events through the reader's understanding of other texts. Casaubon, for example, lives in the world of his scholarly reading, and in the beginning of the novel he reminds Dorothea of a 'living Bossuet' and a 'modern Augustine' (iii, 23). Dorothea herself longs to be the assistant of another Milton or Pascal. Lydgate's relation to

---

98 This is, of course, Hillis Miller's point in his deconstructive reading of *Middlemarch* in 'Narrative and History': that the novel undermines its own foundation in history by revealing the fictionality of that foundation.

99 The long passage preceding this comment depicts a potential vision of historical progress in the community of Middlemarch which simultaneously hints at later plot developments. The passage has occasioned much critical debate, as it discusses the steady continuity as well as the unrestrained changeability of human history. Society exists in continuous flux, the passage implies; but this flux is in itself characteristic, paradoxically demonstrating the unchangeable nature of historical progress that is recognisable from the recordings of 'older Herodotus'. See, for instance, D. A. Miller, *Narrative and Its Discontents* and Sally Shuttleworth, *Nineteenth-Century Science*.

literature consists in his scientific reading, which he first stumbles upon as a young boy browsing in his guardian's library, occasioning the narrator to remark: 'Most of us who turn to any subject with love remember some morning or evening hour when we got on a high stool to reach down an untried volume' (xv, 134). Mary Garth infuriates old Peter Featherstone by spending all her spare time reading, and Will Ladislaw, on his part, infuriates Casaubon because he has some, albeit superficial, acquaintance with German studies, which Casaubon does not.[100]

The list of literary references could go on, but these examples suffice to demonstrate that *Middlemarch* is a novel in which literature is a constant and significant component in the understanding of characters and contexts. Despite this significance, however, and although the novel is full of literary references, *Middlemarch* contains few narratorial comments which explicitly refer to literature. Characters are frequently depicted through literary allusions and associated with literary works and figures, but the narrator's commentary itself rarely engages directly with literature. Even so, considering the fact that *Middlemarch* is such a 'literary' novel, it is relevant to examine one of the few references to literature that do appear in narratorial commentary.[101]

Having flirted – innocently, in his own opinion – with Rosamond, Lydgate is delicately but firmly taken to task by Mrs Bulstrode, and when

---

100 Criticism of Will arose already with the novel's first reviews. Henry James famously called the depiction of him 'the only eminent failure in the book', *A Century of George Eliot Criticism*, ed. by Gordon S. Haight, p. 83 (first publ. in *Galaxy*, 15 (March, 1873), 424-428). George Eliot was aware of the criticism against Will, recording in her journal: 'When I was at Oxford, in May, two ladies came up to me after dinner: one said, "How could you let Dorothea marry *that* Casaubon?" The other, "Oh, I understand her doing that, but why did you let her marry the other fellow, whom I cannot bear?" '; *George Eliot's Life as Related in Her Letters and Journals*, ed. by John W. Cross, 3 vols (New York: 1885), iii, p. 213. Moreover, F. R. Leavis argues that Will represents 'intentions [Eliot] has failed to realize creatively' (89), and Gerald Bullett maintains that Will is simply 'not worthy of Dorothea', *George Eliot, Her Life and Books* (London: Collins, 1947), p. 228. Later assessments have been less severe. For example, Jane Marie Luecke considers Will's role in the narrative significant; see 'Ladislaw and the *Middlemarch* Vision', *Nineteenth Century Fiction*, 19 (1964), 55-64; and Mary Ellen Doyle argues that Will is represented in two ways in the novel: first as a romantic dilettante and then as a 'noble Dante figure, who alone properly worships the perfect Victorian Beatrice' (147). See also Gordon Haight's article 'George Eliot's "Eminent Failure", Will Ladislaw', in *George Eliot's Originals and Contemporaries: Essays in Victorian Literary History and Biography*, ed. by Hugh Witemeyer (London: Macmillan, 1992), pp. 38-57.

101 *Middlemarch* includes more explicit allusions to literature, for example the reference to Bunyan in chapter 85 and to Samuel Daniel's sonnets in chapter 5; but as these comments have been treated in connection with other functions of narratorial commentary, they are not used as examples in this section.

he is a little annoyed with her inferences he finds even Mr Farebrother's friendly joking permeated with insinuations.[102] On Lydgate's petulance, the narrator comments: 'Solomon's Proverbs, I think, have omitted to say, that as the sore palate findeth grit, so an uneasy consciousness heareth innuendoes' (xxi, 280). Referring to the Book of Proverbs, which itself comprises a combination of parables, pithy questions and wise maxims, the comment imparts a sense of scriptural wisdom to the statement, aligning the narrator with Solomon who was, according to the Old Testament, granted wisdom by God (I Kings 4. 29-31). Indeed, the comment even suggests that the narrator remedies an omission of Solomon's. Reinforcing his sage-like status through the literary reference, then, the narrator's comment draws on Proverbs to authenticate its penetration and reliability. The comment is, moreover, itself formulated as a proverb, employing antiquated verb forms such as 'findeth' and 'heareth', which invests it with additional solemnity. Appearing in narratorial commentary, several literary references function in the same manner as historical references – that is, they support the veracity of the narrative and situate the narrator in the company of literary and historical predecessors of the most exalted kind. In this way, they serve to draw the reader into a sense of confidence in the narrator as authority and in the story as authentic.

Religion

When *Middlemarch* was first published some reviewers found it cold and lacking in spirit, implying that Eliot staged a 'wilful denial of any spiritual dimension to Middlemarch society'.[103] Indeed, the community of Middlemarch is a secular sphere where egoistic reliance on providence is far more in evidence than religious sentiment and piety.[104] But the novel

---

102 Coincidentally, Mr Farebrother's joking is in itself a literary reference as he says in answer to Lydgate's decision to stay at home working rather than going to the Vincys': 'What, you are going to get lashed to the mast, eh [...] Well, if you don't mean to be won by the sirens, you are right to take precautions in time' (xxxi, 280), referring of course to the manner in which Ulysses resists the alluring song of the Sirens in the *Odyssey*.

103 See *The Critical Heritage*, pp. 29-30.

104 Peter Hodgson maintains that *Middlemarch* portrays a secular, modern culture where '[r]eligion had for the most part lost its vitality, its ability to integrate all aspects of life' and where 'it had been reduced to routinized custom, a social game, a means of achieving one's privates [*sic*] ends or justifying one's actions' (125). T. R. Wright

also expresses sadness over the loss of a spiritually orientated religious community and analyses the 'religious yearning' of souls in desperate need of spiritual guidance.[105] Both Dorothea and Bulstrode represent such souls, and even though Bulstrode's religious yearning is obscured by his egoistic drive, his religiosity is sincere and credible. Hence, *Middlemarch* is a religious novel in the sense that it is concerned with the individual's desire to find meaning in life and a vocation to live for.[106] However, although the religious aspirations of characters constitute a principal theme, they are primarily depicted through narrative description, FID and dialogue; relatively few narratorial comments in *Middlemarch* broach the issue of religion.[107] When such comments do appear, it is primarily in the latter part of the novel. Prior to investigating these proper narration-now statements, however, it is relevant to observe the manner in which Dorothea's religious ardour is situated in its novelistic context. The way in which she differs from other characters is established already in the first chapter, where the narrator first poses a direct question and then goes into the FID of a potential community voice:

> And how should Dorothea not marry? [...] Nothing could hinder it but her love of extremes, and her insistance [*sic*] on regulating life according to notions which might cause a wary man to hesitate before he made her an offer [...] A young lady of some birth and fortune, who knelt suddenly down on a brick floor by the side of a sick labourer and prayed fervidly as if she thought herself living in the time of the Apostles – who had strange whims of fasting like a Papist [...] Such a wife

argues that 'the novel is historically incorrect' in the respect that 'the absence of God is so noticeable'; 'Middlemarch as a Religious Novel', p. 139; and Thomas Vargish states that several contemporary critics 'felt the cosmic loneliness in *Middlemarch*' (217). Moreover, most clerics in the novel (Casaubon, Mr Cadwallader and Mr Tyke) seem more concerned with worldly matters than with spiritual ones, and Fred Vincy epitomises the young man who has little choice but to unwillingly enter the Church. James F. Scott comments on Eliot's possible Comtean inspiration in Casaubon's character, who, Scott argues, symbolises 'what Comte saw as a loss of status incurred by the priestly class when the feudal aristocracy made its inevitable concessions to secularism'; 'George Eliot, Positivism, and the Social Vision of *Middlemarch*', *Victorian Studies*, 16 (1972), 59-76 (p. 66).

105 In 1949 Mark Schorer famously labelled *Middlemarch* 'a novel of religious yearning without a religious object'; 'Fiction and the Matrix of Analogy', *Kenyon Review*, 11 (1949), 539-559 (p. 556).

106 Katherine M. Sorensen maintains that despite the alleged absence of God in *Middlemarch*, Eliot 'creates an evangelical world through the very discourse of her fiction'. Sorensen argues that 'the evangelical world of *Middlemarch* lies *behind* the explicit text of the novel [...] in the sense that the evangelical world provides the novel's imaginative and moral source'; 'Evangelical Doctrine and George Eliot's Narrator in *Middlemarch*', *The Victorian Newsletter*, 74 (1988), 18-26 (p. 26) (Sorensen's italics).

107 Cf. religious matters in *Daniel Deronda*, which are discussed similarly in narrative description, FID and dialogue, but rarely in narration now.

might awaken you some fine morning with a new scheme for the application of her income (i, 9).

Scholars commenting on this passage have noted that it introduces Dorothea in a tone of blended irony and affection.[108] Dorothea's zealous piety is certainly derided, but not by the narrator; mediating the frame of mind of an unnamed 'voice of society', the sardonic tone emanates through the FID of a persona whose viewpoint serves as a representation of Middlemarch society. It is this voice, in turn, which is ridiculed by the narrator who disparages Dorothea's unidentified critics by imitating their idiom in FID. By mimicking the speech of a collective voice, the narrator satirises the very values which he enunciates.[109] Although conveying a lucid picture of Dorothea's devoutness, the passage primarily serves to depict a community which has lost its sense of religion, which has accustomed itself to valuing the 'keeping of saddle-horses' over any fellow-feeling for a 'sick labourer' and in which the moral model is determined not by ethical and religious principle but by doing 'what their neighbours did' (i, 9).[110] The tinge of ridicule which adheres to the image of Dorothea here, then, is not due to her piety *per se*, but to the contrast between that image and Dorothea's social context. Significantly, the passage appears in the first chapter of the novel, thereby immediately establishing the clash between Dorothea's religious yearning and the conventions of secular society.

The dividing line between the narrator's own speech and the FID in the passage above is important. Addressing the reader directly, the beginning of the passage creates the effect of drawing the reader into the narrative, hinting at the advent of a general reflection. But subsequent sentences stay within story-time now and with Dorothea's particular situation. Instead the general statement, when it does appear a few lines on and moves away from Dorothea's specific character to reflect on an unnamed 'young lady', appears in the form of FID. This general reflection does not appear in a narration-now sphere exclusive to narrator and reader, but voices the potential opinions of a man 'who would naturally think twice before he

---

108 See for instance Sorensen, 22.

109 For FID which conveys an ironical insinuation about the very medium through which it is focalised, see Pascal, pp. 79-80.

110 Clark-Beattie makes a similar point about this passage, arguing that '[t]here is nothing patently absurd in Dorothea's kneeling down beside a suffering man […] as the narrator's heavy-handed irony makes clear, the absurdity consists in a society which takes saddle-horses seriously but dismisses Apostles and sick laborers as unimportant'. Furthermore, Clark-Beattie comments on the 'narrator's man of the world persona', arguing that through him Eliot 'mimics the views of nineteenth-century liberalism in order to reveal the insufficiency to human needs of much of what passes for inevitable law' (203).

risked himself in such fellowship' (i, 9) with someone like Dorothea.[111] The reflection is focalised through the perspective of a communal persona, but voiced through the narrator who attaches a tone of irony and scorn to it.

Unsurprisingly, most of the commentary pertaining to religion in *Middlemarch* appears in connection with Bulstrode and Dorothea. In a sense, these two characters move in opposite directions in terms of their religious persuasions: Dorothea progresses from an exuberant, but confused religious ardour which she cannot make meaningful to finding purpose in a religion of humanity; and Bulstrode slides from a belief in divine patronage to realising his own hypocrisy and its consequences. In both cases, the narrator's commentary considers the importance of fellow-feeling. With regard to the line of reasoning which Bulstrode devises in order to justify his actions to himself, the narrator remarks on the pervasiveness of his calculations:

> This implicit reasoning is essentially no more peculiar to evangelical belief than the use of wide phrases for narrow motives is peculiar to Englishmen. There is no general doctrine which is not capable of eating out our morality if unchecked by the deep-seated habit of direct fellow-feeling with individual fellow-men (lxi, 582).

The comment can be interpreted as a check on the reader's possible response, discouraging his or her potential criticism of Bulstrode on the grounds of his religious persuasion. Bulstrode's way of thinking, the comment suggests, is not typical of evangelical belief nor of other faiths and traditions; rather, it characterises a type of moral order which does not prioritise fellow-feeling in the sense of empathy with individual souls. The remark hence frustrates any sense of superiority the reader might feel in relation to Bulstrode while arguing for the similar nature of seemingly diverse ideologies.

---

111 According to Gerald Prince, FID is usually defined by its inclusion of 'two discourse events, two styles, two voices, two semantic and axiological systems'; *Dictionary of Narratology*, 2nd edn (Lincoln: University of Nebraska Press, 2003), p. 34. However, Ann Banfield disagrees, arguing that FID is defined as the unspoken representation of one subjectivity. See *Unspeakable Sentences: Narration and Representation in the Language of Fiction* (London: Routledge & Kegan Paul, 1982), pp. 65-108 *et passim*. In the case of FID above I would argue that both definitions apply, as the speech represents the subjectivity of 'society' but carries ironic overtones which can be assigned to the narrator. Michal Peled Ginsburg contends that the passage displays a 'dialogical' element which presents 'contradictory intentions' undermining any 'clear position of authority' in the text; 'Pseudonym, Epigraphs, and Narrative Voice: *Middlemarch* and the Problem of Authorship', *ELH*, 47 (1980), 542-558 (pp. 552-553).

The notion of fellow-feeling is a particular thematic concern in *Middlemarch*, both when it comes to distinguishing egoistic characters from altruistic ones and in respect of Dorothea's personal development. The idea of a moral order which is moored in love and fellow-feeling between individuals is reminiscent of Feuerbach's theories on religion. Affixing divine qualities to human nature itself, Feuerbach argues that all those virtues which man ascribes to God are, in actuality, manifest in man himself. Inspired by Feuerbach, Eliot conceived of a religion in which human feeling for others was a foundation for morality and human progress.[112] This is the type of religion which Dorothea moves towards and which conditions the success of her personal development. Accordingly, Dorothea is the novel's ambassador of fellow-feeling as is demonstrated in, for example, chapter 77. Having faith in Ladislaw's love for her, even before the Rosamond incident has been resolved, Dorothea displays great generosity of spirit, and the narrator remarks on the effect her type of character can have on others:

> There are natures in which, if they love us, we are conscious of having a sort of baptism and consecration: they bind us over to rectitude and purity by their pure belief about us; and our sins become that worst kind of sacrilege which tears down the invisible altar of trust (lxxvii, 726).

The effect of fellow-feeling, the comment suggests, resembles that of divine love – human beings experience a feeling equivalent to that produced by divine benediction through the love of another. In a sense, God is replaced by the type of nature Dorothea represents.[113] Drawing the reader

---

112 The 'religion of humanity' with which Eliot is often associated derives primarily from Comte, who attempted to establish such a religion on a scientific basis. Although Eliot agreed with many of Comte's ideas, she was suspicious of dogma and consequently not sympathetic to his theories on a humanist religion. Eliot's 'religion of humanity' thus has more in common with Spinoza and Feuerbach than with positivism. For more on Eliot's 'religion of humanity' and her indebtedness to Feuerbach, see, for instance, Bernard Paris, 'George Eliot's Religion of Humanity'; Valerie A. Dodd, *George Eliot: An Intellectual Life* (London: Macmillan, 1990), pp. 181-190; and U. C. Knoepflmacher, *Religious Humanism and the Victorian Novel*, pp. 51-63. See also Lisa Baltazar, 'The Critique of Anglican Biblical Scholarship in George Eliot's *Middlemarch*', *Literature and Theology: An International Journal of Theory, Criticism and Culture*, 15 (2001), 40-60; and Suzanne Bailey, 'Reading the "Key": George Eliot and the Higher Criticism', *Women's Writing*, 3 (1996), 129-143.

113 In a letter to Mrs Ponsonby Eliot stated that 'the idea of God, so far as it has been a high spiritual influence, is the ideal of a goodness entirely human'; see *Letters* vi, 98. Elizabeth Deeds Ermarth maintains that Feuerbach's theory of a 'transposition between God and the human species is wholly congenial to George Eliot'; 'George Eliot's Conception of Sympathy', *Nineteenth-Century Fiction*, 40 (1985), 23-42 (p. 24).

into the reflection, the comment appeals to the reader's recognition as well as presupposing his or her concurrence with the argument. By reducing the distance between reader and narrator in the use of 'we' and by anticipating his or her ready agreement, the comment elevates Dorothea's character to an almost divine level while blocking the reader's potential objection to that elevation. It is the fellow-feeling in Dorothea that constitutes her divine status, a status which relies on her empathy and on a certain degree of self-abnegation towards which she progresses throughout the novel. It is only when Dorothea attains complete maturity in this religion of humanity that the narrator's veneration for her character is clothed in religious terms such as 'baptism', 'consecration', 'rectitude', 'purity', 'sacrilege' and 'altar of trust'. In other words, though she is depicted as a superior human being throughout the novel, linked to the likes of Saint Theresa of Avila and the Virgin Mary, it is not until she has fully incorporated a religion of fellow-feeling that the narrator makes such unequivocal references to her divinity.[114] Consequently, this latter comment epitomises the idea of an ideal religion – a complete devotion to fellow-feeling and an abandonment of egoism.

It is significant that as these comments remark on various characters' aptitude for fellow-feeling, they are simultaneously eliciting the reader's capacity to 'love' the characters. Accordingly, the narrator's analysis of a 'religion' of tolerance, sympathy and love does not merely amount to a philosophical scrutiny of processes in the novel; it also stimulates the reader's own understanding of and sympathy for diegetic properties. In keeping with the purpose of commentary, then, comments referring to religion purport to affect the reader's response so that he or she will recognise processes and features and thereby come to sympathise with characters.

Gender Issues

The gender theme in *Middlemarch* has already been indicated twice before the reader becomes involved with the story: first in the Prelude, where the narrator refers to the 'social lot of women' (Prelude, 4), and then in the

---

114 Bernard Paris observes that the Prelude prepares the reader 'to approve of Dorothea's search for glory' but adds that the narrator's references to Dorothea's pre-eminence are 'often accompanied by a condescending or satiric attitude toward ordinary mortals'; *Rereading George Eliot*, pp. 27-28.

epigraph to the first chapter, an excerpt from *The Maid's Tragedy* which reads: 'Since I can do no good because a woman, / Reach constantly at something that is near it' (i, 7).[115] The reference is of course to Dorothea, who desperately seeks a vocation in life but who is restricted by her gender from finding it outside of marriage and religion. From the very beginning the reader is alerted to one of the novel's principal themes. Considering the topicality of the 'woman question' in the late nineteenth century, the importance of the subject in the novel is not surprising, nor is it surprising that this particular concern generated much debate among contemporary critics.[116] The novel incorporates stringent criticisms of patriarchal attitudes and social structures, both in the formation of its plot and in its delineation of character. For instance, several male characters voice conventional patriarchal attitudes when referring to women. One is Mr Brooke, who refuses to discuss politics with Mrs Cadwallader, telling her that '[y]our sex are not thinkers, you know' (vi, 50). Others are Sir James Chettam, who assumes that Dorothea will delight in the gift of a Maltese puppy since '[l]adies are usually fond of these [...] dogs' (iii, 28), and Lydgate, who falls in love with Rosamond under the illusion that she is the epitome of 'what a woman ought to be' [...] 'perfectly lovely and accomplished' (x, 87). Reinforcing Lydgate's assessment of the perfect woman and underpinning the conventional idea that a woman's appearance is to be measured and evaluated, Mr Chicely argues that Rosamond's beauty outshines Dorothea's as Rosamond 'lays herself out a little more to please us' (x, 82). The novel furthermore articulates an objection to the limitations imposed upon women in its delineation of Dorothea and Rosamond.

---

115 Jennifer Uglow argues that the Prelude shows part of Eliot's aim, which, she contends, was to refrain from simplifying male and female into distinct characteristics and instead 'to celebrate diversity, to pick out the cygnet among the ducks, and to deny the existence of a norm'. As with her ideas on interpretation and perception, Uglow maintains, Eliot's feminist analysis also strives to attain 'a mode of perception which is at once accurate [...] and can yet contain contradiction and ambiguity' (205).

116 For example, in an early review R. H. Hutton objected to the theme, arguing that 'the attempt of the "prelude" and the final chapter to represent the book as an elaborate contribution to the "Woman's" question, seems to us a mistake' (307). Sidney Colvin approved of the theme, however, asserting that Eliot 'seems to insist upon the design of illustrating the necessary disappointment of a woman's nobler aspirations in a society not made to second noble aspirations in a woman. And that is one of the most burning lessons which any writer could set themselves to illustrate'; *The Critical Heritage*, p. 337. About this criticism, Gillian Beer remarks that it is astonishing how 'the feminist issues of the work were recognised as crucial, and quite specific, by the book's first readers but then, in critics of the next 100 years until the 1970s, were hardly discussed at all'; see *George Eliot*, p. 148. See also Kathleen Blake's article '*Middlemarch* and the Woman Question', *Nineteenth-Century Fiction*, 31 (1976), 285-312 for more on feminist concerns in *Middlemarch*.

Prevented from pursuing an education, Dorothea's unapplied potential causes her distress as she desperately searches for meaning and vocation; Rosamond's character, on the other hand, is to a great extent the outcome of male dictates, but she finds that after marriage her 'female' education does her no good. Despite the right appearance, upbringing and tutoring, Rosamond still fails at what she has striven towards all her life – at being perceived and admired as the perfect woman.[117]

In view of this central concern with gender, it comes as no surprise that several comments deal with gender issues and that these concerns arise throughout the novel. There are two particular matters which emerge predominantly: one is the way in which society regards women in general, and the other is the institution of marriage – both, of course, relating to the dynamics between male and female. Continually situating male and female in relation to each other, the comments demonstrate tensions be-tween the situations that women are in and the patriarchal attitudes which determine what their roles should be.[118] Voices expressing preconceived ideas on the nature of women appear primarily in the first chapters of *Middlemarch*, and already in chapter one the narrator communicates the belief of collective society: 'Women were expected to have weak opinions; but the great safeguard of society and of domestic life was, that opinions were not acted on. Sane people did what their neighbours did' (i, 9). This comment concludes the passage in which Dorothea's religious ardour is assessed by a collective community voice and refers to the risk a man runs by marrying the type of woman Dorothea represents, that is, the type who might have her own ideas as to the 'application of her income' (i, 9). Relying on retrospective privilege here, the narrator decries a historical past which, he implies, conformed to outdated conventions. Speaking from a position of superiority, the narrator informs the reader of past beliefs and anticipates his or her concurrence. The comment condemns the manner in which Middlemarch society regards women, deeming it anachronistic and characteristic of an earlier scheme of things which needs to be explained. It is the community as a whole that is referred to in this comment, and the past tense indicates the narrator's and reader's temporal and cultural detachment.

---

117 Defining Rosamond as a 'tragic satire on the ideal woman' (153), Beer states that '[i]n *Middlemarch* Rosamond Vincy is a woman entrapped so completely that she is hardly aware of it, so smoothly does her compliance fit'; *George Eliot*, p. 169.

118 Beer argues that George Eliot's central theme in all her novels is the relations between the sexes, maintaining that this contradiction between men and women, between 'difference and connection – sustains the tension of her work'; *George Eliot*, p. 14.

It is significant that the comment quoted above establishes a supposed understanding between reader and narrator with regard to gender issues as early as the first chapter. This understanding informs not only the narrator's attitude towards the 'woman question' in the whole novel, but also the attitude the reader is expected to adopt in relation to the community of Middlemarch. By first mimicking the FID of a hypothetical community voice in the passage preceding the statement above, and then remarking disparagingly on it in the statement itself, the narrator attempts to establish the reader's attitude to the community as well as to gender-related problematics in the novel. The gender-specific theme is thus employed not only for its own sake, but for the sake of introducing the narrator's and establishing the reader's attitude towards the community of Middlemarch.

Attacks on patriarchal tradition are not uncommon in *Middlemarch* commentary. Often these comments embody an ironic dimension which allows the narrator to disparage certain phenomena while retaining a light and seemingly carefree tone. By this subtle blend of criticism and sarcasm, the novel protests against the conventions of patriarchal tradition without seeming to do so – that is, without losing focus on the plot and the continuous 'unravelling [of] certain human lots' (xv, 132). For instance, with regard to Sir James's conceited estimation of his own gender, and the manner in which he condescendingly imagines that he 'refrains' from curbing Dorothea's predominance on account of the delight it brings him, the narrator remarks:

> Why not? A man's mind – what there is of it – has always the advantage of being masculine, – as the smallest birch-tree is of a higher kind than the most soaring palm, – and even his ignorance is of a sounder quality (ii, 20).

This passage constitutes one of few in *Middlemarch* that hover between the narrator's commentary and a character's FID. The line of reasoning is evidently Sir James's, but the ironic overtone and the wedged-in 'what there is of it' derive from the narrator's critical evaluation of the argument.[119] In combination with subsequent passages, this comment constitutes a fierce critique of patriarchal tradition. Not only does it insinuate that Sir James's personality is limp and that 'a man's mind' leaves much to be desired; subsequent passages imply that Providence has provided him with the patriarchal tradition according to which he fashions his arguments. In other words, Sir James's line of reasoning originally derives from

---

119 Commenting on Sir James's conceit in this passage, Jennifer Uglow rightly points out that his contentment is deflated within a few pages as Dorothea announces her engagement to Casaubon; *George Eliot*, pp. 206-207.

a tradition which has programmed him to a particular mode of thinking. In effect, the comment does not denigrate Sir James as a character; rather, it criticises the tradition that shapes the ways in which he regards the roles of men and women. By encouraging the reader to recognise the ludicrousness of Sir James's reasoning, then, the comment involves him or her in an understanding with the narrator, thereby evading any potential objections that the reader might have against the criticism.

The institution of marriage is another area of interest in the novel. Although the commentary does not contain frequent assaults on it, the disadvantages of matrimony to a woman nevertheless appear as a concern, and not seldom as a concern which involves human nature in general. On Dorothea's determination to marry Casaubon the narrator comments: 'And certainly, the mistakes that we male and female mortals make when we have our own way might fairly raise some wonder that we are so fond of it' (ix, 67). Drawing the reader into the experience through the first-person pronoun, this narration-now statement relates the particular dilemma which a woman faces before and after marriage to a general consideration which all types of readers, both men and women, are encouraged to recognise. Rather than disparaging a particular phenomenon by situating narrator and reader on a level superior to it, this comment finds a point of contact between the particular gender-specific problem and a phenomenon which most readers can relate to. The comment thus approaches gender issues from a different vantage point than the comments quoted previously. Rather than criticising through irony, it endeavours to link the reader's recognition of a certain human propensity and the pressures placed on women before and after marriage.

The reflection quoted above not only solicits the reader's understanding of Dorothea's situation but also conveys a notion of premonition. As a contrast to this ill-omened anticipation, Rosamond appears as the deluded female whose sole anxiety has been that on entering marriage she might lose the ability to 'make conquests and enslave men' (xliii, 410). Realising that she can still interest the likes of Will Ladislaw, she deems it 'delightful to make captives from the throne of marriage with a husband as crown-prince by your side' (lxiii, 410). These statements, appearing as the narrator's mimicry of Rosamond rather than part of his commentary, demonstrate how Rosamond has in a sense become a creature of patriarchy, always catering to her vanity and only able to perceive herself in relation to the admiring glances she receives from men. But they also demonstrate the narrator's prejudiced attitude towards Rosamond. It is true that her character is very different from Dorothea's. She is, quite simply, an unsympathetic character. But she is also partly a product of her society and subject to the same restrictions as Dorothea. The narrator, however, cannot separate the unsympathetic character from the creature of patriarchy. He cannot, so to speak, see beyond Rosamond's character in order to analyse what it is that creates her vanity. Hence, there is a distinction here between what the novel implies and what can be inferred from narratorial commentary. The novel itself clearly presents Rosamond as a product of patriarchy, but the narrator's commentary makes no acknowledgment of this. Hence, *Middlemarch* presents both Dorothea and Rosamond as products of social structures; but the novel also shows how differently these structures affect the two women, how differently they adapt to the conditions they live in and, most importantly, how differently the narrator understands their situations.

Prelude and Finale

The Prelude to *Middlemarch* includes references to several themes mentioned above. Introducing Dorothea as a latter-day Theresa, it raises issues which relate to concerns such as religion, history, literature and gender. Comparing Dorothea's religious ardour to that of the sixteenth-century saint, the Prelude establishes Dorothea within a historical and religious context. Her 'passionate, ideal nature demanded an epic life' (Prelude, 3); but unlike Saint Theresa of Avila, who finds 'her epos in the reform of a religious order' (Prelude, 3), Dorothea is 'helped by no coherent social faith and order which could perform the function of knowledge for the ardently willing soul' (Prelude, 3). The Prelude implies that the emergence of a modern, secular society, which stifles religious zeal while restricting the advancement of women, sends Dorothea into a state of confusion and frustration. Before the reader becomes involved in the story, he or she is made aware of how Dorothea should be read.[120] A list of hindrances to Dorothea's aspirations for 'spiritual grandeur' (Prelude, 3) is presented, giving reasons for the 'tragic failure' (Prelude, 3) which it anticipates. 'Meanness of opportunity' (Prelude, 3) prevents Dorothea from converting her mental fervour into active realisation, and the lack of 'a coherent

---

120 Bernard Paris contends that the 'Prelude is almost entirely rhetoric', in the sense that '[i]t gives us little information about Dorothea but much about how George Eliot wishes us to see her'; *Rereading George Eliot*, p. 28.

social faith and order' (Prelude, 3) means that there is no framework for action.[121]

The Prelude, moreover, introduces the theme of history and time, beginning by asking: 'Who that cares much to know the history of man, and how that mysterious mixture behaves under the varying experiments of Time, has not dwelt, at least briefly, on the life of Saint Theresa' (Prelude, 3). Suggesting that human lives are determined by particular historical conditions, this initial comment implies that the novel itself is an experiment which can be analysed by a scientifically-minded observer.[122] Judging by the suggestion that the novel might be regarded as an experiment, the narrator could be seen as establishing his detached, analytical relation to the text; but this hint of detachment is immediately undermined by his affectionate relation to the characters he introduces, that is, Theresa of Avila and Dorothea Brooke. Hence, although the passage emphasises a temporal, historical distance as well as suggesting the narrator's detached relation to the story, the Prelude as a whole serves to reduce the distance between the reader and Dorothea's character. The Prelude thus inserts Dorothea into a historical, literary and social context which acts as a filter through which her character is interpreted; but at the same time it introduces the various themes of the novel which keep recurring as concerns in the depiction of all characters, as well as in the communication between narrator and reader.

The first passage of the Finale mentions the idea of non-fixed interpretations, stating that 'the fragment of a life, however typical, is not the sample of an even web: promises may not be kept, and an ardent outset may be followed by declension' (Finale, 779). Referring to the novel as a mere fragment in the lives of characters, the Finale sets out to furnish the reader with a brief summary as to the continued fates of its chief characters.[123] Observing that the lives of the characters do not end where the nar-

---

121 Kathleen Blake explains the feminist concern in the Prelude as an objection to society which 'offers [women] so little to do, expects less, and never imagines that they need work as much as men do'. In this sense, Blake argues, the female protagonist 'offers a paradigm of the novel's theme – lack of vocation as tenuousness of identity' (289).

122 John L. Tucker makes a similar interpretation of this initial passage, adding that it situates the narrator himself as a 'dispassionate observer' outside the narrative; (780).

123 Barbara Hardy refers to this passage as 'cleverly deceptive' as it warns readers not to base judgments on fragmented perceptions; see 'The Ending of *Middlemarch*', *The Collected Essays of Barbara Hardy* (Brighton: Harvester Press, 1987), pp. 102-108 (p. 107). The Finale was changed several times by George Eliot, who wrote the first version in only a few days but made extensive revisions in the subsequent proof copies. Susan Meikle states that the most radical changes between these altered proofs and the manuscript version consist in Eliot's treatment of the feminist concern and relate to Dorothea's 'mistakes'. Meikle maintains that the new versions demonstrate 'a more

rative ends, and implying that the details narrated in the 'fragment' do not necessarily shape what happens afterwards, the comment further indicates the 'realness' of diegetic properties. Disclosing some of the after-stories, the passage returns to the concept of the epic, introduced in the Prelude, presenting the idea of marriage as a 'home epic'. Outlining the subsequent fortunes of the different couples in the text, the Finale suggests the revaluation of marriage as a beginning rather than an end, proposing that 'that complete union which makes the advancing years a climax' serves to define the new type of epic.[124]

This new type of epic also requires a new type of heroine, however, and it is to her that the Finale returns in its last passage. Looking back to Dorothea's unused potential, first mentioned in the Prelude, the Finale again associates her with Saint Theresa; but this time the tone is more optimistic, as the Finale focuses on 'the effect of her being on those around her' (Finale, 785) rather than on her 'tragic failure' (Prelude, 3). In the Finale Dorothea is a person who leaves no record in history, as opposed to Saint Theresa and Antigone; but she is successful in her own right, as her unhistoric acts have added to human progress. The novel ends on this melioristic note, which is communicated as a narratorial comment to the reader:[125]

> [F]or the growing good of the world is partly dependent on unhistoric acts; and
> that things are not so ill with you and me as they might have been, is half owing to

resigned and qualified belief in the efforts of the individual lives to counteract the effects' of Dorothea's social origins. This more resigned approach, Meikle suggests, corresponds to continuous changes and progressions in the women's rights movement at the time of composition; 'Fruit and Seed: The Finale to *Middlemarch*', in *George Eliot: Centenary Essays and an Unpublished Fragment*, ed. by Anne Smith (London: Vision Press, 1980), pp. 181-195 (p. 188). Harriet Farwell Adams comments on the Finale's uneasy connection to the Prelude, arguing that the many revisions to these last passages indicate the carelessness with which they were composed. Adams insists that it is 'a mistake, therefore, to attach too much significance' to them, as they were written in haste and 'separately from the rest of the novel'; see 'Prelude and Finale to *Middlemarch*', *The Victorian Newsletter*, 68 (1985), 9-11 (p. 10).

124 Kerry McSweeney comments on the concept of the 'home epic', contending that *Middlemarch* 'cannot be an epic work in the traditional sense' given that 'the necessary subject matter is lacking'. Hence, the idea of marriage as a 'home epic' provides the story with a 'modern equivalent to epic action'; *Middlemarch* (London: George Allen & Unwin, 1984), p. 33. In his article '*Middlemarch*: The "Home Epic" ', however, Kenny Marotta questions the term, stating that it is an oxymoron, 'combining domesticity with grandeur'. In this respect, Marotta continues, the term exemplifies the vacillating relation the novel has to the epic genre. See *Genre: A Quarterly Devoted to Generic Criticism*, 15 (1982), 403-420 (p. 403).

125 Barbara Hardy also notices the melioristic idea in this last passage and connects it to 'Carlyle's insistence that history is composed of innumerable biographies'; 'The Ending of *Middlemarch*', p. 105.

the number who lived faithfully a hidden life, and rest in unvisited tombs (Finale, 785).

True to form, this last narratorial comment draws the reader into the argument, reducing the distance between narrator and reader, serving to elicit the reader's sympathy for Dorothea's fate. But this last passage adds yet another dimension of complexity to the ontological divide between reader, narrator and character, as it erases the dividing line between fiction and life outside the fiction by fusing the two. In this very last sentence, story-time now and narration now are joined to form a united sphere.

7. Daniel Deronda

The last of the novels, *Daniel Deronda*, published in 1876, represents a new departure for George Eliot as a novelist. Much has been said and written about the novel's parallel plots, its contemporary setting, its underlying social criticism and, in particular, about its pioneering presentation of Jewish life.[1] *Daniel Deronda* takes a new approach ideologically, but it also differs from Eliot's earlier work structurally and narratologically. For example, all of Eliot's fictional work up till *Middlemarch* opens in a traditionally nineteenth-century fashion, that is, by presenting descriptive overviews of settings and characters.[2] Conversely, *Daniel Deronda* dives right into the mind of a character and poses a number of questions in the form of free indirect discourse (FID): 'Was she beautiful or not beautiful? and what was the secret of form or expression which gave the dynamic quality to her glance?' (i, 3). This opening paragraph is preceded by an epigraph which,

---

1 Many early reviewers objected to what they considered idealised representations of Jewish life in the novel, and *Daniel Deronda* was criticised primarily from an ideological point of view. F. R. Leavis's proposal to expunge everything but the Gwendolen story from the novel was the culmination of a long tradition of criticism against the so-called 'Jewish parts'. George Eliot herself was annoyed with these objections, reproving 'readers who cut the book into scraps and talk of nothing in it but Gwendolen' and insisting that she 'meant everything in the book to be related to everything else there'; see *Letters*, vi, 290. In fairness, it should be noted that a considerable number of readers defended Eliot's presentation of Jewish life, not least Jewish readers in Britain as well as abroad. However, apart from finding Deronda's story dull and 'unrealistic', and the Jewish sections sentimental and over-idealised, many critics argued against the structural composition of the two plots, finding the connection between the two laboured and artificial. F. R. Leavis himself later withdrew his suggestion of cutting the novel in half, admitting the inseparability of the two parts, and later criticism has substantiated the close connection between the Gwendolen and Deronda plots. Besides F. R. Leavis and Henry James see, for instance, Joan Bennett, *George Eliot: Her Mind and Her Art* and Jerome Thale, *The Novels of George Eliot*. See also '*Daniel Deronda*', in *The Collected Essays of Barbara Hardy* (Brighton: Harvester, 1987), pp. 109-129; and Harold Fisch, '*Daniel Deronda* or *Gwendolen Harleth?*', *Nineteenth-Century Fiction*, 19 (1965), 345-356.

2 Additionally, the story of *Romola* is preceded by a 'Proem', the story of *Felix Holt* by an 'Introduction', and the story of *Middlemarch* by a 'Prelude'.

by reflecting on 'the make-believe of a beginning' (i, 3), reveals a sense of self-consciousness and fictionality in the narrative which is easier to associate with modernist writing than with nineteenth-century 'realistic' fiction. Moreover, *Daniel Deronda* deviates from the traditionally straightforward chronology common to realistic representation; it experiments with flashbacks and inversions of sequence in order to highlight the seminal scene where Daniel Deronda and Gwendolen notice each other for the first time at the gambling table in Leubronn. Barbara Hardy describes the novel 'as a remarkable instance of T. S. Eliot's definition of artistic development as a series of "wholly new attempts" and "new kinds of failure".[3] Nevertheless, *Daniel Deronda* has much in common with Eliot's earlier works. In essence, it is a novel which, like all her fictional work, is not merely a story but also a psychological investigation into human relationships and individual development, a study of contemporary society and above all an analysis of the human capacity for compassion.

The technical-narratological part of this chapter begins by studying the movements between general and particular in the novel. It goes on to look at references and addresses to the reader and subsequently moves into analyses of epigraphs and meta-narration. As *Daniel Deronda* is a novel in which instances of free indirect discourse (FID) can be difficult to distinguish from narratorial commentary, the relation between these narrative elements is examined in the ensuing section. The narratological part of this chapter is concluded by a discussion of comments appearing within parenthesis. The thematically orientated section begins by looking at discussions of egoism in the novel. These discussions are closely linked to perspectives on gender, an issue raised in the following section. Other themes deal with problems of interpretation and references to history, religion and literature, all of which recur as particularly pertinent thematic concerns in narration now.

Particular-General-Particular

It is a widespread assumption that the number of Eliot's narratorial comments decreases with each novel. The idea might be attributable to the author's improving ability to weave her narrator's commentary into the text, because actually *Daniel Deronda* contains approximately the same number

---

3   Hardy, '*Daniel Deronda*', p. 110.

of comments as several of her earlier works.[4] Most of them move between the particular and the general, between story-time now and narration now, in order to stimulate the reader's recognition and connect it back to the particular case in the text. In *Daniel Deronda*, a novel in which the psychological analyses of characters' inward depths are perhaps more weighty than in any other Eliot novel, the reader's recognition, understanding and sympathy are especially essential for the advancement of the story and for the credibility of the narrative as a whole. *Daniel Deronda* thus includes a significant number of examples where the narrator moves from story-time now to narration now, using general terms to discuss particular phenomena which, according to the narrator, relate not only to the characters in the text but also to the reader, to the narrator himself and to human kind at large.

Regarding Gwendolen's unhappy life as Mrs Grandcourt, the narrator discusses the process of change going on within her as she struggles to reconcile her former rebellious young temperament with the restrictions placed on her under Grandcourt's sadistic authority:

> Can we wonder at the practical submission which hid her constructive rebellion? The combination is common enough, as we know from the number of persons who make us aware of it in their own case by a clamorous unwearied statement of the reasons against their submitting to a situation which, on inquiry, we discover to be the least disagreeable within their reach (xlviii, 516-517).

Including the reader in the consideration, the initial rhetorical question serves to place narrator and reader on an equal footing, so that the mutual understanding which the implicit response establishes conditions the ensuing argument. This argument, in turn, demonstrates some interesting characteristics of narratorial commentary. The first is that the statement makes an assumption as to the reader's ready knowledge or experience. The phenomenon of being torn between rebellion and submission is, according to the narrator, so common that the reader is surely familiar with it. Secondly, besides taking the reader's recognition for granted, the comment determines that this recognition does not necessarily have to be directly related to personal experience. The empirical knowledge which the reader receives through 'the number of persons who make us aware of it' allows him or her to recognise a phenomenon which, although not having personal or direct experience of it, he or she can understand by way of the imagination. Finally, the statement substantiates Gwendolen's own

---

4 Compare approximately 40 comments in the first 100 pages in *Daniel Deronda* to approximately the same amount in *Adam Bede* and 25 in *The Mill on the Floss*.

thoughts concerning her alternatives to being Mrs Grandcourt. Previous to the comment the narrator has conveyed Gwendolen's deliberations, arguing that 'Mrs Grandcourt "run away" would be a more pitiable creature than Gwendolen Harleth condemned to teach the bishop's daughters' (xlviii, 516). The conclusion Gwendolen has arrived at, then, is corroborated by the generalisation, which attempts to fit the phenomenon into the reader's sphere of recognition. The comment thus serves to authenticate Gwendolen's predicament by situating it in the reader's frame of reference and furthermore to establish a common ground on which narrator and reader can meet in the form of the first-person plural pronoun.

Some comments which move between the particular and the general serve not only to inspire sympathy, but also to introduce additional dimensions to particular episodes. As Gwendolen travels back to England from Leubronn, she contemplates her family's misfortune and expresses her own annoyance with men. Her irritation is commented on by the narrator:

> It is one thing to hate stolen goods, and another thing to hate them the more because their being stolen hinders us from making use of them. Gwendolen had begun to be angry with Grandcourt for being what had hindered her from marrying him, angry with him as the cause of her present dreary lot (xxi, 195-196).

Gwendolen's resentment against men is directed against Grandcourt in particular. Her annoyance with him originates not from disgust at his unwillingness to rectify an immoral past, but rather from the realisation that this past prevents her from fending off her impending misfortune. Hence, at this stage Gwendolen's egoism makes no judgment about Grandcourt's morality other than that his lack of it in the past now hinders her from leading the life she has imagined for herself. Significantly, the narrator elucidates the narration-now comment in story-time now, as if he were uncertain whether the idea might be lost without the particularisation. The transfer from general intellectualisation to particular instance is one of the few examples of commentary where the narrator seems to want to clarify the real meaning of the comment in story-time now. Hence, the narrator himself attaches the essence of the comment to the particular situation in the text, rather than letting the reader on his or her own apply the significance of the comment to the specific situation.

The use of imagery, as in the 'stolen goods' comment above, is common in the shifts between general and particular. Employing figurative language, the narrator generalises about the particular instance in the text by sharing symbolic images with the reader. Having communicated some of Daniel's thoughts concerning Gwendolen, informing the reader that Daniel's interest in the future Mrs Grandcourt went beyond compassion to include 'the fascination of her womanhood' (xxviii, 273), the narrator immediately modifies this information by emphasising Daniel's susceptibility and discretion. Addressing the reader in narration now, the narrator gives an illustration of Daniel's character:

> Sprinkle food before a delicate-eared bird: there is nothing he would more willingly take, yet he keeps aloof, because of his sensibility to checks which to you are imperceptible. And one man differs from another, as we all differ from the Bosjesman, in a sensibility to checks, that come from variety of needs, spiritual or other (xxviii, 273-274).

The illustration presents a distinct impression of Daniel's delicacy, acquainting the reader further with the sophistication of his character. The use of animal imagery is pervasive in all Eliot's novels, so the symbolism is not surprising on the face of it.[5] What makes this particular image unusual is that Daniel is likened to a 'delicate-eared bird' – a type of animal not commonly associated with a male hero.[6] But Daniel is different from Eliot's previous protagonists, both male and female, in that he does not learn to become sympathetic through failure and suffering – he is naturally so; a fully developed sympathetic character, he automatically empathises with his fellow mortals. He possesses what in conventional terms would be considered feminine sensibilities, such as compassion, and incorporates these qualities without suffering any loss of his masculine identity.[7] As the

---

5 For more on Eliot's use of animal imagery, see Karen B. Mann, pp. 7, 15-16.

6 There are several references to Daniel's 'femaleness' in the novel. For instance, in conversation with his mother, the Princess Halm-Eberstein, Daniel 'felt himself changing colour like a girl' (li, 535), and the narrator remarks about mother and son that 'all the woman lacking in her was present in him' (liii, 566). Earlier in the novel Daniel is depicted as being 'moved by an affectionateness such as we are apt to call feminine' (xxviii, 271). Tony E. Jackson contends that 'as Gwendolen turns more and more to Daniel for guidance, he becomes the Beatrice to her Dante'; see *The Subject of Modernism: Narrative Alterations in the Fiction of Eliot, Conrad, Woolf and Joyce* (Ann Arbor: University of Michigan Press, 1994), p. 50. For further analysis of Daniel's character, see Carole Robinson, 'The Severe Angel: A Study of *Daniel Deronda*', *ELH*, 31 (1964), 278-300.

7 Tony E. Jackson argues that even though he is 'presented as a womanly man, he nonetheless occupies the social category of a male' (50). Jackson also reviews Daniel's exceptionality in being the only one of Eliot's characters who is not '*becoming* truly sympathetic in an unsympathetic economic and social environment'; Daniel, by contrast, demonstrates 'the difficulty of *being* naturally sympathetic in an unsympathetic society' (51).

emphasis on Daniel's innate compassion is ubiquitous in the novel, he to some extent epitomises Eliot's idea of a fully developed human being.[8]

In all Eliot's novels, the explanatory element of the general analysis is frequently advertised by 'for' used as a conjunction introducing a clause of reason. In these cases, the statement in narration now typically follows immediately after the particular situation it examines, often preceded by a semicolon. Hence, the particular and the general, story-time now and narration now, are juxtaposed within the same sentence, causing the narrator's comment to pass by almost undetected. An example from chapter 59 shows how smoothly the narrator moves between story-time now and narration now. Finding it difficult to confront Sir Hugo Mallinger after having learnt of his true heritage, Daniel struggles with his feelings, and the narrative moves from the particular to the general:

> Daniel's affectionate gratitude towards Sir Hugo made him wish to find grounds of excuse rather than blame; for it is as possible to be rigid in principle and tender in blame, as it is to suffer from the sight of things hung awry, and yet to be patient with the hanger who sees amiss (lix, 611- 612).

'For' serves a causal function here, explaining, through a general principle, the processes guiding Daniel's mind. The purpose is to encourage the reader to understand his anger at having been duped for so long, but more importantly to invite him or her to sympathise with Daniel's reluctance to reproach Sir Hugo for his 'ignorant kindness' (612). Appearing as a truism, yet without becoming simplistic, the statement alerts the reader's attention to a phenomenon which he or she can recognise. Accordingly, the axiomatic tone of the comment, together with the use of 'for', encourages the reader to interpret Daniel's clemency as a natural reaction in view of his situation.

Comments where 'for' is used as a causal conjunction usually refer to whatever situation they are in immediate propinquity to. As well as rais-

---

8 This idea challenges a common criticism directed towards Daniel's character. Several critics have condemned him on the grounds of his infallibility, humourlessness and lack of irony, disliking the almost messianic portrayal of this man. Barbara Hardy, for example, considers the lack of irony in the depiction of Daniel 'a sign of lifelessness' (120); James Harrison suggests that 'seeming to care so little for himself, Deronda in fact cares for so little else – which makes him the prig he so rightly dreads becoming'; see 'The Root of the Matter with *Daniel Deronda*', *Philological Quarterly*, 68 (1989), 509-523, (p. 518); and Mary Ellen Doyle discusses his supernatural representation and 'the narrator's uncritical identification' with him (164). Harold Fisch, on the other hand, defends Eliot's portrayal of Deronda, arguing that the fault lies with the discipline of criticism which cannot accept the possibility that 'a nineteenth century novel might have a genuine hero' (351).

ing issues which have relevance on a general level outside the diegesis, these comments sometimes add further depth to general themes within the diegesis. Analysing a particular episode, the secondary clause relates to a general phenomenon within the reader's frame of reference, but also to a general theme associated with a particular character or argument within the narrative. Such a comment can be found in chapter 10, which depicts the archery meeting where Gwendolen and Grandcourt see each other for the first time. Gwendolen impresses everyone with her precise shooting aim, and she is particularly pleased to notice that she has made an impression not only on Grandcourt, but also on Herr Klesmer:

> It entered a little into her pleasure that Herr Klesmer must be observing her at a moment when music was out of the question, and his superiority very far in the background; for vanity is as ill at ease under indifference as tenderness is under a love which it cannot return (x, 90).

It follows that before the archery meeting, Herr Klesmer's impression of Gwendolen has been formed under unfortunate circumstances connected with her performance as Hermione in *A Winter's Tale* (*Daniel Deronda*, vi). At that time, Herr Klesmer had sensed Gwendolen's wounded vanity and feigned a compliment on her acting skills and so managed to restore her pride. However, the fact that Herr Klesmer is unaffected by Gwendolen's attractiveness makes her uneasy, as his lack of interest renders her powerless over him. Displaying other talents than beauty and refinement, in this case dexterity with a bow and arrow, Gwendolen continues in her attempts to satiate her craving for admiration. But the vanity referred to in the comment quoted above relates to much more than what happens at the archery meeting. In fact, the generalisation applies not only to the preceding sentence but to Gwendolen's narcissistic attitude towards anything she does. As a whole, it serves as an appropriate description of Gwendolen's most salient characteristic – vanity – the most significant guide to her persona. Moreover, the tenderness mentioned, which is uncomfortable with not being able to reciprocate love, is equally significant to Gwendolen's fate, entering at a later stage when Daniel cannot return the same type of love for her that she has for him. Therefore, this almost unnoticeable narratorial comment, wedged as it is into story-time now, serves as an adumbration of Gwendolen's whole character, as well as of what lies ahead of her.

In the same manner as 'for', 'but' is employed to introduce narratorial commentary. In contrast to clauses introduced by 'for', 'but' often signals a statement which demands special attention. In its general analysis the comment escorts the reader onto a new course, either in opposition to the particularities of story-time now or as an expansion of perspective. A particularly interesting example involves Gwendolen's reluctant acquiescence towards the institution of marriage. The statement shows how the narrator reflects on her attitude and intensifies her deliberations with an extended perspective:

> Of course marriage was social promotion; she could not look forward to a single life; but promotions have sometimes to be taken with bitter herbs – a peerage will not quite do instead of leadership to the man who meant to lead; and this delicate-limbed sylph of twenty meant to lead. For such passions dwell in feminine breasts also (iv, 31).

The conjunction in the secondary clause starts off a line of reasoning applicable to Gwendolen. The comment resembles FID, but the language and general perspective emerge from the narrator. As if issuing from Gwendolen's subconscious mind, the comment shows how Gwendolen extends her field of vision to suit her ambitions. Hence, the secondary clause presents an argument which introduces a change of direction. However, although the gist of the argument is Gwendolen's and mediated persuasively by the narrator, the tone is patently ironical, signalling the naïvety of her nature. The 'bitter herbs' refer back to Gwendolen's examination of marriage, which convinced her that it is 'rather a dreary state, in which a woman could not do what she liked, had more children than were desirable, was consequently dull, and became irrevocably immersed in humdrum' (iv, 30-31).[9] The humour in these lines conditions the perception of irony in the ensuing comment, which draws the conclusion that having many children and becoming boring are the 'bitter herbs' which inevitably accompany matrimony, thereby constituting the unattractive side effects of social advancement.[10] The passage thus manages to express the character's beliefs with a certain degree of gravity while imparting an ironic dimension to the situation. In turn, the irony invites the reader to share in the humour, placing both reader and narrator on a level above the diegesis from where Gwendolen can be viewed.

Introducing primary clauses, 'but' characteristically introduces a departure from story-time now where the narrator reflects generally on the

---

9 The reference to 'bitter herbs' brings to mind *The Mill on the Floss*, in which the narrator discusses Thomas à Kempis's *The Imitation of Christ* as a 'small old-fashioned book' which turns 'bitter waters into sweetness' (IV, iii, 291). The phrase is also a reference to the Passover in Exodus 12. 8, and Numbers 9. 11, which should be eaten 'with unleavened bread and bitter herbs'.

10 Although the narrator comments humorously on Gwendolen's naïve ideas about marriage, there is also a serious, feminist undertone which acknowledges her perceptiveness.

particularities of events in the narrative. Rather than reinforcing particular attitudes in the narrative in order for the reader to sympathise, these passages hence encourage the reader to allow the episodes in the text to widen his or her perspective. To grasp the narrowness of Gwendolen's world-view, an extended perspective is essential – a requirement which is acknowledged by the narrator, who repeatedly comments on Gwendolen's outlook on life by providing a larger picture. On being invited to the Arrowpoints of Quetcham Hall, Gwendolen is confident of her own superiority, presuming that everyone will admire her and that she in turn will find them silly and ridiculous. The narrator, however, invites the reader to consider Gwendolen's attitude from another angle:

> Gwendolen, who had a keen sense of absurdity in others, but was kindly disposed towards any one who could make life agreeable to her, meant to win Mrs Arrowpoint by giving her an interest and attention beyond what others were probably inclined to show. But self-confidence is apt to address itself to an imaginary dullness in others; as people who are well-off speak in a cajoling tone to the poor, and those who are in the prime of life raise their voice and talk artificially to seniors, hastily conceiving them to be deaf and rather imbecile (v, 35).

Mrs Arrowpoint, of course, sees right through Gwendolen. But the narrator informs the reader that it is Gwendolen's own tendency to underestimate the people around her that exposes her conceit. The comment, then, reverses the perspective so that instead of viewing the diegetic world through Gwendolen's eyes, the reader perceives the perspective of other characters in the text. Also, by commenting on reprehensible self-confidence, the narrator acknowledges and criticises Gwendolen's arrogance. The presentation of the derogatory ways in which fortunate people address less fortunate ones encourages the reader to perceive the tone of self-importance with which Gwendolen approaches people she believes to be dull and uninteresting. Consequently, in this example, the process of stimulating the reader's recognition serves not to elicit the reader's sympathy, but to motivate him or her to follow the narrator's line of argument as he extends the perspective of the narrative.

Like *Middlemarch*, *Daniel Deronda* contains several narratorial comments which appear within parentheses that serve as topographical indicators of a shared sphere between reader and narrator. The majority of these surface in the first half of the novel and primarily in connection with Gwendolen, investing a particular phenomenon with ironic distance. They serve as asides to the reader, humorously remarking in passing on a particular line of thought or form of behaviour. For example, the narrator interrupts a conversation between Gwendolen and her uncle, Mr Gascoigne, to comment parenthetically on Gwendolen's argument for getting a horse. She has suggested to her uncle that she might renounce some other pleasure if it helps towards paying for the horse, and the narrator interjects before continuing the dialogue: '(Was there ever a young lady or gentleman not ready to give up an unspecified indulgence for the sake of the favourite one specified?)' (iii, 27). The irony undermines Gwendolen's credibility and emphasises her young naïvety. This emphasis, in turn, indicates a mature reader who can recognise *and* remember the phenomenon.

However, not all parenthetic comments in *Daniel Deronda* display irony. In another scene where Daniel and Gwendolen find themselves alone, the narrator employs literary analogy to describe Daniel's demeanour:

> [H]e had a wonderful power of standing perfectly still, and in that position reminded one sometimes of Dante's *spiriti magni con occhi tardi e gravi*. (Doubtless some of these danced in their youth, doubted of their own vocation, and found their own times too modern) (xxxvi, 381).[11]

The spirits referred to are numerous and include, among others, Socrates, Plato, Hector and Electra. There is no irony here, as there seldom is in reference to Daniel, but instead a comment which elevates him to an almost divine level. The parenthetical aside has two dimensions: first, it authenticates the preceding sentence, salvaging it from being interpreted as absurd should the reader think that the narrator's esteem for Daniel has gone too far. The 'spirits' are thus brought down a notch, intimating that even legendary and historical figures were just human once; secondly, there is an element of humour in the very idea of Socrates dancing and worrying about what to do with his life. This vision encourages the reader not to judge the flattering equation too harshly, and to acknowledge the exceptionality of Daniel.

The parenthesis thus signals the approach of a narratorial aside. The comments in themselves do not differ in terms of function from other narratorial comments, but the parentheses indicate a separate level away from the narrative and story-time now, a level to which only the reader and the narrator have access.

Consequently, as in the earlier books, the movement between general and particular in narratorial commentary is facilitated by typographical indicators which can either make the transition from one level to the other seem smooth and effortless or appear as abrupt shifts in tone and perspec-

---

11 The reference is to *Inferno*, iv. 112 and 119, translated in the Oxford World's Classics edition as 'great spirits with grave and serious eyes'.

tive. The major difference between *Middlemarch* and *Daniel Deronda* is that in the latter novel, the narrator is less likely to compel the reader in and out of narrative spheres in a haphazard fashion, appearing more restricted and constrained. In Eliot's last novel, then, narratorial commentary is as common as in the earlier books, but the narrator seems less prone to call attention to the transitions made between story-time now and narration now.

References and Addresses to the Reader

All narratorial commentary in Eliot's novels is to some degree concerned with the reader's response, and most of it serves to influence the reader in one way or another. Normally, these attempts appear as subtle elicitations directed at the reader's sense of recognition; but occasionally it seems subtle attempts do not suffice. Therefore, expecting the reader to respond in a particular manner, the narrator addresses his or her assumed response openly in an effort to authenticate the narrative. Introducing Grandcourt into the story, the narrator engages in a description of the expectations the people in the neighbourhood have of his arrival, but straight away suspects some readers of a failure to accept the validity of the description:

> Some readers of this history will doubtless regard it as incredible that people should construct matrimonial prospects on the mere report that a bachelor of good fortune and possibilities was coming within reach, and will reject the statement as a mere outflow of gall: they will aver that neither they nor their first cousins have minds so unbridled; and that in fact this is not human nature [...] But, let it be observed, nothing is here narrated of human nature generally: the history in its present stage concerns only a few people in a corner of Wessex – whose reputation, however, was unimpeached, and who, I am in the proud position of being able to state, were all on visiting terms with persons of rank (ix, 76).

The narrator presupposes that the reader automatically applies the particularities of the text onto his or her own life as a means of assessing the authenticity of the narrative. Rather than encouraging the reader to recognise a particular phenomenon by relating it to his or her own world, then, the narrator imagines this process to have taken place already and consequently launches his argument on the basis of it. Surprisingly, the defence he offers contradicts the fundamental idea of many other narratorial comments in Eliot's oeuvre. In this example, the reader is requested to regard the particularities of the text not in a general sense, but as unique to the characters in question. The narrator claims to make no reference to 'human nature generally'; he only concerns himself with the chosen characters whose doings may disagree with the reader's experience. It is impossible to overlook the defensive tone in the comment or to help wondering at the narrator's disavowal of the correlation between the particular and the general – a correlation that plays such a vital role in most other narratorial comments. Both elements increase the reader's distance to the narrator and the text; and rather than underpinning the authenticity of the text, the narrator's admonitory tone alienates the reader from engaging in and relating to characters and events.

There is an aspect of meta-narration in this comment, which acknowledges the notion of fictionality while recognising the presence of an addressee. It is clear that the narrator imagines a critical addressee who continuously evaluates the degree of genuineness in the text. This concern with authenticity under the reader's supposed scrutinising eye is evident in most of Eliot's novels, but it is commonly managed by the narrator through applications to the nature of human beings in general, i.e. by relating the particular to the commonplace rather than emphasising the exclusive. Accordingly, references to the general serve as a guarantee of the dimension of veracity in the fiction. In the quotation above, however, the narrator attempts to achieve the same effect by taking the reverse approach. By insisting on the selectiveness of a small group of characters and dissuading the reader from attempting to recognise their motives and actions, the narrator attempts to uphold the authenticity of the narrative. Moreover, the narrator endeavours to erase the impression of fictionality by referring to the narrative as a history. The comment thus insists on the genuineness of characters and events, suggesting that they have taken place in actuality and that the narrator is a historian rather than a story-teller.

The quotation above is an atypical example of narratorial commentary even with regard to its way of considering the reader's response. Characteristically, comments addressing the putative reaction of a reader or readers endeavour to activate the reader's sympathy and guide him or her towards what the narrator regards as the 'right' interpretation. Reflecting on an expected reading, these statements anticipate what the reader's reaction will be, remarking on that hypothetical response. Regarding Daniel's complex relationship to Sir Hugo and to the truth of his parentage, the narrator accounts extensively for his feelings, but then arrests the account to consider the reader's reaction:

> The average man may regard this sensibility on the question of birth as preposterous and hardly credible; but with the utmost respect for his knowledge as the rock from which all other knowledge is hewn, it must be admitted that many well-proved facts are dark to the average man, even concerning the action of his own heart and the structure of his own retina (xxxvii, 402).

Contrary to the comment regarding 'only a few people in a corner of Wessex', this statement serves to induce the reader into an understanding with the narrator. At the outset it does not actually qualify as a comment on the reader's response, as it considers the anticipated response from what is labelled the 'average man'. Initially, it is unclear whether the reader is included in this category of human beings; but considering the mordant irony in the second part of the statement, it seems apparent that the reader is exempted from mediocrity and invited to share in the narrator's scorn for the average man's ignorance. By imagining a hypothetical reader and condescendingly, albeit covertly, criticising his or her assumed interpretation, the narrator attempts to reduce the distance between himself and the actual reader by trying to make him or her feel superior to the average ignoramus. Rather than accusing the reader of a particular interpretation and attempting to convert him or her, then, the narrator applies reverse psychology, rebutting an interpretation which, it is implied, only the average man would arrive at.

Not all comments involving reader response are oblique schemes for manipulating the reader. Occasionally the narrator is strikingly candid. For example, early on in the novel Gwendolen's character is extensively described and her excellent qualities specified. Following this description the narrator presents an analysis of the basis for her authoritarian and queen-like demeanour, playing with the idea that superficial qualities can govern internal characteristics. This idea is immediately rejected, however, and the narrator turns to the reader instructing him or her to 'beware of arriving at conclusions without comparison' (iv, 32). Subsequently, a comparison is presented to illustrate the general caution. In effect, the narrator warns the reader not to form an opinion about Gwendolen's demeanour on the basis of external facts. Instead, the reader is to believe that it is Gwendolen's 'strong determination' and 'total fearlessness in making [herself] disagreeable' (iv, 33), despite being exceptionally beautiful, that underpin her imposing persona. Contrary to many other comments incorporating the reader's imagined response, this direct address makes no assumptions about the reader's 'ready-made' interpretation, nor any indirect intimations as to what an ideal reader would be like. Rather, it serves as a manifestation of that didactic tone for which Eliot has often been criticised, an accusation which she herself fervently rejected.[12]

'We' is frequently used in *Daniel Deronda*, as in all Eliot's novels, and primarily serves to diminish the reader's distance to characters, in order for him or her to feel affinity and so sympathise with certain characters. Broaching human idiosyncrasies or patterns of behaviour which the reader can easily recognise, the narrator's comment facilitates the reader's understanding of characters and events. The typical 'we'-comment justifies character behaviour on the grounds that it is acted out in accordance with human nature. By incorporating the reader into the 'we', thus making him or her subject to the same laws of nature as the characters, the narrator shields the characters from the reader's censure, providing the reader can recognise and agree with the reflection proffered in the narratorial comment. Several 'we-comments' are pooled with direct remarks or insinuations about the reader's response. An example of this type of joint function appears in chapter 59, when Daniel waits for Sir Hugo's arrival in Genoa. Grandcourt has died, and while Daniel waits he finds himself inwardly smiling at the thought of Sir Hugo's estates now being passed on to his own offspring. Naturally this satisfaction collides with Daniel's annoyance with Sir Hugo for withholding information about his Jewish parentage, and with the reality of its being a happiness which emanates from another man's death. But the narrator sanctions Daniel's subdued elation by remarking:

> We should be churlish creatures if we could have no joy in our fellow-mortals' joy, unless it were in agreement with our theory of righteous distribution and our highest ideal of human good: what sour corners our mouths would get – our eyes, what frozen glances! and all the while our own possessions and desires would not exactly adjust themselves to our ideal. We must have some comradeship with imperfection (lix, 611).

Typically for Eliot's novels, this comment demonstrates the precedence that compassion takes before righteousness. Daniel's joy is justified by a general reflection on the benefits of sympathy, and the reader is included

---

12 After her death, Eliot was often accused of being excessively didactic in her novels. Some critics, for example Ford Madox Ford and E. M. Forster, regarded her works as those of a solemn teacher or preacher. In *The Critical Attitude* (1911), Ford claims that '[h]aving studied *Das Leben Jesu* [George Eliot] became inflated by the idea of the writer as prophet'; quoted in *The Oxford Reader's Companion to George Eliot*, ed. by John Rignall (Oxford: Oxford University Press, 2000), p. 127. George Eliot herself was anxious not to appear didactic or preachy, stating in a letter to John Blackwood: 'I have always exercised a severe watch against anything that could be called preaching, and if I have ever allowed myself in dissertation or in dialogue [anything] which is not part of the *structure* of my books, I have there sinned against my own laws'; see *Letters*, v, 459.

into the example so that his or her feelings of affinity with Daniel are boosted. At the same time, the narrator attempts to outmanoeuvre any possible suspiciousness on the reader's part by encouraging him or her to respond positively to the reflection on human nature. By persuasively arguing that Daniel's inability to hold on to his principles is not only right for him in this case, but often appropriate for human beings in general, the narrator undertakes to prevent the reader from criticising Daniel's feelings of joy, and simultaneously to decrease the distance between him and the reader.

It would seem implausible that the same reduction of distance should be sought in connection with the contemptible Grandcourt; but in fact, the narrator does strive to base some of his monstrous behaviour on what is innate in human nature. Describing how Grandcourt spends his days in idleness after dismissing Lush, the narrator points to his contemplative mood, advising the reader not to over-interpret on the basis of superficial impressions:

> We mortals have a strange spiritual chemistry going on within us, so that a lazy stagnation or even a cottony milkiness may be preparing one knows not what biting or explosive material. The navvy waking from sleep and without malice heaving a stone to crush the life out of his sleeping comrade, is understood to lack the trained motive which makes a character fairly calculable in its actions; but by a roundabout course even a gentleman may make of himself a chancy personage, raising an uncertainty as to what he may do next, which sadly spoils companionship (xxviii, 269).

There are two functions working simultaneously in this comment. First, it raises an awareness of the darker side of human nature, taking for granted that the behaviour described is not exclusive to a particular group of mankind, but equally innate in all humans. In turn, this awareness suggests a resemblance between the reader and Grandcourt, implying that both are equally capable of harbouring explosive interiors under well-trimmed and composed façades. By this means the narrator attempts to elicit understanding (but not sympathy) for Grandcourt's character, and to diminish the impression of machine-like callousness that is commonly associated with him. Here, there is an intimation of passion and ardour; and although it is motiveless and capricious, it instils a certain degree of human feeling, albeit malicious, into a character whose interior the reader has little access to.

Secondly, the comment serves as a premonition, forewarning the reader of what Grandcourt is capable of and insinuating that an explosion might take place. Informing the reader of Grandcourt's unpredictability, then, the narrator endeavours to stimulate the reader's curiosity and to stimulate his or her expectations as to Grandcourt's and Gwendolen's marriage. Indisputably, the premonition presages an ominous outcome; but it does so misleadingly, indicating that Grandcourt's 'explosive material' will eventually blow up, which, of course, it never does. Accordingly, the comment sustains the reader's feeling of insecurity with regard to Grandcourt, maintaining the impression of him as a highly volatile character, whose interior material might catch fire and explode at any time.

As in the earlier novels, the narrator invokes the reader's imagination on a number of occasions. Although not continually shifting the reader's perspective of the text as in, for example, *The Mill on the Floss* or *Middlemarch*, references to the reader's ability to imagine scenes in *Daniel Deronda* similarly serve to define the reader's position in relation to the text. When Mirah sings to Daniel for the first time, the reader is encouraged to imagine what she looks like:

> Imagine her – it is always good to imagine a human creature in whom bodily loveliness seems as properly one with the entire being as the bodily loveliness of those wondrous transparent orbs of life that we find in the sea – imagine her with her dark hair brushed from her temples [...] Then see the perfect cameo her profile makes, cut in a duskish shell where by some happy fortune there pierced a gem-like darkness from the eye and eyebrow (xxxii, 314).

Appealing to the reader's power of imagination, the comment confirms the reader's position outside the diegesis, acknowledging the fact that the reader's role in the narrative takes place within his or her imagination. Contrary to earlier novels, then, this appeal to the reader does not form part of a continuous movement which alternately locates the reader inside or outside the diegesis, but rather substantiates the reader's established role beyond the text. Furthermore, these types of comments, which recognise the significance of the reader's imagination in the reading process, maintain an impression of fictionality and weaken the notion that the narrator is retelling a history which he has himself experienced. The comment constitutes an amalgam of story-time now and narration now as it addresses the reader directly in a sphere beyond the narrative world and in the present tense, but simultaneously focuses on the particular properties of story-time now. This interweaving of story-time now and narration now reduces the distance between the reader and Mirah, locating her character vividly in the reader's 'here and now'. Therefore, although the reference to the reader's imagination advances the notion of fictionality and underpins the reader's position beyond the narrative, the same factors serve to situate

Mirah in the reader's immediate imagination, thus decreasing the distance between character and reader and encouraging the latter's active concern for the text.

The type of imagination referred to above is one which involves the reader's capacity to visualise scenes. Accordingly, further on in the comment, the narrator requests the reader to 'see the perfect cameo her profile makes'. In an earlier novel such an application to the reader's visual capacities could be interpreted as an attempt on the part of the narrator to pull the reader into the diegesis. But in view of the fact that *Daniel Deronda* contains so few examples of metalepsis and considering the context of imagination, it seems appropriate to understand the narrator's use of the word 'see' as part of the rhetoric of imagination, i.e. that the vision the reader is encouraged to 'see' is within his or her mind's eye.[13]

Daniel Deronda is not completely exempt from examples of metalepsis, though, and while there are fewer instances of it here than in Eliot's early novels, the narrator nevertheless experiments with transitions between narrative levels. An attempt to include the reader into the diegesis occurs only once, in chapter 17, where the narrator describes Daniel as he rows down the Thames just before preventing Mirah from committing suicide: 'Look at his hands: they are not small and dimpled, with tapering fingers that seem to have only a deprecating touch: they are long, flexible, firmly-grasping hands' (xvii, 157-158).[14] Without forewarning the reader is pulled into the narrative world on the assumption that he or she can actually see Daniel's hands. The request is based on the tacit understanding that narrator and reader exist on the same narrative level from which there is immediate access to the diegetic world. Although sharing the same level with the narrator is no novelty to the reader at this stage, this example presents a difference which depends on the reader's presupposed potential for visually witnessing components belonging to the diegetic world. Such an assumption suggests the 'actuality' of the narrative, implying that there is no barrier between the reader's 'real' world and the world of the text. Furthermore, the reader's assumed visual access reduces the distance

---

13 Brian Swann considers the images of eyesight to be some of the most interesting in the novel. See 'Eyes in the Mirror: Imagery and Symbolism in *Daniel Deronda*', *Nineteenth-Century Fiction*, 23 (1969), 434-445.

14 Compare this entreaty with another in *Adam Bede*: 'Look at Adam through the rest of the day, as he stands on the scaffolding with the two-feet ruler in his hand [...] Look at this broad-shouldered man with the bare muscular arms' (xix, 211). Interestingly, Adam and Daniel are both ideal heroes, prominent among Eliot's protagonists not only for their high morality but also for their physical beauty. The images which the narrator invites the reader to share in are exceedingly physical, almost sensual in their use of adjectives of admiration for the physical frame of both men.

between the narrator and the reader as well as between the reader and Daniel. By 'seeing' his hands and by accepting the favourable description, the reader is encouraged not only to feel closer to Daniel, but to feel his physical presence and to admire his beauty.

As in all Eliot's novels, the narrator refers to himself in the form of the first-person singular on a number of occasions. Although these instances are fewer than in *Middlemarch*, and although they do not transform the narrator's relationship to the story – i.e. he remains in the extradiegetic-heterodiegetic sphere – these occasions nevertheless provide the narrative with a persona, which creates the illusion of personalisation. Furthermore, they frequently carry a tone of humility on the part of the narrator, as if he is deliberating together with the reader on the particularities of the text. Assumptions are common when the narrator's 'I' is involved, and they habitually serve to moderate the narrator's authoritative attitude. For example, in a reflection on Gwendolen's reasons for accepting Grandcourt in marriage, the narrator checks his own opinions as to her motives:

> Gwendolen's ideas were pitiably crude; but many grand difficulties of life are apt to force themselves on us in our crudity. And to judge wisely I suppose we must know how things appear to the unwise; that kind of appearance making the larger part of the world's history (xxix, 282).

The first part of the comment works in the regular manner to extend the reader's sympathy for a type of behaviour which might not at first strike the reader as understandable. The second part serves as an anticipation of the reader's possible response. But rather than present a pertinent reflection in the standard authoritative tone, the narrator reveals a trace of prudence, delicately proposing an alternative response rather than didactically presenting the reader with the 'right' interpretation. Here, there is another psychology at work – 'I suppose we must' includes the reader in the narrator's exclusive sphere, ascertaining his or her place among that elevated group which must have patience with the 'unwise'. By presupposing the reader's place among the wise, the narrator not only places the reader on a narrative level equal to his own, but also – by the power of flattery – attempts to manipulate him or her into agreement. By seeming to relax his hierarchical hold on the narrative and presenting a more personalised attitude, the narrator attempts to influence the reader's interpretation of the situation. Accordingly, the comment reduces the distance between narrator and reader, but here at the expense of the reader's distance to Gwendolen who is, of course, the unwise party in contrast to whom the reader is invited to feel morally and intellectually superior.

In the quotation above, the 'I' appears in narration now and so presents no complications as to the narrative level at which the reader is addressed. However, occasionally the narrator's 'I' addresses the reader in story-time now as well, accentuating the narrator's role as story-teller or historian over that of commentator. This engaged story-teller surfaces in chapter 7 to inform the reader of what happens to Rex and his horse at the fox hunt: 'For I grieve to say that in the search for a gate, along a lane lately mended, Primrose fell, broke his knees, and undesignedly threw Rex over his head' (vii, 59). The rhetoric of this statement gives the impression that the narrator has no control over events in the narrative. This impression in turn rests on the supposition that the text is based on historical actuality and that the narrator is merely giving an account of historical events. The narrator's regret at what happens to Primrose suppresses the notion of narratorial authority. Generally, meta-narrative references emphasise the fictionality of a text, reminding the reader of the act of narration. However, in this example, the narrator's reference to the story-telling act is eclipsed by his acknowledgment of powerlessness over the unfolding of events, and therefore serves to underpin the notion of historical accuracy rather than alert the reader to the aspect of fabrication.

In contrast, another 'I' emerges in chapter 14 in which the roving archery match takes place: 'I am not concerned to tell of the food that was eaten in that green refectory, or even to dwell on the glories of the forest scenery [...] being just now bound to tell a story of life' (xiv, 125).[15] Although there is no suggestion of fictionality – rather the reverse – the statement signals the narrator's command over the narrative, reminding the reader that it is in the narrator's power to choose narrative components. Sustaining the idea of testifying to historical detail by suggesting that the story-teller's objective is to 'tell a story of life', the narrator simultaneously exerts his authority over the text by insinuating that supposed actual events are also subject to remoulding through narration. Consequently, Eliot's narrator directs attention to the inevitable aspects of fiction in the same reader-address in which he proclaims 'to tell a story of life', a statement which implicitly authenticates the actuality of the narrative events.

As in *Felix Holt*, the narrator in *Daniel Deronda* approaches the reader requesting him or her to excuse a character in the text; also, as in *Felix Holt*, these requests invoke different excuses. For example, regarding Sir Hugo's reticence as to Daniel's parentage, the narrator asks the reader to '[l]et Sir Hugo be partly excused until the grounds of his action can be more fully

---

15 Cf. a similar statement in *Middlemarch*, where the narrator claims to be preoccupied with 'unravelling certain human lots' (xv, 132).

known' (xvi, 147). Again, the reader is cautioned not to make a too hasty judgment and encouraged to suspend interpretation until further details have been narrated. These particulars follow directly after the address and concern Sir Hugo's naïvety and inner cheerfulness. The narrator argues that these qualities render it difficult for Sir Hugo to decode Daniel's more serious nature. However, the details offered as to Sir Hugo's actions are not the full reason why he keeps mum – he has also made a vow to Daniel's mother, as the reader will eventually learn. In view of this pledge, the address could be regarded as a portending admonition, indicating that the full story of Sir Hugo's part in Daniel's personal history has not yet been revealed.

Although the narrator's requests for pardon are not expressed in narration now and are hence not, in actuality, part of narratorial commentary, their presentations as direct addresses do serve to establish a contact between narrator and reader. As such, these appeals convey recognition of the reader's involvement in the text and in the interpretational process. By implying the narrator's acknowledgement of a responding reader, they also draw attention to the act of narrating, hence functioning as metanarrative indicators. Interestingly, none of the appeals for the reader to excuse a character in *Daniel Deronda* applies to a female character. Daniel, Sir Hugo, Rex and Hans Meyrick are all held up as deserving to be pardoned, but never Gwendolen – perhaps the one character, apart from Grandcourt, who could use a little forgiveness. Nevertheless, instead of asking the reader to excuse Gwendolen, the narrator refers to her as 'poor Gwendolen' no less than fourteen times. Unsurprisingly, the first instance appears in chapter 23, when Gwendolen's 'spoiled child' days are over and she is forced to make sacrifices. The narrator thus candidly uncovers his attitude towards Gwendolen, indicating to the reader his own high degree of sympathy for her. As mentioned above, these instances do not occur in narration now, although they often form particularisations annexed to a general statement; but they do serve to influence the reader's understanding of Gwendolen and consequently function as narratological means by which the narrator attempts to manipulate the reader's interpretation of the text.

Epigraphs and Meta-Narrative Comments

Daniel Deronda contains just over seventy epigraphs (some chapters are preceded by more than one epigraph). Fourteen of them are statements in prose which presumably derive from George Eliot herself, as no source is indicated.[16] The unaccredited prose epigraph in *Daniel Deronda* differs slightly from other unaccredited epigraphs: it does not indicate a diversity of voices with shifting genres, but instead retains or even adopts the voice of the narratorial commentator although it is, like other epigraphs, deliberately detached from the running text and established on a structural level separate from the framework of the story. However, the unaccredited prose epigraph acquaints the reader with reflections, analyses and premonitions in the same fashion as narratorial commentary; and in the case of prose epigraphs in *Daniel Deronda*, the language and tone employed resemble those of the narrator's comments in the running text. Unlike comparable instances in *Felix Holt*, in which the language of prose epigraphs differs from the language of narratorial comments, both the content and the style of the unaccredited prose epigraph in *Daniel Deronda* indicate the narrator's transgression of narratorial levels. Therefore, although epigraphs are not normally regarded as part of the narrator's sphere of influence, some prose epigraphs in *Daniel Deronda* will be considered in the light of narratorial commentary.

The first chapter epigraph is one which could be considered relevant to the entire novel.[17] Situated at the very beginning of the story, the epigraph instantly challenges preconceived notions about the beginnings and general structure of narratives:

> Men can do nothing without the make-believe of a beginning. Even Science, the
> strict measurer, is obliged to start with a make-believe unit [...] His less accurate

16 Unaccredited epigraphs in George Eliot's novels are generally believed to have been written by Eliot herself. J. R. Tye, who refers to them as Eliot's "unscribed mottoes", mentions the 45 unaccredited epigraphs from Eliot's novels which are included in Alexander Main's *Wise, Witty and Tender Sayings in Prose and Verse Selected from the Works of George Eliot*. Tye argues that this book was compiled with the help of both George Eliot and George Henry Lewes, who, Tye claims, would have objected to the inclusion of work which was not Eliot's; see J. R. Tye, 'George Eliot's Unascribed Mottoes'.

17 The novel is preceded by an epigraph which is repeated with each new volume, but this motto is presented in the form of verse and makes no narratological or structural allusions. Rather, it focuses on the contents of the story and employs allegorical figures to make abstraction concrete: 'Let thy chief terror be of thine own soul: / There, 'mid the throng of hurrying desires / That trample o'er the dead to seize their spoil, / Lurks vengeance, footless, irresistible / As exhalations laden with slow death, / And o'er the fairest troop of captured joys / Breathes pallid pestilence'.

grandmother Poetry has always been understood to start in the middle; but on re-flection it appears that her proceeding is not very different from his; since Science, too, reckons backwards as well as forwards, divides his unit into billions, and with his clock-finger at Nought really sets off *in medias res*. No retrospect will take us to the true beginning; and whether our prologue be in heaven or on earth, it is but a fraction of that all-presupposing fact with which our story sets out (i, 3).

Approaching the reader even before he or she becomes involved with the story, the epigraph preconditions the reading of the text by discussing the impossibility of establishing proper beginnings. Wherever a story begins, the passage states, something has gone before; a narrative always begins *in medias res*. Hence, the epigraph serves as a structural premonition, alert-ing the reader to the idea of a beginning which is merely a 'make-believe unit' in the absence of a 'true beginning'. Additionally, unlike *Felix Holt* and *Middlemarch*, *Daniel Deronda* is not preceded by an introduction or a prelude. Instead, the epigraph constitutes the reader's first contact with a presumed narratorial voice (apart from the voice of the novel epigraph, which belongs to another genre); and as a result the epigraph could be con-sidered a substitute for the conventional introduction. Several aspects of this first chapter epigraph signal a new attitude towards literature along the lines of what is commonly referred to as 'modernist'.[18] First, it challenges the notion of novels constituting independent entities which begin and end within the framework of the book-covers. By suggesting that all nar-ratives, whether they be scientific or literary, are preceded by beginnings, the epigraph implies the indeterminacy not only of narrative beginnings in general, but also of the narrative beginning at hand. Secondly, the epi-graph embodies a degree of meta-narration, acknowledging the fictionality of the ensuing story. Although there are examples of meta-narration in Eliot's earlier work, this meta-narrative statement is distinct from them in that it addresses the reader even before the story begins. As such, it indi-cates an attitude of distance between the reader and the properties of the narrative from the very start.

The reader is invited to recognise, then, that beginnings always build on other beginnings. However, the structural leap which takes place in the chronology of *Daniel Deronda* is not directly heralded by the epigraph: rather, it encourages the reader to appreciate the indeterminacy of nar-rative structures in general. It is significant that the novel's first chapter

---

18 In *Knowing the Past: Victorian Literature and Culture*, ed. by Suzy Anger (Ithaca, New York: Cornell University Press, 2001), George Levine argues that Eliot's first chapter epigraph in *Daniel Deronda* connects epistemology to what he terms 'necessary revisions of the realist form', meaning the notion that access to the 'real' and the 'true' can only be achieved through hypotheses in the forms of fiction (57).

epigraph appears in the form of a long prose motto which adopts the tone and style of narratorial commentary. Appearing as an epigraphic address to the reader, the statement not only intimates the reader's distance to the text but also establishes a contact between the narrator and the reader (presupposing that the reader interprets the voice of the epigraph as that of the narrator) at a level outside the diegesis. Consequently, presuming that the epigraphic voice is identical to the narratorial commentator's, the first epigraph prepares the reader for structural irregularities, establishes his or her contact and feeling of solidarity with the narrator at a narrative level outside the diegesis, and signals the reader's distance to the text as a fictional entity.

The unaccredited prose epigraph does not appear again until chapter 11, however, so the notion of a narratorial domain which extends the framework of the story is not sustained. Yet, it is impossible to disregard the remaining thirteen prose epigraphs on the grounds of structural incompatibility, as they all adopt the same rhetoric and style as narratorial comments. For example, the epigraph to chapter 11, which depicts Gwendolen's and Grandcourt's very first meeting, appears as a proverb-like statement in the same manner as a narratorial comment might: 'The beginning of an acquaintance whether with persons or with things is to get a definite outline for our ignorance' (xi, 91). Again, broaching the subject of beginnings, but with a difference, the epigraph anticipates the meeting which will take place in the chapter. The statement relates directly to Gwendolen's expectations of Grandcourt and proceeds to describe him in terms of what he is not, i.e. the antithesis to what Gwendolen has expected. Aside from its position outside the diegetic structure, there is little to suggest that this statement is not voiced by the same narrator as the one articulating narratorial comments. Significantly, this epigraph commences Book 2 of the novel, as if to re-establish the narrator's relationship with his audience due to the novel's having been first published in eight monthly parts. The epigraph to this second part thus revives the connection between the reader and the narrator which was established in the prose epigraph to the first book. Book 5, which is the first book in volume three of the novel, also begins with an unaccredited prose epigraph which re-enacts the functions of the epigraphs to chapters 1 and 11. Hence, three books out of eight are set off by the epigraphic narrator's address to the reader.

Consequently, unaccredited prose epigraphs in *Daniel Deronda* differ distinctly from those in *Felix Holt* and *Middlemarch* both in terms of number and function. In *Daniel Deronda* the epigraphic voice of several mottoes is undistinguishable from the narrator's commentary voice; tone, attitude and style are the same, and the epigraphs employ similar devices to influence the reader. It is also evident that the novel's lack of an ordinary introduction facilitates the notion of a first chapter epigraph serving as a meeting-place in which reader and narrator can establish contact before entering into the story.

One particularly interesting *accredited* epigraph precedes chapter 42 and is repeated in translation as an introduction to the chapter. Chapter 42 depicts Mordecai and Daniel sitting among 'The Philosophers' at the 'Hand and Banner'. The passage, excerpted from Leopold Zunz's *Die Synagogale Poesie des Mittelalters*, reads:

> If there are ranks of suffering, Israel takes precedence of all the nations – if the duration of sorrows and the patience with which they are borne ennoble, the Jews are among the aristocracy of every land – if a literature is called rich in the possession of a few classic tragedies, what shall we say to a National Tragedy lasting for fifteen hundred years, in which the poets and actors were also the heroes? (xlii, 441)[19]

By translating the epigraph and employing the translation as an introductory passage to the chapter, the author stresses its significance to the text. Although it anticipates the discussions that will take place at the 'Hand and Banner', the statement does not indicate what direction the story will take. Instead, by specifying that 'Deronda had lately been reading that passage of Zunz' (xlii, 441), the narrator signals the direction Daniel himself is taking and the deliberations that occupy his mind.[20] These deliberations are in unbroken progress throughout the chapter. In the first part, Daniel considers the quotation in view of the Cohen family and observes that they do not exhibit any traces of the type of tragedy described in Zunz's text. Eventually, however, as the chapter progresses and Daniel finds himself involved in the discussion at the 'Hand and Banner', his attitude changes along with his increasing fascination with Mordecai and with Jewish tradition. Certainly, the presentation of the passage both in its original form in the epigraph and as a translated introduction emphasises the importance of this particular theory, not only to chapter 42, but to the question of a Jewish Nation in the novel as a whole. The introduction follows chapter 41, in which Daniel has meditated on Judaism in relation to Christianity, and precedes the very episode in which these meditations are openly de-

---

19 George Eliot has added National before Tragedy in this translation. Leopold Zunz was a Jewish historian with a special interest in the medieval period. His work was published in 1855.

20 Tony E. Jackson claims that the reading-as-knowing motif in *Daniel Deronda*, more than in Eliot's earlier works, 'represents literature as a determinative cause in human consciousness' (48).

bated for the first time. Therefore, Daniel's deliberations in chapter 41, the epigraph, the translated introduction in chapter 42 and ensuing discussions of that passage, jointly introduce what is commonly referred to as the Jewish parts of *Daniel Deronda*. Constituting the first two chapters in Book 6, called 'Revelations', these two chapters serve as starting-points for those ideological elements for which Eliot received so much criticism in the early reviews.[21]

Meta-narrative comments generally serve the purpose of directing the reader's attention to the act of narration. By so doing they remind the reader of the fictionality of the text, indicating how it should be understood and signalling the narrator's function as controller and director. In *Daniel Deronda*, these meta-narrative signs are restricted and subtle.[22] Mention was made above of the narrator's depiction of the archery meeting, where he comments: 'I am not concerned to tell of the food that was eaten in that green refectory' (xiv, 125). The statement makes the narrator's management of the narrative clear to the reader and indicates his exclusive position in relation to the text. It reminds the reader not only of the fictional nature of the narrative, but also of the narrator's privileged power of interpretation. In another example the narrator comments on Gwendolen's and Grandcourt's first meeting, stating: 'How Grandcourt had filled up the pauses will be more evident hereafter' (xi, 94). Again, the narrator emphasises his entitlement to the structure of the narrative by making reference to when and how further information will be divulged.

Additionally, however, the advance notice serves to kindle the reader's curiosity, inciting him or her to anticipate the revelation of Grandcourt's inner thoughts.[23] Hence, the same comment which calls attention to the narrator's management of the text simultaneously works as a film-trailer, advertising what will follow in order to rouse the reader's interest. The subtlety of the novel's meta-narrative comments consists in this: they are rarely just remarks on the act of narration, but usually serve additional functions concerning the reader's response to particularities depicted in story-time now.

Meta-narrative statements are also closely associated with the narrator's 'I' and with his role as a writer or historian. The narrator occasionally makes references to the narrative as a historical account, references which both directly and indirectly serve as indications of his role as historian. Commenting on Gwendolen's appearance, the narrator presents an argu-

---

21 Book 5, entitled 'Mordecai', of course broaches the subject of Judaism, but does not do so as comprehensively or with as much detail as Book 6.
22 On meta-narrative comments in *Daniel Deronda*, see also Nünning, pp. 273-4.
23 See Nünning, p. 270.

ment concerning the difficulties of 'truthful' representation in which he juxtaposes literature with art, remarking on the benefits of the latter:

> Sir Joshua would have been glad to take her portrait; and he would have had an easier task than the historian at least in this, that he would not have had to represent the truth of change – only to give stability to one beautiful moment (xi, 96).

Presupposing that the fundamental purpose of both art and literature is to 'represent the truth', the narrator argues that the historian's undertaking is the more difficult because his 'truth' involves an extended process whereas the artist's only applies to a specific moment in time.[24] Constituting a remark on the difficulties of representation, then, the comment is meta-narrative in the sense that it calls attention to the task of telling a tale. However, unlike the type of meta-narrative comment which accentuates elements of fictionality, this statement serves the reverse function by claiming to derive from a historian who is interested in giving a 'truthful' report of 'actual' events. Accordingly, the narrator emphasises the problems of 'truthful' narration in order to underpin the authenticity of the narrative, intimating that the diegetic elements of the narrative are renderings of actual events and people rather than mere figments of the imagination. Simultaneously, however, the statement draws attention to the narrator's potential unreliability. There is a reversed psychology at work here, though. By implying that his narrative can only ever be an interpretation of the 'actual', the narrator admits to unreliability. But that admission, of course, serves to give an impression of sincerity, a quality which serves to establish a notion of trustworthiness, or in other words – reliability. Consequently, the narrator's admission to being guilty of unreliability tends, in effect, to substantiate the opposite.

Another example is offered by a similar meta-narrative comment which serves to underline the authenticity of the narrative, but which approaches the issue of reliability from another angle. Arriving in England, Gwendolen must wait alone at the railway station while a carriage is being prepared to take her to Offendene. The narrator depicts the scene and describes Gwendolen as she is represented through the eyes of a railway official. Almost apologetically, the narrator comments on the description: 'Contemptible details these, to make part of a history; yet the turn of most lives is hardly to be accounted for without them' (xxi, 195). The statement

---

24 In *Middlemarch*, Will Ladislaw expresses a related line of reasoning, arguing with Naumann about the advantages of language over painting. Language, Ladislaw claims, 'gives a fuller image, which is all the better for being vague. After all, the true seeing is within; and painting stares at you with an insistent imperfection' (xix, 179).

forms part of Eliot's commentary on the necessity for authentic rendering, but in its context, it also signals the narrator's attention to detail in order to convince the reader of the authenticity of the text and the reliability of the narrator. Here, then, there is no intimation of the complexities connected to 'realistic' representation; indeed, the narrator rather suggests the reverse – that a rendering of every detail is necessary and inevitable for a comprehensive view of situations and characters. Hence, the comment implies an assumption as to the narrator's trustworthiness with regard to the details that make up that comprehensive view. Again, the meta-narrative comment serves to support the narrator's reliability and strengthen the notion of authenticity. This example, though, does not address the discord between reality and representation; rather, it takes the genuineness of realistic detail for granted.

Free Indirect Discourse vs. Narratorial Commentary

As mentioned above, the distinction between narratorial commentary and free indirect discourse in *Daniel Deronda* is not always straightforward.[25] In his seminal analysis of FID in the nineteenth-century novel, Roy Pascal argues that the problem of differentiating between FID and what he calls 'authorial comments' demonstrates George Eliot's sometimes defective use of FID.[26] Pascal's contention is that George Eliot, on the whole, displays great skill in her use of FID, but that the novels occasionally exhibit the author's failure to distinguish the narrator's perspective from that of the characters. According to Pascal, this indiscriminate overlapping of perspectives appears when Eliot merges a character's language with the narrator's, colouring the FID with a presence of irony or ridicule, and also when the clues that signal FID are the same as those signalling 'authorial intrusions'. Pascal's observations are, of course, interesting to the study of narratorial commentary and FID in *Daniel Deronda*.

25 FID is, of course, used extensively in Eliot's oeuvre, but the reason why it is discussed here in connection with *Daniel Deronda* and not with Eliot's earlier novels is because this is the only novel which presents several instances of ambiguity as to whether a statement is FID or narratorial commentary. Because Daniel's mind is so close to the narrator's, his deliberations are often difficult to distinguish from the narrator's.

26 See Pascal, p. 86. Pascal gives no definition of 'authorial commentary', but seems to limit such comments to so-called 'intrusions'.

Confusion as to whether a particular opinion emanates from the narrator or from a character emerges as early as page five. Daniel is in Leubronn, surveying the throngs of people around the gambling-tables, and the statement appears immediately before he sees Gwendolen:

> Deronda's first thought when his eyes fell on this scene of dull, gas-poisoned absorption was that the gambling of Spanish shepherd-boys had seemed to him more enviable: – so far Rousseau might be justified in maintaining that art and science had done a poor service to mankind. But suddenly he felt the moment become dramatic (i, 5).

Pascal uses the phrase 'linguistic distortion' to signify the confusion which takes place when the narrator's language and attitude seeps through a character's FID.[27] This occurs occasionally, he argues, with FID emanating from lower-class characters. Permeated with the narrator's irony, such a character's FID may actually ridicule thoughts and emotions as they are being presented.[28]

With characters such as Daniel Deronda, however, this phenomenon is less prevalent because he shares the narrator's excellence of language and intellect.[29] Therefore, in the quotation above, it is impossible to judge by the language employed or by the idea presented whether the statement about Rousseau emanates from Daniel or from the narrator. The comment fulfils the criteria for belonging to the narration-now level; but the idea from which it derives clearly originates in Daniel. There is a colon and a dash separating the two sentences, which could be an indication of a break between story-time now and narration now; but the applicability of the statement both to Daniel's preceding thought and to his highly educated persona sustains the ambiguity. Furthermore, it could be argued that FID commonly appears in the past tense and that the present tense of the statement above indicates a narratorial source.

However, Pascal's analysis shows that once the FID form has been established, which it has in the quotation above, 'the present tense can be safely used to convey subjective statements'.[30] Accordingly, the transfer from past to present does not in itself mark a transition away from FID. While it is not crucial to categorise the statement above as either

---

27 Pascal, p. 86.
28 As an example, Pascal points to Bob in *The Mill on the Floss*. In Book First, chapter 6, Bob has a quarrel with Tom, and the emotions this leaves him with are presented in FID. Pascal claims that the language used to convey his FID is far too advanced for his character, containing words which mock and ridicule him.
29 Pascal, 86.
30 Pascal, 83.

a narratorial comment or part of Daniel's thoughts, it is interesting to study the function it may have as either. Belonging to narration now and constituting part of the narrator's attitude, the comment displays ironic distance. It seems unlikely that Daniel, who is an exceedingly humourless character despite or maybe because of his being such a good one, should incorporate the type of irony that the comment presents. If the comment belongs to the narrator, it could serve to strike a chord with the reader in a mutual smirk at Rousseau's radical idea of depriving children of an education in art and science. Naturally, the shared joke establishes a bond between reader and narrator. On the other hand, it could be argued that narratorial commentary generally refers to characters or events in the text, influencing the reader's interpretation in one way or another. Here, there is no applicability to the text; rather, the comment stimulates the reader's attention through ironic distance. As a function of FID, conversely, the statement, although contrary to character, could allow access to parts of Daniel's character which cannot be revealed in any other way. Perhaps the FID enhances the poly-vocality not of the text but of Daniel's character, showing that he can, in fact, be ironic, but only in his thoughts. As early as page five, the reader really has no way of knowing.[31]

Daniel's close association to the narrator, rhetorically and intellectually, is part of the reason for the complexities inherent in the distinction between FID and narratorial commentary. However, *Daniel Deronda* also includes examples of FID which emanate from characters far removed from the narrator in terms of intellectual sophistication, but which all the same display ambiguity as to whom the statements are attributable to. For example, in chapter 13, Mr Gascoigne has taken upon himself to make sure Gwendolen makes the right decision and accepts Grandcourt in marriage. Through FID, the reader is invited to follow Mr Gascoigne's line of reasoning as he convinces himself that Grandcourt is a splendid match and that it is his duty to make sure Gwendolen marries him. However, Mr Gascoigne's thoughts are interspersed with remarks which could be interpreted as narratorial commentary, but which could also be part of Mr Gascoigne's FID:

> But of the future husband personally Mr Gascoigne was disposed to think the best. Gossip is a sort of smoke that comes from the dirty tobacco-pipes of those who diffuse it: it proves nothing but the bad taste of the smoker. But if Grandcourt had re-

---

31 William Makepeace Thackeray comes to mind here, whose novels include a great deal of interplay between free indirect discourse and narratorial interventions. See Roy Pascal for the presence of FID in Thackeray's work.

ally made any deeper or more unfortunate experiments in folly than were common in young men of high prospects, he was of an age to have finished them (xiii, 118).

Again, although the statement could be perceived as a narration-now remark, its substance is so well integrated with Mr Gascoigne's line of reasoning that it is difficult to distinguish it from his FID. However, the profundity of the comment and the idea it promotes – that rumours reveal more about those who spread them than about those subject to them – agrees with the narrator's general attitude. Here, then, is a slightly naïve rector who has little in common with the urbane narrator, but whose inner reflections may still be confused with the narrator's. Of course, one principal purpose of FID is the effect produced by the linguistic combination of more than one voice, i.e. it intensifies the linguistic density of the text by bringing into play a multiplicity of speakers and attitudes. In view of this objective, it could be argued that endeavours to distinguish voices in FID – that is, attempting to trace single sentences to specific agents – in fact renders the overall desired effect of FID ineffective. And as mentioned above, it is not essential to the study of narratorial commentary to ascribe the ambiguous statements in the quotations above to one source.

However, Daniel Deronda contains a number of statements of unspecific origin which express ideas and opinions on the subject of Judaism. Taking into consideration the abundance of criticism involved in the treatment of Judaism in the text, it becomes especially interesting to examine some of the grey areas where beliefs and opinions concerning Judaism are expressed by a non-identifiable agent.[32]

As was pointed out above, chapter 41 forms a turning-point in the novel. Mordecai has been introduced well before this chapter, as has the

---

32 Several critics have argued that *Daniel Deronda* does not idealise Jews in general, but merely the 'refined Jew'. See, for example, Susan Meyer, ' "Safely to Their Own Borders": Proto-Zionism, Feminism, and Nationalism in *Daniel Deronda*', *ELH*, 60 (1993), 733-758, and Carolyn Lesjak, 'Labours of a Modern Storyteller: George Eliot and the Cultural Project of "Nationhood" in *Daniel Deronda*' in *Victorian Identities: Social and Cultural Formations in Nineteenth-Century Literature*, ed. Ruth Robbins, Julian Wolfreys and James R. Kincaid (New York: Macmillan, 1996), pp. 25-42. In his introduction to the Penguin edition to *Daniel Deronda*, Terence Cave states that discrimination and intolerance towards Jews was rife in the 1860s and 1870s, and Peter C. Hodgson argues that the novel centres 'on the oppression and prejudice directed against the people of Israel' (128); *Daniel Deronda*, ed. Terence Cave (London: Penguin Books, 1995), pp. xx-xxi. George Eliot herself commented on attitudes towards Jews in her own age, writing in a letter to Harriet Beecher Stowe: 'But precisely because I felt that the usual attitude of Christians towards Jews is – I hardly know whether to say more impious or more stupid when viewed in the light of their professed principles, I therefore felt urged to treat Jews with such sympathy and understanding as my nature and knowledge could attain to'; see *Letters*, vi, 301.

theme of Judaism; but it is not until chapter 41 that Daniel's intricate cogitations are disclosed and that, in consequence, the reader is introduced to his ideas concerning religion, tradition and philosophy. Here, a change can be discerned in Daniel; hitherto he has displayed an attitude of acquiescence, self-denial and diplomacy, but in chapter 41 he reveals an assertive and authoritative quality. The chapter follows Daniel's first meeting with Mordecai and comprises his deliberations resulting from that meeting.[33] Even though he suspects that Mordecai might be a ranting fanatic and thinks that they have nothing in common – not even 'race' – Daniel is fascinated by him and forced to scrutinise his own tendency to pass judgement. His scrutiny is expressed in the form of FID, but on several occasions the contents of his thoughts are difficult to distinguish from the linguistic signs and clues used to signal narratorial commentary:

> Columbus had some impressions about himself which we call superstitions, and used some arguments which we disapprove; but he had also some true physical conceptions, and he had the passionate patience of genius to make them tell on mankind. The world has made up its mind rather contemptuously about those who were deaf to Columbus. "My contempt for them binds me to see that I don't adopt their mistake on a small scale," said Deronda, "and make myself deaf with the assumption that there cannot be any momentous relation between this Jew and me, simply because he has clad it in illusory notions" (xli, 438-439).

Employing the plural first-person pronoun and articulated in the present tense, the first sentence seems to qualify as an obvious narratorial comment. The inclusion of the reader into the reflection by the use of 'we', and the appropriation of a well-known historical fact as a precedent for a particular phenomenon in the text, are, of course, typical features of narratorial commentary. Hence, the direct reader address seems to emanate from only one voice – the narrator's. However, the direct speech that ensues disputes such a deduction. Materialising as a direct progression of the argument in the comment, Daniel's direct speech implies that the Columbus theory is, in effect, part of his FID. But the impression of ambiguity remains, as the statement applies so well to the narrator's use of narratological devices to address the reader, and to his general philosophy of liberalism and empathy. The ambiguity is deliberate and geared to eradicating the impression of theories, ideas or arguments which emanate from a single source and to ascribing these philosophies to the novel's unspecified but governing thematic principle. A great deal of what the novel declares about Judaism

---

33 It is not Mordecai's and Daniel's first meeting, they have met in the bookshop twice; but it is their first 'real' meeting where they are more profoundly acquainted with each other and where Daniel learns of Mordecai's wish for a protégé.

is expressed in this fashion. In fact, although a common impression among readers and critics of *Daniel Deronda* is that it is a novel dedicated to examining Jewish community and tradition, few narratorial comments actually broach the subject of Judaism. Instead, the greater part of what the reader learns about the attitude towards Jewishness in the novel he or she learns primarily from dialogue between characters, from FID and, indeed, from those instances of FID or narratorial commentary which display a variety of narratological and linguistic signals unattributable to any single agent.

Egoism

The thematic concerns which are raised in the narratorial commentary in *Daniel Deronda* are almost identical with the themes featured in *Middlemarch* commentary. In her last two novels, indeed, it seems as if George Eliot concentrated her narratorial commentary to a number of specific issues.[34] As in *Middlemarch*, the matter of egoism runs like a connecting line of thought throughout the novel.

In *Daniel Deronda*, the dichotomy between egoism and self-abnegation is apparent in the novel's division of plot. Daniel and Mordecai represent embodiments of selflessness or a de-centering of the self, while Gwendolen and Grandcourt epitomise egoism at its most intense.[35] As expected, these distinctive qualities constitute the subject of several narratorial comments which elaborate on the details of each character's relation to the self. Gwendolen's egoism, for example, is closely associated with her vanity and wilfulness and Grandcourt's with his desire for psychological domination. However, although Gwendolen typifies the definitive female egoist, dis-

---

34 These themes are not the only topics dealt with in narratorial commentary in the novels, but they are, as mentioned, the ones which appear as recurring themes.

35 This dichotomy has been discussed extensively in literary criticism. Of particular interest is George Levine's article on epistemology in the novel, in which he argues that *Daniel Deronda* refutes the traditional Carlylean notion that an obliteration of self is necessary for knowing 'the Other'. *Daniel Deronda*, Levine claims, demonstrates that 'only through the filter of a modern self [...] can other cultures become accessible or meaningful' (56). Levine's contention is that rather than annihilating the self, Daniel's knowledge of the self facilitates his knowledge of the other. See also K. M. Newton, who argues that Mordecai represents the opposite of the Romantic egoist as he rejects the elevation of the individual self, preferring the individual's unification with race or nationality, whereas Gwendolen is 'George Eliot's most complex and interesting psychological study of a Romantic egotist'; *George Eliot*, p. 172.

cerned earlier in Rosamond Vincy and Mrs Transome, her relation to her self changes as the novel progresses. Before she marries Grandcourt, her selfishness is of the naïve sort which thrives on the absence of adversity, conceiving of youth, beauty and good fortune as everlasting. Pride and vanity have not yet been wounded. But as often happens with comments regarding Gwendolen in the first part of the novel, the narrator does not refrain from irony:

> Pre-eminence is sweet to those who love it, even under mediocre circumstances: perhaps it is not quite mythical that a slave has been proud to be bought first; and probably a barn-door fowl on sale, though he may not have understood himself to be called the best of a bad lot, may have a self-informed consciousness of his relative importance, and strut consoled (x, 84).

The 'mediocre circumstances' under which Gwendolen experiences her feelings of pre-eminence take place at the archery meeting and refer to the looks of approval and admiration which she receives from the 'male judges in the ranks immediately surrounding her' (x, 84). The irony of the remark hence refers partly to the somewhat superficial details on which Gwendolen's feelings are founded, and partly to her lack of humility or introspection. The two allegorical elements, however, engage contrasting symbolic connotations. Comparing Gwendolen to a slave implies serious criticism from a feminist perspective. The men around her, ogling and passing judgment, evaluating her as if she were for sale, take on the roles of colonisers, and Gwendolen herself accepts the role of slave without understanding that this is what she does. These roles are so well integrated into the traditions of her society that the actors are unaware of their political and ideological implications.[36] Gwendolen's happiness thus emanates from the feeling of being the best among 'slaves'.[37] The continuation of the com-

36 Susan Meyer comments on this quotation, claiming that it exemplifies how Gwendolen, as the novel's foremost representation of a female, is repeatedly referred to in terms of imperialism and conquest. In general this is a correct observation, especially considering the language used to describe the relationship between Gwendolen and Grandcourt. But unfortunately Meyer misapplies the quotation above. Meyer contends that the comment follows after Grandcourt has chosen to be introduced to Gwendolen out of all of the women at the archery meeting. However, at the point of the statement above, Grandcourt has not yet arrived at the archery meeting, not yet met Gwendolen and not yet surfaced as a character in the narrative other than by name. Accordingly, the quotation refers not to Gwendolen's feelings at being chosen by Grandcourt, but to her feelings at receiving admiring looks from the male onlookers at the archery meeting.

37 Carolyn Lesjak argues that Eliot's feminism in *Daniel Deronda* 'becomes a powerful instrument in her critique of imperialism' (27), and that the entire Gwendolen plot 'functions as a microcosm of the larger system of imperialism' (26). Both Lesjak and Meyer discuss the language of 'empire' in relation to Gwendolen and Grandcourt's relationship, but the quotation shows that these allegorical references are used with

ment presents a different allegorical image which counteracts the gravity of the first. Resuming the humorous tone which the narrator repeatedly employs in connection with Gwendolen, the analogy drawn between her and a 'barn-door fowl' emphasises the farcical element of the situation.[38] Her vanity convinces her of her superiority as she 'struts' around.

In addition to satisfying an eager, but passive, vanity, Gwendolen's egoism involves an active exertion of will. In the first half of the Gwendolen plot this will manifests itself erratically in whims and eruptions of impulse, expressions of egoism which Eliot's narrator repeatedly saturates with irony.[39] But with increasing hardships in Gwendolen's life the narrator's attitude towards her mellows, and ironical comments are replaced by appeals to the reader's sympathy:[40]

> What passion seems more absurd [...] than this amazed anguish that I and not Thou, He, or She, should be just the smitten one? Yet perhaps some who have afterwards made themselves a willing fence before the breast of another, and have carried their own heart-wound in heroic silence – some who have made their latter deeds great, nevertheless began with this angry amazement at their own smart, and on the mere denial of their fantastic desires raged as if under the sting of wasps which reduced the universe for them to an unjust infliction of pain (xxvi, 245).

---

regard to conventional conceptions of masculine and feminine roles in general and not just in connection with Gwendolen's and Grandcourt's extreme situation.

38 Karen B. Mann states that animal imagery in George Eliot's novels habitually conveys irony (15). It is natural to compare the analogy drawn between Gwendolen and a fowl to the analogy drawn between Mrs Tulliver and a hen. Both analogies ironically portray the woman's supposedly mistaken notion that she is important. Mrs Tulliver is a hen because she thinks she can make a favourable impression on Mr Wakem, and Gwendolen is a fowl because she is happy under the illusion that she is being admired. In Eliot's novels, hence, animal imagery (and particularly imagery pertaining to birds) is occasionally employed to downgrade and ridicule a female character who displays presumptuousness and confidence.

39 K. M. Newton discusses Gwendolen's egoism, noting that her exertion of will incorporates two elements, namely that of mastering external circumstances and that of controlling aspects of her own character. Newton argues that taken together these two elements generate a sense of self-division in Gwendolen, which escalates into even further complications for her as she attempts to counter-act this sense of self-division with even stronger exertions of will (174). Felicia Bonaparte maintains that Gwendolen's egoism is of the sort which is 'so furiously intent on asserting itself that it happily concedes self-gratification, self-interest, even craves humiliation, as long as it senses itself alive' (98). Graham Martin emphasises that Gwendolen is latently aware of values other than those which she lives by, else there could be no exchange between her and Daniel; see ' "Daniel Deronda": George Eliot and Political Change', in *Critical Essays on George Eliot*, ed. by Barbara Hardy (London: Routledge & Kegan Paul, 1970), pp. 133-150 (p. 142).

40 Compare, for example, the narrator's first reference to Gwendolen as a 'poor thing' in chapter 23.

When Gwendolen arrives back at Offendene after her sojourn in Leubronn, her future looks bleak as she faces the prospect of becoming governess to the bishop's daughters. She no longer has the prerogative of exerting her own will or satisfying her desires, as she has become restrained by circumstances outside her control. The narrator, however, acknowledges the relativity of Gwendolen's misfortune, but nevertheless encourages the reader to recognise, and perhaps even recall, the initial ache felt at an early experience of unfulfilled desires. Assuming the reader's altruistic nature, the comment also urges the reader to excuse Gwendolen's egoism and indirectly implies that she too may eventually look back on this pain and consider it selfish and absurd. The comment thus invites the reader to identify actively with the experience Gwendolen undergoes in order for him or her to sympathise with her feelings, even though they might appear trivial in relation to much else.

The focus on Gwendolen's complexity as a character is intensified as the novel develops, despite the fact that she figures less extensively in the second half. Towards the very end of the book Gwendolen's egoistic personality has changed completely. Her almost unbridled will has made her virtually afraid of herself. With Daniel's help she regains self-control, but at the price of falling unhappily in need of him. This need engenders thoughts which place him in relation to herself, displaying another sort of egoism which the narrator relates to a general phenomenon, remarking that 'we are all apt to fall into this passionate egoism of imagination, not only towards our fellow-men, but towards God' (lxix, 682).[41] Gone is the tentative tone from the quotation above, which timidly invites the reader to recognise Gwendolen's situation. Here, the authoritative voice surfaces in full force, letting the reader know, rather than suggesting, that Gwendolen's display of this type of egoism is universal to human nature. The development of the reader's distance to and sympathy for Gwendolen hence corresponds to the development and transformation of her egoism and to the narratorial commentary pertaining to this change.

Daniel, on the other hand, undergoes no transformation with regard to egoism, although the epic elements of the novel are constituted by his transformation from a sense of alienation in the world to an identification with nationhood and 'race'. His altruism is well developed and estab-

---

41 See Henry Alley's article 'New Year's at the Abbey: Point of View in the Pivotal Chapters of *Daniel Deronda*', *The Journal of Narrative Technique*, 9 (1979), 147-159 for a discussion of how the structure of the novel is worked out to present Daniel's and Gwendolen's alternating points of view. Alley argues that the narrator moves between the minds of both characters, highlighting their awareness of each other and demonstrating how everything is related to everything else.

lished already from the start, so that he, unlike most of Eliot's protagonists, does not need to learn to feel compassion or humility through the act of suffering.[42] Instead, a feeling nature is one of Daniel's most salient characteristics and one closely associated with his intense self-consciousness. His tendency to merge that self-consciousness with a feeling for others sometimes amounts to a de-centering of the self.[43] As a counterpart to the extreme egoists in the novel, such as Gwendolen, Grandcourt and the Princess Halm-Eberstein, Daniel's philanthropy is constant and serves as a moral backbone throughout the novel. Narratorial comments pertaining to his lack of egoism, then, not only elicit the reader's sympathy but also reinforce the general attitude regarding humanity and morality in the novel as a whole.[44] In connection with Daniel's rescue of Mirah, the narrator reflects on his inclination for disregarding his own self:

> The creature we help to save, though only a half-reared linnet, bruised and lost by the wayside – how we watch and fence it, and doat [sic] on its signs of recovery! Our pride becomes loving, our self is a not-self for whose sake we become virtuous, when we set to some hidden work of reclaiming a life from misery and look for our triumph in the secret joy – "This one is the better for me." (xxxii, 319).

Despite the indication of Daniel's loss of self, the comment reveals an intimation of self-satisfaction which contradicts its suggestion of self-abnegation. His 'secret joy' is certainly rooted in the cessation of suffering for the 'other'; but it also involves an element of self-importance which cannot be detached from egoism. Daniel's satisfaction at having rescued Mirah boosts his sense of self-worth, and consequently his own self is no longer de-centered or evaporated.[45] The statement, however, seems aimed at elic-

---

42 Cf. for example Adam in *Adam Bede*. See also Tony E. Jackson's distinction between *being* and *becoming* truly sympathetic, p. 51.

43 For example, as Daniel rows down the Thames, absorbed in thought, the narrator describes how his sense of self seems to evaporate: 'He was forgetting everything else in a half-speculative, half-involuntary identification of himself with the objects he was looking at, thinking how far it might be possible habitually to shift his centre till his own personality would be no less outside him than the landscape' (xvii, 160).

44 Some critics maintain that the narrator's evident favouritism for and identification with the infallible Daniel serves the reverse effect of alienating the reader from Daniel rather than encouraging him or her to relate to him. James Harrison, for example, claims that George Eliot 'clearly stands too close to Deronda' (518), and Mary Ellen Doyle argues that the interpretations of Daniel are 'blindly admiring' (163). On Daniel's innate sympathy, see Nünning, pp. 284-5.

45 George Levine touches on this argument when he contends that *Daniel Deronda* shows how Eliot's considerations of self and 'other' had changed. The novel, he argues, advocates not a complete rejection of the self, but the knowledge of it and the recognition of the marginality of the self in relation to the universe. Only then can the 'other' be truly known (56-58).

iting the reader's recognition for a phenomenon common to humanity, rather than at promoting Daniel's righteous qualities.

As a contrast to this focus on altruism, it is interesting to study the epigraph to chapter 25. Although dealing with the opposite of egoism, it attempts to elicit the same reader response as the quotation above. While that quotation conjures up an image of selflessness which includes the reader through the use of 'we' and 'our', the epigraph reaches out to the reader from another vantage point by discussing the notion of egoism as something 'other' and alien:

> How trace the why and wherefore in a mind reduced to the barrenness of a fastidious egoism, in which all direct desires are dulled, and have dwindled from motives into a vacillating expectation of motives: a mind made up of moods, where a fitful impulse springs here and there conspicuously rank amid the general weediness? (xxv, 236).

Chapter 25 further depicts Grandcourt's active pursuit of Gwendolen and familiarises the reader with the extent of his interest in her. As a premonition, the epigraph serves to pre-programme the reader's attitude towards Grandcourt by referring to his egoism as barren and to his moods as capricious, indicating that his displays of passion in Gwendolen's direction are nothing but fickle streaks of ardour in a character otherwise numbed by the absence of duty or responsibility.[46] Besides, the epigraph lulls the reader into a mutual understanding with the narrator by classifying the type of egoism mentioned as something 'other'. This mutual 'other', then, unites the reader and the narrator in disapproval of it.

Accordingly, the statement reinforces the narratorial approach with regard to egoism, but does so in epigraphic form. Emanating from a narratorial voice outside the running narrative, the statement not only refers to the ensuing chapter; it also serves as a manifestation and fortification of the novel's underlying attitude with regard to the issue of egoism. It is significant that an all-pervading thematic issue – that is, the narrator's concern with egoism – is articulated and manifested in the form of an epigraph, as it visibly demonstrates the narrator's transcendence of diegetic levels. The same thematic concern that is expressed repeatedly in the form of narratorial commentary hence appears in epigraphic form as well, adding emphasis not only to the significance of the issue for the novel in its

---

46 For more on Grandcourt, see Robert McCarron, 'Evil and Eliot's Religion of Humanity: Grandcourt in *Daniel Deronda*', *Ariel: A Review of International English Literature*, 11 (1980), 71-88; and Badri Raina, '*Daniel Deronda*: A View of Grandcourt', *Studies in the Novel*, 17 (1985), 371-382.

entirety, but also to the reader's consciousness of encountering the narratorial commentator's voice on a level outside the actual story.

Gender Issues

The novel's stance with regard to gender issues is primarily presented in the form of plot and dialogue. Gwendolen, of course, constitutes a colourful representation of a woman unwilling to acquiesce in the limitations fixed to her gender; but it is perhaps Daniel's mother, the Princess Halm-Eberstein, who most forcefully and lucidly communicates a viewpoint very much in line with feminist ideology.[47] The princess accomplishes what Gwendolen cannot, but nevertheless both women suffer the consequences of having dispositions ill fitted for the conventional and limiting roles which their societies want to force them into.[48] Contrastingly, Mirah symbolises the reverse ideal by an unremitting adherence to the traditions and maxims of her own faith.[49] *Daniel Deronda* only contains one instance in

[47] In one of her meetings with Daniel, the Princess Halm-Eberstein describes the sense of suppression she experienced at not being allowed to fulfil her potential. Explaining why she left her religion and family to pursue a career, she tells Daniel: 'You are not a woman. You may try – but you can never imagine what it is to have a man's force of genius in you, and yet to suffer the slavery of being a girl. To have a pattern cut out – "this is the Jewish woman; this is what you must be; this is what you are wanted for; a woman's heart must be of such a size and no larger, else it must be pressed small, like Chinese feet; her happiness is to be made as cakes are, by a fixed receipt" ' (li, 541). Interestingly, the princess uses the same imagery as the narrator, i.e. slavery, to describe the oppression she experiences under rigid gender rules.

[48] Gillian Beer argues that Gwendolen constitutes 'Eliot's most radical representation of the oppressiveness of women's lot' and further maintains that 'the fate of Daniel's mother makes her a sad representative of freed women'; see *George Eliot*, pp. 222-225. Moreover, Beer maintains that the brilliant woman's, that is Alcharisis's, escape from constriction does not alter the lot of the other woman, i.e. Gwendolen; but Dorothea Barrett contends that even though the 'ordinary' woman's situation is not altered by the fact that another woman breaks free, 'the exceptional woman can be said to have provided what other women need most of all: a vision of how things might be, or be perceived, otherwise' (175).

[49] Several critics claim that the novel juxtaposes the situation for women in England in the nineteenth century with the situation for people belonging to another faith than Christianity. Pam Hirsch, for example, claims that 'the effect of the doubling of women and Jews in *Daniel Deronda* stresses the sense of *both* groups as being exiles, homeless and powerless' and furthermore argues that Eliot's contemporary readers 'had failed to see the connections she had forged between the condition of Jews in British society and the condition of women in British society'; 'Women and Jews in *Daniel Deronda*', *The George Eliot Review: Journal of the George Eliot Fellowship*, 25 (1994), 45-50 (p.

which Mirah ventures into a male sphere by offering a re-interpretation of a Midrashic text.[50] Gender issues and in particular feminist concerns are thus a primary theme in the novel, which explores the relationships between suppressors and suppressed, be it between British Christians and Jews or between men and women. However, many critics disapprove of Eliot's treatment of the theme, arguing that female characters who do not confine themselves to their appointed roles are punished. The princess, for example, loses her voice and dies unhappy, and Gwendolen's youthful aspirations are shattered as she is forced into humility. This criticism of a female character's failure to rise above and conquer established notions regarding her station and status is reminiscent of criticism uttered about Eliot's earlier protagonists, such as Dorothea and Maggie. But Gwendolen does not die or remarry; her ending is open-ended and her outlook actually encouraging. After all, her last words in the novel indicate an optimistic new beginning: 'I shall live. I shall be better' (lxix, 692).[51]

Although the most pressing gender issues in the novel are addressed in the form of plot, narrative description and dialogue, some concerns regarding male and female are broached in the form of narratorial commentary. For example, regarding Gwendolen's early ambitions to be a leader rather than a follower, the narrator remarks that 'such passions dwell in feminine breasts also' (iv, 31). Another female character in *Daniel Deronda*

---

45). Susan Meyer notices this parallel in the novel too, but remarks critically on it, maintaining that '[t]he novel ultimately does with Jews [...] precisely what it does with female transgressiveness: it firmly ushers both out of the English world of the novel' (735). Meyer contends that the novel is concerned with restoring hierarchies and re-appointing men and women to their traditional social roles. According to Meyer, this ultimate intention explains why characters who attempt to break out of their roles are unsuccessful or unhappy in the end.

50 Mordecai has told the story of a woman who is in love with a king but whose love is unreciprocated. The king loves another woman who has been sentenced to death. Out of love for the king the first woman switches identities with the king's love-interest and dies in her stead, rather like Sydney Carton in Dickens's *A Tale of Two Cities*. Mordecai tells the story as an example of selflessness but Mirah disagrees, interpreting it as a last display of egoism on the part of the dying woman. By dying in order to make the king happy, Mirah argues, she simultaneously proves that she is the woman most worthy of his love. Mirah's analysis fits in well with the consideration of egoism throughout the novel.

51 It is important to recognise that the type of character the reader is mostly encouraged to sympathise with is, in actuality, this type of female protagonist, whose inner nature conflicts with society's expectations of her. The fact that she often fails to prevail against convention does not automatically mean that Eliot's novels criticise these characters' inability to adapt to societal hierarchies, or that they promote the notion of an ideal woman. In fact, Gillian Beer argues that Gwendolen's recognition of her own self and of the not-always-so-good powers within that self makes 'a powerful critique of the idealised woman'; see *George Eliot*, p. 222.

who defies custom is Catherine Arrowpoint, who falls in love with and marries Herr Klesmer under the threat of being disowned by her parents. Considering her disobedience to conventional practice regarding marriage and fortune, the narrator comments:

> [I]n every case it is taken for granted that she will consider herself an appendage to her fortune, and marry where others think her fortune ought to go. Nature, however, not only accommodates herself ill to our favourite practices by making "only children" daughters, but also now and then endows the misplaced daughter with a clear head and a strong will (xxii, 202).

Miss Arrowpoint's defiance seemingly issues from a will as strong as Gwendolen's, but also from a 'clear head' – essentials which the narrator describes in an approving tone, hence implying a favourable attitude with regard to Miss Arrowpoint's insubordination.[52] The comment works out a dichotomy between societal expectations and Nature, humorously and ironically reflecting on the human propensity for disregarding the possibility of a collision between the individual and tradition. The purpose of ironically remarking on this dichotomy is to appeal to the reader's recognition, attempting to entice him or her into acknowledging the comical element of a recognisable and common phenomenon. 'Meeting' the narrator on a mutual level by partaking in the humorous observation, the reader is inspired to agree. By ironically ridiculing a universal phenomenon, the narrator makes it seem absurd. As a consequence, Miss Arrowpoint's defiance is condoned and the reader is encouraged to admire her refusal to submit to rules of convention.[53]

As mentioned above, gender-related issues are a central concern in *Daniel Deronda*. In particular, the Princess Halm-Eberstein's avowals in her meetings with Daniel testify to the conditions under which women lived in the nineteenth century. However, few narratorial comments pertaining to gender issues possess the same solemn tone; instead, a number of them, like the one above, emphasise humorous details with regard to gender. Another example occurs in chapter 35, in which Daniel meets Gwendolen as Mrs Grandcourt for the first time. Inwardly deliberating on how happy Gwendolen could possibly be with a man such as Grandcourt,

---

52 This quotation disproves Susan Meyer's contention that the impetus of *Daniel Deronda* is to reinstate social hierarchies. Miss Arrowpoint is clearly upsetting social hierarchies by marrying the Jewish Herr Klesmer and he in turn is upsetting religious convention by marrying a Gentile, yet the narrator is clearly sympathetic to the union. The couple are never symbolically 'punished' for their overturning of hierarchies, but are depicted as happy in their new roles as man and wife.

53 On the generation of sympathy for Miss Arrowpoint, see Nünning, p. 275.

Daniel speculates about her motives and the narrator addresses the reader:

> In general, one may be sure that whenever a marriage of any mark takes place, male acquaintances are likely to pity the bride, female acquaintances the bridegroom: each, it is thought, might have done better; and especially where the bride is charming, young gentlemen on the scene are apt to conclude that she can have no real attachment to a fellow so uninteresting to themselves as her husband, but has married him on other grounds. Who under such circumstances pities the husband? (xxxv, 346).[54]

Even so, Daniel's reflections as to Gwendolen's motives for marriage, the narrator contends, derive not from his general pity for brides as described in the quotation above but from knowledge of Grandcourt. The statement is followed by the suggestion that Daniel might be excused for not pitying Grandcourt. Hence, the narrator is eager to point out that the reflection above is not completely applicable to Daniel in this case, as his suspicions are well founded. Unusually, however, the humour in the comment insinuates a degree of ironic distance to Daniel's character, establishing a contact between the narrator and the reader through the medium of humorous recognition. That recognition is imbued with irony which is, as a rare instance, at Daniel's expense. The comment thus intimates a different, albeit temporary, position with regard to Daniel, de-glorifying him for a spell and placing him on a level with other fallible characters whose imperfections the reader can recognise and perhaps even identify with. As mentioned, though, this ironic distance is only transitory and almost cancelled out by the narrator's request for pardon on behalf of Daniel. Still, the presence of irony permeates the comment which serves as a general reflection, elucidating and analysing the particular deliberations that occupy Daniel's mind.

As in *Middlemarch*, narratorial commentary pertaining to gender issues in *Daniel Deronda* highlights the conflicts between the situation of women and the traditions that govern their lives. However, these comments are regularly imbued with irony and humour, as if the topic is too hot to handle in a completely serious manner. Again as in *Middlemarch*, therefore, the novel incorporates its grimmest observations regarding gender issues in the form of characterisation and plot.

---

54 This statement could be equally relevant to Edward Casaubon and Dorothea.

Problems of Interpretation

A recurring concern in George Eliot's fiction is the unreliability of outward signs. Deceptive appearances, shifting perspectives and each individual's unique interpretation of signs form a thematic dimension in all the novels. Examples of first impressions which undergo alteration because they were based on mere appearances are frequent in *Daniel Deronda*, from Daniel's initial evaluation of Gwendolen at the gambling tables to Gwendolen's first impression of Grandcourt, after which she deems him 'not ridiculous' (xi, 93). Narratorial commentary also includes observations on the insta-bility of interpretation, frequently reminding the reader of the possibility of several perspectives and different interpretations.[55] One character who fails to perceive the possibility of interpretations other than his own is Mr Middleton, the cleric who falls in love with Gwendolen and who con-strues her blatant lack of enthusiasm for him as evidence of her passion. Remarking on Mr Middleton's erroneous understanding of Gwendolen's signals, the narrator states: 'for all meanings, we know, depend on the key of interpretation' (vi, 46).[56] The presence of 'we know' implies the presumption of a reader familiar with the complexities of interpretation, inviting him or her onto a level with the narrator which is distinct from Mr Middleton's. But apart from referring to the particular episode of Mr Middleton's mistaken assumption, the proverb-like aspect of the comment indicates that it has significance for the narrative in its entirety as well as relevance outside the diegesis. The 'truth' of the statement is indisputable, and it could well be lifted out of its context and function independently as a philosophical reflection.

Similarly, but with added emphasis and complexity, the narrator com-ments on Grandcourt's and Gwendolen's relationship. They have been yachting together for weeks, and the absence of stimulus and company other than her husband's is grating on Gwendolen. Feeling stifled and

---

55 For a discussion of double meanings in *Daniel Deronda* and on how the novel might be deconstructed, see Cynthia Chase, 'The Decomposition of the Elephants: Double-Reading *Daniel Deronda*', *PMLA*, 93 (1978), 215-227.

56 In 'The Apocalypse of the Old Testament: *Daniel Deronda* and the Interpretation of Interpretation', *PMLA*, 99 (1984), 56-71, Mary Wilson Carpenter claims that despite the narrator's evident expectation of a reader more sophisticated than Mr Middleton, as is indicated by the statement, many critics regard the readers of the novel as Mr Middletons who can only read the narrative straightforwardly, and who therefore cannot comprehend the organic unity which the two plots comprise, seeing them as two independent halves.

imprisoned under his supremacy, she broods on her interaction with him, and the narrator perceives a further aspect of interpretation:

> The beings closest to us, whether in love or hate, are often virtually our interpreters of the world, and some feather-headed gentleman or lady whom in passing we regret to take as legal tender for a human being may be acting as a melancholy theory of life in the minds of those who live with them – like a piece of yellow and wavy glass that distorts form and makes colour an affliction (liv, 575-576).

Here, interpretation is not an internal force predicated on external signals, but an external phenomenon which functions as a lens through which the internal world is perceived. The statement works as a general reflection on Grandcourt's impact on Gwendolen, an impact which affects her consciousness in such a way as to influence her every thought. This type of interpretation, then, is distinct from the type which the narrator assumes the reader to be familiar with. Accordingly, the comment serves an explicatory and descriptive function, illustrating the sway Grandcourt has over Gwendolen's interpretation of the world. The sympathy elicited is for Gwendolen whose submissiveness under Grandcourt's authority, the reader learns through this comment, not only places physical and political restrictions on her, but also determines her inner consciousness by affecting her interpretation of the world.

Closely related to matters of interpretation is the signification of language. Approaching an important issue in the novel's commentary, Eliot's narrator repeatedly reminds the reader that words uttered may not correspond to the language of the mind. For example, apropos of Daniel's deliberations with regard to Mirah's family, the narrator contrasts his words with his thoughts: 'these fine words with which we fumigate and becloud unpleasant facts are not the language in which we think' (xix, 176). Even for the ideal Daniel, then, spoken words serve as camouflage for what he is actually thinking but dare not formulate.

As a development of this idea of the relation between spoken words and the language of the mind, the narrator intellectualises the complexities of linguistic description, intimating that 'attempts at description are stupid' and maintaining that '[w]e recognize the alphabet; we are not sure of the language' (xi, 91). The comment should be understood in view of the narrator's theories on interpretation and language.[57] In accordance with other comments on interpretation, the statement makes the reader aware of the fact that signs taken together may not form an accurate whole, as the individual signs in themselves are subject to illimitable interpreta-

---

57 Cf. Nünning, p. 271.

tions. Correspondingly, the words that make up language are subject to interpretation and so may vary in meaning with each individual interpretation. This concern with non-fixed processes of signification, which is in line with much twentieth-century thinking, works as an acknowledgement of the ambiguity of language. Consequently, these comments serve as reminders to the reader, directing his or her attention to the fact that all interpretation is subjective and that language – even the narrator's – can never be a transparent medium through which a universal 'truth' can be reached.

References to History

Daniel Deronda is George Eliot's only novel in which the story takes place approximately at the time of writing. Therefore it is not surprising that the amount of narratorial commentary with historical references is considerably smaller than in the earlier novels. Still, the narrator refers to the narrative as a 'history' and displays attentiveness to the novel's historical present, fictive episodes being arranged against the backdrop of actual historical events such as the American Civil War and the expansion of the British Empire.[58] But of course the most prominent historical issue present in the novel relates to Judaism and to Jewish communities in the temporal and spatial setting of the story.

An indication of the fictional time-period, roughly 1864, appears as early as chapter 3, where the narrator comments on some people's sense of

---

58 *Daniel Deronda* incorporates many references to the American Civil War, both direct as in chapter 9, where the news of Grandcourt's arrival is said to have 'no reference to the results of the American war' (ix, 75), and indirect as in chapter 69, where Gwendolen's shock at Daniel's revelations is compared to the outer mechanisms of war: 'There comes a terrible moment to many souls when the great movements of the world, the larger destinies of mankind, which have lain aloof in newspapers and other neglected reading, enter like an earthquake into their own lives – when the slow urgency of growing generations turns into the tread of an invading army or the dire clash of civil war, and grey fathers know nothing to seek for but the corpses of their blooming sons, and girls forget all vanity to make lint and bandages which may serve for the shattered limbs of their betrothed husbands' (lxix, 689). As always in Eliot's novels, there are references to many actual historical events of immediate interest to the fictive time of the narrative. Another such reference in *Daniel Deronda* is Bismarck's defeat of Austria in 1864 and of France in 1871. In response to Gwendolen's singing, Herr Klesmer argues that at least it is acceptable to *see* her sing, and the narrator comments: 'Was there ever so unexpected an assertion of superiority? at least before the late Teutonic conquests?' (v, 38-39).

grievance: '[I]n Wessex, say ten years ago, there were persons whose bitter-ness may now seem incredible' (iii, 24). In the same manner as in the ear-liér novels, the *Daniel Deronda* narrator makes a distinction between 'then' and 'now', indicating that the motives and behaviours of characters in the fictional time-sphere, although only ten years prior to the act of narrating, need to be explained and authenticated to an unconvinced reader. The suggestion that readers may find the bitterness of some characters 'incred-ible' appears again in chapter 9, where the narrator remarks on a collective group of characters specific to the time and place of story-time now:

> Some readers of this history will doubtless regard it as incredible that people should construct matrimonial prospects on the mere report that a bachelor of good fortune and possibilities was coming within reach [...] But, let it be observed, nothing is here narrated of human nature generally: the history in its present stage concerns only a few people in a corner of Wessex (ix, 76).[59]

The quotation refers to the narrative as a history; but here, contrary to other such references, the narrator is keen to underline the fact that this is the particular history of an exclusive group of people. Earlier references to what can be generally known about people at a certain historical point in time, or to how experiences can be shared by people existing in differ-ent historical times, are irrelevant here. Furthermore, the narrator implies a personal connection to the characters by claiming that these characters 'were all on visiting terms with persons of rank' (ix, 76) and that this was a fact which the narrator was 'in the proud position of being able to state' (ix, 76). The historical reference here, then, is not so much an endeav-our to demonstrate historical accuracy as it is an effort to establish the distinctiveness of this specific history. Should the reader find that some narrative components correspond badly with 'reality', the narrator, in this example, counters criticism by claiming to re-tell a history which is per-sonal rather than general. By implication the narrator momentarily divests himself of his didactic task, as part of which he attempts to elicit sympathy and understanding, instead adopting the role of a mere reporter involved in narrating a distinct history. This alternate attitude is unstable, however. Claiming not to draw any parallels between events in the narrative and the possible 'realities' of a historical past, the narrator's approach to the

---

59 Commenting on the irony in the passage, Nünning contends that it parodies the themes and conventions in the English novel in a meta-narrative manner; see p. 273. Although this quotation has been cited and analysed earlier in my section 'References and Addresses to the Reader', I quote it here again to illustrate how functions in Eliot's narratorial commentary overlap so that one single statement can serve several functions.

relevance of historical authenticity contradicts the essence of a narratorial comment which appears only two pages earlier:

> I like to mark the time, and connect the course of individual lives with the historic stream, for all classes of thinkers. This was the period when the broadening of gauge in crinolines seemed to demand an agitation for the general enlargement of churches, ball-rooms, and vehicles (viii, 74).

Anna Gascoigne's personal persuasion that she would have been able to give up the luxuries of sophisticated society, had she and Rex been allowed to travel to the colonies, is situated in the context of a 'historic stream'. At this point the narrator is eager to establish Anna's individual belief within a larger context and also keen to present himself as a general historian, informing the reader about phenomena particular to the period which he or she is assumed to be unfamiliar with. A direct parallel is drawn between the particularities of the fiction and the alleged 'realities' of a historical past; this parallel serves to reinforce the authenticity of the – fictive – events and to highlight the narrator's role as historian. However, that role is almost instantly challenged, creating the impression that the novel incorporates contradictory narratorial attitudes with regard to the relation between the narrated text and a historical past. In turn, these conflicting narratorial attitudes affect the reader's relation and distance to the text. By purporting to tell a history of personal lives which is unattached to a general history, the narrator diminishes his own distance to the text while increasing the reader's distance both to the text and to himself. With this approach the narrator makes the 'history' his own, accrediting himself with an intimate relation to the text and in consequence alienating the reader from both himself and the text. Contrary to this distancing effect, the latter quotation reduces the distance between narrator and reader through the narrator's attempt to enlarge the reader's understanding. By situating a particular phenomenon in a general context, i.e. by initiating the circular movement of particular-general-particular, the narratorial comment enhances the reader's understanding of the text, inviting him or her to share in the narrator's perspective on it.

These conflicting narratorial attitudes are reminiscent of *The Mill on the Floss* and *Middlemarch*, in which the reader's distance to the narrator and to the text is in constant flux. As a consequence of the narrator's more stable relation to the text in *Daniel Deronda*, however, the reader's distance to the narrator, and in turn to the text, is also less erratic. The example above, then, is an exception to the normally constant relation of the *Daniel Deronda* narrator to the text. Nevertheless, it is a refreshing instance of disagreement and narratorial retrogression in a work where the narrator's attitude to the text is characterised by restraint and discipline.

Religion

History and religion are closely interwoven in *Daniel Deronda*.[60] Deliberations on the state, future and importance of Judaism are simultaneous considerations of Jewish nationhood, of traditions and historical legacies and of relations between Christian and Jewish communities, both from an actual historical perspective and from the perspectives of the characters in the text. One of the most pressing questions which the novel raises, and which is voiced in the discussions held at the 'Hand and Banner', concerns the matter of assimilation. Should Jews in the Diaspora assimilate into existing societies, or should they uphold their own ethnic and religious identity?[61] Other issues concern the different relations

60 Two themes are of particular significance to the relevance of history and religion in *Daniel Deronda*. The first is the theme of the 'Wandering Jew', a principal figure in medieval Christian legend who is made to wander eternally in punishment for mocking Jesus on the Cross; the second is the theme of Jews in exile, wandering in the wilderness in want of their homeland. Mary Wilson Carpenter considers *Daniel Deronda* in relation to 'the Apocalypse of the Old Testament', i.e. 'the Book of Daniel', arguing that the novel incorporates a number of images from this Biblical text. The images, she argues, serve as hermeneutical instruments to the understanding of *Daniel Deronda*. The reader, Carpenter claims, 'needs to know the traditional interpretation of Daniel to grasp George Eliot's new interpretation of prophetic history' (57). Apart from Daniel's namesake in the Old Testament and many other parallels, Carpenter points to numerological symbolisms in her demonstration of how the texts correspond. For example, she claims, the seventy chapters of *Daniel Deronda* are a direct reference to the 'Prophecy of the Seventy Weeks' (60); furthermore chapter 42 of *Daniel Deronda* – in which the history and future of Judaism is being discussed at the 'Hand and Banner' – corresponds to the 42 months of exile in the wilderness retold in the 'Book of Daniel'. The discussion of the men in the 'Hand and Banner', Carpenter states, 'is essential to Eliot's hermeneutical purpose, which is to unite Jewish and Gentile histories' (63). For more on the discussions in the 'Hand and Banner', see Bernard Semmel, *George Eliot and the Politics of National Inheritance* (Oxford: Oxford University Press, 1994), pp. 121-127.

61 This question is also raised with regard to Mirah, who continuously needs to struggle to maintain her Jewish identity in a cultural atmosphere which wishes to forget it. For example, realising that Hans is in love with Mirah, Daniel confronts him asking: 'Have you heard her – of course you have – heard her speak of her people and her religion?' whereupon Hans replies: 'That can't last' (xxxviii, 396). Hans's mother and sisters also have their clandestine desires, which are disclosed in chapter 46: 'Mrs Meyrick had hoped, as her children did, that the intensity of Mirah's feeling about Judaism would

Christians and Jews have to their respective faiths. That topic has caused several critics to claim that *Daniel Deronda* juxtaposes Christianity with Judaism, depicting the former as having lost its intrinsic value, its ability to maintain moral and ethical guidelines and its capacity to serve as spiritual counsellor to individuals and communities, whereas the latter is depicted as a dynamic force in each member's life, giving Jews a distinctive mission in life and offering multiple pathways for becoming morally and spiritually righteous human beings.[62]

Surprisingly few narratorial comments in *Daniel Deronda* consider religious matters, despite the fact that one of the novel's principal themes forms a comprehensive study of the impact religion can have on the lives of human beings. The novel's attitude towards Christianity and Judaism emanates from a combination of dialogue, FID and narrative description, but rarely from a narrator concerned with addressing the reader directly about these matters. Even those instances of narratorial commentary which do consider religion occur within longer passages of FID (usually Daniel's), making the distinction between ideas originating from the narrator or from a character even harder to discern. The majority of these comments on religion appear in chapters 32 and 33, where Daniel visits a synagogue in Frankfurt and then pays several visits to the Jewish quarters in London. His obvious purpose for these visits is to locate Mirah's family, but an underlying curiosity about the Jewish faith reveals a fascination which in a sense anticipates the revelation of his own descent. Partaking in the Jewish service at the Rabbinical School in Frankfurt, Daniel especially enjoys the liturgies. They need no translation, as the narrator explains:

> The most powerful movement of feeling with a liturgy is the prayer which seeks for nothing special, but is a yearning to escape from the limitations of our own weakness and an invocation of all Good to enter and abide with us [...] The Hebrew liturgy, like others, has its transitions of litany, lyric, proclamation, dry statement and blessing (xxxii, 310).

---

slowly subside, and be merged in the gradually deepening current of loving interchange with her new friends' (xlvi, 484).

62 U. C. Knoepflmacher argues that 'it is through the Jewish half of her novel that George Eliot reminds her readers that the nation's desiccated tradition can be replenished only by an essentially religious form of "culture," a spiritual force which must have both a national location, as well as an international authority'; *Religious Humanism and the Victorian Novel*, p. 132. See also Peter C. Hodgson, p. 138, and Barbara Hardy, '*Daniel Deronda*'. Hardy claims that Eliot's depiction of Jewish society is almost unreservedly favourable whereas her portrayal of English society is unsympathetic and critical (116). Contrastingly, Susan Meyer argues that *Daniel Deronda* is 'rife with anti-semitism', distorting Jewish characters into stereotypes and emphasising greed and cunning as typical characteristics (745-746).

This particular instance of liturgy is performed in a synagogue, but the narrator's interest lies with the power of liturgy in general. The tone is one of approval at the invocation not of God but of good, and of the effects that religious ceremony can have. The fact that it is a synagogue which the (as yet) Christian Daniel enters into, and that it is Jewish ritual by which he is inspired and uplifted, is of no consequence; what is significant is that the liturgy has aroused Daniel's spirit.[63] The statement embodies a decidedly favourable attitude towards the power of religious ceremony; seeking the reader's understanding, it stops short of attempting to elicit his or her recognition. Instead, the narrator's voice takes on the authoritative tone of an educator who aspires to inform the reader of the forces incorporated within religious ritual.

The attitude towards Judaism and the Jewish community in the novel has been the subject of much critical debate. Some critics find the depiction of Jews and Jewish religion exaggeratedly idealistic, while others consider the novel downright anti-semitic.[64] As there are so few narratorial comments pertaining to religion in the book, they do not, unfortunately, constitute a sufficient basis for leaning towards either alternative.

---

63 David Carroll argues that Daniel's religious feeling here is an example of negative capability. Daniel is receptive to this 'divine influx' because it has no 'fixed habitation'. Carroll maintains that Daniel 'is able to respond because he has the correct form of pre-understanding, that of a man whose life is the open hypothesis which hasn't yet crystallised into a theory or a character'; see *Conflict of Interpretations*, p. 289. Saleel Nurbhai sees Daniel's entrance into Judaism as a development from 'golem' to wholeness. 'Golem', Nurbhai explains, is a term 'central to mythical creation in Judaism' and means 'unformed mass'. Nurbhai argues that '[b]efore he is given shape, Adam is *golem*: before he receives the inspiriting breath of God'. By entering into Judaism, Daniel receives this inspiriting breath, which delivers, Nurbhai claims, him from 'golem'. See 'Metafiction and Metaphor: *Daniel Deronda* as Golem', *The George Eliot Review: Journal of the George Eliot Fellowship*, 25 (1994), 39-44 (p. 39).

64 Barbara Hardy highlights Mirah and Mordecai, classifying them as model characters with idealised psychological make-ups (116), whereas Susan Meyer points to Mirah's father, Lapidoth, and the Ezra Cohen family as stereotypes of the 'greedy and cunning' Jew (745). Both critics acknowledge the Princess Halm-Eberstein's criticism of Judaism, however. Although venturing into the area of authorial intention entails the risk of misguidedly associating ideas with authors, or of failing to let the text speak for itself, I think that it is important at this stage to remind oneself of Eliot's personal reasons for writing a novel which focuses in such a high degree on the Jewish community. From her letters it is evident that Eliot was opposed to the discrimination against Jews in England and therefore intended to 'treat Jews with such sympathy and understanding as [her] nature and knowledge could attain to'; see *Letters*, vi, 301. The objective of *Daniel Deronda*, then, is to promote the reader's understanding for and sympathy with Jewish communities. Naturally, intentions and results are not always compatible; but it should be noted that those interpretations which we make of the novel now are made through a twenty-first-century lens by which values and ideals over the years have been refined and nuanced to become consistent with present-day sensibilities.

Still, some comments do reveal unambiguous opinions about Judaism and Christianity which deserve closer scrutiny. In his search for Mirah's family in the Jewish quarters of London, Daniel is invited into Ezra Cohen's home to meet his wife and family. Ezra is proud of his business and trade, and as a result Daniel considers him 'the most unpoetic Jew he had ever met with in books or life' (xxxiii, 331). In response to Daniel's aversion to Cohen's contentment, the narrator remarks: 'It is naturally a Christian feeling that a Jew ought not to be conceited' (xxxiii, 331). The statement is strikingly ironical, and there is a dual element to it which concerns the definition of 'Christian'. The term is, of course, an indication of religious affiliation, and as such it encompasses all persons who subscribe to the Christian faith. Denoting a specific group of people, the term functions as a noun. But it is also possible to interpret 'Christian' as an adjective which signifies a set of values and attitudes connected with that particular system of beliefs. In both interpretations of the word, the comment conveys irony, but with varying connotations depending on which interpretation the reader adopts. Regarding 'Christian' as a noun, the reader construes the irony as being directed towards a specific group, possibly the genteel Englishman whom the narrator has mocked earlier in the novel. Considering the term as an adjective, however, the comment implies a slight on the Christian statement of belief, insinuating that the term has lost its meaning and now denotes the opposite of what was originally intended – that is, pre-eminence and condescension have taken the place of humility and fellow-feeling.[65] Whichever way the reader interprets it, however, the remark serves to modify Daniel's criticism of Cohen, reminding the reader that 'Christian feeling' also suffers from imperfection.

Another perspective which adds a further dimension to the narrator's attitude towards Jewishness appears in the next chapter. Again, the comment develops as a remark on Ezra Cohen, but here it occurs in a parenthesis wedged into an account of a dinner-time conversation at the Cohens'. The topic of conversation is the Royal Family, and the narrator comments that '(the Jew is proud of his loyalty)' (xxxiv, 337). Emitting no obvious sense of irony, the comment seems categorical of a collective group, revealing an attitude which, although ostensibly attempting to be open-minded towards Jews, classifies this community as constituting an 'other' which is observed from a distance and which allows no scope for in-

---

65 It is interesting that this ironical comment is prompted by Daniel's impatience with Ezra Cohen. To Daniel's disgust, Cohen is happy and reveals 'no shadow of a Suffering Race' (xxxiii, 331), which Daniel at this stage seems to think every respectable Jew should. Again, the joke is on Daniel.

dividualism or disparity.[66] The parenthesis serves as an informative aside to the reader, supplying him or her with a 'fact'. Furthermore, it presupposes a Gentile reader, an indication of the type of readership the author was expecting. Like other parenthetical comments, it functions as a reminder to the reader of that exclusive connection between reader and narrator which distinguishes them from the characters in the text.[67]

In Eliot's previous novels, narratorial discussions on religion have been inseparable from the idea of fellow-feeling, and indeed fellow-feeling is very much part of religious discussion in *Daniel Deronda* as well. However, the narrator of *Daniel Deronda* is also concerned with similarities between faiths and cultures. Therefore, discussions regarding religion do not so much concern fellow-feeling in individual lives as they do fellow-feeling and tolerance between creeds. Consequently, *Daniel Deronda* differs from the earlier books in the sense that 'religion' is treated not merely as emotions emanating from the individual's self but as something inseparable from nationhood, history and tradition.

Literary References

Daniel Deronda contains a large number of allusions to other literary works. These allusions are of different kinds. For instance, Tony E. Jackson discusses the reading-as-knowing motif, arguing that several characters in *Daniel Deronda* are 'as much determined by their reading as by other influences in their lives'.[68] Most of the characters, he claims, are well-read and interpret their relations to the world around them through their experiences of reading. Indeed, *Daniel Deronda* introduces the relationship between reading a text and knowing reality as a principal epistemological concern already from the very beginning of the novel. Confusion ensues when reading and knowing diverge, as they do with Gwendolen. Her pri-

---

66 This comment is not representative of the general attitude towards Jews in the novel, but it does demonstrate an element of the depiction of stereotypes which Susan Meyer discusses in her article.

67 Presupposing that the reader is a Gentile, it would seem likely that this comment would alienate and disturb Jewish readers. If it did, there are no records of such an effect; on the contrary, *Daniel Deronda's* reception from contemporary Jewish communities was highly favourable. *The Oxford Reader's Companion to George Eliot* mentions that the editor of the *Jewish Chronicle* and the Deputy Chief Rabbi at the time both sent Eliot letters of appreciation; see p. 82.

68 Tony E. Jackson, p. 48.

mary experiences of the world are acquired from an 'uncontrolled reading' (xiv, 131) of romances which, the narrator argues referring to her first encounter with Lydia Glasher, has 'not prepared her for this encounter with reality' (xiv, 131). Literature has served as Gwendolen's primary source for knowing the world (which, considering that her range of reading has been limited to romances, explains much of her naïvety); but it has also functioned as a source for her conception of her own image and character. She conceives of herself as a romance heroine and continually interprets reality through this specific literary genre.[69] The narrator explains how she incorporates the romantic into the 'real':

> [H]er horizon was that of the genteel romance where the heroine's soul poured out in her journal is full of vague power, originality, and general rebellion, while her life moves strictly in the sphere of fashion; and if she wanders into a swamp, the pathos lies partly, so to speak, in her having on her satin shoes. Here is a restraint which nature and society have provided on the pursuit of striking adventure; so that a soul burning with a sense of what the universe is not, and ready to take all existence as fuel, is nevertheless held captive by the ordinary wirework of social forms and does nothing particular (vi, 43).

The factor which renders the discrepancy between reading and reality manageable for Gwendolen is that she imagines romantic expression as belonging to an internal, private sphere. The world she pictures from reading is subdued by social restrictions in reality. Nevertheless, it exists as a concealed but significant part of her being, functioning as a filter through which she interprets her world. The notion that Gwendolen's perspective on the world to a great extent derives from literary romance might have constituted part of the narrator's ridicule or criticism of her. Interestingly, however, the quotation above serves the contrary purpose: to elicit the reader's sympathy for a character whose passion to explore life is restrained by forces beyond her control. Regarding Gwendolen's confusion of reality and romance as a manifestation of a conflict between interior and exterior, the narrator incorporates Gwendolen's particular dilemma within a larger, more general concern which the reader is invited to recognise. Hence, the narrator turns the reader's focus away from the particularities of reality and literature to a more general discussion. Understanding Gwendolen's

---

69 To be fair to Gwendolen, she is not the only character to live through her reading. When Daniel contemplates where to take Mirah after rescuing her, he thinks of the Meyrick sisters as 'three girls who hardly knew of any evil closer to them than what lay in history books and dramas, and would at once associate a lovely Jewess with Rebecca in "Ivanhoe" ' (xvii, 165). For a contextual analysis of 'Gwendolens' in earlier literature, including romances, see Sara M. Putzell, 'The Importance of Being Gwendolen: Contexts for George Eliot's *Daniel Deronda*', *Studies in the Novel*, 19 (1987), 31-45.

situation as a general example of how social structures can operate to suppress the individual spirit, the reader is encouraged to sympathise with her circumstances.

Mrs Meyrick appears as a level-headed contrast to Gwendolen's inability to separate fiction from fact. She has concerns with regard to the search for Mirah's family, feeling less enthusiastic than her daughters about the romantic details of Mirah's background and experiences. Illustrating Mrs Meyrick's feelings about the element of romance that is attached to the search for Mirah's family, the narrator remarks:

> [T]he romantic or unusual in real life requires some adaptation. We sit up at night to read about Çakya-Mouni, Saint Francis, or Oliver Cromwell; but whether we should be glad for any one at all like them to call on us the next morning, still more, to reveal himself as a new relation, is quite another affair (xlvi, 484).

Mrs Meyrick's relation to literature, albeit non-fictive, is of a different sort. Far from interpreting the world around her according to a reading-as-knowing motif, she wishes to keep reality and romance – to which she is by no means immune – apart. The fact that the characters referred to in the quotation do not derive from a romantic literary genre but are historical persons does not alter the argument. Historical figures can only ever enter into a human being's consciousness through the medium of narration, whether fictive or factual. The image illustrates and elaborates on Mrs Meyrick's ambivalence towards the investigation into Mirah's relations. Analogy is used to transform Mrs Meyrick's particular situation into a scene which the reader can recognise, and through this image he or she is encouraged to sympathise with the hesitations that the prospect of finding Mirah's brother engenders.

Direct allusions to literary works are, as mentioned, abundant in *Daniel Deronda*, repeatedly serving to intensify the reader's understanding of a specific episode or character.[70] In connection to the relation between real-

---

70 Herbert J. Levine argues that literary allusions in the novel enable readers to enter into the inner world of [George Eliot's] characters'; see 'The Marriage of Allegory and Realism in *Daniel Deronda*', *Genre: A Quarterly Devoted to Generic Criticism*, 15 (1982), 421-445 (p. 426). See also Marianne Novy, '*Daniel Deronda* and George Eliot's Female (Re)Vision of Shakespeare', *Studies in English Literature, 1500-1900*, 28 (1988), 671-692 for a discussion of the possible ways in which *Daniel Deronda* can be regarded as a rewriting of Shakespeare. Other critics have, like Novy, observed resonances of intertexts in *Daniel Deronda* which, they claim, inspired Eliot when writing the novel, although these resonances do not figure as direct allusions. See, for example, Mary Ann Kelly, '*Daniel Deronda* and Carlyle's Clothes Philosophy', *Journal of English and Germanic Philology*, 86 (1987), 515-530, and Shifra Hochberg, '*Daniel Deronda* and Wordsworth's *The White Doe of Rylstone*', *English Language Notes*, 31 (1994), 43-53.

ity and fiction, one of these allusions is of particular interest as it constitutes a comment on authors. At the news that Catherine wants to marry Herr Klesmer, the narrator depicts Mrs Arrowpoint's state of shock in the following manner:

> Imagine Jean Jacques, after his essay on the corrupting influence of the arts, waking up among children of nature who had no idea of grilling the raw bone they offered him for breakfast with the primitive *couvert* of a flint […] It is hard for us to live up to our own eloquence, and keep pace with our winged words, while we are treading the solid earth and are liable to heavy dining. Besides, it has long been understood that the properties of literature are not those of practical life (xxii, 209).

In an earlier conversation with Gwendolen about her book on Tasso, Mrs Arrowpoint has pointed out that Leonora's decision not to marry Tasso because of her brother's opposition makes Leonora a 'cold-hearted woman' (v, 37). Catherine's news, of course, makes it difficult for Mrs Arrowpoint to practise what she has preached. The comment traces her reaction by a gradual development from the humorous image of Rousseau to the more ponderous reflection on the relationship between literature and life. By depicting a comical scenario where Rousseau is made to experience the consequences of his theories, the comment establishes a contact with the reader through mutual amusement. That contact, however, which bonds the narrator and reader – penetrating possible barriers between them in the way humour characteristically does – is then taken advantage of by the narrator, who includes the reader into his deliberations on the difficulties of living up to one's ideals. The narrator has gradually reversed the argument, from involving a mockery of authors and theorists who cannot endure their visions in practice to raising the reader's consciousness as to how this so easily happens. The last sentence in the quotation is a further argument in defence of Mrs Arrowpoint's inability to view Catherine's decision in the same way she does Leonora's, but it is also a remark on the relationship between fiction and reality and especially on the relationship between 'reality' and the narrative at hand.

Literary allusions also involve direct references to literary figures. For example, chapter 4 concludes with a reference to Shakespeare's Macbeth, incorporating an idea expressed by this character into the narrator's own argument which draws attention to Gwendolen's multifaceted make-up:

> For Macbeth's rhetoric about the impossibility of being many opposite things in the same moment, referred to the clumsy necessities of action and not to the subtler possibilities of feeling. We cannot speak a loyal word and be meanly silent, we cannot kill and not kill in the same moment; but a moment is room wide enough for

the loyal and mean desire, for the outlash of a murderous thought and the sharp
backward stroke of repentance (iv, 33).

The comment reinforces the narrator's description of character as well as
forming the conclusion of the chapter as a whole. Rather than adopting
a ready-made idea and applying it to the primary text, the intertextual
reference elaborates on the idea of contrasting propensities, approaching it
from another perspective. The narrator hence interacts with *Macbeth* as a
literary text in addition to interacting with the reader and the reader's familiarity with the intertext. It is significant that Eliot has chosen to present
and modify such a well-known passage: not only does it influence the
reader's impression of the issue at hand, i.e. Gwendolen's versatile persona;
it may also alter his or her interpretation of the text alluded to. There is a
sense that the narrator wants to impress the reader by exhibiting intellectual sophistication, but at the same time the observation is incontestable
and rhetorically made out to elicit the reader's concurrence.

Although concluding comments in *Daniel Deronda* seldom include
premonitory elements, it is tempting to read an omen into the comment
quoted above. Certainly the intimations of loyalty, murder and repentance
in connection with Gwendolen are no coincidences, and one might argue
that there is an inkling of prophecy in the choice of intertext.[71] Taken together these elements form an advance mention, the significance of which
can only be recognised in retrospect. This hindsight alerts the reader not
only to the significance of the literary reference but also to the narrator's
control of the narrative.

* * *

Such a subtle manifestation of narratorial control is a typical feature of
the *Daniel Deronda* narrator. Compared to the narrators in, for example,
Middlemarch and *The Mill on the Floss*, he is more detached from diegetic
properties. However, several instances of referring to his own 'I', some
examples of metalepsis, numerous references to 'we' and appeals to the
reader's response nevertheless make the *Daniel Deronda* narrator an engaged and occasionally immediately present one. The distinctive feature of
narratorial commentary in this novel is not that it appears less frequently
than in earlier novels, but that the transitions between story-time now
and narration now are smoother. The presence of some characters (and
Daniel's FID is a good example of this) whose intellectual affinity with

---

71 The lines from *Macbeth* are as follows: 'Who can be wise, amazed, temperate and
furious / Loyal and neutral in a moment?' (II. iii. 108-9). It is significant, however, that
Macbeth is lying. By claiming to have killed the chamberlains in rage and shock, he is
covering up his own guilt and trying to excuse the inexcusable.

the narrator is patent, and whose intricate psychological processes lead naturally into the narrator's reflections, facilitates the transitions between story-time now and narration now, making the boundary between the two almost imperceptible. Consequently, in Eliot's last novel, the narratorial comment is perfected: no longer an 'intrusion', it has become an integral part of the novel's structure.

Concluding Remarks

George Eliot employed several narrative techniques in her attempts to shape reader response. One of those techniques – the narratorial comment – has been in the focus of the preceding chapters. Aiming to show how narratorial commentary operates, this study identifies and analyses how comments steer the relationship between narrator and reader in George Eliot's novels. Before embarking on the actual investigation, however, it was necessary to formulate a definition of narratorial commentary. The concepts 'story-time now' and 'narration now' were therefore introduced to demarcate commentary from other modes of narrative. Story-time now, the present in the narrative in which the reader is engrossed, and narration now, a present in which reader and narrator meet on a separate ontological level, facilitate the distinction of narratorial commentary, understood as a narrative form which comes to pass when story-time now is suspended and the reader is invited into a narration-now sphere which he or she shares with the narrator.

Proceeding from this understanding, the principal objective of the present investigation has been to distinguish the ways in which narratorial comments operate to shape reader interpretations. The first and most fundamental operational mode identified here is the generalisation of particular diegetic phenomena. Moving between story-time now and narration now, regarding a particular diegetic situation from a general perspective, narratorial comments appeal to the reader's understanding and/or sympathy by endeavouring to stimulate his or her sense of recognition. The movement between particular instance and general reflection generates a circular process by which the reader is first encouraged to recognise narrative phenomena in his or her own world and then invited to relate that recognition back to the particular fictive situation. In this way the generalisation establishes a relationship between the narrator and the reader which reduces the distance between the two by way of the reader's recognition and presumed concurrence in the norms and values established by the comment. This communication which the generalisation creates also

300

operates to establish the narrator with authority and the text with validity, both of which are prerequisites for shaping the reader's response.

The movement between particular and general usually involves typographical indicators which signal the transfer from one diegetic level to another. These indicators, which appear in all Eliot's novels, may be semi-colons, conjunctions and parentheses; they function as gateways, signalling the boundaries between the diegetic worlds. On entry, the reader reaches a sphere – narration now – which is exclusive to his or her communication with the narrator. It is possible to argue that the circular movement away from the particular instance of the story and back again is the core of narratorial commentary in Eliot's novels. Regardless of whether comments serve to explain, validate, analyse, correct or evaluate characters and events, these functions can only be set in motion by the transfer from story-time now to narration now. Generalisations may serve several functions in George Eliot's narratives, but they are only effective if the reader can recognise and sympathise with the phenomena conjured up in narration now and relate them back to the particulars of the text.

Eliot's novels remain consistent from first to last with regard to the movement between particular and general. Where references and addresses to the reader are concerned, however, the novels present discrepancies. The first two books, *Adam Bede* and *The Mill on the Floss*, contain a large number of direct addresses which remark on expected reader reactions. These comments overtly recognise the reader's part in the interpretative process and furthermore reveal a narratorial concern with 'right interpretation'. Conversely, *Silas Marner* includes no direct references to the reader's response. In terms of narratorial commentary, this novel constitutes something of an exception, examples of the narrator's presence and narratorial addresses to the reader being far fewer in proportion to the length of the book than in any other Eliot novel. *Felix Holt* sees a return of the reader address, but with some modifications in that direct addresses are less explicit in this novel. *Middlemarch*, on the other hand, resembles the first two novels by incorporating a number of explicit narratorial remarks on the reader's anticipated response. *Middlemarch* also contains many references to the reader in the form of the first-person pronoun, as do all the novels, including *Silas Marner* and *Daniel Deronda*, both of which present a narrator who is more personally detached from the diegesis. First-person pronouns operate to include the reader and general human nature in a shared body of experiences, inducing a sense of solidarity between readers and characters on the basis of their connectedness as 'struggling erring human creatures' (*Letters*, iii, 111).

The narrator's references to himself as 'I' vary in accordance with his remarks on the reader's response. In the first two novels the occurrences are manifold, and in both of them the narrator alternates between levels of extradiegetic and intradiegetic narration. Moreover, in *The Mill on the Floss*, two narratorial attitudes can be discerned – one which is emotionally close to diegetic properties, and one which is detached and analytical. *Silas Marner*, *Felix Holt*, *Middlemarch* and *Daniel Deronda* all contain references to the narrator's 'I'; but among these novels, *Middlemarch* stands out in that its narrator's presence and engagement with fictive characters are more intense than in the other novels. In this sense the *Middlemarch* narrator resembles the narrators in *The Mill on the Floss* and *Adam Bede*, although he never departs from the extradiegetic-heterodiegetic sphere.

With regard to references and addresses to the reader and the reader's distance to the text, the narrator seems able to adjust the reader's relation to the narrative as he goes along, without adhering to any fixed pattern. The first-person plural 'we', for instance, draws the reader into a fellowship with narrator and characters based on the notion that all are representatives of human nature. The 'we', therefore, reduces the distance between reader and diegesis, fortifying the reader's bond with the narrator and with particular characters. Thus, 'we' elicits recognition and concurrence from a reader who is required to sympathise with whichever character the narrator has singled out.

The first-person singular pronoun may be used in contrary ways. When drawing attention to the narrator's presence, the 'I' may form part of a humble admission of imperfection and so serve to draw the reader in; 'I' may also emphasise the distinction between narrator and reader, thereby increasing the distance between them.

There are few instances of the second-person 'you' in Eliot's oeuvre, but those that do occur accentuate the presence of a reader more forcefully than any other mode of reader address. These comments display two narratorial attitudes: one expresses the narrator's anxiety as to the reader's interpretation of characters and events, and the second carries a note of reproach, warning the reader to not be overtly censorious in his or her reading of characters.

In this book, the recipient of narratorial addresses is referred to as 'the reader', the purpose being to distinguish between this persona and possible narratees. As with references to 'you', narratees are rather infrequent in Eliot's novels, and those that do appear usually serve as comic figures who give narrators opportunities to comment humorously on them in further attempts to reduce his distance to the 'real' reader. Occurrences of metalepsis materialise in a narrative domain which hovers between story-time now and narration now. This form of narratorial comment can be divided into narratorial and readerly metalepsis. *Adam Bede* and *The Mill on the Floss* are the two novels which incorporate narratorial metalepsis, a narrative device which conveys an impression of historical accuracy – that is, it suggests that diegetic properties are somehow 'real'. Readerly metalepsis also invites the reader into the fictive sphere, taking for granted that he or she can be present in the narrative world. Readerly metalepses transgress the boundaries of the reader's world and the fictive realm, reducing the distance between reader and diegetic characters. *Adam Bede* is the only novel which intimates the reader's actual physical presence in the story. This imagined presence, however, alternates with comments which acknowledge the impossibility of such an ontological transgression. The other novels, although instances decrease in number with each progressing novel, present readerly metalepsis as the reader's ability to 'see' diegetic properties, references which alternate between signifying the reader's actual visual powers and his or her power of imagination.

The meta-narrative comment is yet another mode by which the narrator endeavours to shape reader interpretation. As a statement which draws attention to the narrating act, meta-narration accentuates fictionality. However, many of the meta-narrative comments investigated in this book actually indicate the reverse, as the meta-narrative comment in Eliot's novels frequently coincides with the narrator's emphasis on his role as historian. By promoting the narrative as a historical account, meta-narrative statements authenticate narratives rather than accentuating fictionality, thus reinforcing an impression of accuracy – an issue with which all Eliot's narrators are concerned. Chapter 17 in *Adam Bede* can be regarded as one long meta-narrative comment, involving an argument for a mode of representation which forms a digression from the unfolding of events. Although *The Mill on the Floss*, *Silas Marner* and *Felix Holt* all contain indirect references to the narrating act, the meta-narrative comment as such does not appear again until *Middlemarch*, where the narrator claims to be busy 'unravelling certain human lots' (xv, 132). The *Middlemarch* narrator, true to style, is explicit with regard to the narrative act, but nevertheless stresses the point of historical accuracy by referring to his role as historian. Meta-narrative comments in *Daniel Deronda* are more indirect, in accordance with the narrator's less conspicuous presence in the narrative.

Felix Holt and *Middlemarch* both include introductions ('Prelude' in *Middlemarch*) which serve to contextualise their respective stories, but which can also be regarded as introductory comments. Significantly,

Daniel Deronda begins not with an introduction, but with a prose epigraph which establishes an attitude of detachment towards the story. In *Daniel Deronda*, unlike the earlier novels, prose epigraphs form another mode by which narratorial commentary operates, constituting a separate level at which narrator and reader can 'meet' and where the narrator can pre-programme the reader's attitude towards ensuing situations in the narrative. The epigraph's structural position outside the framework of the running narrative facilitates the notion of the reader's and the narrator's separate sphere outside the realm of the diegesis.

Although they vary in form and frequency, all these different modes in which narratorial commentary operates – movements between particular and general, references and addresses to the reader, metalepsis, meta-narration, and epigraphs – demonstrate the versatility of a narrator who continuously repositions himself in relation to the reader and to the characters in the texts. These modes are the narratological means through which George Eliot, the author, attempts to control her reader's responses to the text. The individual comments in themselves can have various functions; they may serve to explain or clarify particular phenomena in the narrated story, to analyse the grounds for characters' behaviour, to uncover underlying motives for actions or to validate the credibility of certain narrative events. Regardless of function, however, these comments all share the common comprehensive objective to influence the reader's interpretation of the text. Accordingly, these comments continually shift the reader's position in relation to the narrator and to diegetic characters, alternately reducing and increasing the reader's distance to the text. While these shifts occur in all the novels, *Middlemarch* is the one that most consciously experiments with both the narrator's and the reader's movements towards and away from the diegesis.

Adam Bede and *The Mill on the Floss* are much alike with regard to the narrator's and the reader's relation to the diegesis. In both these novels the reader is 'zoomed' in and out of the narrative, alternately situated inside the diegesis and positioned at a level beyond the narrative. *Silas Marner* represents a sudden departure from these oscillations, introducing a more distanced narrator whose position outside the diegesis remains stable throughout. Consequently, the reader is situated firmly beyond the diegetic realm with the exception of one example of metalepsis. It is important to note, however, that although distances are increased in *Silas Marner*, the narrator is nevertheless concerned with eliciting the reader's sympathy, demonstrating that narratorial distance need not entail emotional detachment. In *Felix Holt*, the narrator retains a less personally involved relation to the narrative but resumes communication with the reader in the form of remarks on anticipated responses. In terms of narratorial commentary, *Felix Holt* connects the earlier novels with the later ones, as it restores several types of comment that were omitted from *Silas Marner*. In *Middlemarch* the narrator's engagement with diegetic properties is reminiscent of *Adam Bede* and *The Mill on the Floss*; but although this narrator is personally involved in the story, he is never imagined to be physically so. Moreover, the *Middlemarch* narrator establishes an authoritative presence in the novel, self-consciously shifting his and the reader's relation to the text by employing all the devices of narratorial commentary. *Daniel Deronda*, although comprising several types of commentary, is exempt from the narrator's dominant presence, demonstrating greater consistency with regard to the narrator's and the reader's distance to the narrative.

Having analysed the modes in which narratorial commentary operates, the second part of each chapter in this study has been devoted to situating the device of narratorial commentary in the thematic contexts of the novels. Although each novel is unique and concerned with different and various topics, the themes broached in narratorial commentary show a certain degree of uniformity. Most novels are concerned with manifestations of egoism and altruism, and the developmental processes towards fellow-feeling that several protagonists undergo are frequently reflected in the comments of these novels. With regard to egoism and fellow-feeling, a pattern which applies to all the novels can be discerned. Those egoistic characters that endure suffering and develop into altruistic 'fellow-lovers' – Adam Bede, Maggie Tulliver, Godfrey Cass, Felix Holt, Dr Lydgate, Will Ladislaw and Gwendolen Harleth – are all subject to commentary which encourages readers to understand and sympathise with them through their egoistic stages. These are also the characters who receive the most attention in narration now, the narrator demonstrating particular concern for the reader's interpretation of them.

Gender issues are also approached in most books, although from varying perspectives. In the early works, women and men are discussed from the vantage point of gender-specific idiosyncrasies, often with humorous or ironic overtones at the expense of either gender. With each progressing novel, however, these issues are given more weight, *Felix Holt* being the first to consider them with consistent gravity. Both *The Mill on the Floss* and *Felix Holt* are novels which deal with restricting gender roles, but whereas the former has no serious discussion about these issues in narration now, the latter raises gender issues in commentary as well as in descriptive passages. *Middlemarch* and *Daniel Deronda* follow suit by including criticism of patriarchal traditions in their commentaries; but it is significant that all these novels combine critical commentary on these matters with comments in which differences between the sexes are regarded with humour and irony.

Historical references also form part of the narratorial commentary of each novel, again exhibiting a gradual development from the earlier novels to the later ones. While the early novels often assign these references to story-time now, the later works tend to place them in narration now. Additionally, commentary on history can be divided into two sub-categories: the earlier novels – *Adam Bede* and *The Mill on the Floss* – present narrator/historians who claim to have experiences of the settings and historical time they narrate; and the later novels – *Silas Marner*, *Felix Holt*, and *Middlemarch* – involve extradiegetic narrator/historians who profess to have extensive knowledge about a by-gone era. *Daniel Deronda* is the only novel studied here in which the story takes place at approximately the time of writing; it is hence natural for this book to contain fewer historical references through commentary. Even so, those that do appear are crucial to its elaborations on an ideological and political past which serves as a backdrop to the cultural and religious themes of the novel.

The historical references in Eliot's novels perform several functions. By explaining the differences between the narrative past and the narration present, these comments attempt to reinforce the authenticity of the narrative as well as the narrator's authority. The narrator's position is a privileged one in that he is a historical mediator, allowing him control of the reader's relation to the diegetic world. The result is often that the narrator accredits himself with an intimate relation to the diegetic world which in a sense increases the reader's distance to that world. Depending on the narrator for information about the 'alien world', then, the reader is brought closer to the narrator, while being reminded of his or her distance to the historical time of the story.

The identification of pressing thematic concerns in narratorial commentary has brought out the recurrence of certain issues in Eliot's fiction. In *Middlemarch* and *Daniel Deronda*, these principal concerns are almost identical. Despite being very different in terms of subject matter, structure and form, Eliot's novels are hence connected through a set of narratorial concerns which run like a developing train of thought from her first novel to her last. Similarly, the narratological devices which Eliot employs in order to move between diegetic levels – such as particular to general, references and addresses to the reader, metalepses and meta-narration – remain the same, with minor discrepancies, from her first novel to her last.

While commentary is by no means the only technique through which the narrators in George Eliot's novels attempt to affect readers, it is the narrative device which most forcefully invites communication between narrator and reader. Through this communication, Eliot sought to encourage her readers to be 'better able to *imagine* and to *feel* the pains and the joys' (*Letters*, iii, 111) of their fellow human beings. But that, as this investigation purported to demonstrate, is not all Eliot's novels do. Through narratorial commentary the novels also challenge, unsettle, question and probe readers, extending their understanding of imagined worlds as well as intensifying their awareness of their own. Narratorial commentary furthermore demonstrates George Eliot's critical engagement with the advanced thinking of her own day and reveals the superb imagination that fuelled her artistic genius. To understand the value of Eliot's narratorial comments is thus to understand how they, rather than constituting 'intrusions', form integral narrative components which contribute significantly to the power and intelligence of her art.

Bibliography

Adam, Ian, 'The Structure of Realisms in *Adam Bede*', *Nineteenth-Century Fiction*, 30 (1975), 127-149

Adams, Harriet Farwell, 'Prelude and Finale to *Middlemarch*', *The Victorian Newsletter*, 68 (1985), 9-11

Alley, Henry, 'New Year's at the Abbey: Point of View in the Pivotal Chapters of *Daniel Deronda*', *The Journal of Narrative Technique*, 9 (1979), 147-159

Anderson, Quentin, 'George Eliot in *Middlemarch*', in *George Eliot: A Collection of Critical Essays*, ed. by George R. Creeger (London: Prentice-Hall, 1970), pp. 141-160

Anderson, Roland F., 'George Eliot Provoked: John Blackwood and Chapter 17 of *Adam Bede*', *Modern Philology*, 71 (1973), 39-47

Anger, Suzy, 'George Eliot and Philosophy', in *The Cambridge Companion to George Eliot*, ed. by George Levine (Cambridge: Cambridge University Press, 2001), pp. 76-97

Arac, Jonathan, 'Rhetoric and Realism in Nineteenth-Century Fiction: Hyperbole in *The Mill on the Floss*', *ELH*, 46 (1979), 673-692

Armitt, Lucie, ed., *George Eliot: Adam Bede/ The Mill on the Floss/ Middlemarch: A Reader's Guide to Essential Criticism* (Cambridge: Icon Books, 2000)

Armstrong, Isobel, '*Middlemarch*: A Note on George Eliot's "Wisdom" ', in *Critical Essays on George Eliot*, ed. by Barbara Hardy (London: London University Press, 1970), pp. 116-132

Ashton, Rosemary, ed., *George Eliot's Selected Critical Writings* (Oxford: Oxford University Press, 1992)

Atkins, W. Siward, 'Free Indirect Style and the Rhetoric of Sympathy in *The Mill on the Floss*', in *Perspectives on Self and Community in George Eliot: Dorothea's Window* ed. by Patricia Gately *et al.* (Lewiston, NY: The Edwin Mellen Press, 1997), pp. 163-192

Auerbach, Nina, 'The Power of Hunger: Demonism and Maggie Tulliver', *Nineteenth-Century Fiction*, 30 (1975), 150-171

---. 'The Rise of the Fallen Woman', *Nineteenth-Century Fiction*, 35 (1980), 29-52.

Austen, Zelda, 'Why Feminist Critics Are Angry with George Eliot', *College English*, 37 (1976), 549-561

Auster, Henry, *Local Habitations: Regionalism in the Early Novels of George Eliot* (Cambridge, MA: Harvard University Press, 1970)

---. '*Silas Marner*: A Qualified Redemption of Ordinary and Fallible Humanity', in *Eliot: The Mill on the Floss and Silas Marner*, ed. by R. P. Draper (London: Palgrave Macmillan, 1970), pp. 217-233

Bailey, Suzanne, 'Reading the "Key": George Eliot and the Higher Criticism', *Women's Writing*, 3 (1996), 129-143

Bal, Mieke, *Narratology: Introduction to the Theory of Narrative*, trans. by Christine Van Boheemen (Toronto: Toronto University Press, 1985)

Baltazar, Lisa, 'The Critique of Anglican Biblical Scholarship in George Eliot's *Middlemarch*', *Literature and Theology: An International Journal of Theory, Criticism and Culture*, 15 (2001), 40-60

Banfield, Ann, *Unspeakable Sentences: Narration and Representation in the Language of Fiction* (London: Routledge & Kegan Paul, 1982)

Barrett, Dorothea, *Vocation and Desire: George Eliot's Heroines* (London: Routledge, 1989)

Barthes, Roland, *The Rustle of Language*, trans. by Richard Howard (New York: Hill & Wang, 1986)

---. *S/Z*, trans. by R. Miller (New York: Hill & Wang, 1970)

Beach, Joseph Warren, *The Twentieth Century Novel: Studies in Technique* (New York: Appleton-Century-Crofts, 1932)

Beardsley, Monroe, *Aesthetics: Problems in the Philosophy of Criticism* (New York: Harcourt, Brace & World, 1958)

Beaty, Jerome, *Middlemarch from Notebook to Novel* (Urbana: University of Illinois Press, 1960)

Beer, Gillian, *Darwin's Plots: Evolutionary Narrative in Darwin, George Eliot and Nineteenth-Century Fiction* (London: Routledge & Kegan Paul, 1983)

---. *George Eliot* (Brighton: The Harvester Press, 1986)

Belsey, Catherine, *Critical Practice* (London: Methuen, 1980)

Bennett, Andrew, *The Author* (London: Routledge, 2005)

Bennett, Joan, *George Eliot: Her Mind and Her Art* (Cambridge: Cambridge University Press, 1948)

Berrien, Steven, 'Narrative Commentary in *Illusions Perdues* and *Middlemarch*' (unpublished doctoral thesis: Harvard University, 1989)

Billington, Josie, ' "What Can I Do?" George Eliot, Her Reader and the Tasks of the Narrator in *Middlemarch*', *The George Eliot Review: Journal of the George Eliot Fellowship*, 31 (2000), 13-26

Blake, Kathleen, '*Middlemarch* and the Woman Question', *Nineteenth-Century Fiction*, 31 (1976), 285-312

Bodenheimer, Rosemarie, 'A Woman of Many Names', in *The Cambridge Companion to George Eliot*, ed. by George Levine (Cambridge: Cambridge University Press, 2001), pp. 20-37

Bonaparte, Felicia, *Will and Destiny: Morality and Tragedy in George Eliot's Novels* (New York: New York University Press, 1975)

Booth, Wayne, *The Rhetoric of Fiction* (Chicago: The University of Chicago Press, 1961)

Broek, A. G. van der, 'The Politics of Religion in *Felix Holt*', *The George Eliot Review: Journal of the George Eliot Fellowship*, 30 (1999), 38-48

Brooks, Cleanth and Robert Penn Warren, *Understanding Fiction* (New York: Crofts, 1943)

Bullett, Gerald, *George Eliot, Her Life and Books* (London: Collins, 1947)

Carlisle, Janice, *The Sense of an Audience: Dickens, Thackeray, and George Eliot at Mid-Century* (Brighton: Harvester Press, 1982)

Carpenter, Mary Wilson, 'The Apocalypse of the Old Testament: *Daniel Deronda* and the Interpretation of Interpretation', *PMLA*, 99 (1984), 56-71

Carroll, David, *George Eliot and the Conflict of Interpretations* (Cambridge: Cambridge University Press, 1992)

---. ed., *George Eliot: The Critical Heritage* (London: Routledge, 1971)

---. '*Silas Marner*: Reversing the Oracles of Religion', in *Eliot: The Mill on the Floss and Silas Marner* ed. by R. P. Draper (London: Palgrave Macmillan, 1967), pp. 188-216

---. '*Felix Holt*: Society as Protagonist', *Nineteenth-Century Fiction*, 17 (1962), 237-252

Cartwright, Jerome, David, 'Authorial Commentary in the Novels of George Eliot as Primarily Exemplified in *Adam Bede, The Mill on the Floss,* and *Middlemarch*' (unpublished doctoral thesis: University of Wisconsin, 1969)

Chase, Cynthia, 'The Decomposition of the Elephants: Double-Reading *Daniel Deronda*', *PMLA*, 93 (1978), 215-227

Chatman, Seymour, *Story and Discourse: Narrative Structure in Fiction and Film* (Ithaca: Cornell University Press, 1978)

Clark-Beattie, Rosemary, '*Middlemarch's* Dialogic Style', *The Journal of Narrative Technique*, 15 (1985), 199-218

Clayton, Jay, 'Visionary Power and Narrative Form: Wordsworth and *Adam Bede*', *ELH*, 46 (1979), 645-672

Cohen, Susan R., ' "A History and a Metamorphosis": Continuity and Discontinuity in *Silas Marner*', *Texas Studies in Literature and Language*, 25 (1983), 410-426

Creeger, George R., 'An Interpretation of *Adam Bede*', in *George Eliot: A Collection of Critical Essays*, ed. by George R. Creeger (London: Prentice-Hall, 1970), pp. 86-106

Crosman, Inge and Susan R. Suleiman, eds., *The Reader in the Text: Essays on Audience and Interpretation* (Princeton: Princeton University Press, 1980)

Cross, John Walter, ed., *George Eliot's Life as Related in Her Letters and Journals*, 3 vols (New York, 1885)

Culler, Jonathan, 'Omniscience', *Narrative*, 12 (2004), 22-34

---. *The Pursuit of Signs: Semiotics, Literature, Deconstruction* (London: Routledge & Kegan Paul, 1981)

---. *Structuralist Poetics* (Ithaca: Cornell University Press, 1975)

David, Deirdre, *Intellectual Women and Victorian Patriarchy: Harriet Martineau, Elizabeth Barrett Browning, George Eliot* (Itacha: Cornell University Press, 1987)

Dentith, Simon, *George Eliot* (Brighton: Harvester Press, 1986)

Derrida, Jacques, *Of Grammatology*, trans. by Gayatri Chakravorty Spivak (Baltimore: Johns Hopkins University Press, 1976)

Di Pasquale, P. Jr., 'The Imagery and Structure of *Middlemarch*', *English Studies: A Journal of English Letters and Philology*, 52 (1971), 425-435

Diekhoff, John, 'The Happy Ending of *Adam Bede*', *ELH*, 3 (1936), 221-227

Dodd, Valerie, *George Eliot: An Intellectual Life* (London: Macmillan, 1990)

Dowden, Edward, 'George Eliot', in *A Century of George Eliot Criticism*, ed. by Gordon S. Haight (London: Methuen, 1965), pp. 64-73

Doyle, Mary Ellen, *The Sympathetic Response: George Eliot's Fictional Rhetoric* (London & Toronto: Associated University Press, 1981)

Draper, R. P., 'The Fictional Perspective: *The Mill on the Floss* and *Silas Marner*', in *Eliot: The Mill on the Floss and Silas Marner*, ed. by R. P. Draper (London: Palgrave Macmillan, 1977), pp. 234-251

Dunham, Robert H., '*Silas Marner* and the Wordsworthian Child', *Studies in English Literature, 1500-1900*, 16 (1976), 645-659

Eagleton, Terry, *Criticism and Ideology: A Study in Marxist Literary Theory* (London: Verso, 1976)

Eco, Umberto, *The Role of the Reader: Explorations in the Semiotics of Texts* (Bloomington: Indiana University Press, 1979)

Eliot, George, *Adam Bede*, Oxford World's Classics, ed. by Valentine Cunningham (Oxford: Oxford University Press, 1996)

---. *Daniel Deronda*, ed. by Terence Cave (London: Penguin Books, 1995)

---. *Daniel Deronda*, Oxford World's Classics, ed. by Graham Handley (Oxford: Oxford University Press, 1988)

---. *Felix Holt, the Radical*, Oxford World's Classics, ed. by Fred C. Thomson (Oxford: Oxford University Press, 1988)

---. *Middlemarch: A Study of Provincial Life*, Oxford World's Classics, ed. by David Carroll (Oxford: Oxford University Press, 1997), with an Introduction by Felicia Bonaparte

---. *The Mill on the Floss*, Oxford World's Classics, ed. by Gordon S. Haight (Oxford: Oxford University Press, 1996), with an Introduction by Dinah Birch

---. *Romola*, Oxford World's Classics, ed. by Andrew Brown (Oxford: Oxford University Press, 1994)

---. *Scenes of Clerical Life*, Oxford World's Classics, ed. by Thomas A. Noble (Oxford: Oxford University Press, 1988)

---. *Silas Marner: The Weaver of Raveloe*, Oxford World's Classics, ed. by Terence Cave (Oxford: Oxford University Press, 1996)

Eliot, T. S., *Selected Essays*, 3rd enlarged ed. (London: Faber and Faber, 1951)

Ermarth, Elizabeth, 'Maggie Tulliver's Long Suicide', *Studies in English Literature, 1500-1900*, 14 (1974), 587-601

Ermarth, Elizabeth Deeds, 'George Eliot's Conception of Sympathy', *Nineteenth-Century Fiction*, 40 (1985), 23-42

---. 'Method and Moral in George Eliot's Narrative', *Victorian Newsletter*, 47 (1975), 4-8

---. *Realism and Consensus in the English Novel* (Edinburgh: Edinburgh University Press, 1998)

Fetterley, Judith, *The Resisting Reader: A Feminist Approach to American Fiction* (Bloomington: Indiana University Press, 1978)

Feuerbach, Ludwig, *The Essence of Christianity*, trans. by George Eliot (New York: Prometheus Books, 1989), first publ. in 1854

Fielding, Henry, *The History of Tom Jones* (London: Everyman's Library, 1962)

Fisch, Harold, '*Daniel Deronda* or *Gwendolen Harleth?*', *Nineteenth-Century Fiction*, 19 (1965), 345-356

Fish, Stanley, *Is There a Text in This Class? The Authority of Interpretive Communities* (Cambridge, MA: Harvard University Press, 1980)

Flint, Kate, 'George Eliot and Gender', in *The Cambridge Companion to George Eliot*, ed. by George Levine (Cambridge: Cambridge University Press, 2001), pp. 159-180

Fludernik, Monika, 'Subversive Irony: Reflectorization, Trustworthy Narration and Dead-Pan Narrative in *The Mill on the Floss*', *REAL: Yearbook of Research in English and American Literature*, 8 (1991-1992), 157-182

---. *Towards a 'Natural' Narratology* (London: Routledge, 1996)

Gadamer, Hans-Georg, *Truth and Method*, trans. by Garret Barden and John Cumming (New York: Seabury Press, 1975)

Gallagher, Catherine, 'The Failure of Realism: *Felix Holt*', *Nineteenth-Century Fiction*, 35 (1980), 372-384

Garrett, Peter, *Scene and Symbol from George Eliot to James Joyce* (London: Yale University Press, 1969)

---. *The Victorian Multiplot Novel: Studies in Dialogical Form* (New Haven: Yale University Press, 1980)

Gates, Sarah, ' "The Sound of the Scythe Being Whetted": Gender, Genre, and Realism in *Adam Bede*', *Studies in the Novel*, 30 (1998), 20-45

Genette, Gérard, *Narrative Discourse Revisited*, trans. by Jane E. Lewin (Ithaca: Cornell University Press, 1988)

---. *Narrative Discourse: An Essay in Method*, trans. by Jane E. Lewin (Ithaca: Cornell University Press, 1980)

Gezari, Janet K., '*Romola* and the Myth of Apocalypse', in *George Eliot: Centenary Essays and an Unpublished Fragment*, ed. by Anne Smith (London: Vision Press, 1980), pp. 77-102

Gibson, Walker, 'Authors, Speakers, Readers, and Mock-Readers', in *Reader-Response Criticism: From Formalism to Post-Structuralism*, ed. by Jane P. Tompkins (Baltimore: Johns Hopkins University Press, 1980), pp. 1-6

Gilbert, Sandra M. and Susan Gubar, *The Madwoman in the Attic: The Woman Writer and the Nineteenth-Century Literary Imagination* (New Haven: Yale University Press, 1979)

Gill, Stephen, *Wordsworth and the Victorians* (Oxford: Clarendon Press, 1998)

Ginsburg, Michal Peled, 'Pseudonym, Epigraphs, and the Narrative Voice: *Middlemarch* and the Problem of Authorship', *ELH*, 47 (1980), 542-558

Goode, John, '*Adam Bede*', in *Critical Essays on George Eliot*, ed. by Barbara Hardy (London: Routledge & Kegan Paul, 1970), pp. 19-41

Goodheart, Eugene, ' "The Licensed Trespasser": The Omniscient Narrator in *Middlemarch*', *Sewanee Review*, 107 (1999), 555-569

Graver, Suzanne, *George Eliot and Community: A Study in Social Theory and Fictional Form* (Berkeley: University of California Press, 1984)

Haddakin, Lilian, '*Silas Marner*', in *Critical Essays on George Eliot*, ed. by Barbara Hardy (London: Routledge & Kegan Paul, 1970), pp. 59-77

Hagan, John, '*Middlemarch*: Narrative Unity in the Story of Dorothea Brooke', *Nineteenth-Century Fiction*, 16 (1961), 17-31

---. 'A Reinterpretation of *The Mill on the Floss*', *PMLA*, 87 (1972), 53-63

Haight, Gordon S., ed., *A Century of George Eliot Criticism* (London: Methuen, 1965)

---. ed., *The George Eliot Letters*, 9 vols (New Haven: Yale University Press, 1954-78)

---. 'George Eliot's "Eminent Failure", Will Ladislaw', in *George Eliot's Originals and Contemporaries: Essays in Victorian Literary History and Biography*, ed. by Hugh Witemeyer (London: Macmillan, 1992), pp. 38-57

---. 'Poor Mr Casaubon', in *George Eliot's Originals and Contemporaries: Essays in Victorian Literary History and Biography*, ed. by Hugh Witemeyer (London: Macmillan, 1992), pp. 22-37

Hardy, Barbara, ed., *Critical Essays on George Eliot* (London: Routledge & Kegan Paul, 1970)

---. '*Daniel Deronda*', in *The Collected Essays of Barbara Hardy: Narrators and Novelists* (Brighton: Harvester Press, 1987), pp. 109-129

---. 'The Ending of *Middlemarch*', in *The Collected Essays of Barbara Hardy: Narrators and Novelists* (Brighton: Harvester Press, 1987), pp. 102-108

---. '*The Mill on the Floss*', in *Critical Essays on George Eliot*, ed. by Barbara Hardy (London: Routledge & Kegan Paul, 1970), pp. 42-58

---. *The Novels of George Eliot: A Study in Form* (London: Athlone, 1959)

---. 'Rome in *Middlemarch*: A Need for Foreignness', *George Eliot-George Henry Lewes Studies*, 24-25 (1993), 1-16

Harris, Margaret, 'The Narrator in *The Mill on the Floss*', *Sydney Studies in English*, 3 (1977-1978), 32-46

Harris, Margaret and Judith Johnston, eds., *The Journals of George Eliot* (Cambridge: Cambridge University Press, 1998)

Harrison, James, 'The Root of the Matter with *Daniel Deronda*', *Philological Quarterly*, 68 (1989), 509-523

Harvey, W. J., *The Art of George Eliot* (London: Chatto & Windus, 1961)

---. 'Idea and Image in the Novels of George Eliot', in *Critical Essays on George Eliot*, ed. by Barbara Hardy (London: Routledge & Kegan Paul, 1970), pp. 151-198

---. 'The Intellectual Background of the Novel: Casaubon and Lydgate', in *Middlemarch: Critical Approaches to the Novel*, ed. by Barbara Hardy (London: Athlone, 1967), pp. 25-37

Havely, Cicely Palser, 'Authorization in *Middlemarch*', *Essays in Criticism*, 40 (1990), 303-321

Hawes, Donald, 'Chance in *Silas Marner*', *English: The Journal of the English Association*, 31 (1982), 213-218

Higdon, David Leon, 'George Eliot and the Art of the Epigraph', *Nineteenth-Century Fiction*, 25 (1970), 127-151

Hirsch, Pam, 'Women and Jews in *Daniel Deronda*', *The George Eliot Review: Journal of the George Eliot Fellowship*, 25 (1994), 45-50

Hochberg, Shifra, '*Daniel Deronda* and Wordsworth's *The White Doe of Rylstone*', *English Language Notes*, 31 (1994), 43-53

Hodgson, Peter C., *The Mystery beneath the Real: Theology in the Fiction of George Eliot* (Minneapolis: Fortress Press, 2000)

Holloway, John, *The Victorian Sage: Studies in Argument* (New York: W. W. Norton & Co., 1965)

Holmes, Frederick M., 'The Paradox of Omniscience in *The French Lieutenant's Woman*', in *Metafiction*, ed. by Mark Currie (London: Longman, 1995), pp. 206-220

Holub, Robert C., *Reception Theory: A Critical Introduction* (London: Methuen, 1984)

Houghton, Walter E., *The Victorian Frame of Mind, 1830-1870* (New Haven: Yale University Press, 1957)

Huggins, Cynthia, '*Adam Bede*: Author, Narrator and Narrative', *The George Eliot Review: Journal of the George Eliot Fellowship*, 23 (1992), 35-39

Hussey, Maurice, 'Structure and Imagery in *Adam Bede*', *Nineteenth-Century Fiction*, 10 (1955), 115-129

Håkansson, Sara, 'Influential Voices in George Eliot's Epigraphs', *Vetenskapssocietetens Årsbok, New Society of Letters at Lund* (2005), 5-18

Isaacs, Neil D., '*Middlemarch*: Crescendo of Obligatory Drama', *Nineteenth-Century Fiction*, 18 (1963), 21-34

Iser, Wolfgang, *The Act of Reading: A Theory of Aesthetic Response* (London: Routledge & Kegan Paul, 1978)

---. *The Implied Reader: Patterns of Communication in Prose Fiction from Bunyan to Beckett* (Baltimore: The Johns Hopkins University Press, 1974)

Jackson, Tony E., *The Subject of Modernism: Narrative Alterations in the Fiction of Eliot, Conrad, Woolf and Joyce* (Ann Arbor: University of Michigan Press, 1994)

Jacobus, Mary, 'The Question of Language: Men of Maxims and *The Mill on the Floss*', *Critical Inquiry*, 8 (1981), 207-222

Jaffe, Audrey, *Vanishing Points: Dickens, Narrative and the Subject of Omniscience* (Berkeley: University of California Press, 1991)

James, Henry, *The Art of Fiction and Other Essays* (New York: Oxford University Press, 1948)

---. 'The Novels of George Eliot', in *A Century of George Eliot Criticism*, ed. by Gordon S. Haight (London: Methuen, 1965), pp. 43-54

---. *Partial Portraits* (London: Macmillan, 1899)

Jauss, Hans Robert, *Toward an Aesthetic of Reception*, trans. by Timothy Bahti (Brighton: Harvester Press, 1982)

Jones, Peter, *Philosophy and the Novel* (Oxford: Oxford University Press, 1975)

Kaminsky, Alice, ed., *The Literary Criticism of George Henry Lewes* (Lincoln: University of Nebraska Press, 1964)

Karlin, Daniel, 'Having the Whip-Hand in *Middlemarch*', in *Rereading Victorian Fiction*, ed. by Juliet John and Alice Jenkins (London: Macmillan, 2000), pp. 29-43

Kearns, Michael, *Rhetorical Narratology* (Lincoln: University of Nebraska Press, 1999)

Kelly, Mary Ann, '*Daniel Deronda* and Carlyle's Clothes Philosophy', *Journal of English and Germanic Philology*, 86 (1987), 515-530

---. 'The Narrative Emphasis on the Power of the Imagination in *The Mill on the Floss*', *The George Eliot Review: Journal of the George Eliot Fellowship*, 14 (1983), 86-93

Kettle, Arnold, '*Felix Holt, the Radical*', in *Critical Essays on George Eliot*, ed. by Barbara Hardy (London: Routledge & Kegan Paul, 1970), pp. 99-115

---. *An Introduction to the English Novel*, 2 vols (London: Hutchinson & Co., 1951)

Knoepflmacher, U. C., *George Eliot's Early Novels: The Limits of Realism* (Berkeley and Los Angeles: University of California Press, 1968)

---. '*Middlemarch*: An Avuncular View', *Nineteenth-Century Fiction*, 30 (1975), 53-81

---. *Religious Humanism and the Victorian Novel: George Eliot, Walter Pater, and Samuel Butler* (Princeton: Princeton University Press, 1965)

---. 'George Eliot, Feuerbach, and the Question of Criticism', in *George Eliot: A Collection of Critical Essays*, ed. by George R. Creeger (London: Prentice-Hall, 1970), pp. 79-85

Kroeber, Karl, *Styles in Fictional Structure: The Art of Jane Austen, Charlotte Brontë, George Eliot* (Princeton: Princeton University Press, 1971)

Lanser, Susan Sniader, *Fictions of Authority: Women Writers and Narrative Voice* (Ithaca: Cornell University Press, 1992)

Leavis, F. R., *The Great Tradition* (London: Penguin Books, 1962), first publ. by Chatto & Windus, 1948

Leavis, L. R., 'George Eliot's Creative Mind: *Felix Holt* as the Turning-Point of Her Art', *English Studies: A Journal of English Language and Literature*, 67 (1986), 311-326

Lerner, Laurence, *The Truthtellers: Jane Austen, George Eliot, D. H. Lawrence* (London: Chatto & Windus, 1967)

Lesjak, Carolyn, 'Labours of a Modern Storyteller: George Eliot and the Cultural Project of "Nationhood" in *Daniel Deronda*', in *Victorian Identities: Social and Cultural Formations in Nineteenth-Century Literature*, ed. by Ruth Robbins, Julian Wolfreys and James Kincaid (Hampshire, NY: Macmillan, 1996), pp. 25-42

Lewes, George Henry, *Problems of Life and Mind*, 2 vols. (London: Tübingen & Co., 1874-1879),

Levine, Caroline, 'Women or Boys? Gender, Realism and the Gaze in *Adam Bede*', *Women's Writing*, 3 (1996), 113-127

Levine, George, ed., *The Cambridge Companion to George Eliot* (Cambridge: Cambridge University Press, 2001)

---. '*Daniel Deronda*: A New Epistemology', in *Knowing the Past: Victorian Literature and Culture* ed. by Suzy Anger (Ithaca: Cornell University Press, 2001), pp. 52-73

---. 'Intelligence as Deception: *The Mill on the Floss*', *PMLA*, (1965), 402-409

---. 'Determinism and Responsibility in the Works of George Eliot', *PMLA*, 77 (1962), 268-279

Levine, Herbert J., 'The Marriage of Allegory and Realism in *Daniel Deronda*', *Genre: A Quarterly Devoted to Generic Criticism*, 15 (1982), 421-445

Lodge, David, '*Middlemarch* and the Idea of the Classic Realist Text', in *The Nineteenth-Century Novel: Critical Essays and Documents*, ed. by Arnold Kettle (London: The Open University, 1981), pp. 218-238

Lubbock, Percy, *The Craft of Fiction* (London: Jonathan Cape, 1921)

Luecke, Jane Marie, 'Ladislaw and the *Middlemarch* Vision', *Nineteenth-Century Fiction*, 19 (1964), 55-64

MacCabe, Colin, *James Joyce and the Revolution of the Word*, 2nd ed. (Houndmills: Palgrave Macmillan, 2003), first publ. in 1978

Main, Alexander, *Wise, Witty, and Tender Sayings in Prose and Verse, Selected from the Works of George Eliot* (London: Blackwood & Sons, 1872)

Malmgren, Carl D., 'Reading Authorial Narration: The Example of *The Mill on the Floss*', *Poetics Today*, 7 (1986), 471-493

Man, Paul de, *Allegories of Reading: Figural Language in Rousseau, Nietzsche, Rilke, and Proust* (New Haven: Yale University Press, 1979)

Mann, Karen B., *The Language That Makes George Eliot's Fiction* (Baltimore: The Johns Hopkins University Press, 1983)

Mansell Jr., Darrell, 'George Eliot's Conception of Tragedy', *Nineteenth-Century Fiction*, 22 (1967), 155-171

Marotta, Kenny, '*Middlemarch*: The "Home Epic" ', *Genre: A Quarterly Devoted to Generic Criticism*, 15 (1982), 403-420

Martin, Bruce K., 'Rescue and Marriage in *Adam Bede*', *Studies in English Literature*, 12 (1972), 745-763

---. 'Similarity within Dissimilarity: The Dual Structure of *Silas Marner*', *Texas Studies in Literature and Language*, 14 (1972), 479-489

Martin, Graham, '*Daniel Deronda*: George Eliot and Political Change', in *Critical Essays on George Eliot*, ed by Barbara Hardy (London: Routledge & Kegan Paul, 1970), pp. 133-150

---. '*The Mill on The Floss* and the Unreliable Narrator', in *George Eliot: Centenary Essays and an Unpublished Fragment*, ed. by Anne Smith (London: Vision Press, 1980), pp. 36-54

Mason, Michael York, '*Middlemarch* and History', *Nineteenth-Century Fiction*, 24 (1971), 417-431

Mattisson, Jane, *Knowledge and Survival in the Novels of Thomas Hardy* (Lund: Lund Studies in English, 2002)

Mautner Wasserman, Renata R., 'Narrative Logic and the Form of Tradition in *The Mill on the Floss*', *Studies in the Novel*, 14 (1982), 266-279

McCarron, Robert, 'Evil and Eliot's Religion of Humanity: Grandcourt in *Daniel Deronda*', *Ariel: A Review of International English Literature*, 11 (1980), 71-88

McDonnell, Jane, ' "Perfect Goodness" or "the Wider Life": *The Mill on the Floss* as Bildungsroman', *Genre: A Quarterly Devoted to Generic Criticism*, 15 (1982), 379-401

McSweeney, Kerry, 'The Ending of *The Mill on the Floss*', *English Studies in Canada*, 12 (1986), 55-68

---. *Middlemarch* (London: George Allen & Unwin, 1984)

Meikle, Susan, 'Fruit and Seed: The Finale to *Middlemarch*', in *George Eliot: Centenary Essays and an Unpublished Fragment*, ed. by Anne Smith (London: Vision Press, 1980), pp. 181-195

Mendilow, A. A., *Time and the Novel* (London: Peter Neville, 1952)

Metz, Christian, *Film Language: A Semiotics of the Cinema*, trans. by Michael Taylor (New York: Oxford University Press, 1974)

Meyer, Susan, ' "Safely to Their Own Borders": Proto-Zionism, Feminism, and Nationalism in *Daniel Deronda*', *ELH*, 60 (1993), 733-758

Miller, D. A., *Narrative and Its Discontents: Problems of Closure in the Traditional Novel* (Princeton: Princeton University Press, 1981)

Miller, J. Hillis, *The Form of Victorian Fiction: Thackeray, Dickens, Trollope, George Eliot, Meredith and Hardy* (Notre Dame: University of Notre Dame Press, 1968)

---. 'Narrative and History', *ELH*, 41 (1974), 455-473

---. 'Optic and Semiotic in *Middlemarch*', in *The Worlds of Victorian Fiction*, ed. by Jerome Buckley (Harvard: Harvard University Press, 1975), pp. 125-145

---. 'The Roar on the Other Side of Silence: Otherness in *Middlemarch*', in *Rereading Texts/Rethinking Critical Presuppositions: Essays in Honour of H. M. Daleski*, ed. by Shlomith Rimmon-Kenan *et al.* (Frankfurt am Main: Peter Lang, 1997), pp. 137-148

Miller, Nancy K., 'Emphasis Added: Plots and Plausibilities in Women's Fiction', *PMLA*, 96 (1981), 36-48

Milner, Ian, 'The Genesis of George Eliot's Address to Working Men and Its Relation to *Felix Holt, the Radical*', *Philologica 1: Prague Studies in English*, 10 (1963), 49-54

---. 'Structure and Quality in *Silas Marner*', *Studies in English Literature, 1500-1900*, 6 (1966), 717-729.

Müller, Günther, *Morphologische Poetik* (Tübingen: Max Niemeyer, 1968)

Neale, Catherine, *George Eliot: Middlemarch* (Harmondsworth: Penguin Books, 1989)

New, Peter, 'Chance, Providence and Destiny in George Eliot's Fiction', *English: The Journal of the English Association*, 34 (1985), 191-208

Newton, K. M., *George Eliot: Romantic Humanist; A Study of the Philosophical Structure of Her Novels* (London: Macmillan, 1981)

---. 'The Role of the Narrator in George Eliot's Novels', *The Journal of Narrative Technique*, 3 (1973), 97-107

Norbelie, Barbro Almqvist, *"Oppressive Narrowness": A Study of the Female Community in George Eliot's Early Writings* (Uppsala: Almqvist & Wiksell International, 1992)

Novy, Marianne, '*Daniel Deronda* and George Eliot's Female (Re)Vision of Shakespeare', *Studies in English Literature, 1500-1900*, 28 (1988), 671-692

Nurbhai, Saleel, 'Metafiction and Metaphor: *Daniel Deronda* as Golem', *The George Eliot Review: Journal of the George Eliot Fellowship*, 25 (1994), 39-44

Nünning, Ansgar, *Grundzüge eines kommunikationstheoretischen Modells der Erzählerischen Vermittlung: Die Funktionen der Erzählinstanz in den Romanen George Eliots* (Trier: Wissenschaftlicher Verlag Trier, 1989)

---. 'Steps towards a Discourse-Oriented Narratology of the Fairy Tale: On the Functions of the Narrator in Hans Christian Andersen's Fairy Tales', in *When We Get to the End...: Towards a Narratology of the Fairy Tales of Hans Christian Andersen*, ed. by Per Krogh Hansen and Marianne Wolff Lundholt (Odense: University Press of Southern Denmark, 2005)

O'Gorman, Francis, ed., *The Victorian Novel* (Oxford: Blackwell Publishing, 2002)

Oldfield, Derek, 'The Language of the Novel: The Character of Dorothea', in *Middlemarch: Critical Approaches to the Novel*, ed. by Barbara Hardy (London: Athlone, 1967), pp. 63-86

Palliser, Charles, '*Adam Bede* and "the Story of the Past" ', in *George Eliot: Centenary Essays and an Unpublished Fragment*, ed. by Anne Smith (London: Vision Press, 1980), pp. 55-76

Paris, Bernard J., *Experiments in Life: George Eliot's Quest for Values* (Detroit: Wayne State University Press, 1965)

---. 'George Eliot's Religion of Humanity', *ELH*, 29 (1962), 418-443

---. *Rereading George Eliot: Changing Responses to Her Experiments in Life* (Albany: State University of New York Press, 2003)

Pascal, Roy, *The Dual Voice: Free Indirect Speech and Its Functioning in the Nineteenth-Century European Novel* (Manchester: Manchester University Press, 1977)

Pinion, F. B., *A George Eliot Companion: Literary Achievement and Modern Significance* (London: Macmillan, 1981)

Pinney, Thomas, 'The Authority of the Past in George Eliot's Novels', *Nineteenth-Century Fiction*, 21 (1966), 131-147

---. ed., *Essays of George Eliot* (London: Routledge & Kegan Paul, 1963)

Prince, Gerald, *A Dictionary of Narratology* (Lincoln: University of Nebraska Press, 2003)

---. 'Introduction to the Study of the Narratee', in *Reader-Response Criticism: From Formalism to Post-Structuralism*, ed. by Jane P. Tompkins (Baltimore: Johns Hopkins University Press, 1980), pp. 7-25

---. 'Metanarrative Signs', in *Metafiction*, ed. by Mark Currie (London: Longman, 1995), pp. 55-68

---. *Narratology: The Form and Functioning of Narrative* (Berlin: Mouton Publishers, 1982)

---. 'On Readers and Listeners in Narrative', *Neophilologus*, 55 (1971), 117-122

Putzell, Sara M., 'The Importance of Being Gwendolen: Contexts for George Eliot's *Daniel Deronda*', *Studies in the Novel*, 19 (1987), 31-45

Pykett, Lyn, 'George Eliot and Arnold: The Narrator's Voice and Ideology in *Felix Holt, the Radical*', *Literature and History*, 11 (1985), 229-240

Quick, Jonathan R., '*Silas Marner* as Romance: The Example of Hawthorne', *Nineteenth-Century Fiction*, 29 (1974), 287-298

Rabinowitz, Peter J., *Before Reading: Narrative Conventions and the Politics of Interpretation* (Ithaca: Cornell University Press, 1987)

Raina, Badri, '*Daniel Deronda*: A View of Grandcourt', *Studies in the Novel*, 17 (1985), 371-382

Richards, Christine, 'Towards a Critical Reputation: Henry James on *Felix Holt, the Radical*', *The George Eliot Review: Journal of the George Eliot Fellowship*, 31 (2000), 47-54

Ricoeur, Paul, *Time and Narrative*, trans. by Kathleen McLaughlin and David Pellauer, 3 vols (Chicago: University of Chicago Press, 1984)

Riffaterre, Michael, *Semiotics of Poetry* (London: Methuen, 1978)

Rignall, John, 'Metaphor, Truth and the Mobile Imagination in *The Mill on the Floss*', *The George Eliot Review: Journal of the George Eliot Fellowship*, 24 (1993), 36-40

---. ed., *Oxford Reader's Companion to George Eliot* (Oxford: Oxford University Press, 2000)

Rimmon-Kenan, Shlomith, *Narrative Fiction: Contemporary Poetics* (London: Routledge, 1983)

Robinson, Carole, 'The Severe Angel: A Study of *Daniel Deronda*', *ELH*, 31 (1964), 278-300

Ruskin, John, *Works*, ed. by E. T. Cook and A. D. O. Wedderburn, 39 vols (London, 1902-1912)

Sanyal, Arundhati Maitra, 'Written in Opposition: Narrator-Narratee Relationship in the Major Novels of George Eliot' (unpublished doctoral thesis: The City University of New York, 2000)

Scholes, Robert and Robert Kellogg, *The Nature of Narrative* (London: Oxford University Press, 1966)

Schorer, Mark, 'Fiction and the Matrix of Analogy', *Kenyon Review*, 11 (1949), 539-559

Scott, James F., 'George Eliot, Positivism, and the Social Vision of *Middlemarch*', *Victorian Studies*, 16 (1972), 59-76

Semmel, Bernard, *George Eliot and the Politics of National Inheritance* (Oxford: Oxford University Press, 1994)

Shaw, Harry, *Narrating Reality: Austen, Scott, Eliot* (Ithaca: Cornell University Press, 1999)

Sheets, Robin, '*Felix Holt*: Language, the Bible, and the Problematic of Meaning', *Nineteenth-Century Fiction*, 37 (1982), 146-169

Showalter, Elaine, 'The Greening of Sister George', *Nineteenth-Century Fiction*, 35 (1980), 292-311

---. *A Literature of Their Own: British Women Novelists from Brontë to Lessing* (Princeton: Princeton University Press, 1977)

Shuttleworth, Sally, *George Eliot and Nineteenth Century Science: The Make-Believe of a Beginning* (Cambridge: Cambridge University Press, 1984)

Sicher, Efraim, 'George Eliot's Rescripting of Scripture: The "Ethics of Reading" in *Silas Marner*', *Semeia: An Experimental Journal for Biblical Criticism*, 77 (1997), 243-270

Simpson, Peter, 'Crisis and Recovery: Wordsworth, George Eliot, and *Silas Marner*', *University of Toronto Quarterly*, 48 (1978-79), 95-114

Sircy, Otice C., ' "The Fashion of Sentiment": Allusive Technique and the Sonnets of *Middlemarch*', *Studies in Philology*, 84 (1987), 219-244

Smith, David, 'Incest Patterns in Two Victorian Novels', *Literature and Psychology*, 15 (1965), 135-162

Smith, Jane S., 'The Reader as Part of the Fiction: *Middlemarch*', *Texas Studies in Literature and Language*, 19 (1977), 188-203

Sonstroem, David, 'The Breaks in *Silas Marner*', *Journal of English and Germanic Philology*, 97 (1998), 545-567

Sorensen, Katherine M., 'Evangelical Doctrine and George Eliot's Narrator in *Middlemarch*', *The Victorian Newsletter*, 74 (1988), 18-26

Spady, Carol Howe, 'The Dynamics of Reader-Response in *Middlemarch*', *Rackham Literary Studies*, 9 (1978), 64-75

Starr, Elizabeth, ' "Influencing the Moral Taste": Literary Work, Aesthetics, and Social Change in *Felix Holt, the Radical*', *Nineteenth Century Literature*, 56 (2001), 52-75

Steiner, F. George, 'A Preface to *Middlemarch*', *Nineteenth-Century Fiction*, 9 (1955), 262-279

Stump, Reva, *Movement and Vision in George Eliot's Novels* (Seattle: University of Washington Press, 1948)

Suleiman, Susan R., 'Introduction: Varieties of Audience-Oriented Criticism', in *The Reader in the Text: Essays on Audience and Interpretation*, ed. by Susan R. Suleiman and Inge Crosman (Princeton: Princeton University Press, 1980), pp. 3-45

Swann, Brian, 'Eyes in the Mirror: Imagery and Symbolism in *Daniel Deronda*', *Nineteenth-Century* Fiction, 23 (1969), 434-445

Szirotny, June Skye, 'Maggie Tulliver's Sad Sacrifice: Confusing But Not Confused', *Studies in the Novel*, 28 (1996), 178-199

Thale, Jerome, *The Novels of George Eliot* (New York: Columbia University Press, 1959)

Thompson, Andrew, 'George Eliot, Dante, and Moral Choice in *Felix Holt, the Radical*', *Modern Language Review*, 86 (1991), 553-566

Thomson, Fred C., '*Felix Holt* as Classic Tragedy', *Nineteenth-Century Fiction*, 16 (1961), 47-58

---. 'The Legal Plot in *Felix Holt*', *Studies in English Literature, 1500-1900*, 7 (1967), 691-704

---. 'The Theme of Alienation in *Silas Marner*', *Nineteenth-Century Fiction*, 20 (1965), 69-84

Tompkins, Jane P., ed., *Reader-Response Criticism: From Formalism to Post-Structuralism* (Baltimore: Johns Hopkins University Press, 1980)

Tucker, John L., 'George Eliot's Reflexive Text: Three Tonalities in the Narrative Voice of *Middlemarch*', *Studies in English Literature, 1500-1900*, 31 (1991), 773-791

Tye, J. R., 'George Eliot's Unascribed Mottoes', *Nineteenth-Century Fiction*, 22 (1967), 235-249

Uglow, Jennifer, *George Eliot* (London: Virago, 1987)

Wallace, Martin, *Recent Theories of Narrative* (Ithaca: Cornell University Press, 1986)

Walsh, Richard, 'Who Is the Narrator?', *Poetics Today*, 18 (1997), 495-513

Van Ghent, Dorothy, *The English Novel: Form and Function* (New York: Rinehart & Company, 1953)

Vargish, Thomas, *The Providential Aesthetic in Victorian Fiction* (Charlottesville: University Press of Virginia, 1985)

Warhol, Robyn R., 'Toward a Theory of the Engaging Narrator: Earnest Interventions in Gaskell, Stowe, and Eliot', *PMLA*, 101 (1986), 811-818

Watt, Ian, *The Rise of the Novel: Studies in Defoe, Richardson and Fielding* (London: Pimlico, 2000)

Welsh, Alexander, *George Eliot and Blackmail* (Cambridge, MA: Harvard University Press, 1985)

Wiesenfarth, Joseph, 'Demythologizing *Silas Marner*', *ELH*, 37 (1970), 226-244

Williams, Jeffrey, *Theory and the Novel: Narrative Reflexivity in the British Tradition* (Cambridge: Cambridge University Press, 1998)

Williams, Raymond, *The Country and the City* (London: The Hogarth Press, 1985), first publ. by Chatto & Windus, 1973

---. *Culture and Society, 1780-1950* (London: Chatto & Windus, 1958)

Witemeyer, Hugh, *George Eliot and the Visual Arts* (New Haven: Yale University Press, 1979)

Wormald, Mark, 'Microscopy and Semiotic in *Middlemarch*', *Nineteenth-Century Literature*, 50 (1996), 501-524

Wright, T. R., *George Eliot's Middlemarch* (Hemel Hempstead: Harvester Wheatsheaf, 1991)

---. '*Middlemarch* as a Religious Novel, or Life without God', in *Images of Belief in Literature*, ed. by David Jasper (London: Macmillan, 1984), pp. 138-152

Zimmerman, Bonnie, '*Felix Holt* and the True Power of Womanhood', *ELH*, 46 (1979), 432-451

Index

Italicised pages refer to principal discussions in this volume. Where a person has been indexed in the running text, any additional reference in a footnote on the same page has been omitted.

LUND STUDIES IN ENGLISH
Founded by Eilert Ekwall. Editor: Marianne Thormählen

022 BERTIL SUNDBY. 1953. Christopher Cooper's English Teacher (1687). cxvi + 10* + 123 pp.

023 BJÖRN WALLNER. 1954. An Exposition of *Qui Habitat* and *Bonum Est* in English. lxxi + 122 pp.

024 RUDOLF MAGNUSSON. 1954. Studies in the Theory of the Parts of Speech. viii + 120 pp.

025 CLAES SCHAAR. 1954. Some Types of Narrative in Chaucer's Poetry. 293 pp.

026 BÖRJE HOLMBERG. 1956. James Douglas on English Pronunciation c. 1740. 354 pp.

027 EILERT EKWALL. 1959. Etymological Notes on English Place-Names. 108 pp.

028 CLAES SCHAAR. 1960. An Elizabethan Sonnet Problem. Shakespeare's Sonnets, Daniel's *Delia*, and Their Literary Background. 190 pp.

029 ELIS FRIDNER. 1961. An English Fourteenth Century Apocalypse Version with a Prose Commentary. Edited from MS Harley 874 and Ten Other MSS. lviii + 290 pp.

030 The Published Writings of Eilert Ekwall. A Bibliography Compiled by Olof von Feilitzen. 1961. 52 pp.

031 ULF JACOBSSON. 1962. Phonological Dialect Constituents in the Vocabulary of Standard English. 335 pp.

032 CLAES SCHAAR. 1962. Elizabethan Sonnet Themes and the Dating of Shakespeare's Sonnets. 200 pp.

033 EILERT EKWALL. 1963. Selected Papers. 172 pp.

034 ARNE ZETTERSTEN. 1965. Studies in the Dialect and Vocabulary of the *Ancrene Riwle*. 331 pp.

035 GILLIS KRISTENSSON. 1967. A Survey of Middle English Dialects 1290-1350. The Six Northern Counties and Lincolnshire. xxii + 299 pp.

036 OLOF ARNGART. 1968. The Middle English *Genesis* and *Exodus*. Re-edited from MS. C.C.C.C. 444 with Introduction, Notes and Glossary. 277 pp.

037 ARNE ZETTERSTEN. 1969. The English of Tristan da Cunha. 180 pp.

038 ELLEN ALWALL. 1970. The Religious Trend in Secular Scottish School-Books 1858-1861 and 1873-1882. With a Survey of the Debate on Education in Scotland in the Middle and Late 19th Century. 177 pp.

039 CLAES SCHAAR. 1971. Marino and Crashaw. *Sospetto d'Herode*. A Commentary. 300 pp.

040 SVEN BÄCKMAN. 1971. This Singular Tale. A Study of *The Vicar of Wakefield* and Its Literary Background. 281 pp.

041 CHRISTER PÅHLSSON. 1972. The Northumbrian Burr. A Sociolinguistic Study. 309 pp.

042 KARL-GUSTAV EK. 1972. The Development of OE $\bar{y}$ and $\bar{e}o$ in South-Eastern Middle English. 133 pp.

043 BO SELTÉN. 1972. The Anglo-Saxon Heritage in Middle English Personal Names. East Anglia [1100-1399]. 187 pp.

044 KERSTIN ASSARSSON-RIZZI. 1972. *Friar Bacon and Friar Bungay*. A Structural and Thematic Analysis of Robert Greene's Play. 164 pp.

045 ARNE ZETTERSTEN. 1974. A Critical Facsimile Edition of Thomas Batchelor, *An Orthoëpical Analysis of the English Language and An Orthoëpical Analysis of the Dialect of Bedfordshire* (1809). Part I. 260 pp.

046 ERIK INGVAR THURIN. 1974. The Universal Autobiography of Ralph Waldo Emerson. xii + 288 pp.

047 HARRIET BJÖRK. 1974. The Language of Truth. Charlotte Brontë, the Woman Question, and the Novel. 152 pp.

048 ANDERS DALLBY. 1974. The Anatomy of Evil. A Study of John Webster's *The White Devil*. 236 pp.

049 GILLIS KRISTENSSON. 1974. John Mirk's *Instructions for Parish Priests*. Edited from MS Cotton Claudius A II and Six Other Manuscripts with Introduction, Notes and Glossary. 287 pp.

050 STIG JOHANSSON. 1975. Papers in Contrastive Linguistics and Language Testing. 179 pp.

051 BENGT ELLENBERGER. 1977. The Latin Element in the Vocabulary of the Earlier Makars Henryson and Dunbar. 163 pp.

052 MARIANNE THORMÄHLEN. 1978. *The Waste Land*. A Fragmentary Wholeness. 248 pp.

053 LARS HERMERÉN. 1978. On Modality in English. A Study of the Semantics of the Modals. 195 pp.

054 SVEN BÄCKMAN. 1979. Tradition Transformed. Studies in the Poetry of Wilfred Owen. 206 pp.

055 JAN JÖNSJÖ. 1979. Studies on Middle English Nicknames. I: Compounds. 227 pp.

056 JAN SVARTVIK & RANDOLPH QUIRK (eds). 1980. A Corpus of English Conversation. 893 pp.

057 LARS-HÅKAN SVENSSON. 1980. Silent Art. Rhetorical and Thematic Patterns in Samuel Daniel's *Delia*. 392 pp.

058 INGRID MÅRDH. 1980. Headlinese. On the Grammar of English Front Page Headlines. 200 pp.

059 STIG JOHANSSON. 1980. Plural Attributive Nouns in Present-Day English. x + 136 pp.

060 CLAES SCHAAR. 1982. The Full Voic'd Quire Below. Vertical Context Systems in *Paradise Lost*. 354 pp.

061 GUNILLA FLORBY. 1982. The Painful Passage to Virtue. A Study of George Chapman's *The Tragedy of Bussy D'Ambois* and *The Revenge of Bussy D'Ambois*. 266 pp.

062 BENGT ALTENBERG. 1982. The Genitive *v.* the *of*-Construction. A Study of Syntactic Variation in 17th Century English. 320 pp.

063 JAN SVARTVIK, MATS EEG-OLOFSSON, OSCAR FORSHEDEN, BENGT ORESTRÖM & CECILIA THAVENIUS. 1982. Survey of Spoken English. Report on Research 1975-81. 112 pp.

109   GUNILLA FLORBY. 2005. Echoing Texts: George Chapman's *Conspiracy and Tragedy of Charles Duke of Byron*. 181 pp.

110   GUNILLA LINDGREN. Higher Education for Girls in North American College Fiction 1886–1912. 294 pp.

111   LENA AHLIN. 2006. The "New Negro" in the Old World: Culture and Performance in James Weldon Johnson, Jesse Fauset, and Nella Larsen. 205 pp.

112   MARIANNE THORMÄHLEN (ed.). 2008. English Now. Selected Papers from the 20th IAUPE Conference in Lund 2007. 384 pp.

113   ANNA WÄRNSBY. 2006. (De)coding Modality: The Case of *Must, May, Måste*, and *Kan*. 244 pp.

114   SARA HÅKANSSON. 2009. Narratorial Commentary in the Novels of George Eliot. 326 pp.